REMAPPING EAST ASIA

A book from the

Japan Foundation Center for Global Partnership

and the Social Science Research Council

A VOLUME IN THE SERIES

Cornell Studies in Political Economy

edited by Peter J. Katzenstein

A full list of titles in the series appears at the end of the book.

REMAPPING EAST ASIA

THE CONSTRUCTION OF A REGION

EDITED BY **T. J. Pempel**

Cornell University Press ITHACA AND LONDON

First published 2005 by Cornell University Press
First printing, Cornell Paperbacks, 2005

Printed in the United States of America

Library of Congress Cataloging-in-Publication Data

　Remapping East Asia : the construction of a region / edited
by T. J. Pempel.
　　　p. cm. — (Cornell studies in political economy) Includes
bibliographical references and index. ISBN 0-8014-4276-1 (cloth : alk.
paper) — ISBN 0-8014-8909-1 (pbk. : alk. paper) 1. Regionalism—East
Asia.　2. East Asia—Economic integration. 3. East Asia—Politics
and government.　I. Pempel, T. J., 1942–　II. Series.
JQ1499.A38R46　2004
337.5—dc22　　　　　　　　　　　　　　　　　　2004015299

Cloth printing　　10　9　8　7　6　5　4　3　2　1

Paperback printing　　10　9　8　7　6　5　4　3　2　1

Contents

III REGIONAL LINKAGES: INSTITUTIONS, INTERESTS, IDENTITIES

Preface

Breakfasts at the International House of Japan frequently precipitate the liveliest of seminars. Guests from all corners of the globe drag their caffeine-starved talents, specialties, and curiosities to the breakfast buffet and as their eyes open so do the conversations, table-hopping, and rotating introductions.

This project emerged from one such morning. Mary Byrne McDonnell from the Social Science Research Council (SSRC) and I shared scrambled eggs and a number of equally scrambled thoughts about the rising importance of Asian regionalism and the burgeoning talent-pool anxious to assess its myriad aspects. Soon others were in the conversation, both directly and by inference. Several weeks later the Japan Foundation Center for Global Partnership and the SSRC Seminar Series had funded my proposal for the planning workshop that led to this book. Shonan Village, Hayama, Japan in March 2001 proved to be an excellent location for shaping the key issues that form the core of this book. In attendance were Muthiah Alagappa, Laura Campbell, Yun-han Chu, Paul Evans, Martha C. Harris, Peter Katzenstein, Ellis Krauss, Andrew MacIntyre, Takashi Shiraishi, Etel Solingen, Dennis Tachiki, Toshiya Tsugami, Keiichi Tsunekawa, Meredith Woo-Cumings, and Xinbo Wu. Frank Baldwin of CGP Tokyo, along with his assistant Takuya Toda, handled logistics and staffing, while Lisa J. Sansoucy was invaluable as a rapporteur. Her detailed notes eased the burden of deciphering the lively but frequently conflicting commentary.

A follow-up meeting was held in Portland, Oregon, February 22–24, 2002, at which preliminary drafts were presented, dissected, and remanded for reconsideration. All the contributors to this volume attended, as did Baldwin and Toda, along with Ken Ruoff of Portland State University and Saori Katada.

Finally, on June 21–22, 2002, a smaller conference was held in Berkeley under the sponsorship of the Institute for East Asian Studies at the University of California, Berkeley. Joyce Kallgren and Hideki Hara joined a number of the paper writers, and both provided valuable feedback. Joan Kask and Kumi Sawada Hadler provided valuable local logistical assistance for that conference. Mary Retzinger did more than yeoman service in beginning preparation of the final manuscript for the press. When Kumi returned to the institute after giving birth to her first child, she finished that task with her usual attention to details too easily missed by others.

As he has been for me and for so many others over many years, Peter Katzenstein was an exceptionally conscientious and insightful critic at all stages of this project. Roger Haydon at Cornell University Press reaffirmed his reputation for giving invaluable but always sensitively delivered editorial suggestions and assistance. My contributors and I owe both of them a particular debt of gratitude, as we do to an anonymous reader who provided exceptionally valuable suggestions. Whatever flaws remain would have been far more numerous without their consistent help.

The inevitable victim in a time-consuming project is one's spouse. Kaela Pempel Kory was unendingly tolerant of my continual pleas for "more time to write" and in her unfailing willingness to shoulder tasks that I shirked, particularly the many that came with relocating from Seattle to Berkeley midway through the project. It is to her that this book is lovingly dedicated.

T. J. P.

Berkeley, California

Contributors

Laura B. Campbell is Director and Legal Consultant, Environmental Law International.

Paul Evans is Professor in the Faculty of Graduate Studies at the University of British Columbia, based at the Institute of Asian Research and the Liu Institute for Global Issues.

Natasha Hamilton-Hart is Assistant Professor in the Southeast Asian Studies Programme at the National University of Singapore.

David Leheny is Assistant Professor of Political Science at the University of Wisconsin, Madison. He has worked in the Office of the Coordinator for Counterterrorism at the U.S. State Department.

Andrew MacIntyre is Professor of Political Science and Director of the Asia Pacific School of Economics and Government at the Australian National University. He was previously a professor in the Graduate School of International Relations and Pacific Studies at the University of California San Diego.

Geoffrey McNicoll is a senior associate of the Population Council, a nongovernmental research organization with headquarters in New York. He was formerly a professor in the Research School of Social Sciences, Australian National University, Canberra.

Barry Naughton is So Kwanlok Professor of Chinese and International Affairs at the Graduate School of International Relations and Pacific Studies, University of California, San Diego.

T. J. Pempel is Professor of Political Science and Director of the Institute of East Asian Studies at the University of California, Berkeley.

Etel Solingen is Professor of Political Science and International Relations at the University of California, Irvine.

Dennis Tachiki is Professor of Business Administration, Tamagawa University, Japan, and was formerly with the Fujitsu Research Institute.

Keiichi Tsunekawa is Professor of Political Science at the University of Tokyo, Komaba.

REMAPPING EAST ASIA

1

Introduction:
Emerging Webs of Regional Connectedness

T. J. PEMPEL

An overarching ambiguity characterizes East Asia. On the one hand, the region has at least a century-long history of internal divisiveness, war, and conflict. It also remains the site of several nettlesome territorial disputes. The region, furthermore, is exceptionally diverse culturally, linguistically, and religiously. It is a pastiche of Sinic, Japanese, Islamic, Buddhist, Muslim, and Christian traditions. None provides a significantly unifying cultural-religious cohesiveness across the region, despite the efforts of many to claim the existence of certain overarching "Asian values." Indeed, many countries such as Malaysia, Indonesia, the Philippines, China, and even Australia confront serious internal ethnic, linguistic, or religious divisions impeding agreement on even a single set of national, let alone regionwide, cultural norms.

Population differences in East Asia are also more dramatic than in many other regions. Few countries have substantial immigrant populations; only Malaysia has more than 4 percent foreign born. Widely varied political systems can be found throughout East Asia. Meanwhile, despite an overwhelming economic improvement and the ease with which writers (e.g., Campos and Root 1996; Terry 2002; World Bank 1993) trumpet the "Asian economic miracle," the region is composed of exceptionally diverse national economies, several of which have recently witnessed major setbacks. East Asia is also home to many of the world's most persistently problematic areas of military friction (Emmerson 2001, 104) and an area with one of the world's highest levels of arms imports (Simon 2001a, 49; although cf. Alagappa 1998, 631–33). Moreover, as nonstate terrorism and the proliferation of weapons of mass destruction have become increasingly important shapers of international affairs, their impact has been widely felt across much of East Asia.

Given such wide-ranging diversities, that East Asia has not become as integrated a region as Western Europe, the Gulf States, Central America, or the Southern Cone of Latin America should occasion little surprise. Instead, many would readily endorse Friedberg's contention that the region is "ripe for rivalry," a place likely to emerge as the "cockpit of great-power conflict" (1993, 7).

The focus on East Asia's lack of integration grows largely out of the high level of attention given to the actions of the region's governments and to the cooperative or conflictual interactions of nation-states (e.g., Frankel and Kahler 1993; Mansfield and Milner 1997). Yet a strikingly contradictory view of the East Asian region emerges when one looks at linkages beneath the level of state actions. In that picture, despite the overwhelming structural impediments to integration, East Asia has in recent years become considerably more interdependent, connected, and cohesive. This increased cohesiveness has been driven by developments, among other things, in trade and investment, cross-border production, banking, technology sharing, popular culture, transportation, communication, and environmental cooperation, as well as in crime, drug, and disease control. Such areas illustrate a region that has developed an increasingly dense network of cross-border cooperation, collaboration, interdependence, and even formalized institutional integration.

Also rising sharply and steadily have been measures of personal contact, including intra-regional telephone and mail communication, shipping and aviation, tourism, television and satellite broadcasts, and legal and illegal migration (Cohen 2002). And at the level of popular culture, a bevy of pan-Asian activities span the region, captivating many of its citizens—Japanese cartoons and karaoke, Korean pop music, Star TV, Korean and Chinese soap operas, pop artifacts such as "Hello, Kitty," multinational Asian singing groups, and the like. The mass appeal of such pan-Asian activities was such that early in this century, pop promoters were clamoring to create dozens of multinational Asian singing groups and bands to appeal to this newly emerging sense of regional popular identity.

These transnational webs take many forms, are of differing tensile strengths, and reach more or less deeply into very different parts of the region. Some admittedly prove quite ephemeral and vanish quickly, but many more have been sinking roots and gaining undeniable tenacity within the region. Over time, these webs of connectedness have become far thicker, more numerous, and more comprehensive. Many appear likely to be long lasting and influential. A few have gained significant levels of formal, governmentally ratified institutionalization.

This book is about the people, processes, and institutions that have been weaving webs of connectedness across eastern Asia. Its chapters examine the mixture of complex and often competing agents and processes that, in a host of different functional areas, have been knitting various segments of East Asia together. Such emerging links now counterbalance the lines of potential confrontation, suggesting that rather than rivalry, the region is "ripe for cooperation."

A central contention of this volume is that this latter picture, which stresses increasing cooperation across national borders and increasing coherence as a region rather than ongoing fragmentation, is the more intellectually puzzling as well as the more predictive of East Asia's future. The region remains unquestionably highly diverse and contains numerous trouble spots that will impede easy cooperation. Many governments remain jealous of and competitive with one another. But this point is far less counterintuitive than is the contention that despite such tensions, the region has been busily fostering ever deeper regionwide networks of cooperation and that these in turn are laying the groundwork for a reduction in long-standing national tensions. Not only is this happening, we believe, but multilateral ties and cross-border connectedness have become by far the more prevalent trends in the region.

East Asia and the Question of Regions

Regions, regionalization, and regionalism have, of late, gained considerable attention both in the real world and within academic circles. In an international arena allegedly beset by the surging tide of globalization, certain geographical regions have taken on increased political and economic coherence, acquiring in the process the status of midlevel actors, larger than the nation-state but far smaller and less comprehensive than the entire globe.

This attention to regions derives primarily from the burgeoning number of formal institutional arrangements now linking various geographical regions together. The European Union (EU) is far and away the most thickly institutionalized and comprehensive of these. But the EU has numerous companions such as the North American Free Trade Agreement (NAFTA), the Gulf Cooperation Council (GCC), the Central American Common Market, the Caribbean Community (CARICOM), and the Southern Common Market (Mercosur). From 1947 to early 2002 alone, the General Agreement on Tariffs and Trade (GATT) and the World Trade Organization (WTO) were informed of the creation of more than 250 regional economic agreements; over 170 are currently in force with perhaps 70 others operational but unregistered (WTO website). Most of these were essentially free trade areas or customs unions. Other regional groupings pursue different goals. Central to most, however, is some component of geographical proximity, involving arrangements designed to bring together neighboring countries. In addition, most regional bodies carry at least the implicit notion that such neighborliness generates sufficient common interest to spur enhanced cooperation throughout the "neighborhood." In this sense, the term *region* carries a meaning that is not only geographic but also geopsychological.

Such an image resonates with common usage. There, regions are taken as contiguous territorial areas having sufficiently clear internal cohesion and definitive enough external boundaries as to be readily distinguishable from other neighboring, and purportedly equally easy-to-distinguish, regions of the world. Familiar and popular examples include sub-Saharan Africa, the Caribbean, the Middle East, Western Europe, or Central America.

Contrary to such a largely unproblematized interpretation of regions and presumptions of geographic self-definition, the world for the most part is not, in fact, composed of "natural regions." Almost no region in the world with genuine political and economic significance is so essentialist in its makeup; rarely can any be understood as delimited by simple geographic lines on a map. Regions, instead, are fluid and complex mixtures of physical, psychological, and behavioral traits that are continually in the process of being re-created and redefined (Mansfield and Milner 1997; Katzenstein and Okawara 2000). Hemmer and Katzenstein (2002, 587) quote Georg Simmel to great effect: "A border . . . is not a geographical fact that has sociological consequences, but a sociological fact that takes geographical form. The same can be said of regions." Or, as Richard Higgott (1997b, 238) has put it: "The yardsticks of 'regionness' will vary by the number of policy issues or questions present and above all by what the dominant political actors in a given group of countries at a given time see as their political priorities."

An East Asia characterized by enhanced cross-border cooperation is hardly the prevailing perception among students of comparative regionalism. It is undeniable that East Asia has far fewer legally embedded, broadly encompassing, and deeply institutionalized regional bodies than do other regions of the world, most notably Western Europe but less conspicuously the Middle East, Latin America, or even Africa. Moreover, the Asian economic crisis of 1997–98 revealed the flaccid and feckless nature of the few regional bodies that do link East Asian countries, most prominently the Association of Southeast Asian Nations (ASEAN) and Asia-Pacific Economic Cooperation (APEC). These two did little to buffer the region's economies from the cascadingly destructive tsunami that wiped out billions of dollars in accumulated regional wealth. Furthermore, proposals by Japan to create an Asian Monetary Fund to provide regional economic coordination during the crisis foundered quickly in the face of Chinese, U.S., and International Monetary Fund opposition (Amyx 2004; Henning 2002). Such experiences have driven many to conclude that East Asian regionalism is far less deep, less powerful, less internally cohesive, and less formally institutionalized than its counterparts in many other parts of the world (e.g., Grieco 1997; Katzenstein and Shiraishi 1997; Mattli 1999, 163–78).

In speaking of Northeast Asia, Michael Ng-Quinn (1986, 111) makes a sweeping historical case about the weakness of regional ties and its presumed causes. His argument is based less explicitly on comparative evidence and more on presumptions about the underlying state-centric logic that he sees as driving regional arrangements:

> There have been no rules in northeast Asia that are both regionally derived and applicable to the whole region. . . . The core regional actors lacked internal consolidation and their contact was sporadic. . . . No one actor has been powerful enough to superimpose its rules, and there has been no common external threat to induce regional cooperation or provide an opportunity for a regional protector to emerge. There has also been no issue of conflict or cooperation within the region requiring the generation of regional rules beyond those of alliances and suzerainty.

Using the European or other regional experiences to critique East Asia for being "behind" in its level of regional integration is an impractical, if understandable, mistake. As Breslin and his colleagues have argued (2002, 11), such views "reflect . . . a teleological prejudice informed by the assumption that 'progress' in regional organization is defined in terms of EU-style institutionalization." William Wallace (1995) argues convincingly that the European experience is an exception, not a model, and Miles Kahler (2000a) underscores that point by showing how distinctive and rare Western Europe's deeply legalized institutions are in comparative terms.

Furthermore, the high standard of internally generated goals and regional leadership such as put forward by Ng-Quinn also establishes an unnecessarily abstract and high bar for Asian regional cohesiveness. Demonstrating that East Asia falls short of either comparatively or abstractly established standards for state-to-state regional institution formation sheds little real light on the particular cross-border links that have in fact been forged across the region. Such a privileging of the state as regional or global actor in the forging of regional linkages risks underplaying the importance of alternative engines of linkage. Indeed, as the chapters in this volume by Etel Solingen and Geoffrey McNicoll make clear, both domestic politics and demographic configurations make the East Asian region quite different from most other major regions of the world; certainly, they make it considerably different from Western Europe.

In resonance with such judgments, this book rejects any mix of theoretical standards to determine the extent of "real" regional linkages. Nor does it make any teleological presumptions that Europe's present is Asia's future (Higgott 1998b). Instead, it takes the East Asian region on its own terms, focusing on the particulars of its evolving integration, the vast majority of them driven by actors other than national governments. It presumes that more than one path—not simply state actions—can lead to the development of greater regional cohesiveness. It recognizes that regional integration in East Asia has been historically slow to develop cross-border linkages and regional connections through much of the later nineteenth and twentieth centuries. Nevertheless, despite such a fragmented historical legacy, East Asia has, with varying degrees of depth and speed, and with admittedly numerous reverses over time, begun to put into place an expanding network of webs that span national borders and deepen regional ties. These have become considerably more salient politically and economically since the early to mid-1980s. This network is, however, by no means driven exclusively by state actions.

Indeed to appreciate the linkage mechanisms operating across East Asia, it is useful to recognize that at least three discrete drivers have been spinning webs across East Asia: governments, corporations, and ad hoc problem-oriented coalitions. To focus exclusively on one of these while ignoring the others is to miss the greater multiplicity and complexity of ties that are emerging.

Moreover, these three engines have been spinning their diverse but often complementary webs from two quite different directions. The two major processes stressed in this book are regionalism, the top-down process of government-to-government formation of institutions such as ASEAN, APEC, or the ASEAN Regional Forum (ARF), and regionalization, the bottom-up process of cross-border cooperation driven primarily by nongovernmental actors such as corporations, NGOs (nongovernmental organizations), and track II groups. A more detailed analysis of both the engines and the processes of regional integration is given later in the chapter. But the central point to underscore at this stage is that a host of overlapping and reinforcing regional ties are being built in East Asia—not only through formal, governmentally constituted bodies but also, and more pervasively, by cross-border investment and trade flows, increasingly common cultural experiences, and unofficial links among NGOs and track II bodies. The cross-border linkages created by these latter activities have been far more numerous and far-reaching than those that result in more formal and institutionalized multinational bodies.

To appreciate how much this combination of ties has contributed to enhanced regional cohesiveness, it is important first to establish just how diverse and unintegrated East Asia was during most of the nineteenth and twentieth centuries.

Overcoming Asian Fragmentation

Asian integration at the beginning of the twenty-first century is admittedly less extensive than its more ardent proponents would prefer. Nevertheless, what exists now contrasts sharply with the fragmentation that characterized the region for most of the past century. Before the mid-nineteenth century, a sinocentric world order revolving around cultural exchange and the tributary system wove many parts of Asia into a more cohesive whole (Fairbank 1968; Kang 2003b). Sea lanes simultaneously created trading regimes that linked most of Asia's great port cities through trade, migration, technology, and finance (Hamashita 1997). By the middle of the nineteenth century, however,

Asia, like the rest of the world more generally, had fallen under the preponderant global and regional influences of the Western powers, colonialism, and military conquest. Collectively, these forces fractured most of East Asia's previous cross-border linkages. For the next 150 years, eastern Asia was pockmarked by a fragmented collection of disparate Western colonies. Only Japan and Thailand escaped Western colonial rule. In the years leading up to World War II, the only meaningful Asian challenge to Western predominance across the region, and the only real bid for East Asian integration, came from Japan's unsuccessful efforts to mobilize military force and anti-Westernism in the service of forging its Greater East Asia Co-Prosperity Sphere (although cf. Petri 1993).

In the years immediately following World War II fragmentation prevailed. Two processes perpetuated this division: decolonization and the Cold War. As Asia's former colonies gained national independence, political elites in these countries, from Indonesia to the Philippines, directed their efforts primarily toward nation building at home and defending their newly won sovereignty from the perceived depredations of former colonial masters, menacing neighbors, and regional and global superpowers. With attention concentrated inward, few countries made serious efforts to advance projects aimed at closer regional integration.

As decolonization proceeded, the Cold War kept the region fragmented. The Korean peninsula was cleaved at its midpoint by the United States and the USSR, with Korea's two indigenous governments becoming longtime surrogates for the contending superpowers. The countries of Indochina were riven by a series of wars, first with the French, then with the Americans, and throughout and subsequently, among themselves. Indonesia was subjected to a Cold War–inspired bloodbath in the mid-1960s that left it divided at home and at odds with many of its immediate neighbors. Guerrilla insurrections split Thailand, Malaysia, Myanmar, and the Philippines. Some 15–20 percent of the Cambodian population was liquidated by the Khmer Rouge during the mid-1970s. And most importantly, Mao's victory in 1949 spawned the country's sequestration by the United States and its Cold War allies across Asia (Anderson 1998). Decades of internal war, the Great Leap Forward (1958–60), the unleashing of the Red Guards in the mid-1960s, and the Tiananmen massacre added to China's internal chaos as well as to its economic and political isolation from much of the rest of Asia. And these were just the "big problems" keeping East Asia internally divided ("Billion Consumers" 1993).

The Cold War played out very differently for regional integration in East Asia than it did for Western Europe. In Europe, the United States built its alliance structure around the North Atlantic Treaty Organization (NATO), a multinational and eventually militarily integrated organization that originally included more than a dozen European and North American countries as members. In Asia, by way of contrast, the United States put forth no such integrating alliance structures. Instead it forged discreet and ad hoc "hub-and-spoke" alliances and basing arrangements with each of its anticommunist allies—Japan, South Korea, Taiwan, Thailand, and the Philippines. But there were no pro-U.S. regional security arrangements other than the failed SEATO pact and the somewhat more successful ANZUS arrangements with New Zealand and Australia that brought several Asian governments into cooperative alliances (Hemmer and Katzenstein 2002). Security arrangements provided little basis for Asia's American allies to become more integrated with one another. Instead, their respective capitals were connected along separate bilateral tracks to Washington (Crone 1993; Ikenberry 2001; Kahler 1995; Nau 2002).

In juxtaposition to this American alliance structure in Asia stood the Soviet Union, the People's Republic of China, North Korea, and North Vietnam. Neither the Soviet Union nor China succeeded in establishing any East Asian equivalent to the integrative Warsaw Pact that linked, however tentatively and repressively, the Soviet satellites in Eastern Europe. Thus, the two competing military alliances in Asia provided at best elements of partial integration among each alliance's members, and both were far more tentative than such links in Europe. Virtually no links spanned the ideological chasm that separated the two hostile blocs (Ikenberry and Mastanduno 2003).

Ricocheting between these two blocs, a number of East Asia's recently decolonized countries sought some version of neutrality and nonalignment. This was most notably true of Indonesia, which took a leading role in creating the nonaligned movement. Although often more rhetorical than real, Third World nonalignment and solidarity held loosely together until the 1980s, thereby adding still a third arc of global alignment that kept the countries of East Asia divided from one another.

The American-dominated security order in East Asia had its economic component as well. In the wake of the communist success in the Chinese civil war and China's subsequent military intervention in the Korean War, the United States leveled a variety of restrictions designed to prevent America's allies, but most especially Japan, from trading freely with China, previously Japan's most important trade partner. In 1952, American constraints were tightened further to prevent "any substantial economic relationship between the two" for fear that such links would expose Japan to "Communist blackmail and ideological contamination" (Shaller 1985, 291). In return for shutting down access to the China market, the United States pledged to provide a "satisfactory livelihood" for Japan by enlarging its own markets for Japanese exports, pressing the World Bank and other institutions to lend generously to Japan, and helping to turn the country into the "workshop of Asia." Eventually, the United States opened its own markets asymmetrically to its Asian allies, fostering pan-Pacific economic linkages that tied a number of Asian countries economically and strategically to the United States.

In at least two ways, therefore, the Washington-dominated hub-and-spoke order contributed to fragmentation across East Asia, in sharp contrast with the cross-regional ties that connected America's European allies. First, in Europe both the security and economic structures fostered by the United States, most notably NATO and the predecessors to the European economic union, created a basis for subsequent institutionalization of intra-European ties (Gould and Krasner 2002; Ikenberry 2001; Nau 2002). And second, many of America's Asian allies had far stronger ties across the Pacific than they had among themselves. These differences contributed mightily to the subsequent evolution of regional connections in the two regions: European countries were linked together economically and strategically from the first years after World War II; East Asian countries remained correspondingly divided though many had individual links across the Pacific to the United States.

Not until the late 1960s and early 1970s did this pattern begin seriously to shift. Three important threads then began to converge, collectively enhancing transnational ties across East Asia. First, as Japan's phenomenal economic success became regularized, the country was catapulted forward as an alternative version of capitalism, which gained particularly strong appeal within Northeast Asia as well as in Singapore and Malaysia (Johnson 1987; Pempel 1999a; Terry 2002; Woo-Cumings 1999). Enhanced Japanese wealth also allowed the country to play a larger role in regional economic development through foreign aid, trade, investment, and technology transfer. As Andrew MacIntyre and Barry Naughton analyze this situation in chapter 4, Japan dominated the East Asian region until the early 1990s, its economic success giving the country a quiet but unmistakable leadership role at the head of a flock of East Asian "flying geese." More tangibly, as Keiichi Tsunekawa shows in chapter 5, Japan entered into a series of official agreements with many of its Asian neighbors to pay World War II reparations and to establish regular links through official aid. Both sowed the seeds for greater economic ties between Japan and many of the other countries in noncommunist Asia, and these then catalyzed embryonic growth of the region as a whole.

As Japan, and later South Korea and Taiwan, improved their national economic competitiveness, a host of manufacturing industries within the United States began to wilt under the sudden competition that Asian products posed in American and global markets. By the mid- to late 1980s, the U.S. government had begun a series of protectionist moves in its trade relations with Japan and with Asia more generally. These included "voluntary export restraints," sector-specific market-opening pressures, and demands for structural changes in political and economic practices deemed harmful to U.S. firms, as well as exchange rate realignments. All sought to reduce America's bilateral trade deficits and provide economic protection to politically and economically valuable sectors of U.S. industry. Collectively these undercut some of the easy entry for specific types of Asian exports to the United States. These

American moves thus began to weaken some of the prevailing pan-Pacific ties while simultaneously bolstering economic interdependence within Asia (e.g., Gordon 2001). The old hub-and-spoke system remained dominant in security but lost much of its previous power in trade and investment. Moreover, prior vulnerabilities of individual Asian countries to imbalanced bilateral bargaining with the United States began to be partially offset by their enhanced willingness to turn to collective action and multilateral forums during economic bargaining with Washington (e.g., Katada 2004).

A second big shift bolstered closer ties across Asia. As early as the late 1950s, China began to turn its strategic orientation away from exclusive reliance on the USSR, opting first for autonomy and then later for greater openness to Western capitalist economics. Internal developments in China combined with the normalization of diplomatic relations between the United States and Japan on the one hand and the People's Republic of China on the other began to open the door for China's shift in economic focus and for its reintegration with the other parts of Asia. This Chinese shift also improved the overall security climate across the region, provided an additional intra-Asian counterweight to U.S. influence, and simultaneously enhanced the potential for greater trade and investment throughout the region.

Finally, a third factor contributed to increased Asian integration when Southeast Asia's early wave of anticolonialist nationalisms was overtaken by a collective realization of their common vulnerability to the larger regional and global powers. The result was the creation in 1967 of ASEAN (and the Asia Development Bank) by the governments of Indonesia, Malaysia, the Philippines, Singapore, and Thailand. Begun as a noncommunist arrangement to promote security among its members, ASEAN gradually expanded its collective mission to include economic, social, and cultural cooperation and development (Acharya 2001a).

Initial efforts to give an economic role to ASEAN failed, including preferential trading arrangements, the ASEAN Industrial Project, ASEAN Industrial Complementation, and the ASEAN Industrial Joint Venture (Stubbs 2002). As problems of internal security receded, however, and the wars in Indochina ended and the Cold War cooled, attention within ASEAN turned increasingly to issues of trade, stabilization of commodity prices, market openings, and the effort to attract development assistance from the industrialized countries. During the mid- to late 1980s, domestic political shifts took place in all four of the main ASEAN countries, with economic liberalizers gaining sway in recognition of the benefits that stemmed from Japanese direct investment and the potential to enhance their export prowess. Official opposition gave way to overt support for more liberalized inflows of foreign capital (see chap. 2 in this volume, by Solingen, as well as Acharya 2003; Johnston 2003).

At least three important consequences followed. First, the once highly fragmented countries of Southeast Asia became formally linked through an explicit multilateral institution designed to give them collective bargaining power within international forums. Second, economic and political ties across Southeast Asia were strengthened, with ASEAN eventually expanding to include ten countries. Third, ASEAN developed a bargaining style ("the ASEAN way") that emphasized cooperation despite low levels of formal institutionalization and legalization (Johnston 2003). ASEAN operates not from any set of strict legal procedures that might be viewed as checks on national sovereignty but instead, most typically, by creating sequential issue-by-issue coalitions. In time, this style came to be used by members to resolve internal territorial disputes and to balance collectively against the larger powers (Acharya 2001a; Leifer 1989; Alagappa 1993). The consensual approach to coalition formation also took wider hold across the region. Further, as the region began to record exceptional rates of economic transformation, trade and investment cooperation reinforced the impetus toward closer relations.

Yet even as the countries of ASEAN increased their mutual cooperation, most remained jealous of their national prerogatives. Neither ten-nation unanimity nor agreement on an overarching agenda has been required for ASEAN actions. Rather than surrendering sovereignty to some regional organization, the ASEAN governments have more often proceeded through ad hoc issue-specific coalitions. Yet, as David Leheny makes clear in chapter 10, in more recent times, growing concern about Islamic fundamentalist terrorism in much of Southeast Asia has begun to erode this previously sacrosanct respect for sovereignty. By early 2002, for example, Malaysia and Singapore were pushing ASEAN toward tighter security cooperation, and an informal meeting of foreign ministers in Thailand in February 2002 yielded a pledge of joint action against terrorism.

Over the past twenty to thirty years, therefore, many of the previous barriers against East Asian cooperation have been eroding, and the region's leverage within international politics has been growing. Paul Bracken has suggested that although Asian countries are a long way from developing transnational military forces and most continue to rely on very limited national forces, it is today virtually impossible to imagine the United States or any other Western power using military force to impose its will on any country in Northeast or Southeast Asia in the way that the former colonial powers sought to reestablish their empires in the aftermath of World War II, or the United States intervened in Korea in the early 1950s or in Vietnam and Indochina in the 1960s or 1970s (Bracken 1999). Even American efforts to force "regime change" on North Korea through military threats have been stymied by the cooperative opposition of several major Northeast Asian powers and their collective willingness to engage in Six Party talks to resolve the prevailing issues. Still, few governments in East Asia are now explicit antagonists against America's broad global power position (Ikenberry and Mastanduno 2003, although cf. Mearsheimer 2001b, 373–77, 396–400).

It is in the economic arena, however, not security, where Asia's pan-regional linkages have become the thickest. Throughout the postwar years, the once poor parts of the world have generally become even poorer, while the richer parts have gained larger shares of world GNP. East Asia provides the only noteworthy exception. In 1960, Japan and Northeast Asia accounted for only 4 percent of world GNP, compared with a total of 37 percent for the United States, Canada, and Mexico. By the early 1990s, the combined economies of Japan, Taiwan, South Korea, the ASEAN countries, and greater China contributed roughly 30 percent of world GNP, approximately the same share as that held by North America on the one hand and Western Europe on the other. Asia showed similar jumps in its shares of world trade, attraction of foreign direct investment, and gains in per capita GNP. Much of this came from enhanced investment, trade, and cross-regional production, as noted in the chapters in this volume by MacIntyre and Naughton, Dennis Tachiki, Natasha Hamilton-Hart, and others. Broadly speaking, the region's relative shares of world power expanded militarily, diplomatically, and economically, and most East Asian countries benefited in the process.

At the same time, the collective improvement in Asia's international standing economically has not been accompanied by the rapid eclipse of national self-interest and Westphalian sovereignty. Indeed, few Asian governments have pressed for an extensive institutionalization of their cross-border ties in any field. Nevertheless, numerous new networks are being built across East Asia, particularly through the actions of private and semi-private actors.

Toward Asian Regional Integration: Three Drivers, Two Directions

One major contention of the chapters in this volume is that several different types of actors, or drivers, have been enhancing connections across East Asia. Clearly many of East Asia's more cooperative ventures have been driven by the national governments of the region. At least equally as often, however, the key spinners of East Asia's webs of cooperation (and occasionally conflict) have been nonstate actors, including such diverse players as multinational corporations, NGOs, private citizens engaged in so-called track II processes, and cross-border media, as well as individual workers, students, athletic teams, rock bands, and dance troupes. The former have created various links of organizational cooperation, while the latter have crisscrossed borders expanding previously narrow definitions of national culture into more regionally complex, if often inchoate, mixtures of "Asian identity." This book concentrates on examining these three sets of actors, or drivers, which we contend lie at the core of recent links across East Asia. It is organized around chapters that focus explicitly on each of these three.

Moreover, these three sets of actors have forged ties from two quite different directions—from the top down and from the bottom up. Governments generally operate from the top down, whereas nonstate actors more frequently connect from the bottom up. But as will be much clearer from the detailed analyses that follow, this oversimplifies an inevitably more complex reality.

Three Drivers of East Asian Linkages

The three main drivers of connections across national borders in East Asia have been governments, corporations, and ad hoc problem-oriented bodies. Governments have been among the most conspicuous and well studied of these three. For students of comparative regionalism, particularly students of European integration, the focus on national governments is a given. This is generally also the case for most studies of regional linkages undertaken by political scientists. In most such instances, the focus is on multinational governmental cooperation that results in formal regional organizations.

Without a doubt, governments in East Asia, as elsewhere, have been key agents driving certain of the region's integrative activities. But as is made explicit by MacIntyre and Naughton in their chapter dealing with China, Indonesia, and Japan, and by Tsunekawa in his chapter on Japan, these countries have not always pursued closer regional integration through formal multinational organizations. Hence, East Asia has far fewer of these bodies than many other regions of the world. The reasons for this are straightforward, starting with the earlier analysis of the historical roots of East Asian fragmentation. But in addition, national governments that join in multinational organizations typically surrender elements of their individual sovereignty in the collective quest for a broader and more deeply institutionalized regional integration. As Solingen demonstrates in chapter 2, domestic national politics and the composition of domestic socioeconomic coalitions play a key part in this process. Regional organizations are most likely to emerge, she argues, when government leaders in geographically proximate countries share and pursue common internationalizing agendas that lead them to conclude that cross-border cooperation will be to their collective benefit. To date, many governments in East Asia remain unconvinced of those benefits.

Those who argue that regional ties are weak in East Asia stress that formal multilateral organizations are by no means as extensive or as deeply legalized as their counterparts in other regions, most particularly in Western Europe. Nevertheless, even these organizations have become increasingly more numerous in connecting the countries of East Asia. In several noteworthy instances, the governments of the Asia-Pacific region have institutionalized their cooperation through formal organizations such as ASEAN, the APEC forum, ARF, SCO (Shanghai Cooperative Organization), APT (ASEAN + 3, that is, the ten ASEAN member states plus China, Japan, and South Korea), and the Tumen River Area Regional Development Program with its membership of five communist or former communist countries focused on a variety of issues linked to economic development in continental Northeast Asia (Davies 2000). In Paul Evans's deft wording (2003, 2), "The noodle bowl of Asian regionalism—ASEAN, ASEAN PMC, ARF, SAARC, SCO, APEC, PECC, CSCAP—is not quite as thick or rich as its spaghetti-bowl counterpart in Europe. But in a post–Cold War setting, the noodle bowl is filling quickly." Figures 1.1 and 1.2 show how such formal institutions have been expanding in number and scope just since 1990.

Important as such multilateral bodies are in institutionalizing regional cooperation, they are by no means the only way in which East Asian governments have been weaving cross-national connective webs. They have also cooperated across borders through the use of foreign aid, cultural exchange agreements, technology-sharing arrangements, and ad hoc agreements over particular extra-national problems such as smuggling, piracy, migration,

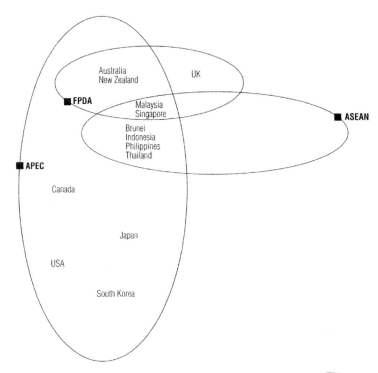

Fig. 1.1. Membership in selected East Asian and trans-Pacific groups, 1990. APEC, Asia-Pacific Economic Cooperation; ASEAN, Association of Southeast Asian Nations; FPDA, Five Power Defense Arrangement.

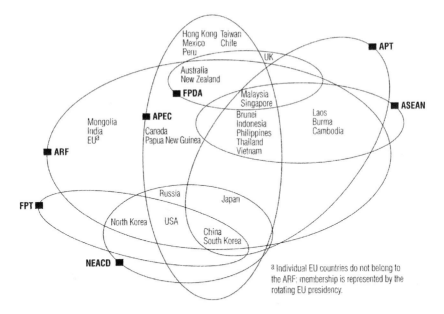

Fig. 1.2. Membership in selected East Asian and trans-Pacific groups, 2002. APEC, Asia-Pacific Economic Cooperation; APT, ASEAN + 3; ARF, ASEAN Regional Forum; ASEAN, Association of Southeast Asian Nations; FPDA, Five Power Defense Arrangement; FPT, Four Party Talks; NEACD, Northeast Asia Cooperation Dialogue.

organized crime, environmental degradation, and the like. Tsunekawa provides a particularly comprehensive analysis of how these different pieces were pursued by the Japanese and other governments in East Asia.

Of particular significance lately has been the explosion of bilateral trade pacts. Hardly in existence as recently as 1998, these were extensive and expanding in number and inclusiveness by 2002 (see figs. 1.3 and 1.4; Dent 2003, 2–4).

Without question, East Asia has also begun to face a number of transnational problems that call for governmental cooperation across borders (Dauvergne 1997a, 2001a; Dupont 2001; Shinn 1996). Under most circumstances, such cross-border cooperation has not been characterized by the creation of deeply institutionalized formal organizations. Nor, as bilateral trade pacts most explicitly underscore, are agreements always reached in ways that involve comprehensive regional memberships. Instead cooperation tends to be problem specific, ad hoc, and involving a limited number of governments. Nevertheless, such governmental actions toward cross-border cooperation complement other actions aimed at developing more fully formalized multinational bodies.

Governments are by no means the only drivers connecting East Asia. A second set of drivers has also been critical, namely, private corporations and

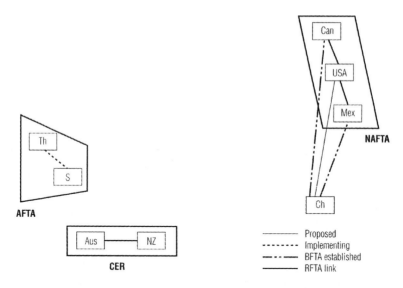

Fig. 1.3. Asia-Pacific free trade agreements before 1998. AFTA, ASEAN Free Trade Agreement; BFTA, bilateral free trade agreement; CER, Australia—New Zealand Closer Economic Relations Trade Agreement; NAFTA, North American Free Trade Agreement; Aus, Australia; Can, Canada; Ch, Chile; Mex, Mexico; NZ, New Zealand; S, Singapore; Th, Thailand; USA, United States.

financial institutions. Tachiki and Hamilton-Hart examine the evolution and import of these networks in their respective chapters. Such actors have been at the core of a second major body of literature on regional ties, one that has been the province primarily of economists. In such cases the focus has been on connections developed through regional trade, investment, and cross-national production networks. Multinational corporations typically act with little overt concern for formal and legalized cooperation. They are usually driven instead by cross-border market incentives and opportunities. More often they follow business plans aimed at enhanced rationalization of their production. To the extent that such actions rely on governments, the underlying assumption by most who analyze corporate activity is that the flag will follow the money; corporations are presumed to engage in cross-border activities less out of consideration for the national interest or well-being of their host government and more in the single-minded pursuit of corporate profitability. When corporate activities are married to investigations of regional ties, the central questions involve the extent to which regional economic arrangements (such as free trade blocs or bilateral free trade agreements) are compatible with global measures designed to enhance economic efficiency and create markets that extend beyond national borders (such as the World Trade Organization, common accounting standards, and the Basel Accord). A key question underpinning such studies is whether a particular

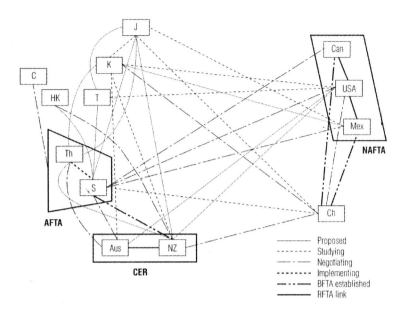

Fig. 1.4. Asia-Pacific free trade agreements by mid-2002. AFTA, ASEAN Free Trade Agreement; BFTA, bilateral free trade agreement; CER, Australia—New Zealand Closer Economic Relations Trade Agreement; NAFTA, North American Free Trade Agreement; RFTA, regional free trade agreement; Aus, Australia; C, China; Can, Canada; Ch, Chile; HK, Hong Kong; J, Japan; K, South Korea; Mex, Mexico; NZ, New Zealand; S, Singapore; T, Taiwan; Th, Thailand; USA, United States.

form of regional economic integration will present "a stumbling block or a building block" toward the ultimate market goal of greater global efficiency and enhanced collective economic welfare (Lawrence 1991).

Regardless of such long-term impacts, numerous multinational corporations in East Asia have created cross-border global production networks and webs of corporate interaction across wide swaths of the region. Moreover, corporations are also regionalizing East Asia through cross-border promotion of products linked to "Asian" popular culture (Leheny 2003). Such bottom-up connections are far less official bridges across national borders than are those constructed by governments, but they carry a huge proportion of Asia's regional traffic nonetheless.

Less well studied and less conspicuous is still a third driver of regional integration, namely, problem-oriented bodies, both semipublic and private, that cooperate across national borders in pursuit of solutions to a host of different types of transborder problems. Yet as the world generally and many of its regions more specifically are discovering, an increasing number of problems defy national solutions and call instead for largely informal, noninstitutionalized cooperation either by governments or by private-sector groups within the same region (Dupont 2001; Shinn 1996). These include problems in the areas of the environment, energy, water, migration, crime, nonstate terror, boundary disputes, or pandemics such as AIDS or SARS, to name only a few of the most conspicuous. Such problems are rarely amenable to comprehensive regionwide solutions, nor do they necessitate multinational regional organizations. Furthermore, for various reasons, many of these problems are not often first addressed by national governments. Diverse problems such as AIDS, water, terror, and migration rarely share common outer boundaries or affect the same groups of countries. Nor do they always follow market patterns of trade or investment. By far the major approach to dealing with such cross-border problems, at least in East Asia, has been problem-specific cooperation involving public, semipublic, and private actors engaged in the search for rolling, ad hoc, but multicountry solutions. Often, but not necessarily, solutions once reached on one problem enhance the likelihood for both geographical broadening and issue deepening at subsequent points in time.

In this context, within Asia, as elsewhere, an emerging cadre of elites from the public, semipublic, and private sectors has been cooperating to address such specific problems and to propose regional solutions. NGOs, religious fundamentalists, professional associations, and track II epistemic communities, to name only several examples, have been cooperating across East Asia's national borders in this way.

Collectively, such actors have led to an increase in regional approaches to a variety of different problems and to a deepening of regional connections, even though few result in formal institutions or multilateral bodies. Rather they are more ad hoc in nature, more limited in membership, and more singularly focused in the problems they address.

In this volume, one exemplary case involves environmental problems such as acid rain, haze, or marine pollution, a problem area addressed by Laura Campbell in chapter 8 as well as by Tsunekawa in chapter 5. Quite parallel, however, are the pan-regional connections that have sprung from efforts to link antigovernmental Islamist groups such as those that are studied by Leheny in chapter 9. Often deeply anchored in localized political disputes, many of these groups have established cross-border nodes of cooperation that forge additional intra-Asian links, albeit not always of the kind welcomed by those now in power. In such cases, regionalization takes a distinctly antigovernmental but nonetheless integrative form. Finally, as explored by Evans in chapter 10, a number of ad hoc organizations and groupings have gained institutional legitimacy through explicitly regional proposals to address commonly perceived problems. Often these emerge as track II groups—epistemic communities of regionally committed private-sector and public-sector individuals who meet regularly and explore possible regional approaches to various specific problems. Or they may involve cross-border cooperation among commonly focused NGOs from several different countries, sometimes in cooperation with, other times at odds with, the affected governments. Within quite different venues, all of these groups work to create sequential coalitions that result in border-crossing links on a problem-by-problem basis. With very different tensile strengths and across very different national boundaries, these ad hoc coalitions have been generating an increasing number of cross-regional linkages.

Building Cohesion from Two Directions

Ties across East Asia have moved forward through two related but analytically distinct processes: *regionalism* and *regionalization* (Breslin 2000, 207; Hurrell 1995b; Gamble and Payne 1996). Regionalism involves primarily the process of institution creation. It occurs most conspicuously when nation-states come together through top-down activities—deliberate projects involving government-to-government cooperation. New institutions are designed to deal with transnational problems that confront several nations in common. In response to common negative externalities beyond their individual capacities to resolve, several presumably rational governments act collectively to reduce transaction costs and individual vulnerabilities while simultaneously furthering their own self-interests (Keohane 1984). Regionalism thus involves national governments concluding that their interests are sufficiently congruent with one another to subordinate elements of their nominal national autonomy. They agree to be bound by a collective set of agreements that are only partly in accord with national preferences. Regionalism, in short, has at least three key elements: it is top down; it is biased toward formal (usually governmental) agreements; and it involves semipermanent structures in which governments or their representatives are the main participants.

In almost all instances, such a decision to act collectively necessitates at least the partial surrender of a nation-state's Westphalian sovereignty. Entering into binding agreements with its neighbors obligates a state to behave according to various collectively agreed upon rules. Any real or theoretical freedom it may have had to act unilaterally is subordinated to acting in concert with others. Formal regional groupings are rarely a nation-state's preferred first strategy, particularly when that state is relatively powerful globally or within the region. Why accept a set of potentially inhibiting rules unnecessarily? Yet when several states agree to be mutually bound, they enhance trust and gain greater predictability about their neighbors' actions.

Regionalization, in contrast, develops from the bottom up through societally driven processes. The corporate behavior discussed earlier is typically one of the most powerful of these processes, providing a major catalyst to regional cooperation in East Asia. In one view, "The most important driving forces [in regionalization] . . . come from markets, from private trade and investment flows, and from the policies and decision of companies" (Gamble and Payne 1996, 334).

Social processes are by no means completely independent of governmental actions and institutional underpinnings. Indeed, as Tsunekawa shows for Japan, and as MacIntyre and Naughton demonstrate for China and Indonesia, East Asia's major governments have frequently taken official actions designed to stimulate or to support behavior by private-sector actors. Furthermore, as Solingen argues, national governments under the control of liberalizing domestic coalitions typically find it beneficial to cooperate with one another in advancing the interests of their core private-sector supporters.

Yet ultimately, even more important engines of regionalization have been hundreds, if not thousands, of individual social and economic actors. Thus the key elements in regionalization are a bottom-up process, social construction, and results that do not necessarily involve governmentally representative bodies. Such linkages rarely involve serious challenges to national sovereignty and as such are typically far less problematic for states to permit, although obviously many particular governments, for reasons linked to the retention of national power by particular elites, would prefer fewer, rather than more, linkages from within to outside their borders.

As noted earlier, explicit top-down government institution building has without a doubt contributed to enhanced Asian cohesiveness. For the most part, however, Asian governments have been reluctant to regionalize in formal and institutionalized ways. This traces back largely to jealousy over the possible surrender of sovereignty. But it is linked as well to the lack of agreement on underlying goals and values. Asian governments have resisted creating new transregional institutions because in large measure they have not seen them as necessary, nor have they agreed on what ends they might serve. As Simon put it:

> No real community consisting of common values, interlocking histories, and the free movement of peoples and firms across national boundaries exists yet in the [Asian] region. Hence the reticence about creating political institutions that would entail policymaking based on legal procedures. Successful institutions require common views of objectives as well as cost and benefit sharing. (Simon 1998, 197)

Until the late 1980s, and arguably even since, the principal impetus toward closer integration in Asia came less through explicit and formal organizations such as ASEAN, ARF, or APEC and more from bottom-up processes tied to economic and problem-solving regionalization. Economic ties were long the most visible and interlaced fibers crisscrossing Asia. Indeed, few of Asia's formal institutions have been central to the organization or functioning of the region's economy; instead, economic links have been driven primarily by private corporate actions (Gilpin 2000, 266).

At least three analytically separate components were vital in weaving Asia's more complex regional economic webs: investment, production networks, and trade. All can be traced to the development and increased utilization of post-Fordist production processes. These are driven by innovation within the production process, by small-batch production and quick changeover of product lines, by the development of long-term supply and subcontracting networks, and by the simultaneous integration of a large number of small- and medium-sized manufacturers. Such production arrangements, particularly in manufacturing, fostered the development of complex forward and backward linkages among contractors and component producers in different countries across Asia and the use of subcontractors and partners across national lines (Bernard 1994).

Pioneered by such Japanese manufacturers as Toyota, these processes spurred substantial investment by Japanese corporations into other parts of Asia, starting in the early 1970s and accelerating dramatically in the latter half of the 1980s. The earliest Japanese investments were made in Northeast Asia—most notably Taiwan and South Korea. These were later expanded into Southeast Asia. Transborder production networks thus developed in products such as textiles, light manufacturing, and raw materials. Tachiki demonstrates in considerable detail the ways different corporations have created these networks, the methods they have used subsequently to function, and the complex boundaries they have developed.

An even stronger wave of intra-Asian investment and trade was unleashed as a result of the currency realignments that followed the Plaza Accord of 1985. Japanese-owned corporations again led the way, setting up extensive and sophisticated production facilities throughout Southeast Asia (Doner 1991; Hatch and Yamamura 1996; Hatch 2000; Pempel 1997).

Transborder investment also flowed from both manufacturing and financial institutions based in Hong Kong and Taiwan. Much of this investment went into China, creating distinctive and cross-national Chinese production networks. Typically based on family and ethnic connections, these networks were more flexible and fast moving than the facilities developed in Asia by Japanese-owned companies (Hamilton 1999; Naughton 1997). Singaporean banks and investors were particularly significant sources of cross-border investments in the financial sector, with Singapore's largest local bank, DBS, acquiring majority shares of banks in Thailand and Hong Kong as well as large shares of a local bank in the Philippines (Hamilton-Hart 2004). Additional outflows of money from companies based in South Korea, Singapore, and Malaysia enhanced the networks of bottom-up connectedness among the Asian economies. In some instances these investments were openly encouraged through government policies by both host and home country; in many others, such as certain Singaporean investments in Indonesia, personal ties across national borders led to investments despite countervailing governmental policies. The importance of such personal and corporate ties is explored in considerable detail by Hamilton-Hart in chapter 7.

Interlaced with these trends was the emergence of both natural economic territories and growth triangles. The former were created, usually within a single country, to provide investment incentives to corporations as well as synergistic concentrations of business talent. Growth triangles, in contrast, span national boundaries as neighboring states pool their complementary comparative advantages in, for example, labor and raw materials (Indonesia), manufacturing facilities (Malaysia), and logistical support (Singapore) in the Singapore–Riau Islands–Johore growth triangle (Katzenstein 2003). The Tumen River Delta project saw subnational governmental actors from Japan, northeast China, North and South Korea, and parts of the Russian Far East acting as the prime movers. Despite its grand scope, however, the project foundered on the complexity and competing agendas of the many national and subnational governmental actors. China's Dailian export zone to Japan and South Korea is another such region, whereas Guangdong Province has forged a virtually microregional economy with neighboring Hong Kong, essentially excluding the rest of China. Fujian has done much the same with Taiwan (Breslin 2000; Naughton 1999).

By the mid- to late 1990s, therefore, a dense web of networks in manufacturing and banking was crisscrossing East Asia. Corporations with quite different types of internal organization and varying degrees of flexibility were involved. Boosted by these investment flows, intra-Asian trade grew substantially, becoming more multidimensional and adding additional layers to intra-Asian linkages. Roughly 30 percent of Asia's total exports were intra-Asian in 1970; by 2001 the figure was 47 percent. Intra-Asian imports increased from 30 percent to 53 percent (Guerrieri 1998, 68–69; McKinnon and Schnabl 2003, 4). A considerable portion, of course, was trade in finished products sold between merchants in different countries—the stuff of Ricardian trade theory and comparative advantages of different national economies—but much of the growth involved intra-firm trade arising from the new ability of individual companies to move components throughout their regional production networks, crossing national borders with increased ease. Economically driven regionalization has created business ties stretching across Asia's political boundaries and vastly enhancing the bottom-up integration of the region.

Ambiguously positioned between top-down and bottom-up processes were many of the actions driven by ad hoc problem-oriented groups. In a host of different arenas, for example, networks of public and private individuals across the region have cooperated in semiformal dialogues to bring about closer regional agreement on solutions to problems involving trade, crime, maritime navigation, health care, and even military interventions. Paul Evans, an active participant in many of track II dialogues, provides a detailed analysis of the most important of these processes. They are also addressed by Tsunekawa and Campbell in their separate chapters. It is clear from their collective analyses that track II dialogues—what Milner (2000) has called a "relentless conversation"—have created a number of pan-area communities of like-minded regionalists whose ongoing interactions have begun to bring forward practical solutions to a variety of problems.

Yet as Campbell and Tsunekawa demonstrate separately within the area of cross-border environmental problems, it is nonoverlapping alliances of Asian governments that have been collaborating (or failing to collaborate)—both institutionally and informally. At times such cooperation has resulted in a formal Memorandum of Understanding; more often it has led to government and private-sector collaboration across national borders in the absence of formal institutionalization. Simultaneously, other environmental issues have been addressed almost exclusively by the private sector through the promotion of regional and global harmonization of environmental standards, often designed to enhance national economic competitiveness. And in still other instances, formal institutions such as ASEAN have been able to generate effective pressures on member counties to address specific environmental problems at the source.

NGOs and other organizations based in civil society, such as professional and business associations, along with regional advocacy groups, have also contributed to the bottom-up regionalization of East Asia, but their overall influence has been far less than that of either corporations or track II participants. Tsunekawa notes that cross-regional NGO networks have been affecting policy since the first Asia-Pacific NGO Environmental Conference was convened in Bangkok in 1991. Nevertheless, NGOs remain far less powerful in East Asia than they have been in North America and Western Europe. Indeed, some governments, including those in Singapore, Malaysia, and China, have been overtly hostile to NGOs. And even in Japan, which is nominally more "pro-NGO" than these others, one powerful Japanese leader, Suzuki Muneo, at the January 2002 international conference to generate funding to rehabilitate war-ravaged Afghanistan, successfully pressed the Ministry of Foreign Affairs to prevent Japanese NGOs from participating. Furthermore, various Japanese government agencies have conducted extensive and secret background investigations on individuals and NGOs that have utilized new sunshine laws in the exercise of their legal rights to gain access to government data. China and many countries in Southeast Asia have been even more draconian in their treatment of NGOs and other organizations outside official party or governmental lines of control.

Even where they are strongest, namely, in the environmental areas, NGOs in East Asia have been only marginally effective, as both Campbell and Tsunekawa point out. In much of the West, NGOs have been the most critical agents promoting tighter regional or global environmental standards. This has not been the case in East Asia. Ironically, however, as Campbell argues, the general inability or unwillingness of East Asian regional institutions to address the transboundary haze problem helped to shift government attitudes about

NGOs. Most notably, Indonesia's failure to stop forest burning was a major reason behind Singapore's promotion of greater Asian and international NGO involvement in regional environmental issues. Additionally, through the Internet, global and regional NGOs have begun to provide valuable information to their counterpart groups in specific Asian countries, allowing many to play an enhanced role in regional problems. Also bolstering NGO significance have been various extra-regional supports such as that of USAID.

Finally, although it is not examined in great detail within the remaining chapters, Asian regional connectedness has been bolstered by popular cultural developments. Unlike recent claims, made by certain East Asian leaders such as Malaysian prime minister Mahathir or former Singaporean president Lee Kuan Yew, that the region is marked by certain timeless and transcendent "Asian values," claims made by local political leaders during the first two decades after World War II emphasized the purported distinctiveness of Malaysian, South Korean, Chinese, or Indonesian culture. Most of these earlier leaders denied that Asia as a whole had any relevant border-spanning culture whatsoever. Indeed, many countries explicitly banned songs, radio programs, and movies produced by their neighbors. As a consequence, for much of the postwar period, East Asia experienced little of the integrative, transborder cultural amalgamations that began to stitch the European countries together as early as the 1940s. Today, the situation is quite different. As McNicoll has noted, East Asia is now marked by middle-class consumerism, fueled by "youth bulges." From cartoons to karaoke and from pop music to Internet sites, such youth-oriented popular culture now bleeds across East Asia's national borders in ways unimaginable two decades ago. The result is an increasingly common template of daily citizen experience in much of East Asia.

The cumulative result of such diverse actions has been to enhance the number, range, and depth of intra-Asian connections. East Asia today is a much more closely knit region than it was at the end of World War II or even a decade ago. At the same time, the inner links across East Asia vary greatly in their nature and their targets of integration. As a consequence of this diversity, the outer boundaries of the region are also highly fluid. This final issue deserves explicit attention.

Fluidity at the Outer Limits: East Asia's Elastic Boundaries

One result of the complex interplay of three such diverse drivers operating from two different directions is that any East Asian "region" manifests very different outer boundaries to viewers observing different drivers or processes. "Regions" are hardly unproblematic, with fixed and clear-cut geographic borders. In fact no region in the world with genuine political and economic significance is so essentialist in its makeup. Rarely can any region be understood as delimited by simple geographic or political lines on a map. Instead, regions are fluid and complex mixtures of physical, psychological, and behavioral traits continually being re-created and redefined. They vary with the policy issues that confront a region and what the dominant political actors in a given group of countries see as their political priorities.

This is certainly true of "East Asia," whose particular composition has been highly contested. No single map of East Asia is so inherently self-evident and logical as to preclude the consideration of equally plausible alternatives. Rather, as with geographical borders throughout history, the composition of East Asia has been highly contested, and different visions of the relevant scope of the region remain in widespread use throughout East Asia and its vicinity. Evans (2000, 7) provides an extensive list of the more frequently used terms that encompass that particular portion of real estate: Asia-Pacific, Asian-Pacific, Asia Pacific, Asia and the Pacific, Asia/Pacific, East Asia, East Asia and the Pacific, East Asia and the Western Pacific, Eastasia, Eastern Asia, Far East, Monsoon Asia, the Pacific, Pacific Asia, Pacific-Asia, Pacific Basin, Pacific Rim, and Western Pacific. Furthermore, there are at least two dozen different definitions for Asia-Pacific. Even more complicating, as Shiraishi (1999, 2) notes, is that few of these labels coincide with internal or external actors' own perceptions of reality.

Without a doubt, different geographical configurations are explicitly used to advance or retard specific political goals. Nevertheless, very different geographical pictures emerge when the focus is on governmental agreements and regionalism, and this picture is different from the one seen when one concentrates on private corporate activities and regionalization. One set of boundaries that is "obvious" from a focus on, say, governmental trade agreements is meaningless if one's regional concerns are with the development of anti-terrorist networks.

The authors in this book most typically employ the term East Asia or eastern Asia. This refers to the region composed of the nation-states of Northeast and Southeast Asia—China, Japan, the two Koreas, Taiwan, and the ten members of ASEAN (Singapore, Indonesia, the Philippines, Thailand, Malaysia, Borneo, Laos, Cambodia, Vietnam, and Myanmar). These countries are geographically proximate, and from many perspectives, such a use is logical. As mentioned in several chapters in this volume, most notably those by Tsunekawa, MacIntyre and Naughton, Tachiki, and Hamilton-Hart, the integration of Northeast Asia, rich in technology and capital, with labor-rich and capital-poor Southeast Asia, has given the area a certain amount of region-defining economic sense. Such a definition also finds explicitly institutionalized form in the so-called APT formulation (ASEAN + 3–China, South Korea, and Japan), as examined by Evans, among others. The APT countries provide the core of what most authors mean by the term East Asia.

At the same time, such a definition does not automatically include such neighboring nation-states as the Russian Federation (especially the Russian Far East), Australia, and New Zealand, all of which have periodically expressed a desire to be treated as parts of East Asia. Whether to include various Pacific Island countries is also an open question. Although a core East Asian region may be identified with only minor controversy, that core is ringed by many others whose inclusion or exclusion is less unambiguous.

Any East Asian region defined by trade dependence or centered on security and defense, however, would have quite different borders. The United States remains far and away the most critical export market for many of the countries of East Asia. Furthermore, U.S. alliances with Japan, South Korea, and Australia, plus its guarantee of Taiwanese autonomy, along with its extensive military presence throughout the Asia-Pacific, argue for considering the relevant region to be more than any narrowly constructed East Asia.

The United States is only one of several extra-regional actors that demand regional recognition in a focus on security. Unquestionably, security and defense define a much wider "regional security order" for East Asia (Lake and Morgan 1997) that includes not just Japan, China, and the other countries typically taken as geographical components of Southeast and Northeast Asia but also the United States, Russia, and most probably central Asia, India, and Pakistan as well (Alagappa 1998). Indeed, many of the countries of central Asia have explicit claims to regional importance particular on security grounds, and this was reflected in the creation of the SCO, linking China, Russia, and four central Asian states. Moreover, Australia provided the bulk of the military force behind the resolution of the conflict in East Timor. And as Leheny's chapter on nonstate terrorism in East Asia makes clear, al Qaeda has also begun to play a substantial "extra-regional" role in support of locally based Muslim fundamentalist groups in various parts of East Asia. The organization is having a profound impact on East Asian regional security, which suggests the need to see East Asian security as linked to several areas that broaden its boundaries.

Such different "maps" of East Asia exemplify the broader issue: no self-evident and essentialist East Asia forms a single logical and self-contained regional unit. Rather, as different problems emerge, most regions take on different geographical parameters. To be sure, changing problems determine which of many possible collectivities within the various definitions of the East Asian region will be most relevant. Different problems "create" different regions. In their individual chapters, the authors explicitly tease out either more expansive or restricted geographical notions, as seems most warranted by the particular problem(s) they examine.

Certainly East Asia's formal multilateral bodies, as is clear from the different orbs circumscribed in figure 1.2, include or exclude quite different countries. In certain cases, such as the ASEAN Free Trade Area agreement (AFTA), a large group of governments that span Northeast and Southeast Asia have been organized into an officially recognized and legalized institution. Yet the Five Power Defense Arrangement (FPDA) is more limited in size, with quite different member countries. The SCO and the Northeast Asia Cooperation Dialogue (NEACD) are described by still different memberships. In yet other instances, ranging from APEC to nonstate terrorist links, formally and informally created connections take shapes that go well beyond any narrow Asia-specific boundaries.

The fast-growing network of bilateral free trade agreements has also created new linkages both within East Asia and across the Pacific (Dent 2003). The patterns they form are quite different from full-scale institutional arrangements. Similarly, individual pollution problems draw in only the two, three, or four contiguous governments most deeply affected by a specific problem such as acid rain while leaving out otherwise unaffected neighbors that might nevertheless be part of agreements on different problems.

Finally, various production networks foster regional arrangements that actually defy existing national boundaries, instead forming investment corridors that span several states but encompass none completely, a point developed at length by Tachiki. He identifies two different "core" corridors—one in Northeast and the other in Southeast Asia—neither of which completely corresponds with existing nation-state boundaries associated with East Asia. Moreover, he locates what he calls "new frontier countries," a term that includes Mongolia as well as parts of China's interior, central Asia, and South Asia, all of which, he shows, are being woven through foreign direct investment more closely into the East Asian economic center. Such moves are almost certain to generate still new outer boundaries for the region.

Tachiki's findings coincide with McNicoll's analysis of East Asia's "urban corridors," which weave together economic nodes and networks centered on the limited number of global cities in the area. McNicoll contends that East Asia may well see the fusion of these two corridors into a non-state-defined corridor that runs from Japan and North Korea to West Java.

A similar pattern of regional fusion with nonnational boundaries was found by Gilbert Rozman (2004), who examined the links forged in Northeast Asia by local and regional (as opposed to national) governments in China, South Korea, North Korea, the Russian Far East and Eastern Siberia, Japan, and Mongolia. Many of these efforts proved stillborn, yet the energies engendered in bringing them forward all proceeded along subnational lines. To the extent that these efforts resulted in actual programs, the shapes were very much at odds with national political boundaries, just as has been true of various East Asian investment corridors.

Thus, for purposes of this book, the notion of an East Asian region has at its underlying center the combination of Northeast and Southeast Asian states noted earlier. Certain intra—East Asian linkages across these core borders are vastly stronger than others, while the outer boundaries remain fuzzy.

In this vein, the chapters in the book take for granted, and reinforce through empirical evidence, that the region known as East Asia has emerged with highly fluid outer boundaries subject to redefinition and reconfiguration. The boundaries vary constantly as problems and attempted solutions change. Nevertheless, within this fluidly changing set of outer limits, an undeniable core of countries is becoming more closely linked as the consequence of a mix of actions by different drivers acting through quite different, and often complementary, processes. At the same time, this core of East Asia retains numerous extra-territorial ties, particularly across the Pacific and increasingly into central Asia. East Asia is thus becoming a more cohesive region, but one whose map is constantly being redrawn, usually in erasable pencil rather than Magic Marker.

It is in this context that the contributors to this volume are using the term *remapping*. Remapping does not imply the erosion or elimination of the standard territorial lines that demarcate the outer boundaries of sovereign nation-states. Instead, remapping suggests that additional lines of cooperation are being developed across East Asia that are complicating, and on occasion competing with, the more traditional lines of sovereign state power. It also implies that these outer boundaries are continually reshaping our perceptions of what we mean by East Asia.

I

REGIONALISM IN COMPARATIVE PERSPECTIVE

2

East Asian Regional Institutions:

Characteristics, Sources, Distinctiveness

배경
(국내정치상황)

ETEL SOLINGEN

East Asian institutions are embedded in a regional economic, political, and social context that has become highly integrated into the global political economy in recent decades. This feature sets East Asia apart from other industrializing regions, although at the same time, the informality of its regional ↔ EU institutions is much less unusual. This informality has become a "puzzle" in the analysis of regional institutions, largely as a result of routine comparisons with the EU, which have helped obscure other important comparisons. As Kahler (2000a) has argued, heavily legalized regional institutions such as the EU are islands, anomalies in a generally less legalized world. Beyond that, whether legalization necessarily contributes to higher levels of compliance is a contested proposition (Lutz and Sikkink 2000; Alter 2000). Nor is openness to resorting to various multilateral options uniquely East Asian.

It is important to underscore what this chapter leaves out by design. I do not dwell here on normative issues regarding whether and how to improve the institutional "strength," "teeth," "fitness," or wherewithal of East Asian institutions. A growing literature focuses precisely on these issues (Leifer 1996; Almonte 1997–98; Jones and Smith 2001; Feinberg 2003). My main concern here is threefold: taking stock of extant characterizations of East | Topic

I thank T. J. Pempel, discussants Andrew MacIntyre and Paul Evans, and other participants at the workshops in Hayama, Japan (March 25–27, 2001), and Portland, Oregon (March 22–24, 2002), as well as Davis Bobrow, Ralph Cossa, and Richard Stubbs, for their useful suggestions. At different stages this research benefited from support from the Social Science Research Council—McArthur Foundation Fellowship on Peace and Security in a Changing World, a SSRC—Japan Foundation Abe Fellowship, the United States Institute of Peace, and the University of California's Pacific Rim Research Program and Institute on Global Conflict and Cooperation.

Asian institutions, tracing them to underlying domestic political conditions, and exploring the extent to which they represent highly unique paths to regional cooperation.

Characteristics of East Asian Institutions

Studies of East Asian regional intergovernmental institutions often converge on the identification of a set of characteristics shared by most of them, despite variations in membership, longevity, and issue area (economics, security, or both). Many of these characteristics are frequently traced to those developed by ASEAN, including informality, reliance on *musjawarah* and *mufakat* (Malay-style consultation and consensus), incrementalism, building on personal and political relations, saving face, avoiding arbitration mechanisms in dispute resolution, and emphasizing process over substance (Acharya 1999). Indeed, the ASEAN Regional Forum (ARF henceforth) and, more recently, the ASEAN + 3 framework replicated many of ASEAN's defining institutional profiles. Even the Asia-Pacific Economic Cooperation (APEC), with yet a different membership composition, shares at least some of these traits. Three core characteristics—informality, consensus, and "open regionalism"—as displayed by ASEAN, the ARF, and APEC, capture the emphasis of East Asian institutions on process rather than outcome.

Informality

Informality complements, and indeed encapsulates, many of the characteristics previously mentioned, such as relying heavily on personal relations, avoiding third-party adjudication, and emphasizing process over substance. According to Lipson (1991, 500), "informality is best understood as a device for minimizing the impediments to cooperation, at both the domestic and the international levels." An informal setting also makes it easier to agree not to raise confrontational or contentious issues. Informality is well matched with those institutions that aggregate members retaining a strong attachment to sovereignty and a commitment to noninterference in domestic affairs. It certainly provides some guarantee that the institutional environment remains free of enforcement mechanisms, such as third-party adjudication. In terms of process, informality favors dialogue, meetings, and consultations; in terms of outcome, it favors general principles and codes of conduct.[1]

ASEAN was no more than a declaration (Bangkok Declaration) after its creation in 1967. In 1971 its foreign ministers signed a Zone of Peace, Freedom, and Neutrality Declaration (ZOPFAN) to develop collective strength,

1. For a detailed characterization of East Asian institutions as nonlegalized, see Kahler 2000b.

solidarity, and "security from external interference." In 1976 the first summit meeting of heads of state adopted two key documents. The Declaration of ASEAN Concord emphasized exclusive reliance on peaceful processes in the settlement of intraregional differences and reaffirmed ZOPFAN. The Treaty of Amity and Cooperation (TAC) in Southeast Asia promoted "perpetual peace, everlasting amity, and cooperation" among the member states.[2] It also established three basic principles: respect for state sovereignty, nonintervention, and renunciation of the threat or use of force in resolving disputes. Thus, ASEAN has not relied on formal dispute-resolution mechanisms and is not a collective security arrangement.[3] There is disagreement about whether or not ASEAN amounts to a security community (Khong 1997a; Acharya 2001a; Leifer 1989; Kahler 1995). ASEAN developed several informal mechanisms known as the "ASEAN way," emphasizing consultation, accommodation, reciprocity, and informal diplomacy.

The informal mechanisms that organize ASEAN's activities include heads of state summits (alternating between a formal and an informal summit every year), an annual meeting of foreign ministers, and a multiplicity of other meetings involving senior officials (senior officials' meetings [SOM], attended by heads of foreign ministries), other ministers, and delegates in a wide range of issue areas. Since 1992, ASEAN Post-Ministerial Conferences (involving the ASEAN 10 + 10 dialogue partners) have expanded to include discussions of conflict resolution and the promotion of transparency and confidence-building measures on security matters.[4] These included bilateral military exercises dealing with common internal and external enemies. The role of a very small central ASEAN secretariat is reduced to that of coordinating among national secretariats sited in member states' foreign ministries. After the Asian crisis, the limits of this secretariat were recognized: "We . . . see the need for a strengthened ASEAN Secretariat with an enhanced role to support the realization of our vision" (http://www.asean.or.id, ASEAN Vision 2020). Finally, there is the ASEAN Standing Committee (ASC), headed by the foreign minister of the state holding the annual ministerial meeting and including all ambassadorial representatives in that state. Clearly, the composition of the ASC changes every year.

APEC began as an informal dialogue but has since become a central institution promoting free trade and practical economic cooperation in the Asia-Pacific, with a combined GDP of more than US $18 trillion in 1999 and 43.85

2. All ASEAN's basic documents and summit declarations can be found at http://www.asean.or.id.

3. A dispute-settlement mechanism of sorts exists under the TAC, but ASEAN states have not resorted to it, favoring bilateral management of conflicts and even the International Court of Justice over this regional option.

4. The ten dialogue partners are Australia, Canada, China, the European Union, India, Japan, Russia, New Zealand, South Korea, and the United States.

percent of global trade (http://www.apecsec.org.sg). ASEAN's opposition to "mandatory directives" was expressed at the outset, through the Kuching Consensus. China was even more opposed to binding codes. Malaysia and Japan have been particularly resistant to a vision of APEC as a free trade area. Thus, APEC did not evolve into a formal institution of the kind the United States and Canada were advancing but rather followed the relatively informal style of other East Asian institutions. There are no coercive mechanisms for implementation or enforcement but voluntaristic commitments (individual action plans), proposals for "concerted unilateral action," and weak evaluation procedures. An Eminent Persons Group first suggested a dispute-settlement mechanism along the lines of the WTO; it was later diluted into a dispute-mediation service and eventually superseded by the explicit embrace of the WTO's Dispute Settlement Understanding.

APEC's small secretariat, established in 1993 in Singapore to serve as the core support mechanism, comprises only twenty-three officials, seconded by member economies for fixed terms and a similar number of locally recruited support staff. The secretariat provides advisory, operational, and logistic/technical services to member states and APEC officials. Many consider it too weak and underfunded to support a more dynamic agenda, even one not focused on trade liberalization but on trade facilitation and economic, technical, and political cooperation. The annual meetings of leaders (heads of state) have been described as the single most important of APEC's achievements. The Bogor Declaration (1994) and the Osaka Summit Implementation (1995) advanced APEC's pledges to liberalize trade by committing its industrialized members to reduce trade barriers by the year 2010 and industrializing ones by 2020. The subsequent Information Technology Agreement liberalized trade in information technology equipment, and the Early Voluntary Sector Liberalization program liberalized trade in nine sectors. An Economic and Technical Co-operation (Ecotech) forum was created to promote sustainable economic growth. Other APEC meetings gather ministers and senior officials for agenda-setting purposes, as well as working groups, seminars, and workshops designed to disseminate norms and develop analytical abilities and sensitivity to gender and the environment (Aggarwal and Morrison 1998; Aggarwal and Lin 2001).

The ARF was created in 1994 to address Asia-Pacific security. ASEAN was initially lukewarm to a regional security institution along the lines of the Conference on Security and Cooperation in Europe, as advocated by others, but it quickly moved to promote a more consultative mechanism along the lines of ASEAN's own, tenaciously reaffirming ASEAN's role as the ARF's driving force. In its relatively brief history, the ARF approved a concept paper identifying an evolutionary approach toward a conflict-resolution mechanism; promoted dialogue on the Spratly Islands dispute and on Korean denuclearization; advanced confidence-building measures, including white papers, on defense policy and exchanges between military academies; and published its first *Annual Security Outlook* in 2000, promoting confidence and transparency. The ARF has not moved from confidence-building measures into preventive diplomacy, largely because of China's resistance to any binding decisions or conflict-resolution procedures. However, China's preference for bilateralism in resolving extant disputes is wholly consistent with ASEAN's own internal modus operandi in this regard, although there is progressively more strategic use of multilateralism in both cases (Christensen 1999; Johnston 1999). Similarly, there are no enforcement mechanisms in the ARF. Indeed, ARF does not even have a secretariat. ASEAN hosts all of the ARF's annual meetings of foreign ministers and the preceding ARF-SOM meetings, but not intersessional workshops on specific topics. At the 2001 meeting (Hanoi), ARF participants discussed the concept and principles of preventive diplomacy, the need to enhance the role of the ARF's chairman in the period between sessions, and the possibility of creating a list of experts and "eminent persons" entrusted with analyzing problems of mutual concern. On the whole, the ARF remains the least institutionalized relative to ASEAN and APEC.

Consensus

East Asian institutions are also consensus oriented. ASEAN pioneered consensual decision making (mufakat) among East Asian institutions. Several sources have been identified to explain this principle, whose origin can be found in Javanese village societies' invoking the need for a leader to seek the community's acceptance of a given decision. At the same time, ASEAN's consensus was found to be pointedly driven by the need to portray a common external front that would strengthen ASEAN's position vis-à-vis major powers (Acharya 1999, 63). The consensual rule allowed the member that benefits the least from an agreement to influence the terms of the agreement, a principle that contradicts the notion of hegemony by most powerful states (Khong 1997a, 330–33). Consensus in ASEAN does not require unanimity, only that the nonsupporting party is prepared to let the decision move forward.[5] In other words, "consensus does not assume that everyone must agree, it assumes at least that no one objects to the proposal" (Chin 1997, 5). The guaranteed voice of every member, as a result of the consensus principle, arguably strengthens loyalty toward the institution (Hirschman 1970). The need for consensus requires a nonconfrontational approach and a willingness to sustain differences while crafting some minimal common understandings. Most importantly, there is a concerted effort to prevent such differences from dominating the public debate.

5. Thambipillai 1994, 120. The "five-minus-one" principle formulated by Lee Kuan Yew allows a decision to move forward provided it does not harm the reluctant party or exclude it from future interactions (Acharya 1999, 63–64).

The ARF has embodied ASEAN's consensus rule writ large, precluding major powers from advancing their agenda at the expense of smaller participants. Consultation tends to pass over divisive issues, relegating them to later resolution as they "achieve ripeness" or are made irrelevant and innocuous by time and events (Almonte 1997–98). The ARF's "weak decision rules," according to Simon (2001b, 284), can also be traced to an effort to make China comfortable in a multilateral security institution. The outcome of this consensual process are decisions that can be implemented in a voluntary, nonbinding way. The consensus principle may prevent coercion and confrontation, but some find it a barrier to institutional change. Decisions are hard to reach when any participant can wield veto power. According to this view, the institution's evolutionary pace is deliberately held back by the lowest common denominator.

APEC operates by consensus reached on the basis of open dialogue geared to define regional objectives rather than binding agreements. This "concerted unilateralism" leaves it up to members to implement those objectives (Gershman 2000). The consensus rule, a derivative of ASEAN's principle, allowed competing visions within APEC (supporters of binding comprehensive trade and investment liberalization versus supporters of informal economic cooperation) to endure since its inception. Even as some continue to criticize decision by consensus in APEC, they also regard it as potentially a long-term strength, by making the process less contentious (Aggarwal and Lin 1991, 183). The consensual principle structures APEC as a horizontal organization with a weak hierarchy, despite colossal differences in members' power and resources.

Open Regionalism

A third key characteristic of East Asian institutions is their open regionalism (Drysdale 1991; Garnaut 1996). In the economic domain, open regionalism seeks to enhance regional economic exchange without violating the legal requirements embedded in the World Trade Organization (most-favored-nation rule) or without discriminating against extra-regional partners. An extension of this approach to security and other issue areas implies an effort to signal openness and inclusiveness in the design of regional arrangements. East Asian regional institutions are said to support, not substitute for, global multilateral institutions (Harris 2000, 501). In 1993, ASEAN agreed on a free trade area (AFTA) designed to allow free trade in manufactured and processed goods by 2003.[6] Yet the 1997 ASEAN Vision 2020 declaration defined ASEAN as "a concert of Southeast Asian nations, outward looking,

---

6. Chia 1996. Six of the wealthier members—Brunei, Indonesia, Malaysia, the Philippines, Singapore, and Thailand—were expected to reduce tariffs down to between zero to 5 percent by 2003, whereas Myanmar, Cambodia, Laos, and Vietnam would do so by 2005. Malaysia expressed its intention to delay tariff reductions in the auto industry until 2005.

living in peace, stability and prosperity, bonded together in partnership in dynamic development and in a community of caring societies. . . . We commit ourselves to moving toward closer cohesion and economic integration, narrowing the gap in the level of development among Member Countries, ensuring that the multilateral trading system remains fair and open, and achieving global competitiveness" (http://www.asean.or.id, ASEAN Vision 2020). The theme of ASEAN's ministerial meeting in Hanoi (2001) was ASEAN: United, Stable, Integrated and Outward-Looking.

APEC's commitment to open regionalism is expressed in pledges to embrace nondiscrimination (extending any cooperation on a most-favored-nation basis) and to accept new members (Haggard 1997, 44; Aggarwal 1995; Drysdale and Elek 1997). At the same time, the pace at which new memberships ought to be extended (to countries such as India, for instance) is contested. The effort to maintain consistency with WTO rules is reflected in all its declarations. The ministerial meeting and the leaders' summit (Shanghai, 2001) reaffirmed APEC's commitment to open regionalism and "strong support for an open, equitable, transparent and rules-based multilateral trading system, as represented by the WTO," while emphasizing the urgency of launching a new WTO round to reenergize the global trading system.[7] As Tay (2001, 2) suggests, both APEC and the ARF are inclusionary frameworks that "often included more states than function would have suggested. . . . The broader groups were favoured."

The prevailing open regionalism of East Asian institutions did not evolve unchallenged (Higgott 1999). In 1990, Malaysia's prime minister Mahathir bin Mohamad advocated an East Asian Economic Grouping that would exclude "non-East Asian" states. Japan, Indonesia, Korea, and Singapore, among others, expressed doubts about this concept. ASEAN eventually rejected the proposal in favor of an East Asian Economic Caucus that retained the principle of open regionalism (consistent with GATT and APEC). In the early 1990s, ASEAN initially expressed reservations about Japan's Nakayama proposal for a security forum because it regarded the proposal as contradicting ZOPFAN, or ASEAN's objective of "regional autonomy." However, this principle had been compromised at birth (1971) when Indonesia called for the exclusion of all foreign military bases, only to be overpowered by the web of United States–ASEAN bilateral relations. The principle of regional autonomy was diluted over the years, and its relevance faded even more with the establishment of the ARF.

The Asia–Europe Meeting (ASEM), including the ASEAN 10, Japan, China, and South Korea, in dialogue with the EU, provided sharper definition to an East Asian regional concept because it required an "East Asian" partner to the dialogue. Not surprisingly, Prime Minister Mahathir became an impassioned advocate of ASEM, which was originally conceived by ASEAN.

---

7. See APEC's website at http://www.apecsec.org.sg.

In the immediate aftermath of the Asian crisis, the creation of an Asian Monetary Fund was opposed by external actors (the United States initially) but also by China and others within the region. However, by late 1997 ASEAN helped launch the first East Asian Summit, which later evolved into the ASEAN + 3 process. The Manila Framework Group, launched in 1997, led to the establishment of an Asian Surveillance Group in 1998. That year the ASEAN + 3 initiated annual meetings of heads of state and regularized meetings of foreign and finance ministers. At a meeting in Thailand (2000), financial officers agreed on the Chiang Mai Initiative, a currency swap system to increase their hard currency reserves. This system was designed to help defend member economies from speculative attacks and avert potential liquidity crises stemming from unexpected capital outflows ("Asian Nations" 2000). The ASEAN + 3 process is an evolving one.[8] It is unclear whether significantly less financial dependence on the IMF and World Bank will result from it. The currency swap facility retains close links to IMF conditionality.

In sum, the extant state of institutional affairs in East Asia does not provide strong evidence for a reversal of open regionalism anytime soon. However, an alternative perspective suggests that the Asian crisis of the late 1990s and a distinctive form of Asian capitalism could weaken open regionalism as we know it (Higgott 1999; Stubbs 1999b).

Permissive Conditions and East Asian Institutional Features

What are the background conditions that underpinned the process of regional institutionalization in East Asia, and how might they affect the specific features it exhibits? Most studies of East Asian institutions converge on the identification of certain key characteristics they share. However, this convergence does not extend to a unified understanding of the sources of these characteristics (Ravenhill 1998; Kahler 2000d). Following T. J. Pempel's call, in chapter 1, for a focus on process rather than structure, I explore three intellectual trends explaining processes of institutionalization in the region. In particular, I examine a coalitional perspective initially designed to understand broader issues of regional conflict and cooperation, which might also shed light on the permissive conditions and processes under which East Asian institutional forms have evolved in recent decades.

There are clear advantages to studying East Asian institutions through cultural lenses.[9] The latter can deepen our understanding of the sociocultural

8. The 1999 ASEAN + 3 declaration can be accessed at http://www.asean.or.id/menu_asean+3.htm.

9. Alagappa 1998 urges the incorporation of political identity and national self-conceptions as important explanations for how security issues are perceived and how states' behavior changes over time.

background that might have led to an institution's particular characteristics.[10] They also sensitize us to an institution's communicative processes and socializing effects, or the ways in which these characteristics are self-perpetuating and regenerative.[11] The evolution of an "ASEAN way" from cultural forms in Javanese village society (musjawarah and mufakat) is at the heart of cultural analysis of East Asian institutions, and both of these forms seem to be entrenched in the plethora of consultations and meetings being held annually. Once embedded in a regional institution, particularly ASEAN, these norms are also ascribed transformative effects that create a new regional identity among members. A positive feedback loop is stipulated, from domestic culture to regional institutions, and back.[12]

Whether these particular norms or any other legal cultural forms are common throughout the region is a highly contested proposition, however. Indeed, some have suggested that it is the very diversity of legal systems that precludes progress toward a more legalized regional framework (Kahler 2000d, 561). If this is true for ASEAN, the more so for the more diverse contexts of APEC and the ARF. Cultural studies might benefit from a systematic understanding of domestic political considerations. It is particularly baffling that cultural studies have disregarded systematic explanations of domestic political changes related to internationalization, despite the region's unparalleled integration in the global economy in recent decades. The emphasis on musjawarah and mufakat is often advanced in detachment from both political-economic realities, material and ideational. Take away markets and the domestic politics that have produced them and one removes the most fundamental feature differentiating East Asia from other industrializing regions.

More sensitive to markets, but not necessarily to domestic politics, are functionalist understandings of East Asian institutions. The latter's main characteristics are explained in terms of potential gains from regional cooperation (such as managing the side effects of economic integration, liquidity crises, contagion effects, terrorism, migration, and others) that are difficult to realize because of collective action considerations. ASEAN's Vision 2020 declaration clearly recognized these needs (http://www.asean.or.id). However, that formal institutions, majority vote, or open regionalism is invariably a corollary of the need to cooperate regionally is contested as well. Haggard (1997, 45) finds "little evidence for the theory that higher levels of interdependence generate the demand for deeper integration," or the theory that trade generates prisoners' dilemma situations that only institutions (or a hegemon) can

10. See, e.g., important contributions by Acharya 1999, 2001a.

11. For an illuminating analysis of the language of Asia Pacific security, see Capie and Evans 2002.

12. Katzenstein and Shiraishi (1997) argue that domestic social and political norms that favor informal political and economic networks account for the relative informality of Asian regional institutions.

resolve. Moreover, to the extent that transaction costs are clearly at work as a barrier to cooperation, shared social norms of the kind addressed by cultural analysis can lessen those barriers, rendering formal institutions redundant.

Even within a rationalistic, functional framework, formal institutions may be less compelling when members' time horizons are long, gains from cooperation are repetitive, and peer pressure is important (Harris 2000, 496). According to Lipson (1991, 500–508), informal agreements facilitate cooperation because they make fewer informational demands on the parties, can be negotiated quickly, and can be rapidly modified as conditions change. Rapid change has particularly characterized East Asia in recent decades. Lipson also recognizes that problems of imperfect information and incentives to defect plague both verbal declarations and more formal agreements. Hence, other sources of informal agreements must be explored. Haggard (1997), for instance, urges a proper understanding of the preferences and capabilities of relevant actors and of the distributional effects of institutions. The differential impact of more binding constraints on different actors is also discussed by Kahler (2000d, 561), who points to the military and state security bureaucracies as having a particular interest in resisting more legalized institutions, whereas business leaders press for more rules to enforce liberalization.[13]

This tack leads to a third analytical possibility hitherto ignored in explaining the permissive background that bred East Asian institutions. Such effort compels a better understanding of key agents of regionalism: domestic ruling coalitions throughout the region. Paradoxically, different accounts of East Asian institutionalism have largely overlooked these underlying dynamics. Worldwide, political leaders rely on material and ideal aspects of internationalization for the purpose of brokering coalitions across the state—societal divide, logrolling both state agencies and societal actors sharing common interests and purpose.[14] The nature of resulting ruling coalitions constitutes an important referent for understanding the political agendas promoting certain regional arrangements but not others. Elsewhere (Solingen 1998) I argued that different domestic ideal-typical coalitions—and the different regional coalitional clusters they constitute in the aggregate—define a region's boundaries as well as its propensity for conflict and cooperation.[15] Driven by different approaches (grand strategies) to both the domestic and global political economy and institutions, different coalitional clusters—

13. This may be highly contingent on the pattern of business interests, however. Industrialists throughout the Middle East, often in tandem with landowners, frequently resist liberalization (Aarts 1999, 206).

14. Internationalization involves increased openness to international markets, capital, investments, and technology. Many perceive internationalization as a threat to local/national norms, cultures, and values, including nationalism. Hence, coalitions include political actors advancing both material and ideal interests and values.

15. For a more complete analysis of ASEAN in coalitional terms, see Solingen 1999 and 2004b, and Jayasuriya 2001.

internationalizing, backlash, hybrid—create regional orders, "identities," and shared expectations about conflict and cooperation.

Once it prevails politically, the dominant coalition's strategy becomes *raison* 국가이성 *d'état.* The grand strategy of internationalizing coalitions emphasizes domestic economic growth, cooperation and stability in the region, and dependable access to global markets, capital, investments, and technology. Macroeconomic stability and international competitiveness are granted primacy because both are expected to reduce uncertainty, encourage savings, and enhance the rate of investment (including foreign). Regional cooperation reduces the need for unproductive and inflation-inducing military investments and for protecting state-owned enterprises under a mantle of national security. Instead, the mobilization of resources for conflict can potentially emasculate domestic macroeconomic objectives via expansive military budgets, government and payments deficits, the rising cost of capital, inhibited savings and productive investment, depleted foreign exchange, overvalued exchange rates, currency instability and unpredictability, and stymied foreign investment.

The grand strategy of backlash coalitions, in its purest form, hinges on the interests of state industry and ancillary military-industrial, inward-looking sectors, as well as of ethnic, religious, and civic nationalist groups threatened by internationalization. Regional insecurity and competition helps sustain these coalitions in power, whereas more regional cooperation has the potential of eroding their resources and undermining their objectives. Backlash state and private actors are generally unconcerned with the prospects that regional instability might undermine foreign investment. Classically, these coalitions rely on populism, active states controlling prices, increasing nominal wages, overvaluing the currency to raise wages and profits in non-traded-goods sectors, and dispensing rents to private firms by discriminating against competing imports through tariffs, controls, and multiple exchange rates. Backlash coalitions flout an array of international economic, political, and security regimes that are depicted as anathema to the economic, national, ethnic, or religious objectives they advance.

As argued, these are ideal-typical coalitional types.[16] In the real world, the strategies of hybrid coalitions bestride elements from the other two, albeit in different degrees and combinations, but nonetheless placing real coalitional forms closer to different ends of the spectrum. For instance, internationalizing coalitions can retain state intervention and industrial policy, but they allow the expansion of private capital—local and international—far more significantly than do backlash coalitions. Despite significant differences among them, the modal East Asian ruling coalition has been closer to an

---

16. Ideal types are conceptual constructs, a limiting concept with which real situations are compared, not a historical or "true" reality (Weber 1949, 93). On Weberian ideal types as deliberately one-sided abstractions from social reality useful as "heuristic" devices in the "imputation" of causality, see Ruggie 1998, 31–32.

export-oriented, internationaliz*ing* strategy than most other developing regions. Overall, their progressive integration with the global economy and piecemeal steps toward regional cooperation and stability conformed to the hypothesized synergies—across the domestic, regional, and global levels—in their coalitional grand strategies. The domestic political and economic circumstances that led to a more cooperative regional order also tended to reinforce further global integration.

To be sure, domestic coalitional variations within East Asia abound. Ruling coalitions in Hong Kong and Singapore embraced free trade or entrepôt models. Coalitions ruling ASEAN states in the early stages were lubricated by state-directed lending and extensive family-owned conglomerates, organizing constituencies favoring foreign direct investment and natural resource and manufacturing exports alongside more traditional import-substituting interests. Internationalizing constituencies, including a burgeoning middle class with vested interests in political stability, grew stronger by the 1980s.[17] Radical nationalist and ethno-religious groups were marginalized to prevent exclusivist political and cultural forms from undermining domestic, global, and regional purposes. Economic growth was the foundation of these coalitions' grand strategy, embedded in the concept of national resilience (*ketahanan nasional*), which, writ large, would endow ASEAN itself with resilience (Alagappa 1995; Emmerson 1996; Acharya 1997). On the whole, export-led strategies in Malaysia, Indonesia, and Thailand succeeded with much less emphasis on industrial policy than was the case in South Korea and Taiwan, let alone in non—East Asian newly industrialized countries (MacIntyre 1994; Haggard and Kaufman 1995). In Japan, a coalition of bureaucratic and private actors retained enormous influence, blocking liberalization (Pempel 1998). All throughout the region, an implicit social bargain provided high per capita growth, employment, high investments in health and education, and increasing returns to small business and farmers. The bargain was pivoted on internationalization, albeit gradual and selective.

Although a far cry from market-based models of political economy, private entrepreneurship flourished throughout the region to an extent virtually unparalleled in other industrializing regions, and perhaps anywhere beyond the Organisation for Economic Co-operation and Development community. Furthermore, none of these other regions embraced the opportunities (and risks) of the international marketplace more fully. East Asian states were active lenders and regulators but less active entrepreneurs than elsewhere in the industrializing world.[18] Some of the weak economic fundamentals character-

17. On the domestic politics that led key ASEAN states to favor economic openness, see MacIntyre 1994 and Bowie and Unger 1997.

18. According to Stiglitz (1996), East Asian states intervened selectively to promote exports, provide credit, and subsidize declining domestic industries, but price distortions were within bounds.

istic of many industrializing states—current account and budget deficits, infla-tion, foreign exchange reserves, sluggish exports—were far more sound even in Southeast Asia. Public-sector fiscal profligacy was far more restrained.[19]

Military expenditures as a percentage of GDP were relatively moderate insofar as they were never allowed to choke the domestic macroeconomic requirements of an internationalizing strategy. There were neither arms races nor offensive buildups that threatened neighboring countries, although China's modernization has made this claim more contentious.[20] Military modernization efforts there can be interpreted as at least partly directed at satisfying one important constituency threatened by this strategy, segments of the People's Liberation Army (PLA). Even so, one might argue that China's estimated military expenses of about 4 percent of GDP (International Insti-tute for Strategic Studies 2000) in the late 1990s—lagging behind a much higher rate of economic growth—were carefully contained to avoid derailing the fundamentals of an internationalizing strategy. A coalitional analysis also helps illuminate realignments away from war on the Korean peninsula, an evolving relationship between the internationalizing South and a backlash North since the 1960s, the sources of cooperative overtures by the South, the origins of alternative nuclear postures (1970s and 1980s), more viable coop-erative convergence by the 1990s, and North Korea's oscillations in response to competing domestic orientations (Solingen 1998).

The expected synergies between domestic and regional stability so central to internationalizing strategies are also evident in emerging regional institu-tional arrangements that reinforced the links between economic and security objectives (Soesastro 1995; Stubbs 1999b). APEC, for instance, evolved natu-rally from preexisting informal institutions such as the Pacific Economic Cooperation Conference, the Pacific Trade and Development Conference, and the Pacific Basin Economic Committee, organized to advance trade coop-eration while taming or co-opting domestic protectionist forces (Ravenhill 2000). Although not designed to deal with security matters, APEC reflects an underlying logic of cooperation that transcends the economic arena. Security issues such the Korean peninsula, United States–China relations, and terror-ism have been discussed informally, and sometimes formally, at bilateral meet-ings and APEC summits. The Auckland Summit (1999) yielded a commitment to provide the UN with a multinational peace force to East Timor. At their 2001 meeting in Shanghai, members committed to prevent and suppress all forms of terrorist acts in accordance with the UN Charter, to

19. For further regional comparisons, see Bowie and Unger 1997.

20. Even Buzan and Segal (1994) acknowledge the absence of highly competitive arms accu-mulations. See also Ball 1993–94 and Mack and Kerr 1995. On arms expenditures as represent-ing a small percentage of GDP and as sensitive to budgetary constraints among ASEAN states, see Solingen 1999 and 2002, Acharya 1999, 73, and for cross-regional comparisons, Solingen 2001a. For a different perspective, see Huxley and Willett 1999.

sign and ratify all basic antiterrorist conventions, and to adopt new antiterrorism financial procedures, among other steps. The integral nature of economics, security, and domestic political objectives is evident in APEC leaders' declaration that terrorism is "a direct challenge to APEC's vision of free, open and prosperous economies, and to the fundamental values that APEC members hold" (http://www.apecsec.org.sg).

Converging coalitional objectives were also expressed in ASEAN's different cooperative phases. In the early and middle stages—through the early 1980s—cooperation was largely geared to protect the domestic political viability ("resilience") of coalitions advancing export-led industrialization. Domestic stability and prosperity via exports and foreign direct investment were the primary objectives. As Acharya (1999, 69) argued, "the attainment of performance legitimacy through economic development is a key element of comprehensive security doctrines found in ASEAN." An inward-looking emphasis on each member's domestic stability (political, macroeconomic) was thus a requirement for an outward-looking (internationalizing) strategy. The most extreme backlash threats to this strategy were perceived to be domestic subversion in the form of Communist insurgencies, separatist movements, and ethnic and religious extremism. As domestic support for an internationalizing strategy grew stronger, other security issues were progressively brought to the fore. ASEAN shied away from external security matters during the Cold War era, but these began being addressed by the 1990s. Later, ASEAN became central to an even broader security framework in the form of the ARF, designed to advance broader Asia-Pacific security cooperation.

The ARF adopted ASEAN's style, including the latter's evolutionary, step-by-step approach, its consensual decision making, and its preference for passing over divisive issues until they had achieved ripeness, while investing the institution with resilience as a viable regional forum for political and security dialogue (Almonte 1997–98). Although a security institution, the ARF in its 1998 communiqué specifically recognized the need to address the socioeconomic impact of post-crisis reforms, particularly their impact on the less privileged sectors of society, noting that certain aspects of the regional financial crisis could impact on peace and security in the region.[21] Similarly, the seventh ARF meeting (2000) addressed important political and security issues bearing on regional peace and stability that emerged as a result of globalization. There was a clear understanding that the ARF's future is inextricably linked to the domestic coalitional foundation that has underpinned ASEAN and other member states.

In sum, this overview of domestic coalitional conditions throughout the region offers a window into the characteristics of regional institutions that have

21. Chairman's statement, fifth meeting of the ARF, Manila, July 27, 1998, at http://www.dfat.gov.au/arf/arf5.html.

emerged in recent decades. Informality allowed coalitions with comparable—but not identical—platforms of engagement with the global political economy and its institutions to advance regional cooperation as a vital component of internationalizing strategies. ASEAN-style consensus was adaptive to a rapidly changing economic and political environment requiring regional and domestic stability, at whatever stage members found themselves on the path toward internationalization. APEC-style consensus similarly allowed the inclusion of states in early phases of internationalization (continental Southeast Asia in particular, but also Russia, Peru, and others). Furthermore, consensus and informality in ASEAN, APEC, and the ARF allowed members to transcend their disparate domestic institutions (democratic and otherwise) and to bind political opponents and successors to institutional commitments of a broad nature, in the direction of internationalization, while progressing at different speeds.

Both consensus and informality were fitted to integrate newcomers, such as erstwhile backlash ruling coalitions in Vietnam and China, because such arrangements were perceived to minimize resistance from lingering domestic backlash quarters. Indeed, China's reluctance to accept anything beyond a nonbinding security institution like the ARF may well be a result of continued domestic coalitional tensions.[22] The ambiguous, hot-and-cold tactics displayed by China over the Spratly Islands, the South China Sea more generally, the Taiwan issue, the U.S. bombing of the Chinese embassy, and the forced landing of a U.S. reconnaissance aircraft in Hainan in early 2001 reveal the protracted domestic competition between China's internationalizing and backlash camps. The former is led by WTO advocates who are also more attuned to some of the advantages of regional institutions; the latter by nationalist segments in the People's Liberation Army, protected state enterprises, agriculture, and local governments, who resist openness (Christensen 2001). Informal multilateral forms have not only assuaged at least some of China's domestic concerns but have also enabled North Korea's inclusion in the ARF process. Particularly noticeable have been efforts by internationalizing South Korea to activate the ARF in support of Kim Dae-jung's Sunshine Policy of accommodation with North Korea, in an effort to tame the latter's backlash factions. The 2001 ARF chairman's statement emphasized the need to hold further rounds of Korean North–South summit meetings.

Consensual decisions shaped APEC as a horizontal organization that is only minimally hierarchical. This enabled coalitions at different stages of internationalization, and with different domestic institutions, to protect their domestic political prerogatives and resources.[23] The informality of East Asian

22. As Simon (2001b, 284) argues, the PLA has resisted any disclosure by China of its order of battle, future arms acquisition plans, or full participation in the UN Conventional Arms Register or a regional arms register.

23. On APEC as the product of domestic political constraints and resulting cross-border regional coalitions, see Krauss 2000.

institutions also allowed ruling coalitions to include business, academic, and other constituencies that might buttress domestic support for their agenda (for example, the APEC Business Advisory Council).[24] East Asia's informal "policy networks" (Harris 1994) were, in essence, a transnational extension of ruling coalitions.

Finally, a commitment to open regionalism was particularly well suited for coalitions aiming at deepening their global ties while strengthening regional cooperation and stability. This strategy is akin to the sort of "trading states" and "virtual states" that had risen in East Asia in the latter part of the twentieth century (Rosecrance 1986, 1999). These institutional forms were rather efficient for coalitions driven to enhance access to global capital flows, particularly in the 1980s and early 1990s (Higgott 1999, 105). As Tsunekawa (in this volume) argues, open regionalism also fit Japan's economic interest as a "commercial state" that was now pursuing bilateral free trade agreements with trans-Pacific partners, even if better examples of open economies can be found in that region.

Notwithstanding these obvious links between the region's coalitional landscape and the institutions it bred, the coalitional argument discussed here was originally designed to explain the extent of regional conflict and cooperation, not the specific nature of regional institutions per se. As such, this coalitional logic leaves ruling coalitions with a wider range of institutional options, and perhaps a noninstitutional (albeit cooperative) one as well. As we have seen, consensus-oriented, informal means to advancing confidence-building measures are well matched to coalitional efforts to enhance regional stability, as are the plethora of informal track II meetings endemic to East Asia's regional institutional scene. But so can bilateral efforts to maintain peaceful and stable relations be held as a clear priority for internationalizing coalitions, for reasons explained earlier. The recent spur of bilateral free trade agreements and negotiations is wholly compatible with internationalizing coalitions.[25] Unilateral steps and private-sector activities (in trade liberalization, for instance) are similarly attuned to internationalizing grand strategies, providing self-binding commitments that facilitate diffuse reciprocity. Other cooperative forms can take shape as informal, ad hoc, issue-specific, flexible "coalitions of the willing" (Tay 2001), within East Asia and between it and other regions. From this perspective, T. J. Pempel's question about the importance of formal institutional arrangements for regional cooperation can be answered quite simply: formal institutions may not at all be required.

---

24. On the growth of ASEAN business networks, see Khong 1997b.

25. Bilateral agreements made or under negotiation include those of South Korea with Japan; Singapore with Japan and South Korea; New Zealand with Singapore and Hong Kong; China and Japan with ASEAN collectively and bilaterally; and several East Asian countries with Chile, Mexico, and the United States. Singapore, a pioneer in this wave of free-trade-areas, has pursued agreements with the United States, Japan, Australia, Canada, Iceland, Norway, Switzerland, and Liechtenstein.

A more constraining (formal) framework that locks in current coalitional preferences might arguably be preferred under certain conditions, but not if it is likely to trigger more stern domestic (backlash) opposition. In any event, the coalitional backdrop even in Southeast Asia is not completely inimical to legalizing verification and compliance mechanisms, as is evident from some recent developments (discussed later in the chapter) and from the 1995 Southeast Asian Nuclear Weapon Free Zone Treaty. The latter not only includes the right to trigger fact-finding missions but also calls for referral to the International Court of Justice when disputes remain unresolved for more than one month (Acharya and Ogubanwo 1998).

The coalitional landscape thus offers only a baseline for potential regional arrangements, and an important one at that. Institutions, however, are made from more than the enabling conditions that may have given them life. Institutional forms may differ from the intended efforts of ruling coalitions, and institutional effects may obtain or evolve unintentionally. Indeed, regional institutions themselves may change the nature of coalitional competition at home, and they can certainly alter the preferences of coalitions in power and in the opposition. They can also create new and competing constituencies and socialize erstwhile adversaries (Haas 1964). They can strengthen certain coalitions at the expense of others by providing political support of the kind APEC has provided to liberalizing forces, even in China and Japan (Aggarwal and Lin 2001, 181). In short, coalitional analysis can study institutions both as intervening and independent variables.

Further research along coalitional analysis must explore these institutional effects. It must also investigate the extent to which alternative coalitions may have led to the same kind of institutional arrangements as the ones we observe today. In particular, would ruling coalitions minimally engaged in the global political economy and representing expansive military-industrial complexes (consuming 25 and 30 percent of GDP, as in other regions) have yielded the same contextual environment that led to ASEAN, the ARF, and APEC? Would such coalitions have been more amenable to more formal institutional arrangements?[26] Kahler (2000a, 672) suggests just the opposite. In his view, the coalitional forms discussed earlier may explain varying positions vis-à-vis the legalization of regional institutions, or the extent to which regional institutions display heightened obligation, greater precision in rules, and delegation of rule interpretation and enforcement to third parties. Thus, he argues, internationalizing coalitions may be more prone to use legalization as a means for regional stability, whereas backlash coalitions may be more likely to resist legalization because of the high sovereignty costs or loss of autonomy.

26. Would Japan's Co-Prosperity Sphere and China's Bandung Conference be better understood as backlash regional forms? What about the Asian and Pacific Council (ASPAC), SEATO, and the Association of Southeast Asia (ASA)?

In sum, approaches building on domestic politics, whether coalitional or not, are a developing research agenda that complements the important contributions made by more conventional understandings of East Asian institutions, functionalist and cultural.[27] The preceding analysis points to possible extensions and potential links between state-based functionalist and domestically based coalitional understandings. Similarly, coalitional and cultural accounts are not inimical, considering that coalitions result from leaders' efforts to coalesce both material and ideal interests (Solingen 1998, 2001a). Furthermore, regional institutions can arguably transform the identity and interests of coalitional entrepreneurs and constituencies, both in power and in the opposition. The claim, for instance, that ASEAN leaders had hoped to develop a regional identity where none existed seems quite plausible. However, what encouraged leaders to converge on that objective in the first place must be explained. Although both domestic threats and reliance on growth and prosperity as legitimizing governing tools are often acknowledged as critical parts of the answer, cultural accounts have rarely formalized them into a coherent argument.

One exception is Johnston (1999), who explains the emergence of the ARF as the result of multiple state interests in the region creating sufficient uncertainty (particularly regarding China) as to require some mechanism for increasing predictability in the security environment. Johnston specifically acknowledges a common interest in maintaining economic prosperity and avoiding costly arms races, which is reminiscent of internationalizing clusters, although he does not stipulate that this common interest resulted from converging coalitional grand strategies. Subsequent developments within the ARF, he argues persuasively, must take into account path dependence and mutual constitution.

Comparative Dimensions of East Asia Institutions

The foregoing survey of the special characteristics of East Asian institutions and of their potential sources suggests several lines of inquiry on regional institutions, in this and other regions. It also raises the need for the analysis of East Asian regional institutions to contend more systematically with comparative dimensions.

First is the extent to which, beyond the common characteristics identified for core East Asian institutions, one can also discern differences among them. According to Kahler (2000d), ASEAN has evolved toward a more legalized

---

27. For further elaboration of the advantages and limitations of cultural and functionalist approaches, and for related potential research designs exploring the behavior of alternative coalitions, see Solingen 2004a.

approach, whereas the ARF and APEC have resisted legalization. Supportive evidence is found in the institutionalization of ASEAN's senior officials' meetings in economic, environmental, social, and other issue areas, in the emergence of national-level secretariats to sustain them, in the agreement to create AFTA, and in the subsequent delegation to the secretariat of increased—but moderate—responsibilities for advancing AFTA. In 1996, ASEAN adopted a dispute-settlement mechanism, in the context of AFTA, requiring a majority vote. ASEAN leaders also agreed at the third ASEAN informal summit (1999) to constitute an ASEAN troika, an ad hoc body of foreign ministers able to address urgent concerns with regional peace and stability. The constituted troika would conduct its work in accordance with the core principles of consensus and noninterference, and make recommendations to ASEAN foreign ministers (http://www.aseansec.org/menu.asp?action=3&content=2).

Despite these modest developments, ASEAN's secretariat continues to be subordinated to the national secretariats, and the organization remains relatively free of binding and precise legal obligations. Parties (Malaysia and Singapore, Malaysia and Indonesia) have not resorted to the existing mechanism of dispute settlement (the TAC's High Council) but have turned instead to the International Court of Justice. Still, relative to the others, ASEAN is the most densely institutionalized in terms of the sheer number of meetings across a wide range of issue areas, incipient inroads into majority vote, and some—albeit tentative—readiness to rely on third-party adjudication. APEC, with many more members, has also grown in the number of seminars and events it organizes, but these are more restricted to the economic arena. The ARF has the thinnest institutional structure, with not even a secretariat to provide coordination between meetings. The consensus rule is strong and resilient in APEC and the ARF, as it is in ASEAN. Finally, with respect to open regionalism, there may be some differences across all three institutions. The ARF and APEC appear to be the most inclusive. Even North Korea was invited to join, as was India, with Pakistan's accession expected in the near future. The ARF does not include Taiwan because of China's opposition, but Taiwan was allowed to become an APEC member. AFTA makes ASEAN much less open than APEC and the ARF. The ASEAN + 3 is yet an uncertain but developing institutional context that may not necessarily weaken APEC or the ARF (Tay 2001, 2).

ASEAN, APEC, and the ARF merely reflect related, and to some extent isomorphic, institutional forms within a much wider range of regional institutions that are amenable to coalitions broadly committed to internationalization.[28] The range logically includes international mechanisms (WTO, International Court of Justice). A tighter understanding of the specific resources and constraints of ruling coalitions at home and in the region may

---

28. On institutional isomorphism, see DiMaggio and Powell 1991.

help elucidate the kind of instrumentalities and strategic behavior they engage in when joining, or relying on, different institutions. Without such understanding, the fallback to broad inferences about behavior from state-level categories often produces less satisfying explanations. As Krauss (2000) has shown, domestic coalitional considerations may dictate different positions with respect to different issues even within the same institution. Can differences across East Asian regional institutions be traced to the imputed stronger entrenchment of musjawarah and mufakat in ASEAN, its cultural source? Hardly so if ASEAN is found to be the most prone to transcend them.

A second comparative dimension compels attention to whether, and the extent to which, East Asian institutions are peculiar in a broader—transregional—sense. The answer to these questions must make allowance for the "relative to what" criteria. As argued at the outset, the overwhelming, nearly exhausted, comparison between East Asia and the European Union may have helped obscure other important comparisons. A broader comparative context reveals less uniqueness than is often asserted. ASEAN's TAC basic principles of respect for state sovereignty, nonintervention, and renunciation of the threat or use of force in resolving disputes are widely accepted by most other regional (and international) institutions. Furthermore, the informality, face-saving, consensus-bound, noninterfering style of East Asian institutions can be found in many other regions, from Latin America to the Middle East and South Asia. There is as much reliance on personalism in the management of regional relations in the Arab Middle East, for instance.

ASEAN and the Gulf Cooperation Council (GCC) share some converging attributes, including an initial concern with domestic stability/internal security as well as (subsequently) external threats, limited economic integration, limited initial common identity, and, above all, the perceived homogeneity of ruling coalitions, at least in their broad grand strategies.[29] The GCC has a supreme council that calls together state leaders on an annual basis, a council of ministers that gathers foreign ministers four times a year, and a secretariat sited in Saudi Arabia. It has made some incipient steps toward internal conflict resolution.[30] Limited as it may appear, GCC's institutionalization has been labeled "one of the most vibrant and multifaceted experiments in

29. The Gulf Cooperation Council was founded in 1981 by Saudi Arabia, Kuwait, Oman, Bahrain, Qatar, and United Arab Emirates. Lawson (1999, 20) traces the first burst of GCC regionalism to a set of new institutions designed by ruling coalitions in 1980–81 to cajole potential opponents of the regime among local entrepreneurs and professionals. Among other things, the Iranian Revolution had incited domestic opposition among Gulf states. See also Acharya 1992.

30. An escalation to war between Qatar and Bahrain in 1986 over Hawar Island was prevented by Saudi mediation, while four GCC states oversaw Qatar's withdrawal from the disputed island. In 1991, however, Qatar turned to the International Court of Justice to rule on that dispute, a step rejected by Bahrain. A Saudi–Qatari border clash in 1992 was mediated by Egypt's President Mubarak.

regional organizations" (Barnett and Gause 1998, 179), a characterization that also places it close to the ASEAN experience.

1) Mercosur has a thinly institutionalized, informal framework emphasizing pragmatism and flexible procedures and negotiation styles.[31] Agreements are negotiated directly by foreign affairs and economics ministers rather than by especially created independent secretariats. Few would confuse this with a supranational framework. Notably, Latin America had a legalistic tradition and a series of far more structured institutions in preceding decades that neither fulfilled their original missions of integration nor created positive "spillover" cooperative effects. They simply "spilled around" reinventing themselves anew (Ferguson 1984), much as in the Arab Middle East. Only a dramatic domestic coalitional reversal in the 1990s infused old regional institutions with new life and created fresh, relatively more effective, and leaner ones. Internationalizing coalitions throughout the region, not institutions, led to Mercosur and to unprecedented security institutions such as ABACC (Agência Brasileiro-Argentina de Contabilidade e Controle de Materiais Nucleares, or Argentine-Brazilian Agency for Accounting and Control of Nuclear Materials) (Solingen 2001b).

2) Another property, the consensus rule, can be found in otherwise highly legalized contexts, such as the WTO and NATO. Because the WTO operates by consensus and not formal voting, any one of the weakest of its 144 members can, at least in principle, thwart an agreement that might otherwise be overwhelmingly favored. In less legalized frameworks, the GCC requires all decisions taken by the Supreme Council and the Ministerial Council to be unanimous, as does the Arab League. Decisions from Mercosur to the Euro-Mediterranean Partnership are based on consensus without formal voting. Nor are confidence-building measures and track II activities unique to East Asian institutions, despite the particularly extensive and active network around the Council for Security Cooperation in the Asia Pacific (see Evans's chapter in this volume). Both were widespread in contexts such as the multilateral Middle East peace process of the 1990s. Indeed, the whole concept of the ARF, including different issue areas (or thematic "baskets"), intersessional meetings, and track II seminars, bears many similarities to the original structure envisaged for the multilateral Middle East peace process in 1991–92 or to the subsequent Euro-Mediterranean Partnership.[32] The main difference

31. Mercosur came into being in 1991 and includes Argentina, Brazil, Uruguay, and Paraguay. Chile, insisting on a single common external tariff of 11 percent, has an "associated status," as does Bolivia.

32. The multilateral Middle East peace process emerged out of the 1991 Madrid conference and gained momentum with the Palestinian–Israeli Oslo agreements but was eventually derailed by domestic coalitional changes in the region (Solingen 2000). It included most countries in the region but excluded, notably, the more extreme backlash forms in Iraq and Iran (Syria was a lukewarm participant). On the Euro-Mediterranean Partnership or Barcelona process, see Solingen 2003.

between these two and the ARF was in the underlying domestic coalitional backdrop in each region, which has been more strongly internationalizing in East Asia than in the Middle East.

What about open regionalism? Some explain East Asia's open regionalism by pointing to regional institutions that presumably have enabled the production of collective goods (thus enhancing trade and security) that can benefit both members and nonmembers (where the latter can free ride on those benefits). Instead, institutions such as NAFTA and the EU better fit the definition of "club goods" producers, in that they are designed to benefit members while precluding free-riding by nonmembers (Gruber 2000; Rosecrance 2001). Seen in this light, open regionalism may turn out to be the one feature that appears stronger in East Asian institutions (APEC and the ARF in particular) than in other regional counterparts, certainly the Arab League (which formally excludes non-Arabs) and the GCC (which in practice has systematically excluded even other Arab states). However, the ephemeral experience of the more inclusive multilateral Middle East peace process—its eventual resuscitation should not be discounted—had strong elements of open regionalism, as do ABACC (which included a partnership with the International Atomic Energy Agency) and to some extent Mercosur, which encourages open trading relations with the rest of the world. Latin American regional institutions more generally appear to have become more compatible with an open global political economy in the 1990s. The recognition of synergies across economic, military, and other aspects of cooperation is common in regional institutions in the industrializing world as well, from the GCC to Mercosur and the Arab Maghreb Union.

Three additional conceptual issues must be considered in order to advance this research agenda. First, the experiences of East Asian and other regional institutions suggest the need to differentiate between processes leading to regional cooperation and those designed to steer political or economic integration. The latter two are only one of many forms that regional cooperation can take, compelling a more comprehensive effort to understand the role of institutions in cooperation. Cooperation can come about even where there is little integration or institutionalization, whereas conflict is possible in the presence of both. As Barnett and Gause (1998, 168) suggest, "simply put, the GCC was about cooperation, not integration," and to a large extent the same can be argued for East Asian and other regional institutions. To be sure, none of these cases fits the profile of collective security arrangements. Indeed, when asked about the need for such an arrangement to protect the Arab world, Saudi Crown Prince Abdullah replied that "the Arab world will be protected by God" (Sciolino 2002).

Second, further comparative research on East Asian regional institutions should address another domestic institutional variable: democracy versus authoritarianism. East Asian institutions bring together varied combinations of regime types (as did the multilateral Middle East peace process, the Euro-Mediterranean Partnership, and the Organization of African Unity), setting them apart from regional institutions gathering all-democratic members (Mercosur, EU) and from those assembling all-authoritarian ones (GCC, Arab League). Such comparisons may shed further light on the conditions under which the nature of domestic institutions may influence reliance on informality, consensual decision rules, and open regionalism.

Finally, any analysis of institutions requires a clearly formulated understanding of the conditions under which institutions may change. For the most part, analyses of East Asian institutions implicitly uphold a belief in their incremental change, with some contending that formality, legalism, and openness are marginally increasing, decreasing, or unchanged, with others perennially foretelling the slow death of a given institution. The possibility of discontinuous "punctuated equilibria," however, and even sweeping departures from the pattern we have observed for the last couple of decades, must be explored as well, for instance, in the context of sharp turns in the global or regional economy or in the security environment. Cultural and functional analyses are better suited to probe into the longer-term evolution of these institutions, whereas coalitional analysis can also accommodate more abrupt or unexpected institutional departures, responsive to domestic electoral and other political changes. The most recent regional financial crisis does not appear to have had a revolutionary impact on the nature of East Asian institutions, although it has given new impetus to the ASEAN + 3 process. But this applies only to the short term. East Asian institutionalism, like all others, is a work in progress.

3

Demographic Future of East Asian
Regional Integration

GEOFFREY MCNICOLL

In contrast to the pace of political and economic events, populations change slowly, their transformations most evident on a time scale not of years but of generations. Hence, demographic conditions are often viewed as background to current events. That perspective does not make demography inconsequential but gives it a role somewhat like that of geography, contributing features to the landscape on which social change takes place and in some measure channeling that change or otherwise narrowing its degrees of freedom. But population dynamics are also active ingredients in the processes of social change, reflecting as they do the unorganized but often predictable behavior of myriad families and individuals—and, in this role, by no means necessarily slow moving. In particular, demographic factors have the potential to play a significant part both in promoting and in impeding regional integration. The case in point is East Asia.

East Asia here refers to the region from Japan to Myanmar (the UN's East and Southeast Asia), which in 2000 had almost exactly two billion inhabitants, one-third of the world's population. It has a wide range of demographic situations, just as it has a diversity of economic conditions and political systems: from China's 1.26 billion population to Brunei's 328,000,[1] and from Cambodia's

This chapter is a revised version of a paper prepared for the Japan Foundation/SSRC Workshop on Regionalization in Asia, Portland, Oregon, February 21–24, 2002. Comments on an earlier draft by T. J. Pempel, Dennis Tachiki, and other workshop participants are acknowledged.

1. Confusingly, UN demographic data for China include Taiwan and exclude Hong Kong (and Macao). On this basis, the population figure for 2000 is 1,275 million. Adding Hong Kong (6.9 million) and subtracting Taiwan (22.2 million) yields 1,260 million. Preliminary results of the 2000 census agree, showing a population of 1,265 million (United Nations 2001a; Lavely 2001).

almost 3 percent per year growth rate, with a forecast population doubling within a few decades, to Japan's 0.2 percent growth rate and its forecast population shrinking. There are large differences in age distributions across the region, reflecting the staggered onset of declines in death and birth rates, which contribute to regional variations in labor demand, dependency rates, and migratory pressures. Urbanization is proceeding at a fast pace, and several decades of strong economic growth have produced a burgeoning and politically important middle class, albeit one that has been buffeted by the economic reverses of the late 1990s. Nevertheless, cultural and communal divisions within and across countries remain salient features of the region's population, with implications for international cooperation and even for stability. These demographic conditions and processes of change have helped shape the East Asian regional present and will influence its future. How much so and through what means are the subjects explored in this chapter.

A comparative perspective is needed in this task. The distinctive conditions and experience of East Asia are brought out by comparing this region with others in terms of such factors as size of states, age structures, urbanization patterns, and growth and distribution of human capital. Comparisons of particular significance are with the regions centered around the European Union, potentially extending over all of Europe, and the United States, extending over the other NAFTA states—and potentially over all the Americas. East Asia is often seen as having, or at least being a candidate for, a similar status in the world. In this it contrasts with South Asia, although perceptions of South Asia's potential have perhaps not caught up with changing realities; with Latin America, where a distinctive regional future may yet be forged beyond the ambit of its neighboring superpower; and with Africa and the Middle East, which are seen as mired in political turbulence and state failure.

Population Relativities and Regional Architecture

In relations among states, differences in population size generally count for little. The doctrine of sovereign equality is one source of depreciation. More important, population size has only a muted effect on a state's power. But its residual influence on economic and military capabilities is nevertheless real: population numbers can partly make up for disadvantages in technological levels and organizational prowess, and among countries at comparable levels of development, population is a simple index of economic weight. And sheer numbers have a certain symbolic significance even where differences are practically unimportant: witness the interest in India's likely overtaking of China as the world's largest country by midcentury, or Indonesia's gratification at moving up from fifth to fourth place with the breakup of the Soviet Union (see McNicoll 1999 on these issues).

Population size matters most when there are large differences within a well-defined geographic region. Those differences contribute to the status hierarchy within the region. More tangibly, within a regionally based free trade area, market size is a salient reality. And population size is a factor in regional migration pressures and responses: the same absolute number of movers that constitutes a trivial rate of emigration from a large population may be far from trivial as an immigration rate to a small population. Plausibly, then, the kinds of interactions that take place among states within a region and the kinds of institutions that emerge to accommodate those interactions are affected by the size distribution of those states. On this dimension, the comparison of East Asia with other regions is illuminating.

Within-region population relativities for East Asia, South Asia, Europe, and the Americas are shown in table 3.1. In Europe and the Americas, the most populous country in the region is around 50 percent larger than the next most populous. The African case would be comparable: with Nigeria set at 100, Egypt would be 60, Ethiopia 55. In contrast, China and India have six and seven times the populations of the next largest countries in their regions. We cannot of course read anything from such simple data about intraregional relationships, but the contrasts signal the special circumstances of East Asia and South Asia: no other major world region has a single member with overwhelming demographic dominance. The same holds true if we consider formal regional associations rather than simple geography: in their size distributions, ASEAN + 3 (APT) and SAARC (South Asian Association for Regional Cooperation) stand in contrast to ASEAN itself, EU, NAFTA, Mercosur, and the others.

Table 3.1. Relative population sizes in four major world regions, 2000

East Asia		South Asia		Europe		Western Hemisphere	
Country	%	Country	%	Country	%	Country	%
China	100	India	100	Germany	100	United States	100
Indonesia	17	Pakistan	14	United Kingdom	72	France	60
Japan	10	Bangladesh	14	France	72	Mexico	35
Vietnam	6	Nepal	2	Italy	70	Colombia	15
Philippines	6			Spain	49	Argentina	13
Thailand	5			Poland	47	Canada	11
Myanmar	4			Romania	27	Peru	9
South Korea	4						
Malaysia	2						
Taiwan	2						

Source: United Nations 2001a.

Note: Population size as a percentage of the population of the largest country in the region, for countries with populations over 20 million.

To complement the demographic picture, we need to look at the analogous economic comparison. This is done in table 3.2, which presents indices of size of economy within each region, in terms of purchasing power, for the same four regions identified in table 3.1. In two of the regions, Europe and South Asia, the economic distribution by this measure is not much different from the demographic. For Europe, this reflects general prosperity across EU states; for South Asia, general poverty across the subcontinent. In the other two regions, the economic lens changes the regional picture, with the U.S. economy twice the size of the rest of the hemisphere put together and China sharing dominance with Japan in East Asia.

According to the purchasing power estimates underlying table 3.2, China's GDP passed Japan's in 1992. By 2000 it was over 50 percent higher, although Japan's labor force is enormously more productive. If market exchange rates are used instead, the China–Japan difference is reversed: by this measure Japan is still by far the larger economy.[2] The relative sizes of economies in the region, replacing those shown in the first column of table 3.2, would be Japan (100), China (27), South Korea (10), Indonesia (3), and so forth (World Bank 2002, 236; data for 2000).

There is no single answer as to which exchange rate is more appropriate for this exercise: purchasing power parity gives a better indication of comparative levels of total consumption; market exchange rates better indicate power in the international economy. Whichever is used, it remains the case that China and Japan each have economies several times the size of the next biggest in the region. Thus the two demographic giants of Asia exist in very different regional economic settings—India dominant, China faced with Japan. The special characteristic of East Asia is the presence of two heavyweight powers.

The rough comparability in scale and technology of the major European powers was a source of their historical rivalries, both within Europe and in their various imperial extensions. The need to prevent those rivalries from reemerging after World War II was a major impetus for the move toward unification, and the steady thickening of EU institutions is intended to make the process irreversible. Plausibly, that comparability is now a source of the EU's strength as a political entity, although the trammeled competition that remains lies behind many of its organizational problems. (With the realist's disdain for

2. Estimates of the absolute numbers in 2000 at purchasing power parity (ppp) and at market prices are as follows:

	Japan	China	Source
GDP 2000 (ppp), billion 1990 dollars	2,669	4,330	Maddison 2003
GDP 2000 (market prices), billion dollars	4,677	1,080	World Bank 2002
Per capita GDP 2000 (ppp), 1990 dollars	21,069	3,425	Maddison 2003
Per capita GDP 2000 (market prices), dollars	36,830	856	World Bank 2002

Table 3.2. Relative sizes of economies in four major world regions, 1999

East Asia		South Asia		Europe		Western Hemisphere	
Country	%	Country	%	Country	%	Country	%
China	100	India	100	Germany	100	United States	100
Japan	63	Pakistan	15	France	79	Brazil	13
South Korea	15	Bangladesh	6	United Kingdom	76	Mexico	9
Indonesia	15	Sri Lanka	4	Italy	70	Canada	8
Thailand	10			Spain	38	Argentina	5
Taiwan	8			Netherlands	22	Colombia	3
Philippines	4			Poland	18	Venezuela	3
Malaysia	4			Belgium	14		
Hong Kong	3			Austria	10		
Vietnam	3						

Source: Maddison 2003.

Note: GDP as a percentage of the largest economy in the region, measured at 1990 purchasing power parity values, for economies amounting to 3 percent and above of the largest economy (for Europe, 10 percent and above). Data for Europe and the Western Hemisphere are for 1998.

supra-state institutional veneers, Mearsheimer [2001a, 50] remarks of present-day Germany that it "has the earmarks of a potential hegemon.")

A region in which a single state has uncontested dominance would seem to have much less need for laborious development of a regional architecture. The dominant power is positioned to set the rules for cooperation, to the extent it chooses. India has a hegemonic role over its low-income neighbors by virtue of the sheer size of its economy, backed by its demographic weight, in addition to its possession of major high-technology sectors much in advance of its neighbors' capabilities. However, although the existence of a dominant state may preclude EU-style regionalism, it is fully consistent with looser NAFTA- or OAS-style institutions. Indeed, Ayoob (1999) argues that South Asia is the best-placed region outside Europe and North America to develop in this direction precisely because of India's willingness and unchallenged ability to provide regional public goods—notably security guarantees—to its smaller neighbors, albeit with Pakistan as a potential spoiler.

In East Asia the presence of two regional great powers makes for a distinctive structural problem for regional architecture. But that situation is a fairly new development, a consequence of two very different growth trajectories. In the 1970s and 1980s, Japan's economic dominance of the region was unquestioned, with forecasts seeming even to justify proclaiming "Japan as number one" worldwide. In the avian metaphor then popular, Japan was the lead goose in the development flight, with China one of the trailing birds—its population size more an encumbrance than a claim to status. (That Japan's leadership in the region remained confined to the economic domain was a lingering after-effect of its pre-1945 relationships.) Several decades of remarkably rapid economic expansion in China, however, beginning with the Dengist reforms of the 1970s, transformed the regional outlook. This expansion, along with Japan's post-1989 stagnation, created expectations of a reversal of leadership, with economics coming more into line with demography. Kenichi Ohmae, as quoted in the *New York Times* (April 21, 2002), has remarked that "In the future, Japan will be to China what Canada is to the United States, what Austria is to Germany, what Ireland is to Britain." Such expectations, even if far ahead of realities, translate into behavior.

Economic forecasts are even more hazardous than demographic forecasts. There is much that could happen both domestically and in the international arena to derail China's economic progress. Restoration of Japan's dynamism is similarly entirely conceivable: the abruptness of the shift to a pessimistic outlook between the 1980s and the 1990s may itself be a sign of the mutability of sentiment and its possible detachment from fundamentals. Most immediately, Japan's confidence has been sapped by the problems of its financial sector, which are refractory but remediable. But at a deeper structural level it is likely that the change in outlook owes something to Japan's demographic situation. With fertility below the rate needed for long-run population replacement since the mid-1970s, Japan will start to experience a population fall within a few years. By midcentury, according to the UN's medium forecast, Japan's population will have dropped almost 20 million below its peak of 128 million (very close to what it is now), back to the level it passed in 1974. More important, the population is aging fast. China too has a low fertility rate, but the country is still decades away from any absolute fall in numbers and well behind Japan in aging.

Could Southeast Asia persist as a coherent East Asian subregion, in the eddies of great power tensions and realignments to the north, or even as a third force in a regional triangle? ASEAN aspires to operate in some respects as such an entity, as implied by its contraction to the A of AFTA and ARF, or, vis-à-vis the north, by its invention of ASEAN + 3. The 2000 population of the original ASEAN members was 377 million; its expansion brought its population to 522 million. That is potential heft, even in the company of China.

Because it relies on consensual decision making rather than formal voting, ASEAN avoids the problems of how to relinquish unrealistic one state/one vote arrangements—problems that have periodically bedeviled the EU and become more pressing as it expands. (The ratio of Germany's population to Luxembourg's, the largest EU differential, is 188:1; Indonesia's to Brunei's, the analogous span in ASEAN, is 650:1.)

But even if decisions were taken more in accord with population-weighted voting, Indonesia's 212 million would be outweighed by the next three largest ASEAN members (Vietnam, Philippines, and Thailand, together 217 million). The not unlikely prospect that its present political and economic difficulties will prove long lasting throws into doubt Indonesia's candidacy for being a "pivotal" state in Southeast Asia. Whether that strengthens or weakens ASEAN's role as a regional entity vis-à-vis China and Northeast Asia depends on what kind of institutional thickening takes place within the expanded ASEAN.

Youth Bulges and Old-Age Dependency

The slow pace of change in overall population size of a country need not be paralleled by slow change in all its components. Particular age groups and particular small geographic regions can expand quite rapidly, with significant effect on national economies and societies and thence on the broader regional context.

Demographic transition is the simple term for the radical declines in death and birth rates associated with societal modernization. Death rates typically fall first, and with greatest effect initially on child survival. The numbers of children in the population rapidly expand, with growing needs for education and employment. Denied opportunity, the same burgeoning youth cohorts may become the disaffected instigators of political unrest (see Goldstone 2001). Later in the transition, fertility starts to fall, lowering the proportions of children, easing the demands on the education system, and potentially allowing, and attracting, higher levels of investment per worker. Later still, continued declines in fertility and mortality—the latter now mostly taking place at older ages—lead to an increasing proportion of elderly in the population, with emerging labor shortages and problems of old-age support. It is widely supposed, though on grounds that are partly speculative, that population aging will be a serious economic drag.

In East Asia, the demographic transition began with Japan, where mortality decline dates from the end of the nineteenth century and fertility decline from the 1920s. For most of the region, however, the major declines came after World War II—starting in Taiwan and Korea in the 1950s, and in mainland China and Southeast Asia in the 1960s and 1970s. The regional laggards are Cambodia and Laos, where high, pre-transition fertility (five or more children per woman) persists.

The economic boost from a lowered burden of child dependency (lasting until the new burden of old-age dependency sets in), when combined with the right policy settings, is what has been termed a demographic gift or bonus (see Bloom and Williamson 1998). In the East Asian case, a demographic bonus is seen as having contributed to the region's stellar economic performance over several decades. East Asian regionalism may have proceeded without this "Asian miracle," but economic success greatly raised the stakes for potential member states in the maneuverings over institutional design.

Within each country the process of urbanization, another part and consequence of development, lends a critical locational dimension to these age-distribution trends. During the transition, urban age structures start to look very different from rural age structures, both because of rural—urban differences in the timing of death rate and birth rate declines and because of the scale and age selectivity of rural—urban migration.

The evolution of Japan's age distribution under its long-established low fertility rate and a continuing rise in longevity is seen in the estimates and projections in table 3.3. Today Japan has more than twice as many people under forty as over sixty. By 2025, according to the UN's medium projections (which are moderately robust over this duration), there will be almost as many over sixty as under forty. Eventually, of course, all countries will likely have age distributions weighted toward the elderly, as proportions of childless and one-child families increase and as lives are further lengthened. Comparisons of trends in proportions of the population over sixty for a number of countries and for a longer time series are shown in figure 3.1. The countries included are the largest members of the three world regions earlier used for comparison. Japan is seen to be on an aging track similar to that of Germany, and both are well ahead of China, India, and the United States. There is no advantage in this kind of precedence.

In age distribution, as in scale, the contrast that matters most for East Asian regionalism, in both the economic and strategic domains, is that between Japan and China. Table 3.4 illustrates some facets of the contrast as of 2000 and as projected to 2025. The first two rows present absolute numbers, with

Table 3.3. Distribution of Japan's population by age group (percentage)

Age group	1975	2000	2025 (projected)
0–19	31.5	20.6	16.8
20–39	33.6	27.9	20.2
40–59	23.2	28.3	27.9
60+	11.7	23.2	35.1
All ages	100.0	100.0	100.0

Source: Estimates and medium-variant projections from United Nations 2001a.

Table 3.4. Japan and China: Demographic contrasts

Item	2000		2025 (projected)	
	Japan	China	Japan	China
Total population (millions)	127.0	1,275.0	124.0	1,471.0
Entrants to labor force[a] (millions)	1.6	19.3	1.2	17.6
Population 20–40 / population 20–65 (%)	44.0	58.0	37.0	45.0
Proportion aged 65+ (%)	17.0	7.0	29.0	13.0

Source: United Nations 2001a.

[a] One-sixth of the age group 18–23.

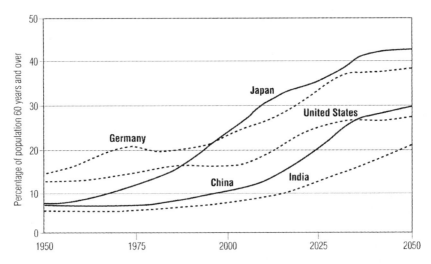

Fig. 3.1. Estimated and projected trends in proportions of persons 60 years and over in selected countries, 1950–2050. *Source:* United Nations 2001a.

the tenfold existing size differences dwarfing the anticipated changes over time. The last two rows show important age structural differences between the two countries at the two times: the proportion of the labor-force-aged population at the prime ages of twenty to forty remains much higher in China than Japan over this period, and although China too has low fertility, rising longevity, and an aging population, Japan's proportion of elderly will remain more than twice that of China through this period. As figure 3.1 indicates, China is about thirty years behind Japan in reaching a given level of the proportion of the population over sixty.

The gradual shift in regional dominance from Japan to China that a continuation of current economic trends, on top of population size differences, would seem to portend is given further impetus by this difference in age structures. Plausibly, Japan's economic travails owe something to the "declinist" sentiments engendered by population aging, as well as to the highly tangible problems for both families and the state of a heavy and still rising dependency burden. (A factor in the lengthy, continuing slump in Japan's economy is the heavy saving by workers anticipating having to rely mainly on their own resources in their old age.) Correspondingly, some part of China's dynamism—like that of the other sometime hypergrowth economies—has come from its still low rates of old-age dependency. When those dependency problems eventually arise, however, China may have to face them with a much less developed social security system than Japan's.

The economic implications of changes in labor supply and demand are mainly felt in the nonagricultural economy, for the most part in the cities.

Thus in addition to the effects of demographic transition on the labor force, we need to consider the labor inflow from the countryside. In China, as in most of Asia, the urbanization process has far to go: in 2000, China was about 30 percent urban (Vietnam was 20 percent, Indonesia 40 percent; United Nations 2001b). The rural sector provides a vast labor pool that can be drawn on by a growing industrial and service economy. A forecast based on plausible assumptions of trends in agricultural productivity has China's farm employment halving, from 259 million to 121 million, during 2000–2025, and nonfarm employment rising from 467 million to 851 million (Johnson 2000, 329). Not all of this anticipated employment shift will result in rural—urban migration: some natural increase in the urban population can be expected, and rural industrialization will probably continue. But a massive relocation of population is under way.

Even though China's aggregate "youth bulge" may have passed—the size of the labor force entry cohort peaked around 1990 and is slowly diminishing—the creation of this amount of nonfarm employment, with numbers of urban job-seekers continually boosted by labor shedding in the countryside, is a formidable challenge. It is exacerbated by a wholly separate channel of labor shedding—the result of cutting back the featherbedding of state enterprises newly exposed to market prices and competition. For an economy growing at 7 percent annually, as China's did in the 1990s, the challenge can probably be met; the problem would come if that growth were to seriously falter.

Japan in 2000, in contrast, was 79 percent urban (South Korea was 81 percent, Taiwan 75 percent). There, urbanization is long completed: the farm population remains as large as it is for political rather than economic reasons. The diminishing ranks of young urban adults cannot be filled from the countryside. There is of course appreciable scope for a response to labor shortages—assuming an economic upturn takes place to generate such shortages—through shifts in participation rates, especially for married women and older people, through continued labor-saving technical progress (even more computers and robots), and through export of jobs. And in a region and a world in which in aggregate there are still more than ample numbers of young adults, there is the option of immigration.

Intraregional Migration and Regionalism

Migration flows between neighboring states, except in refugee situations, almost of necessity reflect a degree of regional integration. The common pattern involves attraction of migrant labor from the less to the more dynamic regional economies, either formally under some guest-worker scheme or informally but with a similar expectation by the receiving states that the migrants would eventually return. Typically too, such expectations do not prevail, and short-term migration shades into permanent settlement. Free trade agreements often tend to promote labor migration, though usually not by intent. Indeed, the intent can be just the reverse, with espousal of free movement of goods and capital meant precisely to limit labor flows.

Countries that are potential destinations for migrants on economic grounds do not necessarily want them, at least not in large numbers. Two polar models of destination countries may be identified, with many gradations in between: one in which migrant labor is drawn on for low-skilled occupations in services and perhaps agriculture, the other in which migrant labor is largely excluded and low-skilled occupations are protected from downward wage pressures through labor market regulation and tariff or nontariff measures. The United States and Japan are the evident exemplars of the two poles; the EU states lie somewhere in the middle.

In proportion to its population, East Asia is not in a migratory ferment. Census-derived data on proportions of foreign-born persons as of 2000–not just migrants from the region—are given in table 3.5. Singapore (and Brunei and Hong Kong) apart, only Malaysia, at 6 percent, has an appreciable foreign-born population. For comparison, estimates of the migrant proportions in 2000 are 7 percent in the United Kingdom, 9 percent in Germany, 11 percent in France, 12 percent in the United States, 19 percent in Canada, and 24 percent in Australia.

In Singapore and Hong Kong, the foreign born comprise both expatriate staff in high-tech production and finance sectors and low-wage service workers. The latter are mainly single women, especially from Indonesia, working abroad for a few years. Malaysia has a substantial number of Indonesian migrants, both skilled and unskilled, responding to the widening income gap between the two countries and eased by absence of visa formalities, a common language, and the long-standing contacts between northern Sumatra and Peninsula Malaysia and across the land border in Kalimantan. Japan's foreign-born population nearly doubled in the 1990s, though this brought it only to 1.6 million in 2000.

The global migration regime, aside from refugee movements, is dominated by migration from developing countries to the West, particularly the United States and the EU. China and the Philippines are the major East Asian sources of such migrants. Within East Asia until recently, only Japan has had the economic scale and level of prosperity to be a potentially significant attractor, and it has chosen to discourage immigration—at least on any track that might lead to citizenship. The largest groups of foreign born in Japan, by official records, are 636,000 Koreans, 294,000 Chinese, and 115,000 Filipinos (Organisation for Economic Co-operation and Development 2001). In comparison, equivalent estimates for the United States in 1999 are 611,000 Koreans, 985,000 Chinese, and 1.46 million Filipinos (and 966,000 Vietnamese).

Table 3.5. Proportion of foreign-born persons in selected East Asian countries, 2000 (percentage)

Country	Foreign-born	Country	Foreign-born
Singapore	33.6	Thailand	0.6
Malaysia	6.3	Indonesia	0.2
Japan	1.3	Philippines	0.2
South Korea	1.3	China	0.2
Taiwan	1.3		

Source: United Nations 2002 and, for Taiwan, http://www.migrationist.com.au.

Census-based country-of-birth data probably omit the majority of "undocumented" or "irregular" migrants. International Organization for Migration data cited by Wickramasekara (2001, 57) give the following estimates of such migrants: Japan (1997): 281,000, two-thirds of whom were from Korea, the Philippines, China, and Thailand; Korea (1998): 96,000, more than half of whom were from China; Taiwan (1998): 20,000, half from the Philippines and Thailand; Malaysia (1996): 800,000, half from Indonesia, one-quarter from Bangladesh; and Thailand (1996): one million, nearly all from Myanmar. Other sources, unsurprisingly, give widely variant numbers.

Looking to East Asia's future, what are the possibilities for significant changes in this limited migration regime? Two might be noted. First, some states might choose to become settlement countries, seeing economic or strategic advantage in numbers or in particular categories of newcomers. Second, some subgroup of states might move toward a common labor market, removing border formalities and work restrictions for their citizens.

As low-fertility, urbanized, and rapidly aging societies with small migrant stocks, Japan, South Korea, and Taiwan might seem to be candidates to establish significant immigration programs. As already noted, Japan is furthest along toward a declining labor force. Although it resists accepting migrants, in practice foreigners in small numbers do manage to enter, finding employment especially in the construction industry. (Japan's agriculture, like the EU's but unlike that of the United States, avoids drawing on a foreign labor force by maintaining high levels of protection against imports.) However, it is a fact of demography, readily demonstrated, that immigration, on any but a large and continually increasing scale, does little to retard population aging. This reality also helps to undermine the popular but somewhat dubious belief that migrants, simply as warm bodies, in some way invigorate an economy. But even if the purpose of migration were indeed to sustain labor force numbers, a migration rate much higher than any that most Asian countries would likely contemplate would be called for.

The UN caused something of a stir in 2000 by publishing calculations of the numbers of migrants that low-fertility countries would need to admit in order to hold constant their populations at labor force ages. These "replacement migration" estimates for Japan came to an average of about 650,000 migrants per year over the next several decades (United Nations 2000). As an immigration rate, it amounts to 5 per 1,000—comparable to the recent U.S. net inflow rate. The analogous estimate of immigration needed for South Korea to maintain labor force constancy was about 130,000 immigrants per year, around 3 per 1,000. (The UN disavowed any intention of policy advocacy, although many observers read that into the exercise.)

Europe, where many countries have an age distribution not unlike Japan's, has also been resistant to increasing immigration, although less effectively so than Japan and with considerable variation among countries. But in comparison with Japan, European countries are already ethnically diverse; for Japan, a migration offset to low fertility would require an enormous effort to acculturate the newcomers and, because that could at most be fractionally achieved, to accept cultural diversity.

The East Asian country that is least resistant to immigration, aside from the city-states, is Malaysia, despite its fertility rate being well above replacement (it averages almost three children per woman) and its population growth rate (2 percent per year) being nearly twice the East Asian average. Malaysia's government has long tended to favor population growth. In a much-quoted statement, the then Prime Minister Mahathir once proposed that Malaysia aim for a population of 70 million (it was then below 15 million), essentially on mercantilist grounds: that was the size thought to be needed to support an automobile industry. (Laos, sandwiched between the much larger and economically more vigorous states of Thailand and Vietnam, and Myanmar, politically isolated, have also tended to be populationist, although ineffectively so: both have generated refugee outflows.) Malaysia's welcome for low-skilled foreigners is withdrawn in bad economic times. In the two years following the 1997 financial crisis, there was a "voluntary repatriation" of some 187,000 undocumented, mainly Indonesian, workers (Kassim 2001, 135).

Are there any prospects for an East Asian version of the common labor market of the EU, or, on a much smaller scale, that of the trans-Tasman economy of Australia and New Zealand? Paradoxically, the probable prerequisite for such an agreement is the strong expectation that any permanent migration under it would be minimal. The richer EU states fear mass immigration, but mainly from Eastern Europe and the developing countries. Within the 15-state EU, migration between countries has been relatively low; experience has shown that regional economic differentials are not great enough to overcome the language and cultural impediments to movement. However, expansion to an EU-25 that includes Poland and other East European states has raised the level of anxiety on this score, and the prospect of the incorporation of Turkey further heightens such concerns. NAFTA, unlike the EU, does not permit the free movement of labor. It stopped short of becoming a common market at least in part because the United States and Canada envisaged a massive, and legal, inflow of migrant labor from the south. The 1985 report of the Royal Commission on the Economic Union and Development Prospects for Canada put it bluntly: "Control over foreign immigration is a basic and very important national policy, and the obvious need for Canada to maintain control in this field is sufficient reason to rule out a common market" (1985, 1:306). This was merely with reference to United States–Canada relations, before NAFTA's extension to Mexico. A fortiori, the objection would apply to a hemispheric common market.

Thus the prospect of a common labor market across major parts of East Asia, such as within an envisaged ASEAN Economic Community, let alone over the whole region, seems remote. Even where there are scant cultural obstacles (as between Indonesia and Malaysia or between mainland China and Hong Kong), the smaller population has an interest in maintaining a firm control of numbers of entrants to avoid being swamped. There may be more possibility of an Asian version of the EU's Schengen Accord, the agreement that permits visa-free movement over an important subgroup of member states. But if so, it would probably come only with prosperity, and even then more as a convenience for tourists, business travelers, and students than as a final stage of economic integration. As to migration from more distant regions, it is hard to imagine even a prosperous East Asia being the kind of worldwide magnet for economic migrants and asylum seekers that the EU has become. The trickle of migrants from Latin America, mostly persons of Japanese descent, to Japan is hardly indicative.

For all the attempts to enforce state control over entry, an appreciable part of international migration eludes regulation. It is notable that the relaxation of visa requirements under Schengen was linked to a tightening of regulations covering non-EU citizens (Geddes 2000, 171). Although much undocumented migration is illegal only in terms of formal immigration law, there is a part that entails more serious criminal activity. Trafficking in economic migrants and asylum seekers is an expanding and profitable sector of the world's black economy. Its East Asian component has mainly to do with illegal migration from China (especially Fujian) to the United States and other Western countries and the transit of others through the region to the same destinations. Another, smaller, regional trafficking operation recruits women and children from Laos, Cambodia, and Myanmar to Bangkok's sex industry—a consequence of which has been the rapid spread of HIV infection in those countries.

Nodes, Networks, and Corridors

Progress in economic integration does not require or even necessarily benefit much from intraregional migration. Mass migration is a highly inefficient process of linking economies, even aside from its brain-drain component and the populist political resistance that large inflows tend to generate. It is far more practical to move capital and technology to where the labor is—and finished goods to where the consumers are—than to move the labor. The relocation of manufacturing from higher- to lower-wage countries is the major dynamic in the spread of economic development. The main East Asian examples are Japanese (and U.S.) investment in Taiwan and South Korea, Japan's investment in Southeast Asia, and, more recently, Taiwan's investment in mainland China. (The balance of social benefits and costs to the capital-exporting country is probably positive too, but clearly factor-price equalization across countries is not a goal endorsed by that country's own workers.)

Even though it involves comparatively few people actually moving, the embodied human capital transferred along with foreign investment may be the basis of strong international ties. Along with a factory comes a transfer of managerial expertise, worker training, and numerous complementary effects on human capital and infrastructure. The countries receiving the investment, if resourceful, can lever themselves up the technology ladder, from basic manufactures to sophisticated products like consumer electronics. Eventually they may be able to do without the foreign management and even to compete technologically with the source countries. Japan did so vis-à-vis the United States; Taiwan and South Korea are doing so vis-à-vis the United States and Japan; China doubtless will do so vis-à-vis all four.

This pattern is the "flying geese" or, more prosaically, product-cycle model of regional development. It was the organizational basis of the vast expansion of Asian exports to Western markets. Japan's initially central role in it lessened as Western buyers increasingly dealt directly with manufacturers, commissioning labor-intensive products subject to specified design criteria and on-time delivery. Service exports too have expanded as communications costs, falling toward zero, have permitted the relocation of parts of rich-country service sectors to low-wage countries. These encompass not only low-income back-office work and customer service operations but also accounting, marketing, design, and engineering services—although, with their greater facility in English, South Asian countries have some evident advantages over East Asia in this sector.

The same kind of linkages also characterizes a second, more distinctively East Asian, production system: that based on the network of business and financial contacts across the region as organized by overseas Chinese firms and families (see the account in Bernard 1996, 653–54). With not much overstatement, Huntington (1996, 170) writes: "Outside Japan and Korea the East Asian economy is basically a Chinese economy." Overseas Chinese-owned firms play a large, even dominant role in the economies of Indonesia, Malaysia, Thailand, and the Philippines. Singapore and Hong Kong serve as major financial hubs for these firms, mobilizing and channeling investment funds, and providing a secure retreat—financial and physical—when (as they sometimes have done) conditions sour. Unlike Japanese (or Korean) companies, these Chinese businesses are family-based firms, even when very large. The networks linking their dispersed parts were and still are of enormous economic significance to the economies of Southeast Asia, a separate source of entrepreneurial dynamism to that coming from Japan or, more diffusely, from the West. With the opening of China to foreign investment following the Dengist reforms, China itself became a vast new recipient of investment funds from Taiwan, Hong Kong, and Singapore. The 1997 currency crisis and resulting economic setbacks in Southeast Asia, which China almost wholly escaped, has further encouraged this redirection of resources.

Economic geographers describe the spatial economy of East Asia in terms of networks of cities and industrial regions rather than of firms. Cities in a network are linked in a hierarchy of functions, with information handling and services at the top and manufacturing at the bottom. In Friedman's (1986) categories, Tokyo is in the top class of "global cities" (along with New York and London), Singapore is in the next (a class that includes Los Angeles and Frankfurt), and Seoul in the third (with Paris, Mexico City, and others). Such hierarchies supposedly operate fairly independent of national boundaries, and independent too of the geographical features that may have originally determined city location. Centrality of functions rather than population size determines a city's place in the hierarchy, and functions can be gained or lost as technology advances and costs change (Yeung and Lo 1996, 22–23). P. G. Hall (1997) has speculated that the concentration of specialized financial and other informational services that define global cities may be diminishing, as these services shed labor or draw on it in distant locations. Newfound awareness of the physical vulnerability of major urban locations is a further likely spur to deconcentration.

East Asia's largest cities in rank of population are shown in table 3.6. Tokyo apart, they lie well down on the world list: Shanghai is only the world's ninth largest city, Jakarta fourteenth. Of course, the ranking in terms of population numbers and administrative boundaries often does not coincide with status in terms of economic geography. Thus, according to Lo and Marcotullio (2001), the nerve centers of the region's urban hierarchy, with "command and control" roles, are Seoul and Taipei as well as Tokyo; Shanghai, Jakarta, and Bangkok are mere industrial centers—doing the grunt work, so to speak. (In a wider Asia-Pacific city system, Lo and Marcotullio even have a category of "amenity cities," represented by Vancouver and Sydney—the term suggesting an R & R role for the region's harried entrepreneurs.)

With rising density of transport and communications links, urban areas merge. The famed "growth triangles" of the region are probably less important

Table 3.6. Populations of major East Asian cities in 2000 and as projected for 2015

City	Country	Population (millions)		City	Country	Population (millions)	
		2000	2015			2000	2015
Tokyo	Japan	26.4	26.4	Ho Chi Minh	Vietnam	4.6	6.2
Shanghai	China	12.9	14.6	Yangon	Myanmar	4.2	6.0
Jakarta	Indonesia	11.0	17.3	Guangzhou	China	3.9	4.5
Osaka	Japan	11.0	11.0	Pusan	S. Korea	3.8	3.9
Manila	Philippines	10.9	14.8	Hanoi	Vietnam	3.7	5.1
Beijing	China	10.8	12.3	Singapore	Singapore	3.6	4.0
Seoul	S. Korea	9.9	9.9	Bandung	Indonesia	3.4	5.2
Tianjin	China	9.2	10.7	Chengdu	China	3.3	4.1
Bangkok	Thailand	7.3	10.1	Nagoya	Japan	3.2	3.2
Hong Kong	China	6.9	7.7	Pyongyang	N. Korea	3.2	3.8
Chongqing	China	5.3	8.9	Changchun	China	3.1	4.6
Wuhan	China	5.2	7.4	Xian	China	3.1	3.8
Shenyang	China	4.8	5.7				

Source: United Nations 2001b.

Note: Table lists cities with a population of 3 million and over in 2000.

than the vast emerging urban corridors—the equivalent of America's Boswash, the name once given the Boston–New York–Washington corridor, or its West Coast parallel from San Diego to San Francisco, or the corridors defined by the high-speed rail network in Europe. China's entire east coast is potentially such a corridor. A still more expansive—or alarming—Asian vision is sketched by Yeung and Lo (1996, 41): "It is not a far-fetched scenario that the coastal region of Pacific Asia will in the future be a continuous urban corridor stretching from Japan/North Korea to West Java." Pyongyang may be slow to join, but the majority of the cities listed in table 3.6 lie in this prospective belt. The exceptions are the major Chinese inland cities: Changchun, Chengdu, Chongqing, Wuhan, and Xian.

Ebullient expectations of this sort assume away possibilities of serious demand problems. Western markets for manufactures and tradable services are not insatiable, even abstracting from business cycle effects. China's now pervasive presence in those markets already puts strong pressure on most other regional suppliers. Continued vigorous growth of industry in East Asia, and of the urban-industrial system that supports it, may increasingly have to depend on the region's own consumption demands. China's domestic market for manufactures is burgeoning along with its economy, but that will not necessarily benefit the other economies of the region—Japan, perhaps, excepted. The growth picture in those other economies, since 1997, is quite variegated. Thus there is no guarantee that the networks and corridors spanning the region that were established in the earlier phases of industrial development will always flourish.

Culture and Consumerism: Formation of Regional Identity

In purchasing power terms, Japan, Singapore, and Hong Kong have per capita incomes slightly above the Western European average, at about 75 percent of the U.S. level (see Maddison 2003). For quality of life, such a gap is inconsequential. Taiwan and South Korea have per capita incomes about half that of the United States; Malaysia and Thailand about one-quarter. In each of these four countries a substantial part of the population is now securely middle class. Even China, Indonesia, and the Philippines, at about 10–12 percent of average U.S. per capita income, have a numerically if not proportionately large number in this category.

Middle-class status is most simply defined by levels and patterns of consumption. What is consumed looks much the same from Seoul to Jakarta: high-rise housing and new durables such as cars and computers. The middle class also have become consumers of entertainment, and of news—of their country, the region, and the world—with values and perceptions echoed, and in some measure shaped, by the media.

An East Asian urban middle class acculturated to Japanese cartoons, Hong Kong martial arts films, and Western computer technology—embodied in equipment increasingly of Chinese manufacture, with the latest, if pirated, software—is recognizably akin to the middle class of Europe or America. The similarity would exist even if those on the Asian side were assigned a work ethic and consensual decision-making style informed by "Asian values," the neo-Confucianism that used to be invoked to account for the region's pace of economic growth and comparative political quiescence (Mahbubani 1998). The particular content of consumption is distinctive, but not sufficiently so to differentiate Asian consumers in any important respect from consumers elsewhere.

Thus any regional identification people carry in their minds—their cognitive regionalism (the term is from Hurrell 1995b)—must have its basis elsewhere. The parallel with Europe is helpful. What does being a European or EU citizen mean to an Italian or a Swede, beyond simple geography? Few would suppose it to mean taking pride in each other's national histories, let alone accepting collective guilt for the death and suffering in past "European" wars and social engineering follies. Those assumed associations and responsibilities appear real only from a great distance. But if ownership of history is not at stake, we are left mainly with administrative matters: identity tied to an EU passport and currency and the constraints of a thickening mesh of regulations from Brussels. Certainly there is the hope (not universally shared) that these will promote an actual sense of European identity, but for the time being, cognitive regionalism in Europe comprises a layering of affiliations and loyalties—to town, province, nation, and, much more vaguely, to the EU. The lesson may be that effective regionalism need only claim a minor part of a person's identity.

It is possible to imagine the slow emergence of an East Asian identity along the same lines, and just as thin in outcome. A strong regional economy would generate the kinds of bilateral links and multilateral institutions that form among neighboring countries on the same path to relative affluence. The various trade pacts and other organizations and associations—on health, environment, fisheries, marine piracy, and numerous other matters, each with their working groups, conferences, and dialogues—covering all or part of the region would serve as a kind of less bureaucratic Brussels. As a regionwide prospect, however, there are evident difficulties, not least the demographic asymmetries discussed earlier in the chapter. Even for Southeast Asia, what had once seemed a likely course toward an eventual ASEAN-based identity appeared less secure with the faltering of economic growth and puncturing of overly optimistic expectations.

Any substantial progress toward economic-cum-administrative regionalism assumes that the many and intricate ethnic, linguistic, and religious divisions in the region would fade into the background. That, of course, is not assured of happening: at least at present they remain alive and at times are decisive for political and economic outcomes. Huntington's is the most prominent voice for a culturalist interpretation of the contemporary world. "Culture and cultural identities," he writes, "are shaping the patterns of cohesion, disintegration, and conflict in the post–Cold War world" (1996, 20). East Asia is a stew of many cultures ("civilizations" in his usage): Sinic, Japanese, Islamic, Buddhist, Muslim, and Christian. ASEAN, for example, had "one Sinic, one Buddhist, one Christian, and two Muslim member states" in its original makeup (132) and has subsequently become even more diverse. Such organizations "could face increasing difficulty in maintaining their coherence" (128). Mahbubani (1998, 131–32) protests such a picture: he acknowledges Southeast Asia as "Asia's own Balkans," but it is a region that for some decades has been vastly successful economically and peaceable politically by reason of the "corporate culture" it has developed—Asian values as manifested in international relations. (He was writing in 1995; the culture experienced some ructions subsequently.)

Clashes of cultures, intense but on a comparatively small scale, are seen in various parts of the region. One source is organized frontier settlement—Han Chinese in Tibet, Xinjiang, and Inner Mongolia; migrants from Java in Indonesia's "outer islands"—or the spontaneous economic migration that grows alongside the official programs and may outlast them. Differences in language, religious traditions, and customary law give rise to communal strains, pitting existing inhabitants—Tibetans and Uigurs in western China, Dayaks, West Papuans, and many other groups in eastern Indonesia, Moros in the southern Philippines—against settlers. China's border conflicts appear largely under control: in Xinjiang, partly because continued migration is swamping the local population; in Mongolia, because a newly impoverished

Russia now faces a flourishing Chinese consumer economy (see Banister 2001, 296–97; Wines 2001). Indonesia, a weakened state in the post-Suharto era, is not as fortunate. A fragile pluralist outcome in some of its settlement areas has been unraveling, in some instances generating extreme communal violence. Dramatic instances are the killings and expulsions of Madurese transmigrants by Dayaks in West Kalimantan and the fighting between Christians and Muslims in parts of Maluku and Sulawesi. Islam is at the base of another violent and long-running Indonesian conflict: that between the government (seen as Javanese and syncretist) and the rigorously Islamist independence movement in Aceh, northern Sumatra.

Huntington's "Confucian–Islamic connection" (1996, 239) was based on links between Pakistan, Iran, and China. Seen from East Asia, such a connection is far-fetched. The regional manifestation of the process of Islamization that has been occurring in many parts of the Muslim world has introduced new difficulties for regional integration. The separatist movements in Aceh and the southern Philippines and the radical Islamic voices on the fringes in both Indonesian and Malaysian politics are exclusivist, tending to be anti-Western but certainly not pro-Chinese. In any event, the Confucian end of the putative axis would hardly need other support. Indeed Huntington, in a provocative vein, refers to "the greater China co-prosperity sphere" (168–69). " 'Greater China' is . . . not simply an abstract concept. It is a rapidly growing cultural and economic reality and has begun to become a political one."

East Asia, 2025

What does a demographic perspective reveal about prospects for regional integration in East Asia? The demographic aspects of regional change, as described in this chapter, consist in (1) the constraints imposed by existing relative population sizes; (2) the conditions set up by the uneven onset, pace, and outcomes of demographic transition across the region, affecting both population growth and age structure; (3) the rapid urbanization that is still taking place and the development of interlinked urban economies; and (4) the emergence of a sizeable and fast-expanding population of middle-class consumers on the one hand, and the persistence and sometimes strengthening of cultural identities on the other, creating a complex layering of values and affiliations.

The big story of regional change, in which demography plays some part, is the changing China–Japan relationship. There are many uncertainties surrounding the economic futures of both countries, despite the temptation to simply project recent trends forward. ("China" in such a comparison can refer just to its Pacific littoral. Countrywide per capita averages would continue to be held down by a backward interior.) The expectation that Japan will *not* become merely a rentier economy depends on its prospects for retaining a technological leadership role in the world, and specifically maintaining an edge over China. For the United States, technological leadership is not in doubt: the United States could plausibly continue to relocate manufacturing jobs abroad but retain its huge advantages in research and development, benefiting from network externalities and other sources of increasing returns in this area. Not least, the United States draws in a lot of intellectual talent from the rest of the world. Japan's parallel inflow of human capital is minuscule in comparison.

The second regional story with a population angle is about culture versus economy as principles of regional organization. Huntington's vision of an East Asian future seems to be of a China-led Sinic regionalization, incorporating Taiwan, Hong Kong, Singapore, and to some extent the Chinese diaspora economies of Southeast Asia. Japan is left out of this ("Japan as a culturally lone country could have an economically lonely future"; Huntington 1996, 134), but so might be a more Islamicized Indonesia and Malaysia and an eastward-looking Philippines. Contrasting with such a culturally influenced kind of integration would be a geographically (or propinquity-) defined entity like ASEAN or AFTA, or further regional extensions of such institutions—perhaps with cultural considerations suppressed far enough to admit Australia and New Zealand. The more organically evolving networks that are tying together Asia's cities into urban hierarchies and regional manufacturing, service, and trading economies—a bottom-up process—have cultural elements but are based far more on an economic logic.

Against the somewhat ominous future of a "co-prosperity sphere" in East Asia is the comfortable bourgeois vision of an array of thriving middle-income economies with fairly similar demographic structures—promising to generate over time huge numbers of reasonably, and eventually very, well-off consumers. For a few countries in the region, demographic modernity is still decades away, but most will soon have to make their way in the new demographic landscape of slowly shrinking labor forces and rising numbers of elderly. Whether regionalism will become a serious matter of economic leverage, and thus acquire political content, or remain a minor component of people's self-definition may largely be determined by events and trends elsewhere. Environmental change, not treated in this chapter, is one potential source of trouble. Strategic change is another: there is little in East Asia's regional future that is not in some measure contingent on the shape and substance of the United States–Japan–China triangle. Geographic regionalism is a kind of holdover from an earlier age, something to do with shaded maps. It should be rendered increasingly obsolete, one might suppose, by modern communications technology and low transport costs. But it is also the default option of geopolitics in an uncertain and hazardous world.

II

DRIVING REGIONAL INTEGRATION

4

The Decline of a Japan-Led Model of the East Asian Economy

ANDREW MACINTYRE AND BARRY NAUGHTON

The dynamism of the Asian economies since the 1950s not only implies rapid growth; it also implies continuous change in the economic relations among East Asian countries. In this chapter we map the changing interests of three key East Asian countries with respect to the main economic issues and explore the way in which those perceived interests shape what those countries have sought to achieve from regional economic cooperation. Specifically, we focus on the interaction between changes within national political economies and changes in the wider regional economy, and the effect these two variables have had on government-to-government economic cooperation in Asia. Our aim is to describe and explain what we see as a basic shift in the pattern of economic issues and economic cooperation in East Asia.

To highlight the changes, we develop a simplifying framework in which East Asian economic interactions are divided into two periods: the first, from about 1985 to about 1994, we characterize as the period of the flying goose model and of "open regionalism," or APEC-style consensual cooperation among governments. The second period, from about 1994 through the present (2002), we characterize as a period of instability in economic hierarchies and economic relations. The new period reflects the emergence of competing interregional production complexes (Japan-centered versus greater China). The result has been great difficulty in converging on patterns of regional cooperation that are seen to be mutually beneficial by the countries involved.

We thank Peter Drysdale, Ross Garnaut, Stephan Haggard, and T. J. Pempel for very helpful critiques of earlier drafts and Pablo Pinto for research assistance.

We develop and illustrate this argument by focusing on the behavior of three Asian countries: Japan, China, and Indonesia. We use these countries not simply because they are the biggest. We use them because, together, they capture much of the essential dynamics of regional economic cooperation across East Asia. In broad terms, we can think of Japan, followed by South Korea, Taiwan, Hong Kong, and Singapore, as representing capital- and technology-rich political economies, which potentially form the nodes of high-level economic development. China represents the most important of the dynamic middle-tier economies whose rapid growth is disrupting traditional economic relationships.[1] The cross-border production networks that link China and Taiwan, as well as Singapore and Malaysia, are creating dynamic economic regions that are closing the gap with Japan. Indonesia shares with Thailand, the Philippines, and Malaysia many characteristics as resource- and labor-rich political economies.

The rough characterizations of economies in the previous paragraph, by themselves, capture much of the fundamental character of Asia's political economy during the earlier period when regional economic relations were more hierarchical. Subsequently, however, as the hierarchical regional structure increasingly breaks down, this taxonomy becomes less satisfactory. But this gets us to the heart of the chapter: the changing dynamics of the Asian regional economy and the implications for attempts by national governments to build regional economic cooperation. This chapter is organized into two main sections, corresponding to the two periods we seek to contrast. For each period, we present five short subsections: the overall economic environment, country sections for Indonesia, China, and Japan, and the implications for international cooperation.

I. The Initial Period: The Japan-Led East Asian System, 1985–94

The Economic Setting

The year 1985 marks a convenient starting point for the acceleration of integration in East Asia. The Plaza Accord of that year and the currency realignments that followed in its wake were key short-term drivers of change. Currency realignments crystallized the economic changes that had been building over the previous couple of decades. By the early 1980s, the remarkable success of Japan had been followed by that of the "four small dragons" (South Korea, Taiwan, Hong Kong, and Singapore) in pursuing export-oriented industrialization. The success of that development strategy created huge export surpluses, which in turn created irresistible upward pressure on the currencies of Japan and some of the dragons. Thus, currency realignments were

---

1. In addition, China shares with Vietnam, Cambodia, and Laos characteristics of transitioning socialist regimes.

simultaneously *consequences* of existing development outcomes and *causes* of further changes in the economic strategy of other East Asian actors.

In the short run, currency realignment made production in Japan, South Korea, and Taiwan much more costly and encouraged firms in those countries to relocate production to less developed parts of Asia. But the receptivity of those other countries was greatly enhanced by three factors. First was the demonstration effect. Countries such as China and Indonesia saw the success of Taiwan and South Korea firsthand and observed the development gap open up between them. The second exogenous factor influencing receptivity was the collapse in raw material prices that began in the early 1980s and culminated in the rapid decline in petroleum prices in 1986. This convinced oil exporters such as Indonesia and China—but also agricultural material exporters such as Malaysia and Thailand—that there was no real future with commodity-based export development. Third, the success of the Japanese economy, combined with the appreciation of the Japanese currency, meant that Japanese capital and technology were available to the rest of Asia.

We use the familiar "flying goose" label to describe this period. The key factors that make the label applicable are the following:

1. There was perceived to be a clear hierarchy of economic development in East Asia at this time. Japan was unambiguously the economic leader, in all respects. Korea and Taiwan were unambiguously second, with Singapore and Hong Kong close behind technologically and bringing superior commercial resources. Malaysia and Thailand came next, and China and Indonesia followed. Potential entrants waited outside the door, Vietnam most importantly.

2. Japan was seen to be the key source of both capital and technology. Japanese investment came both through foreign direct investment (FDI) and through bank lending. Japanese technology made its FDI especially attractive. Japanese corporate networks would integrate firms in other East Asian economies, providing rapid institutional and managerial learning, in addition to "hard" technology transfer.

3. Significant aspects of the Japanese economic policy were seen to be not only successful but also replicable. Protection of some domestic economic sectors was not seen to be an obstacle to export-driven growth. So long as selective trade promotion effectively targeted emerging export sectors—and stable macroeconomic policies provided a predictable, low-inflation environment—countries could gradually emerge into the world economy without the political and economic disruption of across-the-board liberalization.

Like any simple metaphor, the flying goose model falls short of a comprehensive description of the complex Asian reality. It papers over important differences among the various categories or cohorts of developing East Asian economies. For instance, there is important variance in terms of the significance of agriculture and extractive industries, the character of protectionism, the extent of openness to foreign investment, and the basic political economies of foreign economic policy (Bernard and Ravenhill 1995; MacIntyre 1994; Hill 1993; Jomo 1997). But our purpose is not to talk about differing development models around the region. Further, the flying goose metaphor (and, indeed, the very notion of an East Asian economy) clearly does not come to grips with the glaring fact that the United States was a critical part of the underlying economic equation. None of this is in dispute. To be clear, we invoke the flying geese image not to describe the model of economic development in any particular country or to characterize the totality of international economic relations across the greater Pacific, but to capture the *perceived* nature of economic relations among East Asian countries. For our purposes, the utility of the model is that it captures the notion of a hierarchical pattern of economic development across Asia, in which it appeared that national economies could interact without fundamental conflict of economic interests. Japan was the key driver and would stay in front, but the fundamental process was one of an orderly movement of the flock. Each economy, moving forward, would create space for those behind, and indeed make it easier for the follower to fly. The economic policies of national governments would have to be modified to take advantage of opportunities, but the modifications required were feasible, requiring more or less drastic adaptations but maintaining the basics of the selectively protectionist export promotion model. For our purposes, what is important is that the model was perceived at the time as being feasible and attractive to the relevant East Asian governments and capable of being implemented without fundamental conflicts of interest among those countries.

Indonesia

In the second half of the 1980s, Indonesia, like the other resource- and labor-rich economies of Southeast Asia, became increasingly engaged in multilateral economic cooperation across Asia. This was a novel development. Previously, Indonesian policy makers had, for the most part, been inwardly focused, with little serious interest in coordinating economic policy settings with other states. Through the 1970s, except for a few halfhearted efforts at collaboration on joint investment projects and a very limited preferential trade agreement among ASEAN states, Indonesia's priorities were overwhelmingly domestic. From about the mid-1980s the picture began to change as two key factors came together to accelerate the reestablishment of regional trade and financial links between Northeast and Southeast Asia that had been disrupted by the Second World War (Petri 1993; Hamashita 1997).

One fundamental consideration was that, like the other resource- and labor-rich Southeast Asian economies, Indonesia was in the process of unilaterally deregulating and opening its economy. This began with major financial reforms in 1983 and intensified from the mid-1980s with trade and investment reforms following the collapse in commodity prices. Indonesia's earlier import-substituting strategy for industrial development had run its course, and a severe external shock was forcing it to search for a new engine for growth and new ways of mobilizing capital. Increasingly, the burden of policy swung in the direction of lowering barriers to the flow of capital and goods. Indonesia became much more welcoming to foreign capital and was anxious to develop new export industries that could compete in world markets. The second key factor here was the realignment of exchange rates. Where Indonesia was pushing its exchange rate down, Japan was pushing its exchange rate sharply up as a result of the Plaza Accord with the United States. This, together with rising costs at home, led to a wave of investment from Japan and the other capital-rich and increasingly high-cost labor economies of Asia in the latter 1980s.

These two forces intertwined and were mutually reinforcing. Growing volumes of direct investment and bank lending were coming into Asia from Japan as well as South Korea, Taiwan, Hong Kong, and Singapore, and the economies that chose to open their borders received it.[2] Together, these two forces were pushing the leading Asian economies toward each other, promoting a measure of economic regionalization. This, in turn, had important consequences for regional cooperation. With Indonesia now having a much greater stake in the regional economy, it became more interested in and more sympathetic to proposals for an official framework to facilitate a stable and expanding regional business environment. Reinforcing this broader conception of national economic interests was the country's increasingly stable domestic political situation. With internal security concerns much reduced, policy makers increasingly lifted their sights to the wider external environment in Asia. And here, broad commercial and politico-security interests all pointed to the potential benefits of facilitating regional cooperation among the key governments of the East Asian region. With some local variation, roughly parallel dynamics were at work in the other leading resource- and labor-rich Southeast Asian countries (MacIntyre 1997).

In 1989 we saw Indonesia warily agree to join the new Pacific-wide forum being promoted by Australia and Japan, Asia-Pacific Economic Cooperation (APEC). Indonesia (and its Southeast Asian neighbors) was initially concerned about the possibility of APEC being dominated by Japan and the United States. But entrenching an agreement that every other year the peak annual meeting should be hosted by a Southeast Asia country and, more importantly, institutionalizing ASEAN's consensual and nonbinding organizational practices for APEC (the so-called Kuching Consensus) helped to allay those concerns.[3] In this period of relatively easy growth and improving

2. Not all did. The Philippines, for example, was less involved because it did not liberalize until much later. This is even more clearly the case with Laos, Cambodia, and Myanmar.

3. As a further hedge, Indonesian and Southeast Asian neighbors agreed in 1992 to a schedule for creation of the ASEAN Free Trade Area (AFTA) in an effort to prevent ASEAN from being completely overshadowed by the United States, Japan, and increasingly China.

regional familiarity and trust, Jakarta was soon not simply comfortable with the APEC framework but an active supporter. In 1991, in an unusual move for a member of the diplomatically restrained world of ASEAN, Suharto publicly and bluntly rejected the proposal of his Malaysian counterpart, Mahathir bin Mohamad, for an East Asian Economic Group, which was widely interpreted as a challenge to APEC and a call for a more restrictive framework for economic cooperation. And in 1994, Indonesia not only hosted the second APEC summit but played an active role in facilitating the plan to establish a free trade and investment regime in the Pacific by 2010 for high-income countries and 2020 for others.

Indonesia's interest in an economically open framework for regional cooperation quickly strengthened. It turned from being the most protectionist and statist of the nonsocialist Southeast Asian economies to one that played an active role in promoting liberal and outward-looking plans for regional economic cooperation. Indonesia's interest in APEC lay in its potential to promote regional trust and stability and loosely facilitate a peaceful pro-commerce regional environment. This interest in promoting trust and stability among the key countries and facilitating regional commercial links was shared by the other Southeast Asian governments, and it was pursued both at the level of East Asia as a whole as well as more narrowly within Southeast Asia with the development of the ASEAN free trade area.

China

China, like Indonesia, had engaged in a process of market opening well before the Plaza Accord. The success of its East Asian neighbors—and especially Taiwan and Hong Kong, fellow "Chinese" economies—was an important goad to China (Naughton 1995, 63). Closed for two decades, China returned to the world economy at the very bottom of the chain of economic and technological sophistication. Special economic zones created enclaves in which foreign firms could operate with less tax and regulation than in the main economy. Chinese firms carried out processing contracts for firms based in Hong Kong that had the knowledge and access to carry out commercial transactions.

Chinese involvement stepped up drastically after 1985. Enough of the early reforms had been successful that Chinese domestic firms were able to develop the minimally necessary responsiveness to interact with transnational actors. The dramatic policy response, begun in 1986, and fully in place by 1988, was the Coastal Development Strategy. Under this strategy, China threw open all its coastal provinces to foreign direct investment and export processing contracts. Foreign businesses were allowed to go outside the state sector and deal with less bureaucratic, more market-responsive township and village enterprises (Naughton 1996, 2). The correspondence in time between these measures and the external opportunities provided by the East Asian economic system is exact.

At the same time, international organizations were eager to have China—the big "new kid" on the block—enter, so they offered concessionary terms. China entered the World Bank and IMF in the early 1980s and applied to resume membership in the GATT in 1987. The Asian Development Bank allowed Taiwan to remain a member under the "Chinese Taipei" rubric.

It was understood in China at this time that Japan was the dominant external player, economically speaking. Incoming investment from Hong Kong was always larger than that from Japan, to be sure, but this reflects proximity and "suburban" investment. Japan was always the number two source of incoming FDI, through 1992. Moreover, Japan was China's largest trading partner, and far and away the largest source of bilateral development assistance. It was unthinkable that China could seriously rival Japan's economic predominance in Asia.

At the same time, China stood apart from serious engagement in most multilateral organizations. China was peripheral for the APEC process, though expressing verbal support. China did not, for example, join multilateral cooperation agreements on the Mekong River, despite being the key upstream country. China's government consistently calculated that it had more to gain by exploiting its "special" position in a series of bilateral relationships. China concentrated on special pleading, emphasizing its size and enormous potential, while at the same time stressing its enduring poverty and transition-related problems. Special claims on the consideration of the developed countries would only get submerged in a one country/one representative multilateral organization. At the same time, China's peripheral position reflected its relatively shallow integration in the Asian international economy in the 1980s. China had begun to fly with the flock, but it was still content to follow along in the wake of the leaders.

Japan

During the 1970s and 1980s, Japan developed a very clear sense of its own economic position and its own interests. Moreover, there was a fairly high degree of consensus within Japanese political circles about those interests. As a result, Japan was able to articulate a vision of regional cooperation that was highly consistent with the consensus view of its economic and regional diplomatic interests. Because Japan was economically successful, and Japan's interests in cooperation did not yet directly contradict the interests of other countries in the region, it is not surprising that Japan was able to achieve many of its regional cooperation interests. Japan sought continued access to natural resources and expanded access to both growing local consumer markets and cheap labor for the production of goods for third markets. Japan's government was not throwing open its own borders to foreign capital or manufactures, but it was keen to see open and pluralistic economic arrangements across the rest of Asia. This objective was pursued by the various arms of Tokyo's foreign economic policy bureaucracy in a quiet but vigorous manner (Drysdale 1988; Funabashi 1995; Yamazawa 1992; Arase 1995).

Open regionalism served Japan's core commercial interests. By incorporating the United States and other developed countries into regional institutions, it undermined protectionist impulses directed at Japan, and it avoided the danger that regionalism would be met with discriminatory trade policies in countries outside the region. By colluding in the creation of relatively weak, consensus-based institutions, it ensured that its own domestic protectionism would not be seriously challenged. Thus, Japan maintained its freedom of maneuver. At the same time, open regionalism served as a convenient framework to coordinate some aspects of economic policy and to lower the transaction costs faced by Japanese corporations (as investors) and Japanese financial institutions operating in other Asian economies. Thus, the fit was perfect with the notion of Japan acting as the "lead goose," maintaining its own economic model intact, while gradually incorporating what were (mistakenly) perceived as junior versions of its model into an Asian community. In this conception, each economy would move forward in the flock behind Japan, but no economy would be directly challenged by more rapid integration or more intense competition. This model was also reasonably appropriate in a Pacific economy in which most economies had much stronger market orientation toward the United States than to each other. Despite steady increases, intra-Asian trade was outweighed by cross-Pacific trade (Frankel and Kahler 1993).

APEC ✓ ✗

The Development of APEC and Consensual-Style Regional Cooperation

The combination of favorable regional economic circumstances and conducive national political and economic conditions underpinned the emergence of APEC as a framework for regionwide government-to-government interaction. We do not suggest that these conditions alone explain the emergence of APEC. To be sure, there were many obstacles to the birth of APEC, and it was by no means a foregone conclusion. As many have noted, the region was indeed riven by multiple divisions and suspicions that can be traced back, variously, to the Second World War, the Cold War, and great disparities of wealth, size, political form, and social composition. But the prospect of continued prosperity provided a powerful shared incentive for governments to try to overcome these obstacles with a view to nurturing regional economic development.[4] APEC's consensual and nonbinding pattern of policy cooperation suited perfectly. It helped members overcome mutual distrust (just as it had

4. This logic was scarcely a secret. Policy-oriented scholars from Australia, Japan, and the United States had been discussing it for decades (Crawford and Okita 1976; Drysdale and Patrick 1979; Krause and Sekiguchi 1980).

earlier for ASEAN members) and, at least for the East Asian countries, the roughly hierarchical structure of the regional economy meant that there were few big divisive economic issues requiring major adjustment and binding res- olutions. The glaring exception to this was, of course, the United States. Not being enmeshed in the East Asian regional economy in the same way, the United States had economic interests that conspicuously conflicted with those of the others. And, importantly, it prosecuted these interests through other channels, with muscular approaches to bilateral economic relations and mul- tilateral agreements at the global level through the GATT. If the United States was a goose, it had a very different flight path.

In this period of easy growth—greatly facilitated by Japanese capital and technology—APEC-style cooperation made a lot of sense. It cost very little, and no great economic interest turned immediately or directly upon it. Rhetoric notwithstanding, its role was to begin the process of bringing the governments of the region together in a way that helped ease suspicions. It did not matter that APEC didn't actually do much in terms of concrete policy adjustments. Its contribution was to bring governments to the table and open the way to the possibility of more serious policy cooperation in the future.

II. The Contemporary Period: 1994 to the Present (2002)

The Economic Setting

Despite the initial enthusiasm, the much-vaunted conception of a Japan-cen- tered East Asian economic system never developed. The flying goose pattern disintegrated, and the countries of East Asia were left to search for other mod- els and definitions of their self-interest. The single most important cause of this was the bursting of the Japanese "bubble economy" at the beginning of the 1990s, which fatally undermined the system in two ways. First, and most important, as Japanese domestic growth slowed, Japanese corporations became increasingly reluctant to export jobs. Fearing the "hollowing out" of Japan's industrial capability, corporate and government leaders dramatically slowed the restructuring of Japan's core industries. Japan held on to the "full set" of industries.[5] For complex reasons—including their commitment to employment in Japan and their distrust of developments in China–Japanese corporations neglected the potentials for cost-saving, relocating only the most labor-intensive stages of production to other parts of East Asia. For example, the Toshiba corporation had virtually no overseas employees as late as the year 2000. Second, Japanese banks dramatically slowed the expansion of their

---

5. For a vision that did not come true, see Seki 1994.

Fig. 4.1. Japanese bank lending to other East Asian countries, 1986–2000. *Source:* Barclays Capital, reprinted in *Financial Times,* January 16, 2002, 12.

lending in East Asia, and in some cases they began recalling loans to compensate for increasingly shaky finances at home.[6] Figure 4.1 shows that total Japanese overseas lending peaked in 1994 and has declined virtually every year since then. With Japanese economic dynamism slipping, the critical element in the conception of a Japan-centered system was removed. The key driving force of robust financial and technological flows out of Japan to neighboring East Asian economies faltered.

The decline in Japan's foreign direct investment in East Asia has been much less abrupt. Overall, Japanese outgoing FDI tumbled in the early 1990s, from a peak of $66 billion in 1989 to only $35 billion in 1992. Most of the decline, however, was in investment in the developed country economies of the United States and Europe. As figure 4.2 shows, investment in the rest of Asia held up fairly well during this period. But after 1995 in the case of China or 1997 for the rest of Asia, Japanese direct investment declined substantially. With both bank lending and direct investment sinking after 1995–97, Japanese economic influence waned substantially.

While the Japanese economy stumbled, the Chinese economy gained strength. The proximate cause was the enormous surge of FDI into China beginning in 1992 (see fig. 4.3).

China was not able to challenge Japan, South Korea, or Taiwan as sources of technology and investment. It quickly posed a challenge, though, to those recipients of FDI that had been "ranked" ahead of China in the early years of

6. Much Japanese overseas lending was in fact lent to Japanese corporations through Hong Kong and other offshore centers, so the decline in lending and the slowing of outgoing FDI were related.

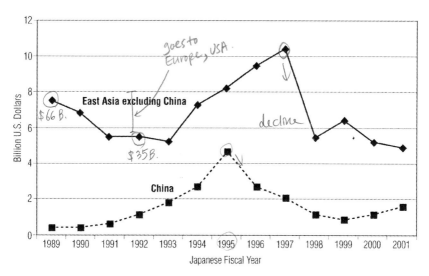

Fig. 4.2. Japanese foreign direct investment in East Asia, 1989–2001. Data are for Japanese fiscal years, which begin in April of the year named and end in March of the following year. Values have been converted from Japanese yen to U.S. dollars at the prevailing exchange rates. *Source:* Ministry of Finance, Tokyo, http://www.mof.go.jp/english/fdi/reference01.xls.

Table 4.1. China's share of total FDI inflows to ASEAN + China

Year	Share (%)
1988–92	36%
1995–96	57%
1999–2000	72%

the flying goose model, the ASEAN nations. China's share of the total FDI inflow into ASEAN + China increased dramatically.

This was a major concern to Indonesia and the other ASEAN states and prompted them to accelerate their plans for AFTA. But if China's challenge had merely been to displace the ASEAN economies bringing up the rear of the "flock," it would be of only local importance, threatening to ASEAN but not especially important to the overall East Asian picture. Instead, the rapid growth of investment into China corresponded to increasingly robust economic capabilities based on cross-border production networks.

China's increased importance was not simply as an attractor and competitor for incoming foreign investment. As a trading partner as well, China began to play an increasingly important role in both intra-Asian trade and exports outside the region. By the mid-1990s, production and trade networks among China, Taiwan, and Hong Kong had developed real regional weight. Total

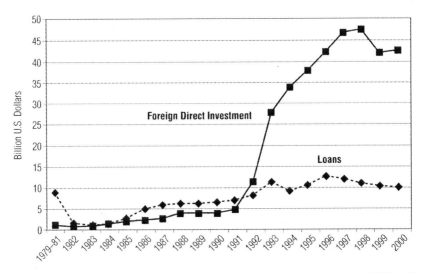

Fig. 4.3. Foreign direct investment in China, 1979–2000. *Source:* National Bureau of Statistics, PRC, 2003, 671.

external trade of these three, after netting out trade among them, amounted to $810 billion in 1999, surpassing Japan's total of $731 billion. More crucially, in some sectors, these networks began to seize technological and competitive superiority from Japan. These changes are most important in the electronics industry and are especially evident in computer and telecommunications equipment. In some industries—including notebook computers and hard disk drives—the combination of American research and "greater China" production networks has displaced Japanese corporations from their preeminent position (McKendrick, Doner, and Haggard 2000). Virtually all the economies of East Asia have taken advantage of the rapidly growing electronics sector. But the "greater China" economies have reaped the greatest relative advantage, and Japan has seen an erosion in its relative position. Japan remains the most important source of high-technology components, but China is now second. Moreover, China has surpassed Japan as the most important Asian market for exporters from South Korea, Taiwan, and Singapore and has gained ground among other exporters (Ng and Yeats 2003, 56–58, 6–7).

The shift in the relative position of Japan and greater China is by far the most important change in overall trade patterns in Asia during the 1990s, which have otherwise been fairly stable. The trend in the previous decade toward increased intra-Asian trade has been moderated: it was abruptly reversed by the 1997 Asian crisis, but then it resumed. The share of intra-Asian exports in total Asian exports increased from 43 percent in 1992 to 49 percent in 1996, dropped back to 43 percent in 1998, and then recovered to 47 percent in 2001. The long-run trend is still toward greater intra-Asian

trade, masked not only by the Asian crisis but also by the declining importance of Hong Kong as an entrepôt for Chinese trade.[7]

The overall trade trends are easiest to see in Asian exports to the rest of the
world. Overall, Asian exports to the rest of the world have grown strongly,
averaging 5 percent per year. There has been a huge drop in Japan's share of
these exports, from 45 percent to 30 percent, while China's share has
increased from 6 percent to 21 percent, so that apparently 15 percentage
points have shifted from Japan to China in a single decade. This comparison
could be somewhat misleading, though, because the growth of China's share
is magnified by the shift of final stages of assembly to China from Taiwan and
Hong Kong, and particularly by China's beginning to directly export goods
that formerly were routed through Hong Kong. Figure 4.4 consolidates trade
data on China with those from Hong Kong and Taiwan to account for the high
degree of integration among the three Chinese economies. The Chinese
three increased their share of Asian exports to the rest of the world from 28
percent to 38 percent, and in aggregate their share now clearly overshadows
Japan's contribution.

Changes in Japan's role in the Chinese economy reflect the broader shifts in
Japan's global economic position. From the beginning of China's opening
through 1991, Japan was the second largest foreign investor in China (after
Hong Kong), accounting for 13 percent of total investment. As investment
poured into China from 1992, Japan completely failed to keep up. In 1993,
Japan accounted for only 5 percent of total investment. Japanese investment
rebounded somewhat after 1993, but for the entire 1993–2000 period, Japan
was only the fifth largest investor in China, after Hong Kong, Taiwan, the United
States, and the EU. Given Japan's industrial prowess, strength in the industrial
sectors driving much Asian investment (especially electronics), proximity to
China, and overall economic size, this is an extremely poor showing.

In other respects as well, Japanese primacy has been shaken. Although
Japan remains by far the largest economy in the region and has by far the
greatest technological capabilities, it is no longer so distinctive in terms of its
actual economic roles. Both South Korea and Taiwan now specialize in
machinery exports to the same degree as Japan, and both have reduced their
dependence on labor-intensive manufactures (textiles, shoes, and so forth)
to the same low level as Japan. Although there is still a quality premium for
Japanese goods, South Korea, Taiwan, and Singapore produce the same type
of goods. Meanwhile, China's rapid economic ascent has upset the hierarchy
from the bottom. As China has emerged as a more attractive destination for

---

7. Throughout the 1980s, the share of Chinese trade going through Hong Kong had actually
increased, despite China's opening, because of Hong Kong's efficiency and because of the importance
of foreign-invested firms (often based in Hong Kong) in China's export performance. But as China's
opening has continued, exporters in China, even foreign-invested firms, have less need to export indirectly through Hong Kong, and imports to China transit Hong Kong less frequently as well.

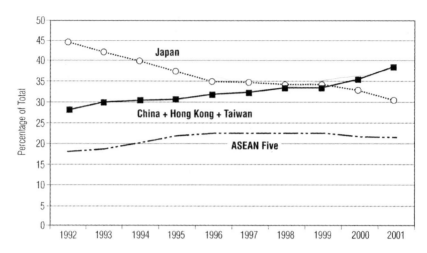

Fig. 4.4. Share of total exports from Asia to the rest of the world for three East Asian countries or regions, 1992–2001. ASEAN Five, Indonesia, Malaysia, Philippines, Singapore, and Thailand. *Sources:* International Monetary Fund 2002; Directorate General of Customs, Ministry of Finance, Republic of China, *Monthly Statistics of Exports,* http://www.dgoc.gov.tw.

FDI, relative to Malaysia and Thailand, for example, it has developed capabilities that in some areas are clearly superior to those of all the ASEAN economies except Singapore.

The collapse of the flying goose model, then, takes two forms. As a result of the weakness of the pulse of the Japanese economy at the "heart" of the model, the circulation of capital and technology through the system is too weak to organize the system around it. Moreover, the unambiguous hierarchy no longer exists. The division of labor is more complex. Different economies have developed strong capabilities in different sectors, and there is no longer a clear ordering among economies in terms of sophistication. Instead, we have the embryonic emergence of a pattern of rival production systems. The Japan-centered system has gone into decline, while the greater China networks have been in the ascendant. It is not really China versus Japan, although the two may sometimes see themselves this way in geopolitical terms. China and Japan scarcely compete at all in export markets. Japan's U.S. exports, for example, only overlap with Chinese exports in categories accounting for 20 percent of the total (less than 10 percent if a crude adjustment is made for quality and product type) (data from the Research Institute of Economics Trade and Industry of Japan, as cited in the Lex column, *Financial Times,* November 26, 2001, 16). But Japan has traditionally cooperated with labor-intensive Southeast Asia, while the China networks have of course found their labor-intensive production bases in China itself. The dynamism of China and the weakness of Japan have therefore especially hurt the Southeast Asian economies, because their competitor economy has grown in strength, while their complementary economy has declined. These patterns unleash new possibilities of competition and cooperation that cannot be remotely contained within a simple hierarchical model of regional economic relations like that of the flying geese.

Indonesia

In many ways, for Indonesia, the 1994 Bogor summit was the high point in terms of movement toward official economic cooperation across Asia. As the 1990s progressed, the momentum in this direction declined, as was evident even before the Asian economic crisis. After the surge of unilateral liberalizing economic reforms of the preceding years, Indonesia's appetite for further adjustment slowed markedly in the mid-1990s. The economy was booming, and the increasingly sclerotic Suharto regime was more likely to focus on the concerns of narrow economic interests threatened by the prospects of competition on the one hand and growing rumbles of popular complaint about inequity on the other. It was not that Indonesia no longer had an interest in facilitating commerce and regional cooperation, but with the economy doing so well and with the increase in sectional domestic political concerns, Indonesia was simply less interested than before in paying the costs of actively pursuing such an agenda. Certainly it had little interest in a binding regime of strictly reciprocal economic agreements of the sort proposed in the APEC Eminent Persons Group and vigorously promoted by the United States. Like most other countries in Asia, Indonesia was already concerned about trade policy bullying from the United States. But more than this, the growth of economic linkages with Japan had now slowed with the bursting of Japan's bubble economy. On the financial front, Japanese investment and bank lending slowed, and on the trade front Indonesia was becoming increasingly conscious of barriers to exporting to Japan.

The economic crisis of 1997–98 radically intensified this trend. APEC was seen to be irrelevant to addressing the country's dire problems, the United States was uncompromising in its insistence on the strict economic remedies articulated by the IMF, and Japan was unable or willing to provide a real alternative source of policy leadership. More fundamentally, Indonesia's political and economic situation had been utterly destabilized internally. On the political front, the country has struggled to construct a viable democracy from the rubble of the Suharto regime. This alone has been an enormous undertaking, consuming the energies and attention of the political elite. Unfortunately for Indonesia, the particular political configuration that took shape in the immediate post-Suharto years provided for weak and ineffective government. In quick succession, two presidents (Habibie and Wahid) labored with little effect in managing policy even in the executive branch, much less in managing policy negotiations with the legislature (MacIntyre 2003; Malley 2002).[8] On the economic front, the corporate sector has been held back by prolonged problems with debt restructuring and the rebuilding of the banking industry. Not surprisingly, apart from natural resource processing and a few other reliable export industries, there was little private-sector support for opening the country's economy to increased foreign economic competition. Indeed, the prevailing pattern in the industrial sector has been to call for a slowing of earlier plans for reducing trade barriers and encourages an emerging pattern of creeping protectionism (MacIntyre and Resosudarmo 2003).

In the longer run, Indonesia's underlying interests in deepening economic linkages across Asia will reassert themselves, but in the wake of the financial crisis, any serious consideration of regional cooperation and coordinating economic policies has been pushed well down the agenda of national priorities.

China

The domestic political economy of China was undergoing important changes at about the same time. After 1993, Chinese policy making began to be associated with much greater decisiveness than had been the case previously. Many of the key outputs of the policy reform process shifted, as central-government policy makers gained greater apparent control over the levers of the policy process. From a consistent trend toward decentralization in the 1978–92 period, selective recentralization has characterized the post-1993 period. Budgetary revenues declined (as a share of GDP) through 1994 but then began to grow rapidly. Macroeconomic policy tilted toward austerity. Reform policies increasingly included measures designed to foster competition on a level playing field, policies that imposed substantial costs on hitherto sacrosanct interest groups, including workers in state-owned enterprises. Bankruptcies of state-owned enterprises soared, and urban unemployment increased substantially. The Chinese government began behaving in a fashion that was much less constrained by particularistic interests and that showed itself to be capable of more authoritative, decisive decision making (Naughton 2001).

These changes corresponded temporally with the flood of FDI into China, which took off after 1993. The more decisive policy-making process in China is important because it has leveraged the external impact of China's sustained rapid economic growth. China has as many economic problems as any member of the East Asian community, probably more. But since about 1993, China has consistently evinced an ability to begin to address the most important problems, an ability that surpasses many of its neighbors. As Overholt has

---

8. More recently, continued political reform has helped to reduce some of these problems; see MacIntyre and Resosudarmo 2003.

described it, "China is in a bigger hole, but it's digging out faster" (1999, 3). China's apparent ability to mobilize swift and decisive action in some areas has accelerated the growth of its economic and political weight in the region. China may have problems, but its political leaders have shown that they are capable of moving to deal with them at a more impressive rate than their counterparts in the Japan or the Indonesia of recent times.

China's serious attention is often directed inward. Even WTO membership is seen primarily as a driver of a further stage of domestic reforms. Indeed, China is big enough and growing sufficiently rapidly that it cannot realistically expect to drive its economic growth primarily with exports to the U.S. market. It would be both politically and economically unrealistic. China's domestic demand will have to be the main driver of China's future development, and that means it might also be the driver of development in other East Asian countries. Yet China is still very backward; it has virtually no dynamic, "competitive" multinational firms, so it is not really in a position to push for meaningful concessions or privileges for its firms in foreign markets.

At the same time, with the relative decline of Japan, China's attitude toward participation in the various international organizations has shifted. Clearly, the World Trade Organization has been the focus of China's trade negotiators since the early 1990s. Since those WTO negotiators, particularly those from the United States, have demanded serious concessions from China, WTO has unavoidably become the focus of China's steps toward liberalization. Nothing in the APEC process is remotely as important as WTO membership. At the same time, ironically, the magnitude of China's concessions for the WTO give it greater credibility in the East Asian policy arena. After WTO membership, China's economy will be more open to FDI, foreign service providers (finance and telecommunications, for example), *and* trade than Japan's economy has ever been. Inevitably, that gives China an extra lever in its interactions with other East Asian economies: market access. China gains an additional measure of credibility from its market opening.

Japan

By the mid-1990s, Japan's vision of itself as the driver of East Asian restructuring was seriously out of date. The inability of successive governments to take effective steps to tackle the country's prolonged economic problems undermined any potential for Japan to assume a true leadership role in Asia.[9] The arrival of the Asian financial crisis in late 1997 brought this home, without really producing any meaningful response in terms of Japanese policy. In 1998, Japan was simultaneously proposing that it serve as the banker of East

---

9. We do not explore explanations for Japan's immobilism in the 1990s here, but for a range of views, see the following: Pempel 1998; Schoppa 2001; Bevaqcua and Iwahara 2002.

Asia and watching passively as its currency dropped to 145 yen/dollar, creating consternation in the rest of Asia. By 1999–2000, with the Japanese economy and the whole Japanese model under enormous pressure, there finally emerged some signs that the entire regional framework was being rethought as Tokyo's international policy makers pushed to regain some initiative.[10] Not accidentally, it was about this time, say 2000–2001, that major Japanese corporations began to accept the inevitability of moving significant steps of the production process offshore, primarily to China.

The Weakening of the Regional Cooperation Centered on APEC

Given the changing regional economic context and the interests of the individual countries, it is unsurprising to find APEC faltering, with the loss of dynamism coming well before the Asian financial crisis. In retrospect, the Bogor declaration in 1994 can be viewed as something of a high-water mark of the APEC process. Few discernable results have been achieved since that time, with subsequent summits proving successively less impressive. The collapse of the Early Voluntary Sector Liberalization program in 1998 marked the first overt failure of an APEC initiative and one of the first major cases of open substantive discord within APEC (Krauss 2004). It is not a coincidence that the first big rupture should have involved the United States. Indeed, the only surprise is that this did not happen sooner. But in terms of the wider East Asian economy, more remarkable is that it pointed to the emergence of serious divergences between Japan and the ASEAN economies. The sudden devaluation of the Japanese yen in 1998, during the darkest hours of the Asian financial crisis—combined with the lack of concern evinced by Japanese policy makers at that time—contributed to seriously undermining Japanese claims of regional leadership. Indirectly—but inevitably—this affected APEC as well.

Changes in the economic environment have shifted the focus of regional cooperation away from APEC. The ASEAN + 3 consultation, initiated in December 1997, responds to a genuine felt need to engage in a manageable framework for dialogue among the main East Asian entities. At the May 2000 Chiang Mai meeting of finance ministers, ASEAN + 3 achieved a substantive result when it established a network of currency swaps among members to help ensure against future financial crises. ASEAN + 3 was also the venue for the events of November 2001 that thoroughly upset the traditional relations among the Asian economic powers.

At the 2001 meeting, Chinese premier Zhu Rongji proposed the establishment of a China–ASEAN free trade agreement within ten years. It was remarkable that China made such a proposal, completely ignoring Japan, and the

---

10. See the following chapter by Keiichi Tsunekawa and, more broadly, Inoguchi 2002.

response, too, was remarkable. The ASEAN countries overwhelmingly (if cautiously) welcomed the proposal, and Prime Minister Koizumi replied that Japan was, at least temporarily, preoccupied with domestic restructuring and would not be in a position to respond. Within weeks, as Koizumi realized he had allowed China to completely seize the initiative on the East Asian diplomatic front, he was scheduling a visit to Southeast Asia to talk about closer economic cooperation. The visit came off (in January 2002), but the damage had been done. Despite some progress on a free trade agreement with Singapore (the only Southeast Asian economy without an agricultural sector), Koizumi's visit produced embarrassingly little.

The regional and national political economies of East Asia are changing in basic ways that have powerful implications for the pattern of multilateral cooperation among governments. We can see this operating at a number of levels.

The most basic implication is that the pattern of regional economic interactions can no longer be expected to pull East Asian countries into an easy APEC-style framework for economic cooperation. The appearance of a clear regional economic hierarchy is now gone. The interactive effects of processes of industrial specialization in individual countries, the prolonged recession in Japan, and the continued rapid rise of China have created a much more complex reality. To a much greater extent than before, there are conflicting economic interests that will require hard bargaining. We have long seen this between the United States and the capital- and technology-rich East Asian economies. Similar dynamics are increasingly conspicuous among the main East Asian economies. The most prominent have been the growing trade frictions between Japan and China on agricultural and some industrial issues. The same is also true of Japan and Southeast Asia. And among the Southeast Asian states themselves, there are certainly specific areas of trade competition and friction, as there are with China too.

Along with the hierarchical order of the flying geese conception of East Asian economic relations, the convenient distinctions we drew among three categories of East Asian economies are also breaking down. For instance, China is becoming a source of not just cheap labor but also industrial design talent for Japan and a source of capital for Indonesia (and other parts of Southeast Asia).[11] It is not surprising that this should be the case, although this is a change in the established picture of the East Asian economy, and it has important implications for the pattern of regional cooperation. The East Asian economy is becoming more densely interconnected, there is greater specialization taking place, and relative economic positions among various countries—most notably, the big three examined here—are shifting. And along with new areas of economic friction, there are also many areas of economic opportunity. One of the challenges for East Asia as it seeks to adapt to

11. See, e.g., "Japan Braces" 2002; "China Investment" 2002; and Dhume 2002.

this changing environment is that it does not have an institutional framework for tackling the divisive issues. The loose, consensual-style rules of APEC are ill equipped for coming to grips with the nitty-gritty of the sectional economic differences that are increasingly arising. On the other hand, none of the other initiatives launched—including ASEAN + 3—is any better positioned to tackle these issues.

Second, if we drop to the national level, in varying degrees we can see country-specific factors also pointing to a reshaping of state preferences toward regional economic cooperation. With a prolonged recession, continued political turnover, and an imploding banking sector, Japan has had little appetite for volunteering significant concessions on electorally sensitive trade issues (in advance of any global settlement under the WTO). Tokyo certainly remains interested in trying to play a diplomatic leadership role in shaping the regional agenda (Inoguchi 2002), but it has had little interest in contemplating serious economic adjustments under APEC. Indonesia is in a similar position. Its willingness to undertake unilateral reforms had already cooled in the mid-1990s, and the financial crisis has thrown it into complete disarray. Regional economic cooperation was simply off the agenda in Jakarta. APEC proved useless in Jakarta's hour of need, and even AFTA obligations are beginning to look unappealing in the current economic climate. But where Japan and Indonesia are in the doldrums, China continues to move strongly ahead. It continues to be willing to adjust important economic policy settings and remains keen to use any and all frameworks for regional economic cooperation (APEC, ASEAN + 3, ASEAN + 1) to advance its leadership aspirations. For China, economic initiatives are seen as coinciding strongly with diplomatic and even national security objectives. The enticement of the Chinese market can serve to reconcile ASEAN countries to China's increasing economic strength, build confidence politically, and wean Southeast Asia away from dependence on Japan and the United States (Lawrence 2002).

Third, and more generally, at the more amorphous level of ideology, the Asian economic crisis has affected the climate of ideas about regional economic cooperation. The crisis produced complex and multifaceted reactions across the region, ranging from anger toward local political and economic elites to anger toward the IMF and the United States. The latter has taken the form of a quasi-nationalist, or perhaps regionalist, desire to have greater Asian control over Asian destinies and to ensure that this never be allowed to happen again. And this, of course, has been a powerful force behind the growth of the ASEAN + 3 framework.

The economic and political forces driving the decline of the APEC process and promoting the rise of the ASEAN + 3 framework are very powerful. The shift in relative strength sometimes encapsulated as "China's rise and Japan's fall" accounts for only part of it. Powerful regionwide economic changes are also an important part of the story. But although it is fairly straightforward to track those changes, it is not at all easy to project them into the future. That is the subject of our final section.

Conclusion: Economic Integration, Regional Cooperation, and Leadership in East Asia

Our primary purpose here has been to highlight the changing dynamics of the political economy of East Asia through a contrast between two time periods. The image of a Japan-led regional economy—enshrined in the flying goose metaphor—became widespread in the literature and popular discussion of the 1990s. But as we show, even as a perception it only really pertained for a short period and has been a very poor guide to the reality of regional economic relations from the mid-1990s on. In analytic terms, we tie our argument about the changing structure of the East Asian regional economy to the changing economic and political circumstances of various East Asian countries. The interaction of these two variables has many important implications for the wider international political economy of the region. In this chapter, we have connected it with efforts by governments to develop official economic cooperation across the region. We see this as helping to explain the rise and fall of APEC-style cooperation.[12]

But what of the future? How are governments likely to behave over the next half decade or so? Anticipating the emerging trends of the political economies of the individual countries of the region is beyond the scope of this chapter, but we can offer some general thoughts about the structure of the regional economy and the question of regional leadership. We suggest that regional cooperation will be in flux for the next decade, because no available set of regional cooperative institutions will be able to accommodate the rapidly changing and still uncertain economic realities.

First, as already suggested, we expect to find harder bargaining as countries face tougher trade-offs between their economic objectives and the kinds of concessions they are willing to make. It is important to be clear that this is at least as great a problem—if not greater—for the ASEAN + 3 framework as for the APEC framework. Both are soft, consensus-based frameworks. And thus although the afterburn from the Asian economic crisis has encouraged East Asian governments to come together on their own, they will be hard-pressed to achieve any more in this configuration. The same is true for the

12. Again, as noted earlier, notwithstanding our focus on East Asia here, it would be silly to think that the style of cooperation embodied in APEC is a function of factors deriving just from East Asia. APEC was not and is not simply a function of East Asian preferences. The United States has also been pivotal. Even though a weak or consensus-based framework for regional cooperation was not the first preference of the United States, Washington has been willing to go along with this because it has had robust options for pursuing its economic interests in East Asia at both the bilateral and global levels.

ASEAN + China and ASEAN + Japan initiatives. The evolution of the East Asian regional economy increasingly requires a more structured and binding framework for policy coordination, whatever the membership of the group. And yet, ironically, precisely because the United States is absent from the various East Asians—only frameworks, geopolitical asymmetries and suspicions among members are likely to make it difficult for them to agree to a set of decision-rules that would enable serious bargaining to take place.

In the short run, this points to the likelihood of diverging trends in regional economic cooperation. On the one hand, we are likely to see continued soft, consensual frameworks at the regional level as various geographical configurations are explored. On the other hand, we are likely to see hard bargaining—which is increasingly necessary—take place on either a bilateral or global level, through the WTO. Complicating the picture here has been the loss of momentum for global trade negotiations under the Doha Round of the WTO, combined with the push by the United States for bilateral "free trade" agreements. Because these bilateral agreements have clear and important preferential trading implications, they have triggered a nervous flurry of other proposed bilateral and subregional free trade arrangements, as countries scramble for fear of being left out. All of this points to tangled and competing trading arrangements around the region (Findlay, Pei, and Pangestu 2003).

Second, the future leadership role of China is still extremely uncertain. In the absence of a clearly defined economic hierarchy, it is unclear what leadership roles are emerging. China's size and rapid economic growth give it a leadership claim, because of the shadow of the future. That leadership claim has credibility because of the record of decisive policy making China has established since 1993, because of the offer of market access that gives China an additional bargaining tool, and because of China's growing commercial reach into the rest of Asia. There are anticipations that China will emerge as an alternative source of final market demand for the rest of Asia, taking up the slack from Japan's declining demand, and that this will allow East Asia to grow more rapidly than the absorptive limits of the U.S. market might otherwise imply. An early illustration of this is the growing involvement of China in Indonesia's energy markets. Moreover, China is already—through the present—more deeply integrated into cross-border production networks than is Japan. Finally, China's commitments to WTO, in some important respects, will make it more open to international trade than Japan (notably in agriculture). This is reinforced by China's status as a continental-size economy, which is likely to predispose it toward a more or less liberal international economic order. Thus, China's commitment to use its economy to drive closer East Asian cooperation appears credible.

But China is not really in a position to be a leader, in terms of its current resources. China's $1 trillion economy is only one-fourth the size of Japan's $4 trillion economy. China has nowhere near the financial resources that allow Japan to deploy foreign assistance in support of its national objectives. China's technological capabilities are still substantially behind those of Japan, although the gap is narrowing. Thus, when China acts like a leader in East Asia, this often involves an element of grandstanding. Indeed, both China and Japan have engaged in a great deal of grandstanding over the issue of free trade agreements with Southeast Asia. The fact that Chinese gestures are treated with somewhat more respect by the nations of Southeast Asia is interesting, but it does not necessarily translate into genuine and effective leadership.

Furthermore, China's economic power, today at least, is an expression of cross-border economic networks in "greater" China rather than just in mainland China. Thus, when Gloria Macapagal Arroyo welcomes an ASEAN free trade pact with China, we are permitted some skepticism ("China, ASEAN Pact" 2002). After all, the Philippines sent only 4 percent of its exports to China in 2001, so it is hard to see that such a pact would make much difference. But closer inspection reveals that the Philippines sent fully 18 percent of its exports to Taiwan and 10 percent to Hong Kong, so that greater China accounted for 32 percent of total exports, exactly the same proportion as sent to Japan. Thus, the Philippines' enthusiasm for a China free trade pact is more an expression of support for deeper integration with Chinese economic networks than for increased exports to China per se. But a significant source of uncertainty exists in China–Taiwan relations. Will the two sides of the Taiwan Straits be able to come to a stable accommodation that will enable these economic linkages to continue to develop? It remains to be seen.

Finally, Japan's economic position remains fluid. This is perhaps most evidently visible in Japan's economic presence in China. We argued earlier in the chapter that Japan essentially missed out, during the 1990s, on the opportunity to restructure output by moving production to China. There are clear signs that since about 2000, the interests of Japanese corporations in China have been reawakened, and there is an increasing effort to accelerate the production and technology transfer process. Companies such as Toshiba, NEC, and Honda—all hesitant to invest seriously in China in the past—are now making major commitments. These trends are showing up in corporate strategy before they show up in the aggregate investment flows, but the change is unmistakable. It would be foolish to underestimate the potential of this movement. Even as it creates anxiety within Japan, it creates new economic opportunities from the combination of Chinese capabilities with Japanese technology, capital, and organizational skills. In the medium run of five to ten years, this could create sufficient economic dynamism to begin to reshape political attitudes and relationships.

For all these reasons, East Asian economic cooperation is likely to remain in flux, and highly uncertain, over the next few years. With a fundamental reshaping of economic relations under way, it will take years for cooperative efforts to catch up and find appropriate forms to facilitate closer relations. Under these circumstances, it is inevitable that there will be rivalry between China and Japan without a clear outcome and instability among the various forums of regional cooperation. The concerns of other East Asian nations will be, to some extent, subordinated to the interests of the new great powers, as they struggle to define their economic interests and their relations with each other.

5

Why So Many Maps There?

Japan and Regional Cooperation

KEIICHI TSUNEKAWA

As transboundary flows of goods, money, people, pollution, arms, and harmful drugs expand in East Asia as in other parts of the world, the ability of individual nations to solve economic, social, political, and environmental problems has declined. Japan and other East Asian countries need to work together to cope with trade impediments and territorial disputes as well as transnational crimes and environmental degeneration. In contrast with Europe, East Asia lacks well-institutionalized frameworks for regional cooperation. Although frequent mention is made of the ASEAN + 3 (APT) grouping, the prospect that East Asia will develop something similar to the European Union remains as dim as ever. However, there are contrasting views about the effects of such institutional scarcity upon the problem-solving capabilities of East Asian governments.

Optimists believe that cross-border activities of private enterprises and businesspeople are so pervasive and dynamic in East Asia that governments do not need permanent regional institutions to cope with problems impeding additional transactions. For example, Hatch and Yamamura (1996, 35) see ASEAN's brand-to-brand complementation program of 1988, by which member countries mutually reduced import duties on auto parts, as facilitating the businesses of Japanese carmakers without a formal free trade agreement. Because ASEAN countries amply benefit from Japanese direct investment, the Japanese government and companies can cope with remaining impediments through ad hoc, piecemeal negotiations with East Asian governments. Such market-based de facto integration came to be called open regionalism and is characterized by concerted unilateral liberalization and most-favored-nation treatment for everyone.

101

From a slightly different angle, Peter Katzenstein (1997, 3, 31–32) argues that comparing European "success" with East Asian "failure" in terms of institutionalization would be a great mistake. East Asian countries may lack formal regional institutions, but they are blessed with abundant, although informal, network structures that greatly facilitate transactions and communications.

By contrast, Joseph Grieco (1998, 242–43) casts doubt on the feasibility of consensus-based informal integration. Addressing Asia-Pacific Economic Cooperation (APEC), he argues that its unilateral, nonbinding commitments are unlikely to lead to meaningful liberalization of economic relations in Asia and the Pacific because certain members over time will feel that others are benefiting disproportionately. Grieco's concern is shared by the U.S. government, which has never been persuaded of the usefulness of "concerted unilateral action" and the principle of most-favored-nation treatment for everyone (Funabashi 1995, 141–43).

In practice, optimism concerning the Asian approach to regional cooperation turned to pessimism toward the end of the 1990s. The APEC process slowed down after the Osaka meeting of 1995. The failure of the Early Voluntary Sectoral Liberalization program at the Kuala Lumpur meeting of 1998 further underscored the standstill of the APEC process (Ohba 2001, 278–79). Both ASEAN and APEC proved powerless in face of the monetary and financial crisis of 1997–98.

Furthermore, although discussions about regional cooperation in East Asia have focused mostly on economic and security matters, East Asian nations increasingly face a variety of unconventional problems such as environmental degeneration, illegal immigration, the spread of HIV/AIDS, drug trafficking, and other organized crimes, all of which have transboundary causes and effects. The lack of an integrated institutional framework has forced the East Asian governments to rely on ad hoc multiple mechanisms, including unilateral, bilateral, regional, and supra-regional schemes. These are frequently redundant and slow in bringing meaningful results. Consequently, many contend that more institutionalized solutions may be advisable to allow East Asian governments to face their common challenges.

This chapter does not evaluate the feasibility of open regionalism but rather focuses on the divergent characteristics of regional cooperation among East Asian governments in various issue areas. Although EU-like agreements and institutions with binding obligations are absent in East Asia, the extent and the depth of cooperative commitment vary from one issue area to another. In some areas, East Asia-wide cooperation is observed, whereas in others, only bilateral or supra-regional frameworks exist. The strength of members' commitment to cooperation schemes also differs from one area to another. This chapter analyzes how cooperative mechanisms vary across issue areas and the factors that shape these differences.

Before discussing our theoretical framework, we need to clarify our country focus and time frame. To explain regional cooperation in East Asia, we need to consider at least five major players: Japan, the United States, China, ASEAN, and nongovernmental actors. This chapter, however, is written from a Japanese perspective, and the regional policies of the other players are touched on only when they are relevant to Japan's policy. Still, many important initiatives for regional cooperation have been taken by players other than Japan. Although mention is made of earlier periods, I emphasize the decade of the 1990s and thereafter, for it was then that regional cooperation was multiplied and intensified in diversified issue areas.

Diversities of Regional Cooperation in East Asia

Cooperation schemes in East Asia differ in terms of their geographical coverage as well as the relative strength of participants' commitment.

To analyze the geographical extension of cooperation in East Asia, we need to distinguish the areas of East Asia, Asia-Pacific, and supra-regional Asia. Important studies trace the history of the concept of "Asia-Pacific" in Japan (Watanabe 1992, 108; Ohba 2002, 97) and show that "Pacific" was originally used to indicate the group of high-income countries such as Japan, the United States, Canada, Australia, and New Zealand. So when Kiyoshi Kojima, a Japanese economist, proposed a Pacific free trade area in 1965, those five countries were the presumed members, although "Asian and Latin American developing countries would gather around this nucleus, just like many African countries associated themselves with the contemporary European Economic Community" (Korhonen 1998, 27). For Japan, therefore, "Asia-Pacific" meant the combination of these two groups of countries (Asia and "liberal" countries). These were designated its most important partners by the first Blue Book on Foreign Policy (Ministry of Foreign Affairs 1957, 7–8).

Both bilateral and regional cooperation have occurred within the "Asia-Pacific" framework. Bilateral cooperation usually involves the United States and a single East Asian country; regional cooperation occurs among several East Asian countries and the United States (and possibly some other "Pacific" countries).

On the other hand, within Japan during the 1940s and 1950s, "Asia" meant not only Northeast and Southeast Asia but also the Indian subcontinent. In the 1960s, however, Asia, as Japan's partner of regional cooperation, came to refer to Northeast and Southeast Asia, excluding the Indian subcontinent. Therefore, regional cooperation in Asia can be subdivided into bilateral ties, Northeast Asia (China, the Korean peninsula, Taiwan, Mongolia, and the Russian Far East), Southeast Asia (the ten ASEAN members), and East Asia (ASEAN + 3 and possibly some other Northeast Asian countries).

Finally, there have been geographical extensions of cooperation that went beyond East Asia and the Pacific, reaching the Indian subcontinent, the Middle East, or the EU. Such cases are referred to as supra-regional cooperation in this chapter.

Geographically, bilateral cooperation is too narrow to be called regional, whereas the presence of the Pacific or supra-regional countries dilutes the "East Asian" nature of cooperation. Regional cooperation in East Asia is thus defined as involving more than three East Asian countries. The case studies that follow demonstrate that "East Asian" frameworks are used in some issue areas, whereas they are seldom observed in others in which bilateral arrangements dominate or non-Asian participants are noticeable.

Cooperation also varies according to its depth. Members' commitments are deepest when a formal agreement exists stipulating mutually binding obligations. East Asia has seen many agreements that require member countries to take actions in pursuit of common purposes, but sanctions such as expulsion have never been stipulated against noncomplying members. Agreed-upon measures are expected to be implemented by individual participating governments in response to peer pressure. This does not necessarily mean, however, that all agreements among East Asian governments are useless.

Peer pressure will be more or less effective according to the way cooperative actions are defined in the agreements. When they are defined in general, ambiguous terms, they do little to help peer pressure work effectively. They can contribute largely to information exchange and confidence building. By contrast, when agreements are specific and concrete enough to make members' expected actions obvious, peer pressure can have greater impact.

In East Asia, besides action-inducing agreements, plenty of groupings or networks are based on no more than conferences, seminars, joint research, and human exchanges. These schemes are less action inducing, but cooperation deepens when the conferences and other dialogue measures are organized by joint agreements of the participating countries rather than being based on one country's unilateral initiatives. Furthermore, joint research or technical cooperation can affect policy when it is organized in a scientifically authentic manner, and the results point strongly to the need for immediate actions by the participants. When peer pressure of this kind is strongly felt, member countries are induced to implement domestic measures "unilaterally" even without a clear-cut action-oriented agreement.

Previous literature on Asian regionalism fails to distinguish these differences in geographical extension and cooperative depth among various regional schemes of intergovernmental cooperation. This chapter relies on three variables to assess different patterns of cooperation: East Asian countries' relationship with the United States, transnational transactions and communication, and domestic constraints and opportunities. Theoretically, these variables are eclectic because each is based on plural approaches dominant in the international relations literature: realist, liberal, constructivist, and "domestic structure."[1]

The first variable, the United States–Asia relationship, is linked to both realist and liberal approaches. On the one hand, emphasis on many East Asian countries' dependence on the United States for security reflects the realist view. This dependence originated because of weak regional cooperation among East Asian countries for security during the early postwar era. Once established, however, bilateral ties came to be viewed by the United States as its preferred framework for security arrangements in East Asia. Dependence on the United States for security has constrained the security policies of many East Asian countries.

Protagonists of the liberal approach stress the fact that many East Asian countries including Japan also depend deeply on the U.S. market. They ship on average 20 to 30 percent of their exports to the United States, and for many of them, the United States has been the single largest market for their products. This trade dependence limits East Asian countries from enacting regional policy measures that could jeopardize their economic relations with the United States. In contrast with commercial dependence, financial and monetary dependence on the United States has been much lower thanks to the overall external-sector strength and credit worthiness of the East Asian economies. Only during a highly serious economic crisis such as that of 1997–98 did U.S. influence through the IMF constrain the policy alternatives of the East Asian governments.

The second variable, transborder networks, is based on liberal and constructivist views. There is a broad consensus that transnational integration of private businesses preceded intergovernmental cooperation in East Asia. Private companies and business people connected by business networks came to be powerful promoters of governmental cooperative measures aimed at reducing transaction costs and other business impediments. This is a typical liberal view. Another liberal case of transborder connectedness leading to intergovernmental cooperation involves transnational networks of noneconomic NGOs, such as groups seeking environmental protection. These networks have also led to intergovernmental cooperation through concerted pressures on individual governments.

The spread of organized cross-border crime is another example in which networks precipitate intergovernmental cooperation. In this case, however,

---

1. Ravenhill (2002) distinguishes three approaches that try to explain the nature of regional cooperation: realist, liberal, and constructivist. We can add the "domestic structure" approach, which emphasizes the importance of domestic power relationships (coalition politics) or state–society relations. Solingen's works (1998 and in this volume) belong to the former version, whereas Katzenstein's argument (1997, 35–37) that Japan's domestic network structures such as keiretsu and administrative guidance shape the "distinctive patterns of Japanese penetration of Asian economies" belongs to the second.

intergovernmental cooperation is aimed at squelching the activities of trans-border crime networks.

Epistemic communities in the field of environmental protection do not have power to influence government policy directly. Their influence is based on the prestige and scientific knowledge of the experts comprising the community. Their views can affect national policy only by affecting the ideas and identity of national policy makers and public opinion in general. This is a constructivist view.

The third variable, domestic constraints and opportunities, is based on the constructivist and "domestic structure" approaches. First, as constructivists would argue, people's value and sentiment affect the regional policy approaches of East Asian governments. In China, South Korea, and some Southeast Asian countries, distrust of and animosity toward Japan persist, based on historical memory. These governments, therefore, are cautious about regional schemes in which Japan could emerge as hegemonic. The Japanese government itself, fearing backlash from its Asian neighbors, hesitates to take measures that could appear imposing or interventionist.

Legal and social norms have constrained the security policy of the Japanese government (Katzenstein 1996a, 115–21). The postwar constitution is called pacifist because it explicitly prohibits Japan from having and using military forces to solve international conflicts, but its "pacifist" content has been diluted through reinterpretation. Thus, Japan started to rearm itself in the early 1950s under an interpretation that self-defense is not international war and the forces for self-defense are not ordinary military forces. The period after the early 1990s saw further reinterpretation of the constitution, according to which Japan's Self-Defense Forces can now be sent abroad to help with UN peacekeeping operations or to join multinational efforts in Afghanistan and Iraq, because those missions are supposed to be aimed at domestic peacekeeping and reconstruction, not at solving international conflicts. In the missions, the use of weapons is to be severely restricted. Except for the case of the U.S.-led war in Iraq, the majority of the Japanese people have supported these reinterpretations of the constitution, although they are hesitant about the use of actual Japanese military forces abroad and want the government to work mostly for civilian purposes.

The domestic structure approach has two lines of argument. On the one hand, Solingen (1998, and her chapter in this volume) distinguishes liberal-internationalist and statist-nationalist coalitions in individual countries and argues that the relative strength of these coalitions determines whether a regional order will be liberal, nationalist, or mixed. Talking about Japan's "regime shift," Pempel (1998, 216) also observes "an underlying socioeconomic bifurcation—between deregulation and internationalism, on the one hand, and regulation and nationalism on the other." Japan's future regime will be shaped by the relative strength and mixture of these two sectors of the population. Thus domestic structure, in Solingen's and Pempel's sense, plays an especially influential role in trade negotiation. Many East Asian governments including Japan's face tenacious resistance from internationally uncompetitive sectors whenever trade liberalization is placed on the table. Such resistance at home is, in no small number of cases, stronger than the liberal pressure from regional business networks.

Another line of argument in the domestic structure approach emphasizes the importance for regional policy of the nature of the state–society relationship. For example, Katzenstein (1997, 29–31) argues that the osmotic ties between the state and society in many East Asian countries contribute to shaping the "network" of regional order. The case of drug control, however, demonstrates that there are areas in which osmotic ties between the state and society can reduce incentives for regional cooperation by enhancing the opportunity for domestic solutions.

In short, the constructivist and domestic structure approaches point to domestic constraints and opportunities for regional cooperation in East Asia. Together with bilateral relationships between the United States and individual East Asian countries as well as pressures from transnational networks, the nature of domestic factors has helped determine the geographical extension and the strength of participants' commitment to regional cooperation in five issue areas, which are analyzed in what follows.

Military Security

Regional cooperation in the security field has been heavily shaped by the pacifist norm in Japanese society, the animosity of the Chinese and other East Asian countries toward the expansion of Japanese influence, the dependence of Japan and several other Asian countries on the U.S. military forces, the preference of the United States for bilateral arrangements, and intermilitary connections between the United States and Japan.

Unlike West Germany, Japan could not envisage a NATO-like regional organization immediately after World War II. Instead, Japan as well as many other Asian countries came to depend for their security on bilateral ties to the U.S. military. Several factors impeded the East Asian countries from having a collective regional security mechanism.

First, during the early postwar era, the U.S. government sought to deprive Japan of war-making capability by dissolving its military forces and encouraging Japanese legislators to adopt a new constitution that prohibited the use of military power to solve international conflicts. The constitution was later reinterpreted as permitting the use of force for self-defense. Even under this interpretation, however, it was still constitutionally impossible for Japan to participate in any collective security agreement that would oblige it to use military might to defend its partners. When the Cold War set in and a hot war broke out on the Korean peninsula, the U.S. government changed its policy and encouraged Japan to rearm itself and cooperate with U.S. war efforts. However, the "pacifist" interpretation of the constitution had become firmly endorsed by the Japanese population, following a traumatic war and foreign occupation. Prime Minister Yoshida, responding in part to public opinion and also in part from his own conviction, opted for a light rearmament and a unilateral dependence on the U.S. military through the Japan–United States Security Treaty (Mendl 1995, 3–4).

Second, unlike in Western Europe, where during the first decade after World War II France and Great Britain provided a counterbalance to West Germany, in East Asia during that time many countries were just gaining independence, and their economic and military capabilities were far less than the potential power of Japan. This power differential strengthened the concern of East Asian countries, which had suffered from Japanese military occupation, for Japan's resurgence as a regional power. Their distrust has persisted, marked by sporadic outbursts over the Yasukuni Shrine and history textbooks provoked by conservative politicians and right-wing intellectuals in Japan.

Thus domestic norms and sentiment within both Japan and other East Asian countries impeded regional cooperation for military security. Facing these regional constraints, the U.S. government took no initiatives to form a NATO-like organization in East Asia but instead opted for separate bilateral treaties with Japan, the Philippines, Australia/New Zealand, South Korea, and Taiwan during the first half of the 1950s. Thailand and the Philippines joined the U.S.-led SEATO (Southeast Asian Treaty Organization) in 1954 (Yamakage 1991, 23). Together with large U.S. military forces stationed in Japan, South Korea, the Philippines, South Vietnam, and Guam, these bilateral security treaties became the backbone of the U.S. strategy of a "hub and spoke" network to contain Communist forces in East Asia.

The first initiative for East Asia–specific regional security cooperation came from ASEAN during the 1970s when the U.S. military capability appeared to be declining. The Guam Doctrine of 1969 had announced a reduction of U.S. forces stationed in East Asia, and the U.S. retreat from Vietnam enhanced the Asian concern, forcing Japan and other East Asian countries to reconsider their security policies (Ogasawara 1998, 164). Most noticeable was ASEAN's peace initiative in Indochina and the endorsement given to that initiative by Japan.

ASEAN was begun in 1967 in an attempt at peaceful dispute resolution and cooperation among five Southeast Asian countries. It was no more than an annual foreign ministers' meeting until the secretariat was set up in Jakarta in 1976. In that year, the first summit meeting was convened, and it adopted the Treaty of Amity and Cooperation. This treaty stipulated, among other things, noninterference in the internal affairs of member countries, settlement of differences and disputes by peaceful means, and renunciation of the threat of use of force (Yamakage 1991, 204–5; Acharya 2001a, 47).[2] ASEAN called for a peaceful engagement policy among its members as well as toward its members' neighbors. It began to pursue peaceful coexistence with Vietnam after North Vietnam defeated the Saigon government. Japan, with huge economic resources, decided to cooperate with ASEAN. Prime Minister Fukuda announced in Manila in 1977 that Japan was ready to help promote peaceful coexistence of the ASEAN and Indochinese countries, and Official Development Assistance (ODA) money would be used to induce cooperation. The Japan Ministry of Foreign Affairs insists that this Fukuda Doctrine was "the first positive diplomatic initiative that Japan took after the war" (Hatano 1998, 101). Although this joint initiative was hampered temporarily by the Vietnamese invasion of Cambodia, ASEAN and Japanese efforts for a peaceful solution to the regional problem came to fruition through the peace-building process in Cambodia during 1988–93.

Besides its peace initiative in Indochina, ASEAN initiated a regional framework for political dialogue and consultation as early as 1978. ASEAN established a series of senior officials' meetings with important economic partners such as the EC, Japan, Australia, New Zealand, the United States, and Canada between 1972 and 1977. In 1978, the ASEAN + Japan Senior Officials' Meeting (SOM) was upgraded to a foreign ministers' meeting at ASEAN's insistence. ASEAN had not been happy with the slow progress of the SOM in responding to ASEAN requests for an expansion of economic assistance from Japan. In upgrading the meeting, ASEAN tried to push Japan toward a quicker and more substantial commitment. The following year, ASEAN invited foreign ministers not only from Japan but also from the United States, Australia, New Zealand, and the EC. This meeting came to be called ASEAN-PMC (or ASEAN Post-Ministerial Conference) because it was held immediately after the ASEAN meeting (Yamakage 1997, 289–90).

When the question of an Asian security framework was raised as a serious subject of discussion in the early 1990s, it was again ASEAN that became the focal point, although the kickoff this time was made by Australian foreign minister Evans. He proposed, in July 1990, to form a forum similar to the Conference on Security and Cooperation in Europe (CSCE) that included participation by socialist countries. This proposal, however, met with a negative reaction from

2. However, the leaders explicitly confirmed on this occasion that ASEAN should not become a military alliance. This is why the member countries needed to rely on extra-regional forces for their security. Thailand and the Philippines had participated in SEATO since 1954. After SEATO was dissolved in 1977, the two countries continued to rely on the United States through bilateral agreements. Malaysia and Singapore, on the other hand, concluded the Five Power Defense Arrangements with Great Britain, Australia, and New Zealand in 1971, according to which Australia has maintained a small air force in Malaysia, and Britain, Australia, and New Zealand stationed a ground force in Singapore. The latter force, however, completely withdrew from Singapore by the end of the 1980s (Acharya 2001a, 53).

the United States, Japan, and ASEAN. The U.S. government continued to take the position that the hub-and-spoke network of bilateral agreements and the military presence of the United States should be the basis for military security in the Asia-Pacific region. Japan and ASEAN insisted that a CSCE-like framework was unrealistic in light of the economic, political, and historical diversities of Asia (Yamamoto 2001, 45; Acharya 2001a, 170).

In June 1991, the ASEAN-ISIS (Institutes of Strategic and International Studies), an important track II network in Southeast Asia, published a report titled "A Time for Initiative," which recommended that a new meeting be organized following the annual ASEAN-PMC to discuss political and security matters among the Asia-Pacific countries. The report also recommended that in addition to the ASEAN-PMC countries, China, Russia, Vietnam, and North Korea should be invited (Soeya 1997, 117). China and Russia had already been invited to the ASEAN Ministerial Meeting held in July 1990 as "guests" of the host country.

On the occasion of the PMC of this ASEAN meeting, Japan's Foreign Minister Nakayama proposed to use ASEAN-PMC as the forum for "political [i.e., security] dialogue." In spite of their apparent similarities, Japan's proposal was different from that of the ASEAN-ISIS. Japan wanted to limit membership to the original members of the ASEAN-PMC, namely, the six ASEAN countries plus Japan, South Korea, the United States, Canada, Australia, New Zealand, and the EU. Japan's main purpose was to alleviate the concern among its East Asian neighbors about its increasing political and even military presence, as exemplified by its extensive involvement in the Cambodian peace process (Yamakage 2001, 64). ASEAN-ISIS, on the other hand, was more concerned with its members' own regional security following the possible withdrawal of U.S. forces from the Philippines, Russian withdrawal from Vietnam, and China's military reinforcement. They, therefore, wanted to involve Russia, China, and Vietnam as well.

Secretary of State Baker first opposed Nakayama's proposal because the United States wanted no regional framework that could jeopardize the hub-and-spoke arrangement it dominated. However, when President Bush visited Tokyo in January 1992, the two countries agreed that the security issue would be discussed at the ASEAN-PMC. The Japanese government allegedly assured Bush that it did not intend to hastily replace the current security arrangement based on U.S.-led security treaties with a new regional framework for collective security (Soeya 1997, 123).

That same month, the ASEAN summit meeting agreed to use ASEAN-PMC as the forum for security-related dialogue (Yamamoto 2001, 48). However, the problem of membership remained unresolved. Australia and some ASEAN countries wanted to include former and current socialist countries, whereas the United States and Japan were less enthusiastic about that idea, preferring a forum of like-minded countries to avoid the complications that would stem from heterogeneous membership. As a compromise measure, ASEAN proposed to establish a new forum that would parallel the ASEAN-PMC (Yamamoto 2001, 50). At ASEAN's insistence, this proposal was finally accepted at the ASEAN-PMC held in July 1993, and the first ASEAN Regional Forum (ARF) meeting was convened in Bangkok in July 1994 with the participation of the ASEAN 6 plus Japan, South Korea, the United States, Australia, New Zealand, Canada, the EU, China, Russia, Vietnam, Laos, and Papua New Guinea. India and North Korea were also admitted in 1996 and 2000, respectively. ARF was thus formed as a supra-regional forum for security-related dialogue that would not jeopardize the U.S.-led security networks but that would satisfy ASEAN's search for broader engagement. Japan was a halfhearted participant.

At the second ARF meeting in August 1995, a concept paper was circulated that envisaged three categories of security cooperation: confidence building, preventive diplomacy, and conflict resolution. In concrete terms, the ARF meeting approved a number of confidence-building measures, including the voluntary exchange of annual defense postures; dialogues on security issues on a bilateral, subregional, and regional basis; and the establishment of senior-level contacts and exchanges among military institutions. In practice, the first meeting of the heads of the military colleges of the participating countries was held in October 1997.

Preventive diplomacy and conflict resolution, however, did not develop easily. China opposed the ARF's role in preventive diplomacy as a violation of the noninterference principle. China also rejected the notion of conflict resolution, taking the position that any international dispute should be dealt with bilaterally. Because of strong Chinese insistence, the concept of conflict resolution was changed to a meaningless "elaboration of approaches to conflicts" (Acharya 2001a, 177). China's position stemmed from its fear that it could be forced to make compromises in the disputes over Taiwan and the South China Sea islands if the cases were to be put on the ARF agenda (Wang 2000, 79).

In addition to ARF, Japan participated in two other security-related forums, the Council for Security Cooperation in the Asia Pacific (CSCAP) and the Asia Security Conference (ASC). Other than ASEAN-ISIS, CSCAP is probably the only major nonofficial forum for security dialogue. Developed in June 1993 by the research institutes for strategic studies belonging to ten countries (five ASEAN countries plus Australia, Canada, Japan, South Korea, and the United States), CSCAP is a track II forum in which defense and foreign relations officials participate, as "private citizens," together with scholars. CSCAP thus provides a semi-official mechanism for dialogue. It has been more flexible than ARF, as testified to by the admission of North Korea in 1996, four years before the DPRK was admitted into ARF. Taiwanese representatives were also accepted as "individuals" on the condition that the Taiwan issue would not be put on the agenda of CSCAP (Shigemasa 1998, 73). Because of strong opposition from China, however, Taiwan has not been admitted to ARF. In practice, CSCAP has served as a supplemental mechanism for ARF. To help ARF, the CSCAP established four working groups dealing with confidence-building measures, maritime security, North Pacific security cooperation, and cooperative and comprehensive security (Acharya 2001a, 176). A fifth working group was added in 1997 to cover transnational crimes.

ASC is also a semi-official forum of high-level officials from defense ministries as well as security specialists and journalists. Its first meeting was hosted by the British Institute of International Strategic Studies at Singapore in June 2002. Seventeen countries including Japan, the United States, South Korea, China, several ASEAN countries, India, and Australia sent delegations (*Asahi Shimbun,* June 3, 2002).

In spite of various kinds of frequently convened meetings, ARF, CSCAP, and ASC continue to be no more than the supra-regional forums in which participants exchange opinions and information. They are far from serving to prevent or solve international military conflicts. It remains to be seen how much they can foster confidence building among participants.

Besides participating in the ARF, CSCAP, and ASC processes, the Japanese government has recently tried to institutionalize bilateral frameworks for consultation and cooperation with Russia, South Korea, and China for the purpose of building mutual trust.

Senior officials of the defense ministries of Japan and Russia have met annually since 1992; in the same year, Japan's secretary of its Defense Agency made his first visit to Russia, with his Russian counterpart reciprocating the following year. The research institutes affiliated with the military in both countries have engaged in research exchange programs since 1993. The battleships of both navies have visited each other's ports since 1996 and engaged in joint training for search and rescue since 1998 (Japan Defense Agency 1999, 179–80).

Defense ministers of Japan and South Korea began mutual annual visits in 1994. Senior officials of the defense ministries also started to meet in the same year. The General Staff Office and the army, navy, and air force of both countries also engage in dialogue, research, and personnel exchange programs. Mutual visits of battleships began in 1994. Joint training by the navies for search and rescue began in 1999. Finally, senior officials of the foreign and defense ministries of the two countries started to meet with each other for security-related talks in 1998 (Japan Defense Agency 2001, 212–13).

Senior Japanese foreign and defense ministry officials have met with their counterparts from China since 1994, and they have participated in research exchanges since 1998. The meeting of top military leaders began only in 1998, with the mutual visits of defense ministers (Japan Defense Agency 2001, 215).

In addition to these bilateral consultations, Japan has organized a variety of unilaterally convened conferences, seminars, and research meetings whose purpose has been confidence building, and it has invited mainly Asia-Pacific countries to participate. For example, the Defense Agency started to organize an annual forum in 1996. The Defense Academy has also convened seminars since 1996, whereas the National Institute for Defense Studies started to organize its own seminar in 1994 (Japan Defense Agency 2001, 218–19).

Notwithstanding Japan's participation in the ASEAN-centered supraregional forums and more recent measures taken at bilateral and unilateral levels, the alliance with the United States continues to be Japan's most important mechanism for national security. On the occasion of the second ASC meeting in May 2003, Japan's secretary of the Defense Agency emphasized that the bilateral treaties between the United States and various East Asian countries continue to be "critical for the stability of the region" (*Asahi Shimbun*, July 27, 2003).

Ironically, the U.S. stance toward Japan was not necessarily consistent, especially after the first half of the 1990s. Within the context of the easing Cold War tension and the frequent trade disputes that had characterized the United States–Japan relationship during the preceding decade, a 1990 U.S. Department of Defense policy paper argued frankly that the United States should deter the development of Japan's capability of power projection and its ability to develop autonomous weapons systems and should keep Japan within the framework of U.S. strategy (Soeya 1997, 119). This is the famous argument that the United States is a "cap on the bottle," with the United States–Japan Security Treaty and the U.S. presence in East Asia impeding any increase in Japanese military power that could threaten the power balance in Northeast Asia.[3]

Five years later, however, the Nye Report reappraised the role of Japan and argued that economic friction should not jeopardize security cooperation between the United States and Japan and that close bilateral cooperation was crucial to effective engagement with China (Nye 1995, 99; 2001, 99). Behind this change in U.S. policy was the renewed threat of North Korean and Chinese military buildup. North Korea refused to accept the surveillance by the IAEA and threatened to withdraw from the Nuclear Non-Proliferation Treaty in 1993. The Chinese government, after experiencing international isolation following the Tiananmen incident, began a drive for the rapid modernization of its military forces. In 1992, the Chinese government enacted the Law on Territorial Waters, unilaterally claiming sovereign right over the Senkaku (Diaoyu) Islands, the Paracel Islands, and the Spratly Islands, and

---

3. In 1990, a Marine Corps general stationed in Japan pointed out the importance of a continuing U.S. troop presence in that country, saying "no one wants a rearmed, resurgent Japan. So we are a cap in the bottle, if you will" (Washington Post, March 27, 1990, quoted in Pyle 1998, 133).

its navy continued to make aggressive moves in both the South China Sea and the Taiwan Straits (Manning 1996, 26).

U.S. concerns were substantiated by China's resumption of nuclear weapons testing in 1995 and its large-scale navy training operations, with actual missile launchings, during the Taiwanese presidential election of March 1996.

In the following month, the U.S. and Japanese governments issued a Joint Declaration on the Security Alliance for the Twenty-first Century in which the two countries recognized that their bilateral security cooperation would continue to be the basis for the stability and prosperity of the Asia-Pacific region. In the same declaration, the Japanese government pledged to revise the guidelines for U.S.–Japanese defense cooperation (Soeya 1998, 214–15). The old guidelines, adopted in 1978, stipulated only the Japanese role in the case of a direct attack against Japanese territory. The new guidelines, agreed to in 1997, added stipulations on the Japanese role in the event of an incident that, if left unattended, could lead to a direct attack against Japan (Kamiya 1998, 135–36). China reacted negatively to the new guidelines, fearing that its reach could extend to Taiwan.

Defense cooperation between the United States and Japan further deepened in 1998 when North Korea launched the Taepo Dong missile over Japan. The Japanese government quickly decided to cooperate with the U.S. plan to develop the Theater Missile Defense system (Wan 2001, 35). China again reacted negatively (Harris and Cooper 2000, 43).

The close connections between the military forces of the United States and Japan have further strengthened bilateral security ties between the two countries. Because the Self-Defense Forces of Japan have come to depend so deeply on the U.S. military for weapons systems, personnel training, and intelligence, their structure and mission are now "an integral component of U.S. military strategy in the Pacific" (Katzenstein 1996a, 102–3, 137).

In short, most of the region's security-related agreements carrying mutual obligations are bilateral ones between the United States and individual East Asian countries, including Japan. Many factors have impeded any deeper institutionalization of "East Asian" security mechanisms. Once the United States had consolidated the hub-and-spoke network of bilateral security treaties, it had a strong interest in preserving that arrangement because, in this way, it could better maintain leadership and a free hand in security-related matters in the Asia-Pacific region. It accepted the ARF and other supra-regional forums as mere supplements to the bilateral security network.

Deep dependence on the U.S. military capability, together with concern about possible adverse reaction from East Asian neighbors, also impeded Japan from taking the initiative to form a CSCE-like organization in East Asia during the post–Cold War era. Japan simply participated in the ASEAN-led ARF, a jointly established supra-regional mechanism of consultation and confidence building. In response to new post–Cold War conditions, Japan also engaged in bilateral dialogues with Russia, South Korea, and China to build mutual confidence. For the same purpose, it has hosted a number of unilaterally organized conferences, seminars, and research meetings with invitees from the Asia-Pacific countries. In the face of the military buildup of China and North Korea, however, Japan's most important mechanism for national security continues to be its bilateral relationship with the United States. This relationship is reinforced by close functional and technological ties between the military forces of the two countries. Those ties are equivalent to the transnational economic and ideational networks that have induced transboundary cooperation in other issue areas. The only difference is that military connections cannot be treated as "nongovernmental" ones.

Drug Control

Regional cooperation to help control drugs in East Asia has been shaped by factors similar to those shaping regional cooperation around military security. The U.S. government has taken an active bilateral approach, while the Japanese government has been cautious about its involvement in the internal security matters of its East Asian neighbors, attitudes matched by those countries' concerns about being policed by Japan. In contrast to the issue of international military security, however, regional efforts to control drugs have met no opposition from the U.S. government. Instead, the United States only shrugs its shoulders in the belief that regional schemes are of little use but are largely harmless. In countries where the United States lacks bilateral leverage (such as Myanmar), however, it welcomes regional initiatives. As for Japan, its regional weakness has been compensated for by its domestic strength. The government has been able to rely on full cooperation by its citizens to cope with the drug abuse problem. Also, antidrug NGOs are in practice semi-governmental bodies, and their international network has failed to mobilize social forces to press their governments to cooperate more closely. Ironically, the spread of drug traffickers' networks beyond national borders has fostered intergovernmental cooperation because it is increasingly clear that the governments of both producer and consumer countries need mutual cooperation to cope with the serious threat drugs pose to the life and health of their citizens.

The U.S. government took the first initiative to control drugs in Asia after World War II, encouraged mostly by the drug abuse problem it faced at home. In the 1960s, drug consumption in the United States increased rapidly under the social conditions fostered by the counterculture and the Vietnam War, so that by 1971, 24 million Americans were believed to have tried marijuana. Consumers of heroin also increased—from 50,000 in 1960, to 250,000 in

1969, and to 500,000 in 1971 (Stares 1996, 24; McCoy 1991, 392). The Nixon administration declared a "total war on drugs" in 1969. Heroin was regarded as especially dangerous because of the devastating physical effects and its high rate of addictiveness. Heroin consumption was widespread among American soldiers stationed in Vietnam—especially a drug called China White, which was produced in the Golden Triangle and smuggled into Vietnam by the Hong Kong mafia (Stares 1996, 26)—and the habit followed many soldiers home. At the time, the main supplier of heroin for the U.S. market was the Corsica mafia (the so-called French Connection, which smuggled heroin produced in Turkey), yet the U.S. government focused its drug control measures in Southeast Asia as well as in Europe by increasing the number of the Drug Enforcement Administration (DEA) agents stationed in Southeast Asia from two to thirty-one during the first half of the 1970s (McCoy 1991, 391). Importation of heroin from Southeast Asia decreased during the following decade but came back to dominate the U.S. market by 1990. After the Reagan administration declared the second "war on drugs," an overwhelming amount of resources was used to control Latin American cocaine, with little effort made against Asian heroin (Stares 1996, 33; McCoy 1991, 388). Furthermore, when the Myanmar military suppressed democracy in 1988, the relationship between the United States and Myanmar was so strained that DEA agents were temporarily forced to leave the country (McCoy 1991, 434). During the same period, opium production spilled over into Yunnan, Sichuan, and other inner provinces of China (Flynn 1998, 21), where drug control from outside was particularly difficult.

Throughout the 1990s, however, heroin from Columbia and Mexico gained market share in the United States, thereby reducing the importance of Southeast Asia as a target of international U.S. drug control policy (U.S. Department of State 2000, 20). Still, the presence of the United States in Southeast Asia is larger than that of any other advanced industrial country, and the U.S. government almost always takes a bilateral approach to drug-related problems. It maintains DEA offices in several countries, including the Philippines, Thailand, Indonesia, Laos, and China (U.S. Department of State 2000, 44, 47, 78, 90), and in many other countries, DEA officers are stationed in U.S. embassies. All are actively involved in information gathering and law enforcement in close cooperation with the host-county police. Only in Myanmar, where strained diplomatic relations made the bilateral approach difficult, has the U.S. government joined the multilateral effort led by the United Nations Drug Control Programme (UNDCP).

U.S. efforts have been especially successful in Thailand. There, production and smuggling of heroin were reduced dramatically during the 1990s. The success was so impressive that the U.S. government established a regional training center for law enforcement officers in Bangkok. This center, called the International Law Enforcement Academy (ILEA), started to receive trainees in 1999 from ten countries: ASEAN 10 minus Myanmar and China (ILEA 2001, 3–4, 24–25).

Compared with the U.S. government, the Japanese government was a latecomer to drug control efforts in East Asia. The suppliers of the most harmful drug in Japan, methamphetamine, have been neighboring Asian countries, so Japan's slowness in instituting a regional drug control policy is peculiar but perhaps understandable for two reasons. First, the Japanese government feared that its attempts at law enforcement in East Asia might create antagonism between itself and its neighbors because of Japan's prewar role in the region. The National Police Agency (NPA) was thus one of the Japanese government agencies whose "internationalization" was most delayed. Not until 1975 did the NPA establish a small Division of International Criminal Affairs within the Bureau of Criminal Investigation, primarily to facilitate information exchange with Interpol. Only in 1994 was this division upgraded to a department belonging to the minister's secretariat (NPA 2000, 80).

Second, the Japanese police can count on the cooperation of its citizens for its internal drug control efforts. The classic book by David Bayley, *Forces of Order* (1978), depicts how deeply the Japanese police are embedded in society. In a book published thirteen years later, Katzenstein and Tsujinaka (1991, 84–104) argue that police and society are as interwoven as ever through a variety of institutions including local police stands (*koban*), residential surveys, and crime prevention associations. Watchful eyes against crime are pervasive, and citizens are usually very cooperative with police officials. Although arrest rates reportedly have been declining rapidly in recent years, Japan still has one of the safest societies in the world. As a result, unlike in the United States, harmful drugs have never become a serious national issue in Japan. The UNDCP (now renamed UNODC or United Nations Office of Drugs and Crime) estimated that in 2000, the addiction rate in Japan was somewhere between 0.4 percent and 1.8 percent of the population and that most addicts were methamphetamine consumers. In the United States, the total number of addicts of cocaine, methamphetamine, and heroin reached 4.0 percent of the population in the same year (UNDCP 2002a). In Japan, domestic police effectiveness has reduced the incentives to pursue a more active regional policy against narcotics transactions.

Because of the NPA's timidity, drug-related cooperation was first conducted jointly by the Japan International Cooperation Agency (JICA) and NPA as a part of ODA programs. Most of these involve unilaterally convened conferences and seminars or the dispatch of trainers and specialists in various techniques of investigation. Today, several seminars are held annually as joint JICA-NPA initiatives, on subjects such as international cooperation for criminal investigation, gun control, organized crime, and drug control. The participants are not necessarily Asians, however, and seventeen Asian and Latin

American countries have joined together to participate in a seminar on drug control (NPA 2001, 237).

In 1988, the NPA started to organize its own seminars, although the number of meetings was limited. Four were listed in the 2000 police white paper: seminars on citizen security systems (such as *koban*), gun control, drivers' licenses, and organized crime (NPA 2000, 260). One of the seminars' main purposes is to foster trust of Japan by its neighbors and to build personal networks among Asian police so that future cooperation is easier and more substantial.

NPA has also tried a bilateral approach to the drug abuse problem in Japan. During the 1970s and 1980s, its main partners were South Korea, Taiwan, and Hong Kong, the major suppliers of methamphetamine at that time (Friman 1993, 45; 1999, 182). By the 1990s, these countries had stopped being the major suppliers. The Japanese initiative was less important than that of South Korea and Taiwan, however, both of which instituted tough measures to cope with their drug abuse problems at home (interview with a high-ranking NPA official, September 7, 2000).

By the middle of the 1990s, China and North Korea had emerged as the main bases for the production and export of the methamphetamine entering Japan. Out of 3,492 kilograms of methamphetamine confiscated in Japan between 1998 and 2002, 51 percent came from China and 35 percent from North Korea (*Asahi Shimbun,* July 30, 2003), although in the singular year 1999, 80 percent (amounting to 1,967 kilograms) originated from China. Japan has had no official way of dealing with the highly uncooperative North Korean government, many of whose agencies are strongly suspected of being involved in the narcotics trade, but the Chinese government has seemed more open to negotiations. As a result, China has become the main focus of Japan's bilateral cooperation. The head of the Department of International Affairs of NPA visited his counterpart in Beijing in 1994, the first visit paid to China by a senior Japanese policeman (*Sankei News,* http://www.sankei.co.jp/databaox/paper/, January 5, 2000). Although China had established the National Narcotics Control Commission four years earlier, cooperation did not come quickly. Only in the late 1990s did China become more accommodating, largely because of the seriousness of the drug abuse problem in China itself rather than as a result of Japanese persuasion. Between 1991 and 1999, the number of officially registered drug addicts in China increased from 148,000 to 681,000, although the actual number is estimated to be no less than 7 million. Even more alarming was the fact that 72.4 percent of those who were infected with HIV/AIDS were drug users. Yunnan Province, home of the largest number of Chinese drug addicts, accounts for 51 percent of all HIV positive cases in the country (*People's Daily Online,* http://j.people.com. cn/, June 26, 2000; UNDCP 2000a, 14).

In this context, Japan and China decided to establish three-joint Japan—China frameworks for consultation and cooperation. One is the annual meeting of vice ministers of the two countries' national police agencies, which began in 1997 (NPA 1999, 37). The second is the meeting of customs officers from the two countries, which began in May 2000 (Ministry of Finance Customs Bureau website, http://www.mof.go.jp/jouhou/ kanzei/, January 24, 2002). The most important, however, is that of the Japan–China Consultation for Domestic Security, which started in 1999 with the participation of representatives from various ministries. From Japan, the ministries of Foreign Affairs, Justice, Finance, and Welfare and Health, and the Maritime Safety Agency have participated and talked with their Chinese counterparts about human smuggling, drugs, guns, and other sorts of organized crime. At the first meeting, both sides agreed to strengthen cooperation in criminal investigations against mafia groups (NPA 2000, 257).

Japan's NPA has succeeded in realizing three joint crackdown operations with the police—in Hong Kong (1997), Hong Kong and Guangdong (1998), and Shanghai (1998)—against groups that were smuggling Chinese workers into Japan (NPA 1999, 37). In December 1999, based on information provided by the Japanese police, the Chinese arrested two drug traffickers, one Japanese and one Korean, in Dalian, in northeast China (Japan Institute of International Affairs 2000, 11–12). However, such concrete results from bilateral cooperation remain limited and sporadic.

Another focal point of regional cooperation for narcotics control is Southeast Asia. There two major efforts are progressing, and Japan participates in one of them.

One endeavor involves subregional drug control efforts by Thailand, Myanmar, Laos, China, Cambodia, and Vietnam. The first four countries, encouraged by the UNDCP, signed the Greater Mekong Subregion Memorandum of Understanding (MOU) on Drug Control in 1993. Cambodia and Vietnam joined the group in 1995, and the group came to be called MOU6. This framework for cooperation is extremely important because the subregion covers the Golden Triangle, a major heroin production center. Previously, Myanmar had been the main producer, and the surrounding countries served mostly as transit routes to the United States and Australia. By the 1980s, however, the surrounding countries saw their own heroin production increasing. During the 1990s, as counter-heroin operations, including opium eradication, were repeatedly conducted in Thailand and, to a lesser degree, in Myanmar, drug producers in the Golden Triangle started to shift their production from heroin to methamphetamine. Now the production of methamphetamine has spread to Thailand and China. Without regional cooperation, it would be impossible to intercept drug trafficking in this part of the world.

Under the MOU6 agreement, the member countries approved a subregional action plan comprising eleven collaborative measures in the areas of demand reduction, supply reduction, and law enforcement. At their 1999 meeting, MOU6 governments approved a new strategy incorporating an expanded cross-border cooperation program, a large-scale computer-based drug law enforcement training project, and new initiatives to fight the increasing abuse of methamphetamine and other synthetic stimulants (UNDCP 2000c, 11–12). Such cross-border cooperation has already produced tangible results. Between 1999 and 2002, there were ten cases of offenders being handed over to the Chinese authorities by their Myanmar counterparts. One of these led to the seizure of more than three tons of heroin and the apprehension of eighteen accomplices (*Eastern Horizon,* March 2003, 16).[4] MOU6 projects have been funded primarily by Japan, the United Kingdom, the United States, EU, and the Scandinavian countries (*Eastern Horizon,* June 2001, 14). The Japanese government announced its intention to cooperate with UNDCP to help MOU6 on the occasion of the Asian Drug Law Enforcement Conference cosponsored by NPA and the Ministry of Foreign Affairs and held in Tokyo in February 1999. Although the smuggling of methamphetamine from Southeast Asia is still limited, Japan's cooperation with MOU6 did not come exclusively from altruism, and seizures of methamphetamine tablets originating in Southeast Asia have been growing in recent years (UNDCP 2002c, 9). Japan donated $1.82 million dollars to the UNDCP to buy jeeps, wireless communication equipment, and other items for MOU6's Cross-Border Law Enforcement Cooperation Project (*Eastern Horizon,* June 2003, 18). It had hesitated to donate jeeps and communication equipment directly to the MOU6 police for fear that these materials would be regarded as "military" (interview with a high-ranking NPA official, September 7, 2000). Because the conservative government of Japan, in response to pacifist norms, had repeatedly promised to be cautious about any export of weapons, JICA and NPA officials could have faced harsh questioning from the opposition parties in the Diet if they had handed over the equipment directly to the MOU6 police.

The Japanese police also have been cautious about stationing personnel in East Asian countries. Unlike the DEA, the NPA maintains no offices there for its law enforcement officers, and NPA officers are stationed in some Japanese embassies only as police attachés. When the NPA finally decided to station its staff in Southeast Asian countries, it sent specialists on signature analysis of confiscated methamphetamine instead of criminal law enforcement officers. Thus, in November 1999, the first NPA signature analysis specialist was sent to Thailand's Office of the Narcotics Control Board (ONCB) for a two-year mission (NPA 2000, 261). In September 2000, another specialist was sent to Cambodia, also for two years. Eight NPA specialists were also sent to Myanmar, but for a shorter period of time, in January and November 2000 (NPA 2001, 93).

---

4. Eastern Horizon is a monthly journal published by the Regional Centre for East Asia and the Pacific of the United Nations Office on Drugs and Crime in Bangkok.

Furthermore, JICA approved a large-scale drug-related assistance program for Thailand in 2001, according to which JICA and NPA would help the ONCB organize a training seminar on drug-related identification techniques for police officers from not only Thailand but also Laos, Cambodia, Vietnam, and Myanmar (direct information from JICA Tokyo office, August 24, 2001).

Preference for alternative-crops projects is another characteristic of Japan's drug control policy in East Asia. The Japanese government took a less harsh line against the Myanmar military government than did the United States (Watanabe 2001, 78–79). JICA continued to help the alternative development project in the Kokan region of Myanmar, where Japanese specialists taught locals how to cultivate buckwheat for export to Japan (interview with a JICA official, Bangkok, September 2001).

Apart from the MOU6 projects, regional cooperation in Southeast Asia has also been pursued by ASEAN, which agreed to establish an Experts' Group on Prevention and Control of Drug Abuse as early as 1972. In 1984 this forum was renamed the ASEAN Senior Officials on Drug Matters (ASOD), which, as the name indicates, is a meeting of senior officials engaged in drug prevention and control in the member countries. Although ASOD has issued several recommendations for supply-and-demand reduction measures and the enhancement of the legal control system, its actual activities at the regional level were mostly limited to joint training courses for drug-related specialists. The ASEAN Training Center for Narcotics Law Enforcement was established in Bangkok in 1979, followed by the ASEAN Training Center for Preventive Drug Education in Manila, the ASEAN Training Center for Treatment and Rehabilitation in Kuala Lumpur, and the ASEAN Training Center for the Detection of Drugs in Body Fluids in Singapore (ASEAN Secretariat website, http://www.aseansec.org/, January 22, 2002). However, no regional action plan for law enforcement was adopted, and actual measures for demand and supply reduction were entrusted to individual governments.

By the latter half of the 1990s, the drug abuse problem was recognized as a serious national problem in traditionally drug-free countries such as Malaysia and Indonesia. In Malaysia, twenty-six clandestine methamphetamine laboratories were seized between 1997 and 2000, a new phenomenon (UNDCP 2002c, 8). According to the Indonesian National Narcotics Board, there was a threefold increase in the number of drug users between 1997 and 1999. The Ministry of Health also estimated in 2001 that there were one million drug abusers, of whom 60 percent injected drugs and 6.3 percent were HIV positive (UNDCP 2002b, 12, 15–16).

The ASEAN Vision 2020 adopted by the second informal summit of ASEAN leaders in 1997 embraced for the first time the idea of "a Southeast Asia free of illicit drugs, free of their production, processing, trafficking and use." The first ASEAN Ministerial Meeting on Transnational Crime was also convened in 1997. At its second meeting in 1999, it adopted the ASEAN Plan of Action to Combat Transnational Crime. This called for a cohesive regional strategy to cover information exchange, cooperation in legal and law enforcement matters, institutional capacity building, training, and extra-regional cooperation. In July 2000, the ASEAN foreign ministers agreed to advance the target year for a drug-free ASEAN from 2020 to 2015. As a part of this effort, ASEAN cosponsored, with the Thai government and UNDCP, the International Congress in Pursuit of a Drug-Free ASEAN, held in Bangkok in October 2000. Besides the ASEAN 10, twenty-four countries including the United States, Japan, and China attended the meeting. The most significant result of this conference was the adoption of ACCORD (ASEAN and China Cooperative Operations in Response to Dangerous Drugs), which sets out various action plans covering civil awareness, demand reduction, law enforcement cooperation, and alternative development programs (UNDCP 2000b, 10–14). Several task forces were later set up to monitor and facilitate cooperation and coordination. ACCORD, however, contains no concrete action plans such as MOU6's cross-border law enforcement cooperation. As of early 2004, the implementation of the online regional drug data collection network and the establishment of the ACCORD website are its sole concrete accomplishments (*Accord e-News,* January 2004, available at http://www.unodc.un.or.th/publications/ACCORD-04–01.pdf, March 14, 2004).

The issue area of drug control is characterized by two opposing transnational networks. On the one hand, there are drug-trafficking connections among organized Asian crime groups, including Japan's Yakuza. Their intensified activities inside and across national borders worsened the drug abuse problem so seriously that bilateral and regional schemes for East Asian cooperation flourished during the 1990s.

On the other hand, the International Federation of Non-Governmental Organizations for the Prevention of Drug and Substance Abuse (IFNGO) was organized in 1981 as an umbrella forum of NGOs from Malaysia, Singapore, Thailand, the Philippines, Indonesia, Australia, and Hong Kong. Other members joined later, and the organization now has 36 registered members from 19 countries, including the United States and Japan. Besides organizing annual conferences, IFNGO cooperates with international organizations such as WHO and UNDCP to realize needs assessment, resource identification, and epidemiological monitoring. However, although ASEAN explicitly calls for cooperation with NGOs, there is no evidence that the activities of IFNGO or any other NGOs contributed to pushing East Asian governments to take more positive stances on regional cooperation. Rather, the national NGOs, including IFNGO members, serve as auxiliaries to their governments in the fields of education and prevention. In fact, the first page of the IFNGO's website has a photograph of Malaysia's Mahathir bin Mohamad with a caption identifying him as the "patron" of the organization (http://www.mmserve.com/drugs/ifngo/structur.htm, March 14, 2004).

Japan's Drug Abuse Prevention Center (DAPC) is one of the associate members of the IFNGO. It was established in 1987 with assistance from the Ministry of Health and Social Welfare, and its aims are prevention and rehabilitation. The center organizes JICA-funded training courses mainly for drug prevention officers from Asia and the Pacific region (DAPC website, http://www.dapc.or.jp/info/, March 14, 2004). Another major semi-official organization that deals with the drug control problem in Japan is Asia Crime Prevention Foundation (ACPF). ACPF was established in 1982 by former Japanese trainees of the United Nations Asia and Far East Institute for the Prevention of Crime and the Treatment of Offenders (UNAFEI), located in Tokyo. This organization has close cooperative relations with the Ministry of Justice and organizes training seminars for criminal law enforcement officers from Asia and other developing areas. These seminars are held three times a year using Japanese ODA money (ACPF website, http://www.acpf.org/, March 14, 2004). DAPC and ACPF, therefore, are little more than arms of the Japanese government, supporting its unilateral policy for confidence building among Asian police and other drug-related officials.

In short, both the U.S. and Japanese governments have been poor practitioners of regional cooperation for drug control. Moreover, because they are mostly passive semi-official entities, NGOs provide little pressure for quickened regional policy coordination. Both the U.S. and Japanese governments have mostly relied on unilateral or bilateral approaches, but for different reasons.

The U.S. government, as the most powerful government in the world, believes that, except for rare cases like that of Myanmar, it can pursue its drug control policy most effectively if it deals with any producing or transit country unilaterally or bilaterally. It stations DEA officers in several Asian countries, where they exchange information with and give advice to their counterparts in the host countries. The U.S. government also invites law enforcement officials from those countries to attend training courses given in the United States or at the Bangkok-based ILEA. However, unlike in the case of military security, the U.S. government has not opposed regional initiatives such as MOU6 and ACCORD. It has simply shown benign neglect.

In contrast, Japan's unilateral and bilateral stance is an expression of its weakness in the region. The Japanese government fears East Asian reactions against any increased presence by Japanese law enforcement officers. It must also comply with the pacifist norm at home by avoiding any "military" component in its drug control efforts in the East Asian countries. Japan's regional weakness has been compensated for by its strength at home. The Japanese police can mobilize social support for their antidrug campaign, and drug abuse has never been as acute as in the United States. This strength at home, however, weakens Japan's motivation to be active abroad.

For all these reasons, the Japanese government started its regional drug control policy by simply inviting Asian police officials to the ODA conferences and seminars offered in Japan. When it became involved more directly in drug control efforts in Southeast Asia during the 1990s, it avoided engaging in law enforcement activities. Instead, it helped Myanmar's alternative-crops projects and sent technical staff to several MOU6 countries. Courses and seminars offered in Japan overwhelmingly focus on techniques of criminal identification and investigation. The Japanese government also donated a lump sum to UNDCP so that the organization could take up the "burden" of buying jeeps and communication equipment for local police.

The Japanese police have been even more cautious in Northeast Asia, despite the fact that they urgently need cooperation from their Chinese counterparts since China today is the largest producer/exporter of the methamphetamine smuggled into Japan. With no regional framework available, Japan has sought Chinese cooperation through bilateral channels established after 1997, but these serve only as arenas for information exchange and confidence building and show few meaningful results in terms of drug-trafficking control.

Drug control is thus characterized by bilateral cooperation between the United States and individual East Asian countries as well as between Japan and China. Unlike the case of military security, however, that of drug control has seen two East Asia-specific schemes for regional cooperation, MOU6 and ACCORD. The former started to bring about tangible results thanks to the benign neglect of the United States, an active UNDCP initiative, and Japan's financial (but not direct law enforcement) assistance, and clearly specified action plans.

Liberalization of Trade and Investment

Compared with the two issue areas already discussed, that of trade and investment has been characterized by much more extensive and intensive participation of private players such as enterprises and individual business people. It is frequently argued that such players contributed to de facto regional integration in East Asia through market transactions, despite their lack of help from formal regional institutions such as the EU and NAFTA (Hatch and Yamamura 1996; Guerrieri 1998, among others).

In addition to individual enterprises, several NGOs or track II forums such as the Pacific Basin Economic Council (PBEC) and the Pacific Economic Cooperation Council (PECC) also function as "private" players in the trade and investment field. They have contributed to strengthening the general atmosphere for closer economic cooperation among Asia-Pacific countries. However, a detailed study of APEC shows that the Japanese and Australian initiatives leading to its formation were not directly expedited by input from such private or semi-official forums.[5] Once APEC started, however, PECC was admitted as the sole official observer of APEC, where it frequently presents concrete policy proposals.

Notwithstanding the importance of such private agents, East Asian governments, especially Japan's, have also tried to promote cross-national economic transactions. Such efforts, however, have met constraints such as the high dependence of Japan and many other Asian countries on the U.S. market as well as domestic protectionist pressures. In addition, many East Asian people were not happy with the protruding presence of Japanese enterprises in their territories, as seen by the anti-Japanese riots in Bangkok and Jakarta in 1974. However, unlike their diffidence around security issues, where military and police are involved, East Asian governments have been much less hesitant in welcoming Japanese goods and investment, as long as these contribute to national prosperity and the Japanese government does not use economic leverage to impose specific policies.

During the postwar period, the Japanese government took the first initiatives to establish closer economic relationships in East Asia. At least until the 1960s, the main motive was self-interest. It is well known that the Japanese government used reparation payments and ODA money to promote Japanese exports to the rest of East Asia (Arase 1995, 28–30, 51; Orr and Koppel 1993, 2). To further strengthen economic ties, the Japanese government also invited Southeast Asian countries to set up a permanent minister-level forum in 1966, which was reportedly the first international conference hosted by Japan after World War II. However, Southeast Asian countries, disliking Japan's emphasis on agricultural development and fearing the resurgence of a domineering Japan, showed little enthusiasm, and the forum soon lost its momentum (Ohba 2001, 264). East Asian countries also disappointed the Japanese government when they chose Manila, not Tokyo, as the location for the headquarters of the newly established Asian Development Bank, despite the fact that Japan was one of the largest contributors to the bank. Apparently, East Asian leaders were reluctant to see an expansion of Japanese influence in the region (Yamakage 1991, 174).

As ASEAN gained strength as a regional organization, the Japanese government chose to work with it in the latter half of the 1970s, as was discussed in the section on military security. When Japan's Ministry of International Trade and Industry (MITI; which was reorganized in 2001 into the Ministry of Economy, Trade, and Industry, or METI) envisaged an Asia-Pacific framework for cooperation in the latter half of the 1980s, one of its first efforts was to persuade

5. There was a sharp conflict between MITI and the Australian foreign minister Hawk, two principal promoters of APEC, on the one hand, and PECC on the other with regard to who should take leadership as well as who should be included and what subjects should be dealt with in a new Asia-Pacific dialogue (Ohba 2002, 234–36). The ministry responsible for PECC in Japan was not MITI but the Ministry of Foreign Affairs.

the ASEAN countries to participate. This initiative finally led to the formation of APEC, but from the beginning there was a difference of opinion among East Asian governments regarding its membership. Australia, another promoter of APEC, envisaged a purely "East Asian" framework that excluded the United States, a proposal strongly endorsed by Malaysia, whereas Japan urged including the United States and Canada (Ohba 2002, 234; Funabashi 1995, 97). MITI, the principal promoter of APEC in Japan, hoped to keep U.S. protectionism in check by enclosing the United States in an Asia-Pacific framework of cooperation and by promoting the growth of East Asian economies—so that they could import more American products (Yamamoto and Kikuchi 1998, 195–97; Mochizuki 1995, 141).

The U.S. government reacted strongly against the Australian proposal. Secretary of State James Baker protested to Australia's Foreign Minister Evans during the latter's visit to Washington, D.C., in March 1989. The following month, senior MITI officials visited the United States to insist that APEC was not intended to be an anti-U.S. bloc. Finally, Secretary Baker expressed official U.S. endorsement of APEC in June 1989 (Funabashi 1995, 94–95, 98). APEC thus came into existence in November 1989, with Japan, Australia, New Zealand, South Korea, the ASEAN 6, the United States, and Canada as its original members.

The U.S. government also reacted fiercely against Mahathir's proposal to form an ethnically "East Asian" entity, to be called the East Asian Economic Grouping, in late 1990. The Bush administration requested the Japanese and South Korean governments to reject Mahathir's idea. Baker continued to oppose Mahathir even after the latter accepted an Indonesian suggestion to rename the group the East Asian Economic Caucus within APEC (Funabashi 1995, 105–6). Heavy dependence on the U.S. market meant that neither Japan nor any other East Asian country would stand by Mahathir and resist U.S. pressure. During the first half of the 1990s, Japan and most other Asian countries were not yet ready to exclude the United States from the framework of economic cooperation in East Asia.

At the same time, the Japanese government opposed the U.S. attempt to use APEC as a platform to negotiate a NAFTA-like regional free trade agreement. Japan supported ASEAN's approach of voluntary, nonexclusionary liberalization that came to be called open regionalism. Open regionalism meant two things for Japan: Japan opposed excluding the United States, but it also opposed an exclusive regional free trade regime.

Open regionalism fit Japan's economic interest as a "commercial state." It feared any economic bloc in which Japanese firms and products could face discriminatory treatment. It preferred the nondiscriminatory, multilateral GATT/WTO framework. This position, however, was contradicted by Japan's own domestic protection in the agricultural and fishery sectors. Throughout the 1990s, open regionalism increasingly degenerated into an excuse for domestic protection.

Although the APEC meeting at Bogor in 1994 called for free trade and investment by 2010 for the developed members and 2020 for the entire group, the Japanese government failed to propose feasible measures that built on these goals when it hosted the Osaka conference the following year. The 1997 meeting at Vancouver agreed to implement the Early Voluntary Sectoral Liberalization program in nine sectors, but that scheme proved to be a failure at the 1998 meeting, when Japan and several other countries objected to the liberalization of certain sectors in the aftermath of the economic crisis (Feinberg and Zhao 2001, 178). APEC came to be regarded as no more than a regional framework supported by a number of jointly organized consultative meetings.

In the meanwhile, ASEAN agreed in 1992 to create AFTA (ASEAN Free Trade Area) by 2008. In fifteen years, ASEAN members would mutually reduce import duties to a Common Effective Preferential Tariff (0–5 percent). Later, the target year was advanced to 2002 for original members and 2003–7 for new members. In 1999, the ASEAN Economic Ministers' Meeting agreed to lower import duties to zero by 2015 for original members and by 2018 for new members. Three months later, these targets were also advanced to 2010 and 2015, respectively (Ministry of Foreign Affairs 2003a, 1–2).

AFTA met no U.S. opposition. There was no reason for the U.S. government to reject it because it did not put American enterprises in a disadvantageous position vis-à-vis their Japanese or European competitors. On the contrary, AFTA would help American companies rationalize their own regional production networks. For the same reason, Japanese companies also enthusiastically welcomed the AFTA process (Hatch and Yamamura 1996, 35). The mutual reduction of import duties, however, did not proceed smoothly. Although the agreements contained quantitative targets, the reduction itself was dependent on concerted unilateral actions by each member country. Furthermore, each country was allowed to present a temporary exclusion list and a general exception list. Naturally, member countries tried to delay liberalization of certain goods in response to domestic protectionist pressures. Yamakage (1997, 202) cites the Indonesia–Thailand conflict over agricultural products. Authors such as Acharya (2001a, 143, 199–200) and Ravenhill (2002, 181–82) remain skeptical about the economic effects of the AFTA process.

Among the original ASEAN members, however, 44,160 tariff items, or 98.35 percent of the total, attained the target of 0–5 percent by the middle of 2003. Although approximately two hundred automobile-related items in Malaysia are exempted for three more years, AFTA has been virtually realized. The average, although not the weighted, tariff rate for six original members under the Common Effective Preferential Tariff scheme is 2.39 percent in 2003, down from 12.76 percent in 1993 (ASEAN Secretariat website, July 23, 2003). AFTA is a typical scheme whose realization depends on concerted unilateral actions under peer pressure. Thanks to positive encouragement from

Japanese and other multinational businesses and with specifically and quantitatively stipulated agreements, peer pressure has worked and brought about a great deal of progress.

Not all AFTA members are satisfied with the results so far, however. Singapore, for example, hopes for quicker liberalization. Dissatisfaction with AFTA and the standstill of APEC have stimulated two new approaches for regional cooperation: the search for bilateral agreements and cooperation on nontrade matters.

The first bilateral free trade agreement (FTA) in East Asia was the Australia New Zealand Closer Economic Relations Trade Agreement (ANZCERTA), signed in 1983. Among other East Asian countries, Singapore has been the most assertive in its search for FTA partners. As one of the most open Asian countries in terms of trade, Singapore had few obstacles to prevent a bilateral approach. Singapore signed FTAs with New Zealand in 2000, with Japan and the European Free Trade Association in 2002, and with the United States and Australia in 2003. It is negotiating FTAs with several other countries, including Canada, South Korea, and Mexico. South Korea is also interested in bilateral FTAs, signing an FTA with Chile in 2003 and contemplating another with Japan.

Even in Japan, where the multilateral approach had been almost a religious belief among policy makers and businesspersons, increasing skepticism about open regionalism started to be heard in 1999 in the face of the stagnation of the APEC process and the flourishing of FTAs in other parts of the world. In April 1999, the Federation of Economic Organizations, the largest business association in Japan, published a report calling for a Japan–Mexico FTA (*Keidanren*, October 2000, 25). This report was intended to suggest ways to offset the disadvantages Japanese companies faced in Mexico under NAFTA. The following month, MITI's white paper admitted, for the first time, that regional integration was compatible with a multilateral approach (MITI 1999, 289–95). MITI's white paper of 2000 made a full-scale study of the effects of regional integration and came to the same conclusion (MITI 2000, 123). In December 1998, a research group was organized within the MITI-affiliated Institute of Developing Economies to study the possibility of concluding an FTA with South Korea; another research group for an FTA with Mexico was formed in JETRO, another MITI-affiliated entity, three months later. A joint research team was formed in March 2000 to explore an FTA with Singapore. Later the same year, a new research group was formed in JETRO envisaging an FTA with Chile (MITI 2000, 121). Within the Ministry of Foreign Affairs— a governmental body usually more cautious about the regional and bilateral approach—the number of officials who endorsed this approach increased throughout 2000 and 2001.

The Japanese government signed its first-ever FTA with Singapore in January 2002 (Ministry of Foreign Affairs website, http://www.mofa.go.jp/, May

26, 2002). Ten months later, it began FTA negotiations with Mexico, but progress there was not as smooth as it had been in Singapore due, among other things, to agricultural protectionism in Japan.[6] By contrast, Singapore, with no agricultural and fishery products to compete with Japanese producers, was an easy partner. Still, Japanese promoters of the agreement with Singapore avoided calling it an FTA and instead named it an Economic Agreement for a New Age Partnership. "New Age" here means that the agreement emphasizes nontrade issues such as policy harmonization in certification and standards, e-commerce regulations, cooperation in financial and information technology businesses, and human exchanges. The Japanese government expects such an approach to alleviate concerns among politically powerful forces of domestic protectionism, while requesting as much exemption from tariff concessions as possible.

The Japanese government's stumbling on both the regional and bilateral fronts was in sharp contrast to/the active regional initiative taken by the Chinese government. Previously, China had shared with ASEAN its dislike of formal institutions because, in China's view, these tend to impose the preferences of some countries upon others. However, as the Chinese economy developed rapidly throughout the 1990s and China successfully negotiated entry into the WTO in 2001, the Chinese government became an active promoter of regional FTAs. On the occasion of the ASEAN + China summit held in Singapore in November 2000, Premier Zhu Rongji suggested the idea of free trade between China and ASEAN. A year later, Chinese and ASEAN leaders who gathered again in Brunei approved a report submitted by the Experts' Group for ASEAN + China Economic Cooperation, suggesting that China and ASEAN establish a free trade area within ten years (*Nihon Keizai Shimbun*, evening ed., November 6, 2001). In November 2002, Chinese and ASEAN heads of government signed a framework agreement in which both sides pledged to complete FTA negotiations by the middle of 2004 (Ministry of Foreign Affairs 2003b, 1–2).

In January 2002, Japanese prime minister Koizumi, as if pressed by the China–ASEAN rapprochement, visited Singapore to sign the bilateral FTA mentioned above, and on the same occasion proposed a similar agreement for "comprehensive economic partnership" (CEP) between Japan and ASEAN. Later that same month, the Japan—ASEAN Experts' Group, composed of officials from economic ministries, gathered for the first time to prepare recommendations for the ASEAN + Japan Economic Ministers' Meeting scheduled for fall 2002. In its second meeting, held in March 2002, officials from Japan's Ministry of Agriculture explained how difficult it was for Japan

---

6. The Japanese and Mexican governments agreed on basic lines of the bilateral FTA in March 2004 (Asahi Shimbun, March 11, 2004) but are expected to need several additional months before signing it.

to liberalize agricultural trade. ASEAN representatives retorted that an agreement without liberalization of agriculture would be useless for ASEAN (METI website, www.meti.go.jp/policy/trade_policy/, June 2, 2002). In October 2003, Japan and ASEAN signed a framework agreement in which both sides agreed that they would "make maximum efforts to commence the negotiation on the CEP Agreement" from the beginning of 2005 and would "endeavor to conclude the negotiation as soon as possible" (Ministry of Foreign Affairs website, March 14, 2004). In the face of the slow progress of its talks with ASEAN, Japan started negotiating separate bilateral FTAs with South Korea, Malaysia, Thailand, and the Philippines between late 2003 and early 2004 (METI website, March 14, 2004).

In short, based on de facto economic integration by private enterprises and preceded by nongovernmental organizations such as PBEC and PECC, Japan and other East Asian countries agreed to establish APEC. Australia's initial proposal to form an entity for economic cooperation that excluded the United States failed in the face of fierce U.S. opposition. Mahathir's venture of forming an exclusively East Asian Economic Grouping (EAEG) was also aborted. However, almost all East Asian countries, including Japan, fearing adverse impacts on domestic producers, resisted the U.S. approach of using APEC to negotiate legally binding trade agreements. Instead, they supported a gradual, voluntary approach. This approach, however, proved futile by the second half of the 1990s, leaving APEC as no more than a talk shop.

AFTA has experienced a much more meaningful trajectory, successfully lowering member countries' tariffs on a great majority of goods. Multinational businesses naturally welcomed AFTA. Unlike in the case of the initial Australian proposal for APEC or Mahathir's EAEG, the U.S. government has no reason to oppose AFTA because economic competitors from Japan and Europe are not on the membership list. The only impediment to the AFTA process is domestic protectionism such as that shown by Malaysia's automotive industry. This protectionism, however, is being overcome gradually under strong peer pressure based on quantitative and specific stipulations of the AFTA agreements,

An AFTA + China FTA, though still in negotiation, is also characterized by similar favorable conditions. Private companies, especially overseas Chinese businesses, will be able to rationalize their production networks in the new FTA region. Little opposition is expected from the U.S. government. Still, domestic protectionism might be much greater in the face of huge economic gaps between China and the ASEAN countries.

Japan and South Korea stand as exceptions to regional integration on trade. Obstructed by the persistent agrarian protectionism at home and constrained by the continuing dependence on the U.S. market, both governments have failed to take much active initiative to deepen trade liberalization at either the Asia-Pacific or the East Asian level. New approaches now emphasize bilateral agreements and, in the case of Japan, nontrade issues. However, domestic protectionist forces continue to impede the process of bilateral negotiations for both countries, each of which had concluded only one FTA agreement by early 2004.

Financial and Monetary Cooperation

Financial integration in East Asia shares many characteristics with economic integration based on trade and investment. First, private banks have played a primary role in the integration, although public banks such as the Export-Import Bank of Japan also cooperated with private banks in strengthening financial and economic ties between Japan and other East Asian countries (Wan 2001, 83). As in the trade and investment field, East Asian governments have not hesitated to welcome the increasing presence of Japan in the financial sector so long as no political conditionalities are attached to money. As for the role of the United States, the monetary and financial crisis of 1997–98 revealed the U.S. government's strong influence, through the IMF, on individual countries. Still, compared with East Asia's commercial dependence on the United States, its dependence on U.S. money is not insurmountable because many, if not all, East Asian countries have enjoyed healthy hard-currency reserves except during the crisis years, and also because Japan can serve as the hard-currency provider of last resort. Furthermore, thanks to the financial deregulation and liberalization implemented after the late 1980s in many East Asian countries including Japan, domestic protectionism hampering regional cooperation in financial and monetary matters has become weaker. Thus, unlike what happened in the trade/investment field, financial and monetary cooperation has come to be supported by an East Asia-specific formal agreement with enforceable commitments.

The Asian Development Bank (ADB), established in 1966, was the first regional institution in the financial sector. It has, however, received financial contributions not only from the East Asian countries but also from the United States, Canada, and European countries. It is therefore an organization with supra-regional membership, although the largest contributors are from the Asia-Pacific region.

Thirty-one years later, in the middle of the Asian financial crisis, the United States opposed a Japanese proposal to create a strictly East Asian mechanism for monetary cooperation. Actually, the search for an East Asian framework for cooperation had started one and a half years earlier. In April 1995, when the ASEAN ministers of economy invited their counterparts from Japan, China, and South Korea to attend an unofficial meeting, Japan sought to invite Australia and New Zealand to avoid giving the impression that it accepted Mahathir's vision of an exclusively East Asian grouping. ASEAN and

Japan could not reach an agreement, and as a consequence, this meeting did not materialize. However, when the Asia–Europe Meeting (ASEM) was launched in 1996, Japan ended its resistance to the idea of an East Asian grouping; the result was ASEAN + 3 (APT). This time when Malaysia opposed inviting Australia and New Zealand, Japan backed down (Yamakage 2001, 66). Because ASEM was a forum not for economic cooperation within East Asia but for dialogue with a non-Asian region, Japan did not have much leverage. As a result, the first, though informal, meeting of the heads of the ASEAN + 3 governments was held in February 1996 to prepare for the first ASEM. APT covers the major part of Northeast and Southeast Asia.

The Asian financial crisis in 1997–98 served to strengthen East Asian solidarity on finance. Japan's proposal to create an Asian Monetary Fund was first made in September 1997 and faced strong opposition from both the United States and China, each fearing that Japanese influence would increase disproportionately in the financial market of East Asia. Moreover, China, with a huge trade surplus, did not need Japanese help as much as other East Asian countries did. The Japanese government gave up the idea and agreed to a cofinancing arrangement with the IMF in November 1997. In total, it committed $19 billion to help Thailand, South Korea, and Indonesia.

The first formal summit of APT was convened in December 1997, and the meeting was routinized thereafter. Meanwhile, the seriousness of the crisis and the perceived slowness and ineffectiveness of the IMF's and the United States's response pushed Japan and other East Asian countries toward further regional cooperation. The Japanese government felt obliged to act quickly because Japanese banks and companies had business networks throughout East Asia and were among the victims of the crisis. Therefore, it offered further assistance, in October 1998, with the New Miyazawa Initiative amounting to $30 billion. The second stage of the New Miyazawa Initiative was announced in May 1999 with the offer of an additional ¥2 trillion (Kishimoto 2001, 292–99).

On the occasion of the APT finance ministers' meeting in May 2000, the Japanese government proposed to strengthen the network of bilateral agreements for currency swaps in order to avoid another monetary crisis. It had already concluded bilateral swap agreements with South Korea and Malaysia as a part of the New Miyazawa Initiative projects. The Japanese proposal was aimed at expanding and combining bilateral agreements among East Asian countries (Kishimoto 2001, 294, 305). When adopted, it came to be called the Chiang Mai Initiative. Although the mechanism is based on a series of bilateral swap agreements, it is actually a regional framework covering the bulk of Northeast and Southeast Asia. The number of bilateral swap arrangements reached twelve with a total of $31.5 billion committed by August 2003 (Joint Ministerial Statement of the ASEAN + 3 Finance Ministers Meeting, August 2003).

The Chiang Mai accord contains another important line of cooperation. The ASEAN + 3 governments agreed to establish a network of "contact persons" as the first step in institutionalizing a well-coordinated system for monitoring the economic and financial situations of member countries. Members also agreed to facilitate a timely exchange of data and information concerning capital flows (Joint Statement of ASEAN + 3 Finance Ministers Meeting, in Suehiro and Yamakage 2001, 460). APT finance ministers agreed in August 2003 to set up the APT Finance Cooperation Fund to support an ongoing peer review process and economic surveillance (Joint Ministerial Statement of the ASEAN + 3 Finance Ministers Meeting, August 2003). Without adequate financial and economic data, it would be difficult for individual East Asian governments to commit their financial resources to help each other in times of crisis.

One important factor that enabled the ASEAN + 3 governments to begin mutual surveillance was the financial deregulation and liberalization that many had implemented since the late 1980s. South Korea, Thailand, and Indonesia were especially positive in liberalizing their domestic financial markets, opening offshore markets, and deregulating foreign currency and other transactions. They implemented those policies, expecting to maintain high economic growth through a smoother intake of foreign capital (Abe, Sato, and Nagano 1999, 79–83; Higashi 2000, 126; Osada 2001, 340). The financial crisis of 1997–98 only strengthened the trend because opaque financial and business transactions were blamed for worsening the crisis. Japan was no exception. Japan's notoriously protected financial market was gradually dismantled by a series of liberalization/deregulation policies that culminated in the financial Big Bang of 1998. As a result, resistance among uncompetitive banks and Ministry of Finance officials to the "internationalization of the yen" declined (Jin 2003, 84–85). Although such internationalization is not feasible for now, regional cooperation requiring transparency in business practice has become more acceptable for Japan and for many other Asian countries, especially in the financial sector.

Facing increasing Asian criticism of IMF-led and U.S.-supported programs, the U.S. government accepted both the Miyazawa and Chiang Mai initiatives. The latter was acceptable to the United States because, unlike the proposed Asian Monetary Fund (AMF), it is not a permanent institution that can routinely affect individual countries' financial and monetary policy. China accepted the initiative for the same reason. However, it can eventually develop into an AMF once China is convinced that such a formation will not strengthen Japanese hegemony in East Asia.

In short, Japanese and other East Asian governments have faced fewer domestic and international constraints in the financial/monetary field than they have in the area of trade. They depend less on the United States for financing and foreign-currency supply than they do for trade. Unilaterally implemented liberalization and deregulation of the financial market have weakened protectionist pressures at home. These factors, together with close financial ties among Japanese and East Asian banks and companies, have led to the Chiang Mai Initiative, so far the only ASEAN + 3 agreement involving concrete commitments.

Environmental Protection

Environmental protection in East Asia has been characterized by the active participation of nongovernmental actors: public-purpose promoters, victims of environmental degeneration, and environmental scientists. Their activities have prompted some East Asian governments, including Japan's, to take positive steps toward protecting the environment. Although the historically based distrust of Japan is present in environmental matters too, the Japanese government has helped alleviate it by using environmental ODA only as a carrot, not as a stick, and by emphasizing technical and technological cooperation. Finally, the U.S. government has had little reason to oppose the East Asian countries' regional efforts at environmental protection, unlike its approach to Asia-Pacific regional military security and trade, but perhaps similar to its approach to regional drug control. It has, however, as in the other issue areas, taken unilateral or bilateral approaches as demonstrated by the Bush administration's 2001 withdrawal from the Kyoto Protocol of the Framework Convention on Climate Change. Such factors have resulted in a proliferation of regional frameworks of cooperation. In addition, at least two initiatives put exceptionally strong peer pressure on participants, despite the absence of legally binding agreements.

Before 1989, most environmental protection measures were enforced by individual governments. The United Nations Economic and Social Commission for Asia and the Pacific (UNESCAP or simply ESCAP) and ASEAN were the sole regional organizations that took any initiative on the matter. ESCAP created an Environmental Coordinating Unit in its secretariat in 1978 (Schreurs 2000, 149). In 1985, it started to host the Ministerial Conference on Environment and Development (MCED), an event characterized as "a milestone in Asian environmental cooperation" (Takahashi 2002, 223). This conference, convened every five years, issued nonbinding regional action programs.

ASEAN, on the other hand, adopted its first regional programs—Environmental Education and Training, Marine Environment, and Environmental Management—in 1981 and issued the Declaration on Heritage Parks and Reserves in 1984 (Schreurs 2000, 147; ASEAN website, January 22, 2002). However, the ASEAN governments' commitment to environmental protection was found to be fragile. The "developmentalist states" in East Asia had long put an overwhelming emphasis on economic development and turned a blind eye to environmental consequences. So, although they signed the Agreement on the Conservation of Nature and Natural Resources in 1985, half of the ASEAN countries failed to ratify it (Springer 2002, 298).

Toward the end of the 1980s, Japan emerged as a major regional player in environmental protection. By the 1970s, the Japanese government, pressed by public opinion and court decisions, had established relatively stringent standards for environmental protection at home and had institutionalized protective mechanisms, including the Environment Protection Agency (now Ministry of the Environment). However, its environmental policy abroad came late. Japan started to consider regional policy seriously only in the face of strong criticism from domestic and foreign NGOs about the weakness of its commitment to environmental protection outside the country.

The development of autonomous NGOs has been hampered by unfriendly governments in countries such as Singapore and Malaysia (Mittelman 1999, 78–79). Still, NGOs in the field of environmental protection are much more numerous and autonomous than those in other issue areas. Partially encouraged by U.S.- or European-based NGOs such as WWF (World Wildlife Fund or Worldwide Fund for Nature), Friends of the Earth, and Greenpeace, many national NGOs in East Asian countries emerged after the 1980s. The editorial committee for the White Paper on Asian Environment lists major environmental NGOs in East Asian countries: 27 in the Philippines, 20 in Thailand, and 25 in Indonesia (Japan Environmental Council 2000, 358–59).

Democratic transformations after the late 1980s helped enlarge the space for NGO activity. The best example is South Korea, where civil society groups flourished after the democratic transition of 1987. By 1993, environmental organizations had created the Korea Federation for Environmental Movement, with one central office and twelve regional offices (Kim 1999, 295–96).

A network of East Asian NGOs took shape when the first Asia-Pacific NGO Conference on the Environment was convened in Bangkok in 1991. That conference has been held several times since in various East Asian cities (Japan Environmental Council 2000, 396). Another NGO network specializing in climate change and transboundary air pollution was formed in 1995. Such regional networks of NGOs, however, are still not powerful enough to influence many governmental policies, primarily because NGOs in authoritarian and socialist regimes have had limited political leverage. It is only the NGOs in democratic countries such as Japan and South Korea that have been instrumental in pushing for regional cooperation through their influence on their home governments.

The Japanese government was frequently accused by NGOs of being excessively permissive toward private companies that cut down rainforest trees for export to Japan or built polluting factories in Southeast Asia. Such accusations became especially common in the latter half of the 1980s, with the expansion of Japanese direct investment into Southeast Asia. In 1986, rain-forest destruction at Sarawak and Kalimantan became a hot issue in both Southeast Asia and Japan. Activists from several NGOs in Japan, responding to the worldwide movement to protect the tropical forest, formed the Japan Tropical Forest Action Network (JATAN) in January 1987 and started a national campaign to press Japanese commercial companies and government agencies such as JICA and the Export-Import Bank to stop timber projects at Sarawak (JATAN website, http://www.jca.apc.org/jatan/jatan10year.html, January 22, 2002). The national newspaper *Asahi* joined the campaign and contributed to awakening the general public to Japan's responsibility for environmental destruction in Southeast Asia (*Asahi Shimbun*, January 27–February 3, 1987).

Other NGO complaints were directed toward Japanese ODA, which placed special emphasis on infrastructure projects such as roads, ports, dams, and power plants. These projects, by their nature, lead to large-scale environmental changes and dislocation of people. Public criticism became so strong that several Diet members, including those from the governing Liberal Democratic Party, felt obliged to participate in a dialogue with NGO people for the first time (*Asahi Shimbun*, June 7, 1987).

To respond to those criticisms, commercial companies in Japan began to establish independent divisions to deal with environmental problems (JATAN website, February 8, 2002). Government agencies such as the Overseas Economic Cooperation Fund and the Export-Import Bank adopted their first environmental protection guidelines in 1989 (Dauvergne 2001b, 59–60). In the same year, within its Department of Planning, JICA established a Section on the Environment, which was upgraded to the Division on Environment and Gender in 1993 (JICA 2001, 7).

On the occasion of the Paris Arch Summit of July 1989, the Japanese government pledged to use up to ¥300 billion for environment-related ODA in the following three years. This goal was more than accomplished, with ¥407.5 billion actually spent. The Japanese government pledged another ¥900 billion to ¥1 trillion at the United Nations Conference on Environment and Development (the so-called Rio Summit). Part of that money was used to form the Japan Fund for Global Environment to support the activities of environmental NGOs. JICA's environment-related expenditures increased from 10.1 percent in 1989 to 19 percent by 1999 (JICA 2001, 2–4). Such figures, however, should not be accepted at face value because traditional infrastructure aid such as water and sewage projects were reclassified as environmental aid (Dauvergne 2001b, 52).

In the face of growing public consciousness about environmental problems, furthered by the Rio Conference, the 1990s saw a flourishing of regional-cooperation initiatives on environmental protection. Envisaging the coming Rio Summit, Japan's Environment Protection Agency, in 1991, invited minister-level officials engaged in environmental protection in the Asia-Pacific countries as well as representatives from international and regional organizations such as ESCAP and the ADB to the first Environment Congress for Asia and the Pacific (EcoAsia) (Ministry of the Environment 2001, 338). This meeting was convened annually thereafter for information exchange and the identification of suitable policies. The APEC's Environmental Ministerial Meeting, which started its annual meeting in 1994, is similar (Takahashi 2002, 226–27).

Within the Northeast Asian subregion, the Northeast Asian Conference on Environmental Cooperation (NEACEC) was inaugurated in 1992, following the Japan–Korea Environmental Symposium of 1988. Besides Japan and South Korea, China, Mongolia, Russia, the United Nations Environment Programme (UNEP), and ESCAP participated to exchange information, share experiences, and discuss future actions on common environmental problems. The following year, another intergovernmental forum named the Northeast Asian Subregional Program on Environmental Cooperation (NEASPEC) took shape with the participation of Japan, South Korea, North Korea, China, Mongolia, and Russia. Although the hosting organization was ESCAP, the South Korean government was a positive promoter of this venture (Takahashi 2002, 224–25). Since 1997, this forum has been engaged in three technical projects (data collection, training, and power-plant improvement) with financial assistance from the ADB (ESCAP website, http://www.unescap.org/enrd/envionment/, June 20, 2003).

Still another subregional forum is the UNEP-sponsored Northwest Pacific Action Plan (NOWPAP). Under its aegis, Japan, South Korea, China, and Russia pledged in 1994 to cooperate in tackling the marine contamination problem in the Sea of Japan (East Sea) and the Yellow Sea. However, partially due to the Japan–South Korea dispute over the name of the ocean between their two countries as well as over the location of the secretariat, the progress of NOWPAP has been extremely slow (Nam 2002, 179; Takahashi 2002, 243). Each participating country agreed in 1999 to establish a regional action center to monitor and assess seashore contamination (Ministry of the Environment 2001, 355). Except for this modest accord, NOWPAP is for now no more than a series of seminars and workshops for officials and experts.

Parallel to its participation in regional forums, the Japanese government began a bilateral approach to persuade China to become more serious about environmental protection. Before the early 1990s, Japan's ODA initiatives sought either to alleviate international and domestic criticism against environment-compromising activities by the Japanese government and companies or to contribute to solving "global issues." By the 1990s, however, Japanese policy makers realized that Japan itself was a victim of transboundary pollution.

③ 국내 환경문제 (by 중국)

As China industrialized, it increased its emission of sulfur dioxide into the air, causing an acid rain problem not only in its own country but in Korea and Japan. In 1992, the Japanese government gave grant assistance to its Chinese counterpart to build and equip the Environmental Protection Center in Beijing for research and training, with air pollution as one of its main areas of interest. Japan has provided additional equipment and technical training since then (JICA 2001, 8).

In 1994, Japan concluded a bilateral Agreement of Cooperation for Environmental Protection with China to foster joint research and information exchange. When Japan's prime minister visited China in September 1997, he and his Chinese counterpart entered into an agreement titled Japan–China Environmental Cooperation for the Twenty-first Century. Two big projects were begun under this agreement. One was a project to rebuild model cities in ways compatible with environmental protection. Chong Quing, Dalian, and Guiyang were chosen as the sites, and the contract for the first concession loan, amounting to ¥16 billion, was signed in March 2000; the second, amounting to ¥15 billion, was signed in March 2001. The second project involved grant assistance to build a computer network connecting a hundred cities, to gather and disseminate environment-related information. The agreement for this project was signed by both governments in March 2000 (Ministry of the Environment 2001, 343).

Besides those big projects, the Japanese government offered China as well as Southeast Asian countries technical and technological assistance in energy conservation and pollution cleanup. The Green Aid Plan initiated by MITI in 1991 was typical of such assistance (Schreurs 2000, 152; Dauvergne 2001b, 59). After the third Conference of the Parties of the UN Framework Convention on Climate Change admitted the Clean Development Mechanism in 1997, the Japanese government broadened bilateral programs for energy conservation and reforestation, mostly with East Asian countries.

Such a technical approach is convenient for the Japanese government for two reasons. First, it does not obstruct the aspirations of many East Asian governments and Japanese companies that hope to continue constructing industrial infrastructure and exploiting mines and forest for export. Second, just as in the area of drug control, the Japanese government, by taking a technical approach, can avoid giving the impression of directly intervening in domestic policy making within the host countries.

The technical approach does not necessarily undermine environmental protection efforts in East Asia. It has served to strengthen pressures on uncooperative governments when it takes the form of authentically organized scientific research into the sources of pollution. The best example is the case of acid rain in East Asia.

Between 1993 and 1997, Japan's Environmental Protection Agency hosted a series of meetings for experts on transboundary air pollution, inviting China,

South Korea, Mongolia, Russia, Indonesia, Malaysia, the Philippines, Singapore, and Thailand. In 1998, on the basis of these meetings, the agency successfully persuaded the participants to form the Acid Deposition Monitoring Network in East Asia (EANET), which covers almost all areas of East and Southeast Asia. China, as the main source of transboundary pollutants in Northeast Asia, was naturally reluctant to join such a permanent network but finally decided to participate in the "preparatory phase" (Nam 2002, 186; Takahashi 2002, 235–36). The inclusion of Southeast Asian countries somewhat alleviated China's uneasiness. For the Japanese government, bringing China into a broader regional framework of cooperation was a way to press China to take more serious antipollution measures without causing the negative nationalist reactions that might have been provoked by bilateral pressures.

EANET is composed of research institutes in the participating countries that use shared guidelines and technical manuals to compile and evaluate data on acid deposition collected at national monitoring sites (Takahashi 2002, 236). After three years of provisional activities, the network entered a "regular" phase in 2001. Although its secretariat is located at the UNEP office of Bangkok, the center of the network for information gathering and training is located at the Acid Deposition and Oxidant Research Center (ADORC) at Niigata, Japan (Ministry of the Environment 2001, 354). This center belongs to the Japan Environmental Sanitation Center, a public-purpose entity working under the auspices of Japan's Ministry of Health, Labor, and Welfare.

In the early phase of research and monitoring, the participating countries blamed each other as the main sources of pollutants. However, scientifically sound research based on common techniques contributed to clarifying the patterns of transport and the deposition of harmful air pollutants. A nonofficial scheme named Model Inter-Comparisons of Long-Range Transport and Sulfur Deposition in East Asia (MICS-Asia) supplements EANET in this respect. This project, launched in 1998, was co-funded by the International Institute for Applied Systems Analysis located in Austria and the Central Research Institute of the Electric Power Industry of Japan. Its aim is comparing and improving the models for long-range transport and deposition of sulfur compounds. In 2000, its scope of research was expanded to cover nitrogen, ozone, and aerosols in addition to sulfur. Participants include six research institutes from four countries: Japan, China, Austria, and the United States. Three, including ADORC, are from Japan (ADORC website, http://www.adorc.gr.jp/adorc/mics.html, July 20, 2003). Although it has non-Asian participants and the number of the participants is still limited, this network may eventually develop into a rare case of an "epistemic community" in the Asia-Pacific region.

Yellow dust is another transboundary pollutant from China, although China did not initially admit that the dust carries polluting agents. Particularly strong, harmful effects are observed in South Korea. The yellow dust problem has been one of the main themes of the Tripartite Environment Ministers' Meeting (TEMM) proposed by the Korean government and established by Japan, South Korea, and China in 1999. In the fourth TEMM meeting of 2002, "substantial measures to control yellow dust were discussed in detail" (Lee 2002, 211). Here again, China has been forced to admit the harmful effects of yellow dust, although research cooperation has not yet reached the level that it has for acid rain.

Intergovernmental environmental cooperation in Northeast Asia is paralleled by an NGO network named Atmosphere Action Network East Asia (AANEA), which was formed in 1995 by seventeen NGOs from Japan, South Korea, China, Taiwan, Hong Kong, Mongolia, and Russia (Takahashi 2002, 240). However, the main promoters of environmental cooperation in Northeast Asia have been the governments of Japan and South Korea, where national NGOs have been especially active and vocal.

In Southeast Asia, the environmentally compromising governments were forced to be more serious about environmental problems in the face of the disastrous haze in 1997. The thick haze, resulting from fires that burned throughout Kalimantan and Sumatra in Indonesia and to a lesser extent Sabah, Malaysia, affected Singapore, southern Malaysia, and Brunei, threatening inhabitants' health and obstructing social and economic life. Damage was especially serious in Singapore, where total costs are calculated to have been $164–286 million (Quah 2002, 430).

There was widespread public anger in those countries, but the national NGOs of the ASEAN countries were not strong enough to force their governments to take immediate action. In contrast, international NGOs such as WWF were actively involved from the early phase of the fires, both monitoring it and informing the global media (Springer 2002, 300).

Facing a discontented public as well as international criticism, ASEAN adopted a Regional Haze Action Plan in late 1997 that called for more strict enforcement of existing laws against companies and others who set fires to clear forests for agricultural or agro-industrial purposes. It also called for the establishment of national plans for more effective fire response. Enforcement in Indonesia became stricter than before but was still not strict enough to satisfy other ASEAN members. When new fires seemed to threaten Brunei, which was hosting the Southeast Asian sports games in 1999, the country threatened to sue Indonesia (Springer 2002, 299, 304). ASEAN adopted a zero-burn policy in April 1999, urging member countries to enact and implement necessary laws and regulations to enforce this policy. To encourage the policy, ASEAN convened a number of dialogue sessions with plantation companies and timber concessionaries, the major culprits in the burning. A workshop on the enforcement of laws against the setting of land and forest fires in Indonesia was also held in September 2000 in Riau Province to develop a common understanding among judges, prosecutors, police, NGOs, and the

mass media and to build social control and public awareness of law enforcement against open burning (ASEAN Secretariat website, January 22, 2002).

The negotiation for a formal agreement to prevent and control fires started
in 2001 with the legal assistance of the UNEP. The ASEAN Agreement on
Transboundary Haze Pollution, signed by environment ministers in June
2002, mandates among other things strict enforcement of existing laws and
enactment of new laws to regulate open burning (ASEAN Secretariat website,
July 20 2003). There are no sanctions for noncompliance, but the obligations
listed in the formal agreement are detailed and concrete, and have placed
constant and strong pressure on the Indonesian government to comply. In
various ASEAN meetings, Indonesia "routinely tries to reassure its neighbors
that it will take action when the threat of widespread fire appears" (Springer
2002, 303).

In short, the issue area of environmental protection is characterized by
abundant unilateral, bilateral, and regional initiatives and frameworks,
although regional institutions with legally binding obligations have yet to be
established. One of the reasons for the density of cooperation is the exceptionally active involvement of NGOs and scientific institutions. Although their
regional networks are not yet strong enough to influence the regional
process, national NGOs of certain East Asian countries, especially Japan and
South Korea, have been instrumental in pushing their governments to pursue more environmentally conscious policies. In Southeast Asia, where NGOs
are weaker, international NGOs such as WWF as well as the anger of the general public played important roles during the haze debacle of 1997–98.

Another characteristic of environmental protection in the Asia-Pacific
region is the abundance of East Asia-specific schemes, especially in the Northeast Asian subregion. As with drug control, the U.S. government has pursued
benign neglect. In not a single case has the U.S. government intervened to
abort a regional initiative, although it continues to take unilateral and bilateral approaches to its own environmental policy.

Another reason for the abundance of "East Asian" initiatives is that China's
persistent resistance to Japanese leadership has been alleviated by careful
Japanese approaches. In its bilateral cooperation with China, the Japanese
government has avoided taking any policy stance that looks imposing. It has
focused instead on a technical approach, giving China abundant technical
and technological assistance to enhance its own research and monitoring
capability and to clean up its own cities and factories. The Japanese government also brought China into several regional frameworks for cooperation by
emphasizing the initially harmless purposes of information exchange and scientific research.

Although most of these regional schemes continue to be forums for information exchange and policy dialogue, EANET supplemented by MICS-Asia is
becoming a powerful peer-pressure mechanism thanks to its scientifically

sound research activities. On the other hand, the haze incident of 1997–98 made ASEAN more ready to try influencing the policy of individual member countries through a well-defined agreement on land and forest fire control. Today, the Indonesian government has come under strong peer pressure as a consequence.

Explaining the Diversities — "critic"

The analysis in this chapter confirms that East Asia lacks a firm institutionalization of regional-cooperation schemes. In spite of the innumerable bilateral, subregional or regional frameworks for cooperation, East Asia has few intergovernmental or supra-national entities with decision-making mandates. Many frameworks involve simply information exchange, policy dialogue, or joint research. When formal agreements stipulating members' obligations exist, they are not supported by sanctions against noncompliers. Implementation, therefore, depends entirely on peer pressure.

The East Asian region is not very well endowed with suitable conditions for legally binding regional institutions. Regional business networks set up by Japanese corporations, and overseas Chinese businesses are so thick that East Asia has seen a market-based integration. This virtual integration, however, has lowered incentives for intergovernmental integration. As exemplified by ASEAN's brand-to-brand complementation program, for example, economic integration can proceed through piecemeal coordination among East Asian governments. Open regionalism emphasizes voluntary, nonexclusionary liberalization and was born of this success in market-based integration. On the other hand, transnational networks among nonbusiness, nongovernmental actors have been too weak to foster regional integration.

The powerful influence of the United States also adversely affects regional integration in East Asia, especially in the issue areas of military security and trade regime. The U.S. government almost always prefers unilateral or bilateral approaches in the region and therefore is not enthusiastic about regional schemes in general; it is particularly hostile to any regional schemes that exclude the United States.

Still another factor obstructing regional integration in East Asia is found among norms, protectionism, and policy effectiveness within individual East Asian countries. In China, Korea, and some Southeast Asian countries, historical distrust of Japan persists; the concern for nationalist backlash from its East Asian neighbors, together with legal and social norms in Japan itself, makes the Japanese government highly cautious about taking on regional leadership. Strong protectionist pressures in many East Asian countries make general liberalization beyond piecemeal adjustments difficult. Finally, policy effectiveness at home, which is affected by the nature of state–society relations, has reduced the incentive for the Japanese government to be more active in its regional policy in certain issue areas.

All these factors have impeded the development of well-institutionalized mechanisms for regional cooperation in East Asia. However, we must not overlook important diversities among various regional schemes and across the different issue areas in East Asia. In spite of the mounting difficulties, East Asian governments have elaborated a variety of regional schemes with different levels of geographical extension and different degrees of cooperative depth to cope with common challenges stemming from the increasing transboundary flow of goods, money, people, pollutants, and drugs.

At the one extreme are unilateral actions by a single country. Japan, as the most resourceful country in the region, has used its ODA money to organize seminars and training courses for police and environmental researchers invited from other East Asian countries. Unilateral actions are not necessarily useless. They can cultivate personal ties and foster confidence building, but they have not been able to induce regional integration directly.

At the other extreme are supra-regional forums such as ARF, ASC, ASEM, MCED, or EcoAsia in which "East Asian" cooperation is diluted by participants from Europe, the Indian subcontinent, central Asia, or even the Middle East. Generally speaking, these forums are so heterogeneous that discussions there cannot go much beyond information exchange, proclamation of common policy objectives, confidence-building dialogue, and identification of small projects with limited funds.

In between those extremes are found "Asia-Pacific," "East Asian bilateral," and "East Asian regional" frameworks of cooperation. Most of the Asia-Pacific ties rest on bilateral connections between the United States and individual East Asian countries. Bilateral security treaties are a typical example. In the area of drug control, many East Asian countries also have established bilateral cooperative relations with the United States by allowing DEA agents to establish a presence in the country's offices or in a local U.S. embassy. Moreover, many developing countries in East Asia once enjoyed or still enjoy the Generalized System of Preferences status offered by the United States. Their economies are highly dependent on the U.S. market.

APEC is a rare case of an Asia-Pacific multilateral forum. It came to a standstill, however, when the U.S. government tried to use it to push legally binding trade liberalization, which met fierce resistance from Japan and certain other Asian countries.

East Asia has developed many bilateral schemes of its own. Japan's cooperation with China has been noticeable in many issue areas, including drug control and environmental protection. The Japanese government also cooperates with some Southeast Asian countries in drug control efforts, though on a much smaller scale. The 2002 Japan–Singapore agreement was East Asia's first and so far sole bilateral FTA. Even in the military security field,

Japan started a series of confidence-building exchanges with South Korea, China, and Russia.

Bilateral cooperation has brought about limited but not negligible results, such as several arrests of drug traffickers and the installation of pollutant-removing equipment in power plants, both in China. Although the actual impacts on the partners' economies are expected to be small, the Japan—Singapore Agreement on Economic Cooperation is a rare case of a legally binding accord in regional trade. Bilateral cooperation, however, remains too narrow to contribute to fostering broader regional cooperation.

Finally, East Asia–specific regional frameworks of cooperation can be divided into subregional and regional ones. Subregional schemes cover either Northeast or Southeast Asia, whereas regional schemes cover both. The latter include ASEAN + 3 and EANET, whereas the former are represented by ASEAN (for haze control), MOU6, and AFTA in Southeast Asia and NEACEC, NEASPEC, NOWPAP, and TEMM in Northeast Asia. The ACCORD and ASEAN + China are intermediate cases.

Among the eleven frameworks listed, six (EANET, ASEAN, NEACEC, NEASPEC, NOWPAP, and TEMM) are in the area of environmental protection. The remaining five include two (AFTA, ASEAN + China) in area of trade and investment, two (MOU6, ACCORD) in drug control, and one (ASEAN + 3) in financial and monetary cooperation.

Although none of these schemes contains sanctions against noncompliers and implementation depends on simple peer pressure, the strength of that pressure is different from one scheme to another. The ASEAN Agreement on Transboundary Haze Pollution, MOU6 for drug control, AFTA, the Chiang Mai Initiative of ASEAN + 3, and EANET for acid-rain monitoring have been much more effective than other regional or subregional schemes. Common to the first four schemes is that all are based on very specific, well-defined commitments. EANET is notable for its scientifically rigorous research organization. These characteristics help pressure member countries into complying with the agreements.

In short, although East Asia as a region is characterized by a general lack of well-institutionalized cooperative frameworks with binding agreements, we should not overlook the tremendous diversities in the geographical extension of and participants' compliance in these schemes. In this sense, we have many "maps" in East Asia instead of a single well-drawn one. But why so? Why are "East Asian" frameworks for cooperation more abundant in the area of environmental cooperation than in those of trade/investment liberalization, drug control, or financial/monetary cooperation, and why does none exist for military security? And why have the five schemes just listed—the ASEAN Agreement on Transboundary Haze Pollution, MOU6 for drug control, AFTA, the Chiang Mai Initiative of ASEAN + 3, and EANET—come to be more effective that the others? This chapter insists that these diversities of regional cooperation in East Asia, as well as the general characteristics of such cooperation, are mostly explained by three variables: transnational ties among nongovernmental actors, East Asian countries' dependence on the United States, and domestic constraints and opportunities.

Military security and environmental protection are two extreme cases. In the former, no East Asia–specific framework exists but only bilateral treaties between the United States and individual East Asian countries, and supraregional forums such as ARF and ASC. By contrast, the issue area of environmental protection is blessed with plenty of East Asian regional and subregional schemes. Furthermore, two of the five most effective regional schemes in East Asia (EANET and the ASEAN haze agreement) belong to this issue area.

The contrast is first explained by the policy stance of the U.S. government. After the United States established the network of anti-Communist bilateral treaties with East Asian countries during the early postwar years, this hub-and-spoke arrangement, together with U.S. military bases in several East Asian nations, became the backbone of U.S. military strategy in East Asia and the Pacific. When initiatives for regional institutions appeared after the end of the Cold War, the U.S. government continued to press for bilateral frameworks, opposing both Australian foreign minister Evans's proposal for a CSCE-like entity and Japanese foreign minister Nakayama's proposal to use ASEAN-PMC for security dialogues. The compromise arrangement was the ARF, a supra-regional forum whose heterogeneity allows only general discussion and information exchange in the interests of trust building. The newer ASC is similar.

The U.S. government also takes bilateral or unilateral approaches in its international environmental policy. However, because regional cooperation for environmental protection in East Asia does not jeopardize U.S. economic or strategic interests, the United States has not opposed any regional initiatives in this issue area.

Second, transnational ties among nongovernmental actors foster regional cooperation for environmental protection but not for military security. Environmental NGOs emerged in East Asia as important national players during the 1980s. They even created regional forums during the 1990s. They became influential enough to affect public policy in democratic Japan and democratized South Korea. Yet they could not gain such influence under the authoritarian developmentalist regimes of Southeast Asia. Their weakness there, however, was supplemented by the active involvement of international NGOs and the general discontent among citizens living with serious environmental degeneration such as forest fire and its haze. As a result of their explicit or tacit pressures, ASEAN finally reached the formal Agreement on Transboundary Haze Pollution, which stipulates detailed obligations of ASEAN members with regard to the prevention, warning, and control of land and forest fires. Northeast Asia has also seen a proliferation of subregional inter-governmental schemes to cope with transboundary pollution.

In the military security case, close connections between the military forces of the United States and individual East Asian countries are equivalent to the transnational networks discussed here, although military forces are hardly nongovernmental actors. Such connections rest on East Asian dependence on the United States for weapons systems, training, and intelligence, which have only strengthened bilateral, not regional, ties.

Third, domestic constraints on regional cooperation are heavier in the area of military security than environmental protection. Japan's postwar constitution was interpreted as prohibiting that country's participation in any collective security arrangement. Social norms in both Japan and the East Asian countries made it extremely difficult for Japan to expand its military-based role in East Asia. With only a dim possibility for regional security cooperation in the near future and with such hot spots as the Korean peninsula, the Taiwan Straits, and South China Sea islands, many East Asian countries including Japan have no alternative but to rely on U.S. military capability for their security.

The Japanese government was cautious to avoid any nationalist backlash from its East Asian neighbors in the field of environmental protection too. By taking a technical approach, it succeeded in bringing China, the main source of transboundary pollutants, into regional frameworks for joint research and monitoring. The results of scientific research, especially that conducted by EANET, now impose relatively heavy pressure on the Chinese government to comply with its findings.

In conclusion, all three variables favor regional cooperation in area of environmental protection. By contrast, all three variables have worked against regional cooperation in the field of military security.

In the other three issue areas, conditions stimulating regional cooperation fall somewhere between those of environmental protection and military security. Transnational networks of private businesses, including banks, have helped foster virtual regional integration in East Asia. Ironically, smooth market-based integration reduced the incentives for intergovernmental integration. However, transnational businesses have been always supportive of further economic integration, de facto or de jure, whenever such initiatives emerge. The IFNGO, a regional forum for antidrug NGOs in East Asia, has not had as high a region-forming capability as private business networks have. Antidrug NGOs in East Asia are mostly semi-official entities that help administer government policy rather than influence policy formation. What really pushed the governments into regional cooperation was the spread of drug addiction and concomitant HIV/AIDS. Governments could not leave the problem unattended and so formed MOU6 and ACCORD in Southeast Asia.

Benign neglect by the U.S. government, a condition not applicable to the economic cases, also helped the subregional efforts for drug control. As in the

Sth that does not Jeopardize the US' interest
that US does not opposed,
not exclue US
constraints imposed by US.

Why So Many Maps There?   **147**

case of environmental protection, regional efforts at drug control jeopardized no U.S. interests. On the contrary, they had the potential to supplement U.S. bilateral efforts in the region.

By contrast, the U.S. government jealously opposed any regional scheme for economic cooperation that excluded the United States. The only exception has been subregional integration by developing countries, as was the case with AFTA. The U.S. government accepted AFTA because it does not place American firms or products at a disadvantage vis-à-vis their Japanese or European rivals. The ASEAN + China trade negotiation, though still in the incipient phase, is also among the developing economies and so far has met no negative reaction from the United States. An ASEAN + Japan FTA, however, might well cause a more substantial reaction from the United States. Yet the prospect of success there is low due to Japanese protectionism at home.

The strength of the constraint imposed by U.S. policy preferences also varies according to the degree of East Asia's economic dependence on the United States. East Asia is less dependent on the United States in the field of finance than in that of trade. As a result, ASEAN + 3 succeeded in agreeing on the Chiang Mai Initiative, whereas EAEG was aborted.

Domestic factors have also helped regional efforts at financial and monetary cooperation, although not those for trade liberalization. Domestic resistance to trade liberalization is extremely high. It is much weaker in financial and monetary cooperation, partially because most East Asian countries have unilaterally implemented deregulation and liberalization of their financial markets.

Therefore, the issue area of financial and monetary cooperation is favored with intimate transnational networks, favorable domestic conditions, and less dependence on the United States. It is not by chance that this issue area saw one of the only two East Asia–wide schemes for cooperation, the Chiang Mai Initiative. The other scheme, by EANET, belongs to the area of environmental protection.

Domestic factors are less favorable for regional drug control efforts. Japan, though the most resourceful country in the region, has been timid in its regional policy because it feared negative reactions from its East Asian neighbors. When MOU6 was formed in 1993 by Thailand, Myanmar, Laos, Vietnam, Cambodia, and China, Japan simply made a limited financial contribution through UNDCP to support MOU6's border cooperation program.

In conclusion, environmental protection, which has the most favorable terms in the three variables, has seen the largest number of regional schemes for cooperation, two of which are among five of the most effective. The area of financial and monetary cooperation follows suit, with close transnational networks and favorable domestic conditions. There the only obstacle was the U.S. position preventing an Asian Monetary Fund. East Asian countries needed to be satisfied with the looser mechanism of currency swaps arranged by APT. Still, this is one of the five most effective and one of the two East Asia–wide schemes of cooperation. The three variables have been less favorable in trade/investment liberalization and drug control. These two fields have seen only a small number of subregional frameworks, although even these remain superior to the issue area of military security.

Conclusion

Weak transnational ties outside of the economic sphere, strong U.S. bilateralism, and heavy normative and protectionist constraints have obstructed a firm institutionalization of regional-cooperation schemes in East Asia. This general feature, however, should not blind us to the diversities observed across the five issue areas. Regional-cooperation mechanisms can be distinguished in terms of their geographical extension and the degree of members' commitment. Lacking a well-institutionalized organization like the EU, East Asian governments have relied on ad hoc, multiple schemes, or "maps," to cope with problems stemming from the intensifying process of globalization. They make their institutional choices according to different constraints and opportunities in each case. By paying attention to the diversities of these schemes and the conditioning factors behind them, we can understand better the driving forces and obstacles to regional cooperation in East Asia.

The three variables used here to explain the diversities are based on four theoretical approaches dominant in the contemporary international relations literature. In this sense, our theoretical framework is extremely eclectic. However, no complex phenomenon such as the regional integration in East Asia can be explained by a single approach. Such an eclectic approach seems inevitable and desirable.

6

Between Foreign Direct Investment and Regionalism: The Role of Japanese Production Networks

DENNIS TACHIKI

Foreign direct investment (FDI) plays an unintentional bottom-up role in integrating East Asia. Through FDI, many multinational corporations (MNCs) now extend their global reach to numerous parts of the region in an effort to exploit their competitive advantages (e.g., see Dunning 1992). East Asian governments, on the other hand, sometimes cooperate with neighboring countries in attracting FDI in an effort to promote their own economic development (Woods 1993; Ravenhill 2001). An increasingly important link between these mutually exclusive starting points lies in the global production networks of MNCs.

A global production network (GPN) results from a business strategy for spreading different stages of production across national borders. GPNs may or may not involve equity ownership (Ernst 1994; Borrus, Ernst, and Haggard 2000), and they unfold within an institutional environment (Henderson et al. 2002; Fruin 1998). This contrasts with notions that MNCs target individual countries to exploit firm-specific advantages (Hymer 1976), to internalize transaction costs (Buckley and Casson 1985), or to incorporate them into an MNC's product life cycle (Vernon 1971). Matsushita Electric Industries (MEI), for example, has a particularly large FDI stake in the Malaysian economy; however, in recent years, this investment has typically been part of the company's larger regional business strategy. MEI spreads different segments of its products and production across East Asian countries, often in joint ventures, to tap local technological and business capacities and assemble final products ultimately destined for local and global markets (Toyo Keizai 2003).

As MNCs relocate products and services to an overseas production base, the complications of coordinating relevant business functions (procurement, personnel, sales, etc.) across national borders become just as important as finding the right country in which to locate a plant. Where MNCs pursue this business strategy, we can begin to speak about GPNs as a force in the *regionalization* of East Asia—that is, a mostly economic process, in which the collective actions of individual actors lead to regional integration from the bottom up (Pempel, chap. 1 in this volume).

Locating production in countries with roughly similar socioeconomic profiles only marginally improves a corporation's bottom line. Hence, the relative absence of GPNs reveals an overlap in the comparative advantage of East Asian countries. On an index of trade complementarity, many Southeast Asian countries and China, for instance, produce similar low- and medium-level technology products (Kwan 2001), with MNCs relatively free to choose one or the other as a production base. Nevertheless, these countries have negotiated a framework agreement for free trade to commence in 2010, creating potentially broader channels for subregional trade and investments. In contrast to theories of comparative advantage, then, to the extent that East Asian countries seek collective solutions to offset their individual perceived comparative *dis*advantages, they participate in the process of *regionalism*—that is, a formal top-down process of regional integration (Pempel, chap. 1 in this volume).

This chapter attempts to get behind the cross-sectional FDI statistics and sketch a more dynamic picture of MNC activity in Northeast and Southeast Asia. Japanese GPNs in East Asia provide a good case study of how the pursuit of corporate self-interest sometimes leads to economic regionalism.

FDI Snapshot

A straightforward reading of the longitudinal FDI data shows that for the first thirty-five years of the postwar era, outward Japanese FDI was rather modest and mainly limited to the extractive and labor-intensive industries (Mason 1999). In contrast, at the end of the five-year period after the 1985 Plaza Accord, both the number of cases and the value of Japanese FDI are nearly double what had been achieved during the previous thirty-five years, according to the Ministry of Finance (2003) statistics (see table 6.1). These figures peaked in 1990, fluctuated downward until the 1997 Asian financial crisis, and then stagnated into the new century (excluding the special case of Japan Tobacco, which acquired R. J. Reynolds International in 1999). Several Japan Bank for International Cooperation surveys suggest, however, a nominal increase in Japanese FDI over the subsequent three years (FY2002–2004) as companies relocated and reorganized their overseas operations (Kaburagi et al. 2002; Marugami et al. 2003).

Table 6.1. Japanese foreign direct investment by region and industry

Region/Industry	1951–1985 Case	Amount[b]	1986–1988 Case	Amount[c]	1989–1991 Case	Amount	1992–1994 Case	Amount	1995–1997 Case	Amount	1998–2000 Case	Amount	2001–2003[a] Case	Amount
North America[d]	13,242	$26,966	5,712	$48,126	6,988	111,206	2,745	55,088	1,800	74,574	799	55,283	555	27,068
Manufacturing Total					1,366	30,794	700	15,186	662	27,268	456	31,864	271	16,044
Chemical					231	4,484	63	2,717	50	2,883	56	2,569	32	5,149
Machinery					182	2,490	83	1,771	107	1,667	84	1,776	30	1,214
Electrical					239	8,365	138	3,492	171	10,943	94	19,413	50	6,351
Transport					140	3,669	84	1,529	62	4,414	74	1,589	74	1,763
Asia-Pacific	11,530	$19,463	3,897	$12,764	4,483	29,453	4,052	26,072	4,019	39,958	1,538	23,128	1,330	17,748
Manufacturing Total					2,372	12,849	2,666	13,569	2,779	24,258	957	13,746	938	12,184
Chemical					204	1,999	168	2,772	243	3,238	130	1,963	105	1,504
Machinery					203	1,203	178	1,192	235	2,043	88	965	103	897
Electrical					395	3,691	368	3,159	476	6,673	286	3,498	223	3,090
Transport					87	1,001	137	941	267	2,766	125	2,337	165	2,669
Europe	3,921	$11,003	1,633	$19,161	2,675	53,354	1,332	24,905	751	30,335	1,616	73,956	2,780	40,971
Manufacturing Total					735	14,618	409	7,065	272	8,184	204	24,747	208	15,685
Chemical					85	1,445	52	1,528	31	1,852	34	1,965	23	1,191
Machinery					90	2,413	81	1,304	46	1,109	29	540	32	1,312
Electrical					123	5,128	51	1,384	78	2,432	40	2,615	43	4,028
Transport					63	2,372	25	1,342	26	1,438	44	4,750	49	7,900
Latin America[e]	4,991	$15,636	1,447	$15,981	1,050	16,827	937	12,913	860	16,526	695	22,458	417	20,128
Manufacturing Total					82	1,709	76	1,996	99	2,800	89	3,718	33	2,647
Chemical					10	348	9	97	4	29	30	382	2	276
Machinery					7	93	9	160	17	155	9	400	4	49
Electrical					12	269	12	152	8	667	12	470	4	709
Transport					14	560	15	928	10	552	9	1,931	12	415
World Total[f]	38,517	$86,928	13,857	$102,706	17,016	230,728	9,707	128,635	7,859	169,899	5,046	180,970	5,183	109,192

Source: Ministry of Finance 1989, 2004.

Note: Case = number of companies. Amounts for 1989–2003 are in 100 million yen. Figures are on an approval basis—that is, investments were approved by the Ministry of Finance for overseas investment but companies might not necessarily have spent the full amount. The manufacturing total includes not only the chemical, machinery, electrical, and transport industries, but also the food, textile, lumber and pulp, metal, and other industries. The Ministry of Finance industry data by country before 1989 are not comprehensive enough to compare with the post-1989 data and are not presented.

[a] 2003 data are for first half of year; [b] Figures given in US$. Yen/dollar exchange rate was Y360 from 1951 to 1971; from 1971 to 1985 it fluctuated, settling at about Y240; [c] Figures given in US$. Yen/dollar exchange rate was Y240–260; [d] United States and Canada; [e] Includes Mexico; [f] Includes regions listed in table plus Middle East, Near East, Africa, and Oceania.

Compared with two or three decades ago, is Japan now more connected to East Asia than it is to other regions of the world? According to the Ministry of Finance (1977, 1991, 2004) statistics presented in table 6.1, Japanese FDI has been skewed toward the developed countries. The largest amount of Japanese FDI by value has gone to North America, primarily to tap the large United States market. From 1998, the European Union moved ahead of the United States as the major destination for Japanese FDI by value and was second overall by number of cases. Nevertheless, since the mid-1980s, Japanese FDI has become more geographically dispersed. East Asia now accounts for the largest number of manufacturing FDI cases, indicating that leading companies are drawing their affiliated small- and medium-sized firms out into this region. This trend emerged first in Northeast Asia (South Korea and Taiwan) and Singapore, shifted toward Southeast Asia (Indonesia and Thailand), and more recently appeared in China. Since 2000, a nominal increase in direct investment in the liberalizing Latin American countries of Mexico and Brazil is adding to the weight of developing regions in Japanese FDI figures.

If table 6.1 is reformatted into a scattergram to display the distribution of Japanese FDI by industry and level of economic development, companies are concentrated around a diagonal regression line that runs from the capital-intensive industries and tertiary-sector quadrant of the member countries of the Organisation for Economic Co-operation and Development down to the light industry and primary-sector quadrant of the developing countries (Ministry of Finance 2004). Between these two poles of economic development, Asia's newly industrializing economies attract Japanese FDI in medium and medium-high industries such as computers, metal products, and chemicals, whereas countries such as Malaysia and Thailand attract investments in medium technology items such as agri-products, nonferrous metals, electrical goods, and automotive parts and components.

The common perception holds that Japanese companies are becoming more involved in East Asia, but the statistical FDI snapshot does not make an obvious case that they have any special link to this region compared with other regions of the world. Petri (1993) argues that the current biased flow of Japanese FDI to developed countries is roughly similar to its prewar overseas investment patterns. Moreover, the "intensity" of Japan's FDI in East Asia (i.e., the ratio of intra-regional versus interregional FDI) has hovered around 20–25 percent, marginally lower than its FDI in North America and the European Union (Bank of Japan 2003; Dobson and Chia 1997). In turn, Japan has not received significant amounts of FDI from East Asian countries, underscoring a lack of reciprocity (Encarnation 1999). Indeed, Hatch and Yamamoto (1996) argue that Japanese FDI promotes regional integration in East Asia, but only as it is skewed toward Japan's "embrace."

Global Production Networks

A clear picture does not emerge from FDI statistics because they are based on bilateral transactions providing only a static snapshot. A more dynamic picture is required to represent the multilateral transactions and interactions that constitute Japanese GPNs; this picture reveals Japan's deepening economic ties to the East Asia region. One way to trace these linkages is to examine a company's business plan and then observe how its GPNs unfold.

Business Plan

A business plan is an organizational document stating a company's goals and the means for achieving those goals. In large companies, the formulation of a business plan is captured in the practice of *hoshin kanri* or policy deployment (Akao 1991). Small- and medium-sized firms are less likely to have a comprehensive business plan than are large firms, but key suppliers in a vertical *keiretsu* (intra-industry corporate grouping) are often drawn into the planning activities of the lead company if the latter moves abroad.

Two basic themes dominate a company's business plan: rationalization and diversification. Rationalization involves business activities designed to eliminate waste and to reduce operating costs. Diversification refers to a company's move up the value-added curve within an industry or its application of existing proprietary technology to produce new products in another industry (Urata and Nakakita 1991).

Over time, companies play these two themes out in their business plans. Rationalization is normally a central theme in the current-year and medium-term business goals. Examples include Japan's renowned *kamban* and just-in-time delivery systems, human resource management, concurrent engineering, and quality function deployment practices (Tachiki 1985). Top management expects eventually to reach a point of diminishing marginal return from rationalization activities, and so companies also strive to sequence the introduction of new products. For this reason, diversification through product development comes to dominate in medium- and long-term business goals. Kodama and Branscomb (1995) showed how companies have been relatively successful in either diversifying *within* their industry by moving up the technological ladder (e.g., using integrated circuit chips in calculators and then in computers) or diversifying *across* industries by applying an existing technology to create a new product in another industry (e.g., using integrated circuit chips in automobiles). Effectively balancing these dimensions has given many Japanese companies their competitive edge.

Until the late 1970s, rationalization plus diversification was the conventional business formula for executing an export-oriented strategy. Companies leveraged Japan's external dependence on energy and raw materials to turn out higher value-added intermediary and finished goods (Nakamura 1981). To be sure, large companies as well as small- and medium-sized firms have introduced a number of hit products over the years on the diversification side of the equation; however, what has distinctly set them apart from other foreign companies is their excellence in deploying the QCD function—that is, high quality, low cost, and short delivery times—the rationalization side of the equation (Womack, Jones, and Roos 1990). One need only contrast the consumer image in the 1950s of the label "Made in Japan" with that of the present to understand how successful this strategy has been.

In the 1980s, with the rise of mega-competition in their traditional product markets and the diffusion of their total quality methods to other countries, Japanese companies began to lose their competitive advantages, which pressured many of them to add geographical diversification to their management repertoire: to produce overseas those products that still retain strong consumer demand but cannot be competitively produced in Japan (Tachiki 1999). From a company's perspective, however, exploiting its "firm-specific advantages" is complicated and time-consuming. Usually there is a trade-off between a target country's production base profile and the operational demands required by a product: To procure from Japan, locally, or from a third country? To use expatriates or local managers? To use internal funds, debt, or equity financing? To tap local or international capital markets? To make business decisions at which location and by what means? One way they select among the trade-offs is through cross-functional management activities to vet an overseas production plan (Kurogane 1993).

When small- and medium-sized firms are drawn into the lead company's move overseas, the factors under consideration expand exponentially. Consequently any initial cost–benefit analysis usually ends with a company delaying plans to produce a product overseas. Working through these issues, however, leads eventually to an action plan that is a mix of domestic, regional, and global operational solutions for configuring the relocation of production overseas and which top management ultimately incorporates into the company's business plan (Tachiki 1999).

Segmentation Strategies

Depending on the mix of overseas business opportunities and the availability of organizational resources, an FDI strategy is skewed toward one of two generic types: segmentation by product or segmentation by function. Each has different implications for both regionalization and regionalism.

The most common GPN configuration is based on product segmentation. A company breaks down its product line from low to high value-added and manufactures each one in the most efficient location. In practice, this strategy results in manufacturing high value-added products in the home country, with low value-added products becoming candidates for either overseas production or discontinuation. Take the case of the videocassette recorder (VCR).

In the early 1980s, when the VCR was the latest consumer electronics innovation, all production was located in Japan. Soon after, as competitors from the Asian newly industrializing economies entered the consumer electronics market, Sanyo Corporation and later other electronics manufacturers began moving their VCR production to South Korea and Taiwan. At that time, these countries represented low-cost production bases with preferential access to markets in developed countries. Both characteristics reduced the intensifying competition and trade friction Japan was facing. Meanwhile, the nascent social and economic infrastructures in Southeast Asian countries made most of them less attractive destinations for such products (Mason 1999). When factor input costs rose in the Northeast Asian production bases in the early 1990s, however, Sharp Corporation was the first in what would become a procession of electronics companies shifting VCR production to their subsidiaries in selected member countries of ASEAN that had by then improved their trade and investment environment (Chowdhury and Islam 1993; Felker and Jomo 1999). Subsequently, as industrial restructuring proceeded in Japan, electronics manufacturers transferred production of ever more sophisticated electronic goods (e.g., audio equipment, large-screen televisions) to their subsidiaries in the Asian newly industrializing economies (Urata 2001).

This much of the economic regionalization story is consistent with theories of the product life cycle except for one important twist. Rather than the wholesale transfer of production for a product to an overseas subsidiary, the product itself can be further segmented, leading to intra-product segmentation. For instance, VCR components include nonmechanical parts, electric/electronic components, and core technologies. A company may procure the nonmechanical parts and the electric and electronic components locally when the VCR is assembled in Northeast Asia. But when the same company moves such production to developing Southeast Asian countries, many of these parts and components come from Japan and/or third countries. Regardless of location, the traditional Japanese supplier is usually exclusively responsible for manufacturing the key technology, in this case the magnetic head. An intra-product segmentation GPN leads initially to "technologyless industrialization" (Yoshihara 1988), but as a country moves up the technological ladder, this picture begins to change (Urata 1999). For example, in the mid- to late 1990s, as part of its Look East policy, Malaysia became not only the major manufacturing site for Japanese VCRs, with magnetic heads now procured from Singapore, but also, in the case of Toshiba Corporation, the main center for the related R & D, design, and engineering.

A perusal of the Toyo Keizai directory of overseas Japanese companies for the past few decades shows that such a product segmentation strategy occurred in a wide variety of industries, particularly those related to textiles and apparel, industrial machinery, electric machinery, chemicals, and transport equipment (Toyo Keizai 1985, 1990, 1995, 2000). The basic strategy was to "move the product, not the factory." As this approach gained momentum in the mid-1980s, a horizontal division of labor emerged within East Asia, with developing countries receiving FDI from companies in low technology products, the dynamic economies of Thailand and Malaysia from companies in low to medium-low technology products, and the Asian newly industrializing economies from companies in medium to medium-high technology products (Parker and Lee 2002). Paving the way for this pattern of economic regionalization were a company's interfirm networks as well as Japanese overseas development assistance (ODA) (Hatch and Yamamura 1996, Arase 1995). Following these contours, the GPNs for many individual companies in low- and medium-technology products began to stretch across East Asia.

A very different GPN configuration is based on the segmentation of business functions that involves taking products from concept to market (i.e., R & D ——➤ design and engineering ——➤ manufacturing ——➤ marketing and sales). A company usually reverses this sequence when moving overseas by starting with the sales and after-service segments, thus minimizing the initial direct investment exposure while acclimating the company to the nuances of a new market (Tachiki and Aoki 1992).

The automobile industry is a representative example. Into the early 1960s, the emerging but small market and weak supplier base in the East Asian countries led Japanese automakers to export rather than manufacture vehicles in the region. Toyota Motor's initial presence in Thailand, for example, began in 1956, with the establishment of the Toyota Motor Sales Company. In 1964, Toyota opened its first plant in North Samrong to assemble completely knocked-down vehicles for a nascent local market. Through the 1970s, as consumer demand grew, Toyota expanded plant capacity and increased local procurement of auto parts. The Toyota Motor case is consistent with a "transaction cost" approach, under which MNCs move between hierarchy and market, deciding whether to perform specific business functions in-house or to outsource for operational efficiency.

This host-country story gained a subregional dimension in the 1980s when the ASEAN governments adopted a brand-to-brand complementation scheme. Under this scheme, for example, Mitsubishi Motor, in local partnership with Proton Motor, began to procure vehicle parts and components from different Southeast Asian countries, import them to Malaysia at preferential tariff rates, and use them to meet local content rules for final assembly. Subsequently, Nissan and Hino in heavy trucks, Toyota in passenger cars and pickup trucks, and Honda in multipurpose vehicles pursued a similar subregional strategy, but with a regional headquarters, usually in Singapore, coordinating most of the related cross-border transactions and with final assembly plants located in Indonesia, the Philippines, and Thailand (Doner 2001). The ongoing interplay between global business strategies and national policies, then, sometimes takes unplanned detours toward economic regionalism.

The Thai government has leveraged this subregional trend to further position itself in the center of the automobile industry's GPNs. In 1993, it authorized the Board of Investment to grant preferential treatment to companies investing in fifty-seven underdeveloped provinces outside Bangkok. Foreign auto assemblers have been taking advantage of this rule to increase their direct investments to use Thailand as their manufacturing base for exporting specific vehicle models. Foreign suppliers, in turn, have been establishing niches in the manufacturing segments of raw material handling, casting and molding, pressed parts, and components in anticipation that Thailand will become the center for automobile assembly across Southeast Asia and beyond (Mukoyama 1994, Mori 2002).

Where this iterative interaction between business strategy and national policy gives rise to an industrial cluster, local companies have a better opportunity to position themselves in the backward (procurement) and forward (sales) cross-border segments of a GPN and reach out to the regional and global economy (UNCTAD 2001). Initially, an asymmetrical relationship existed between Japanese companies and local suppliers (Bernard and Ravenhill 1995), but Ministry of Economy, Trade, and Industry annual surveys of overseas subsidiaries show that they are deepening procurement and sales linkages in host countries and third countries, particularly in the industrial machinery, electrical machinery, and precision instruments industries in Northeast Asia, and the metal, electric machinery, and transport equipment industries in Southeast Asia (METI 1999, 2001, 2003). There are similar clusters of computer-related component suppliers in southern China (Mathews and Cho 2000; Zhu 2000); of IC chip design, engineering, and fabrication expertise in the Hsinchu Science-Based Industrial Park in Taiwan (Saxenian 1999; Amsden 2001); of consumer electric and electronic assembly in Penang and Johore in Malaysia (Urata 1999; Linden 2000); and of the auto parts and component suppliers in Thailand, especially along the East Coast (Doner 2001). In short, the concentration of Japanese FDI in a particular country portrayed in investment statistics is often embedded in a broader subregional GPN.

Network Governance

A segmentation strategy creates a dilemma for Japanese managers: how to coordinate geographically dispersed segments of a GPN for getting a product to market. In this regard, the governance structure for coordinating the product and business function segments escapes notice in most studies. For example, much of the total cost of a product is due to logistics and warehousing.

In moving its products across borders to reach the American market, Sony has established its own logistics company to reduce the cost and time for transporting goods between Malaysia and Singapore, but it is still dependent on independent shipping lines and airlines for eventual transport to the United States. Sony is also adopting new digital technologies (e-mail, mobile phones, etc.) for its information system, but these communications channels are not seamless within and across the developing East Asian countries, requiring continued dependence on analog technologies (telephone, fax machine, etc.). Moving in the opposite direction from goods is the payment system. To hedge against foreign currency risks, subsidiaries invoice nearly all transactions in U.S. dollars, and Sony's operational headquarter's finance division acts as the capital intermediary for all subsidiaries. These business practices reflect the underdeveloped capital and financial markets in East Asia (Tachiki 2000). To integrate the disjunctures in GPNs, Japanese companies rely on two common denominators for conducting business in East Asia: first their interfirm network of expatriates, and second their interpersonal network of ethnic Chinese (Tachiki 1993).

Japanese companies use expatriates where enforcement of intellectual property rights and coordination of business functions are weak. Expatriates provide a secure channel for transferring and protecting technology to an overseas subsidiary. In addition, where expatriates can fill the positions of senior managing director, plant manager, accountant, procurement, and quality assurance/control manager, there is better coordination over the flow of goods, people, money, and information across national borders (Tachiki and Aoki 1992).

Japanese companies commonly tap the interpersonal and business–government connections of the ethnic Chinese business community where their own interfirm relations are weak and/or the Japanese or host government fails to provide public goods. The chapter by Hamilton-Hart in this volume elaborates on the variations in the adaptive strategies of ethnic Chinese companies to fill these vacuums in the regional economy. Indeed, they played more than a bit part in Japanese FDI during the 1980s and 1990s. Among the Mitsui Group, for example, ethnic Chinese took part in an overwhelming majority of the joint ventures in East Asia (Tachiki 1993).

Sony's efforts to bridge the weak links in its GPNs, for example, center on its operational headquarters, Sony Electronics (SONIS before incorporation in 1999), located in Singapore. Sony Electronics consists of five companies covering corporate and regional services, sales and marketing, engineering and manufacturing, and professional support. It has an equity stake in the corporate subsidiaries operating in Southeast Asia. Among them, it has a 23 percent stake in Sony Electronics (Malaysia), located in the Prai Industrial Estate near Penang. A local partner owns 30 percent and the Sony Corporation the remaining 47 percent. Japanese expatriates manage the subsidiary and have introduced advanced operational and maintenance technologies. This plant produces consumer electronics goods, with high local content, mainly for the local and American markets. Sony Logistics delivers parts from suppliers for its Prai plant; it then picks up the finished products and delivers them by land transport to Johor Bahru, where it sorts and consolidates shipments through the Port of Singapore (formerly performed by Mitsui Soko), using Singapore's TradeNet customs clearing network. It then sends goods on regular shipping lines to the west coast of the United States. The parent company and the Singapore headquarters are linked to the point-of-sale system of major American retailers, such as Circuit City, enabling them to monitor consumer preferences and plan production schedules in the Prai Industrial Estate plant, bringing closure to its GPN for consumer electronics products.

Whether to take a majority or minority stake in a subsidiary and where to locate decision-making authority, then, depends on the degree of risk for disruptions in the product and business function segments of GPNs rather than a cultural business propensity. To be sure, the parent company in Japan still exercises control over its subsidiaries. Nevertheless, wholly owned subsidiaries account for only one-third of the Japanese FDI cases; the remaining joint venture cases are split equally between majority (greater than 50 percent) and minority ownership (Toyo Keizai 2003). Across these cases, we find that companies are willing to take less than 100 percent ownership of a subsidiary either where they want to spread their risks to a local, usually ethnic Chinese, partner or where a regional headquarters partially centralizes the decision-making process over government relations, financing, procurement, logistics/warehousing, and sales activities of all subsidiaries under its purview (Tachiki 1993). This more dynamic picture of business in East Asia is not captured by traditional FDI statistics.

Institutional Environment

Japanese companies must not only extend their GPNs across national borders, but they must also manage the opportunities and constraints in their business environment. In particular, changes in political, social, and legal frameworks shape the business environments that confront Japanese companies. Comparing these contextual factors before and after 1985 provides an analytical prism for understanding both the opportunities and the constraints on geographical location of GPNs.

The Plaza Accord triggered currency realignments in East Asia, but it is not a sufficient explanation for the surge in Japanese FDI after 1985. The 1970s saw not only yen shocks but also a series of oil shocks and intense trade conflicts, and these did not result in a high volume of FDI. Instead, Japanese companies successfully pursued domestic rationalization and diversification business plans. The main difference before and after 1985 is the institutional environment (Sumiya 2000). Company business plans sort through a complex mix of people, institutions, problems, and possible solutions. Before 1985, the institutional environment was defined by Japan's domestic iron triangle (Lincoln 1984; Trezise and Suzuki 1976). By the 1980s, however, the public and private sectors had developed an international dimension that opened the door for regional actors and solutions to enter the iron triangle.

Bottom-Up Linkages

Table 6.2 presents the key business organizations representing the interests of particular corporate constituencies. The Japan Chamber of Commerce and Industry (JCCI) has the broadest reach, with local chapters throughout Japan serving the needs of small- and medium-sized firms, whereas the Nippon Keidanren represents some of the most influential companies and associations in Japan. The Keizai Doyukai (Japan Association of Corporate Executives) provides a vehicle for business leaders of major corporations to express their individual opinions, and the Kankeiren (Kansai Economic Federation) consists of the major companies in the important industrial Kansai region of Japan. These institutions play an important intermediary role in strengthening the bottom-up linkages between Japanese companies and the Japanese government.

The key business organizations in the iron triangle have developed the organizational capacity to engage the emerging regional "epistemic communities" described in Evans's chapter in this volume through various organizations. The Japanese national secretariat for the Pacific Basin Economic Council (PBEC) is housed in the JCCI. The Japan National Committee for Pacific Economic Cooperation (JANCPEC) is housed in the Japan Institute for International Affairs, a foreign policy–oriented think tank affiliated with the Ministry of Foreign Affairs. Nippon Keidanren (Japan Federation of Economic Organizations after its merger with Nikkeiren) hosts the Japanese Supporting Council for the Asia Pacific Economic Cooperation (APEC) Business Advisory Council in cooperation with the Ministry of Economy, Trade, and Industry (METI, formerly called the MITI) and the Ministry of Foreign Affairs. The JCCI, Keizai Doyukai, and Kankeiren are major members of the supporting council.

In the 1980s, it became common to find someone seconded for two to five years from a keiretsu company, especially from the *sogo shosha* (general trading companies) and corporate-affiliated think tanks or research departments, to support these organizations and ministries in their economic cooperation activities. Because good business information is not always in the public domain and interpersonal relations are usually defined by keiretsu boundaries, a company's seconded personnel gain greater access to people and

Table 6.2. Partial listing of organizations promoting foreign direct investment

Government	Private
Japan	Industrial associations[a]
Ministry of Economy, Trade, and Industry: Institute of Developing Economies; Japan External Trade Organization; Research Institute of Economy, Trade, and Industry	Consultants: Engineering Consulting Firms Association, Japan; International Development Center of Japan; International Engineering Consultants Association; International Management Association of Japan, Inc.; Japan Port and Harbor Association; Japan Transport Consultants Association
Ministry of Foreign Affairs: Association for Promotion of International Cooperation; Foundation for Advanced Study on International Development; Japan Foundation; Japan Institute for International Affairs; Japan International Cooperation Agency	Think tanks[b]
	Training organizations: Association for Overseas Technical Scholarship; International Tourism Development Institute of Japan; Japan International Cooperation Exchange Center; Japan International Training Corporation; Overseas Vocational Training Association; Pacific Resource Exchange
Other economic ministries	
Financial agencies: Japan Bank for International Cooperation; Japan Development Bank	
Asia-Pacific Economic Cooperation (ASEAN) Centre	Companies and corporate foundations: Fujitsu; Mitsubishi; NEC; Nippon Foundation; NTT; Toyota Foundation
Key business organizations: Keizai Doyukai; Japan Chamber of Commerce and Industry; Kankeiren; Nippon Keidanren	
East Asia	Regional organizations: Pacific Asia Free Trade and Development Conference; Pacific Basin Economic Council; Pacific Economic Cooperation Council
Regional organizations: ASEAN; ASEAN + 3; Asia-Pacific Economic Cooperation	
Investment promotion agencies	Bilateral business councils; friendship committees and associations

[a] See Shiba 1991.
[b] See NIRA 2003.

information across the corporate world and in public institutions. Although this information-gathering channel does not always play a crucial role in corporate decision making, it does provide early warning for spotting emerging business trends in East Asia, such as ODA developments related to regional infrastructure (e.g., the Mekong Delta River project) as well as governmental policy shifts (e.g., liberalization of industrial sectors, changes in regulations). Companies can inject their economic interests into the policy arena through these channels.

By the mid-1980s, the keiretsu companies and their corporate networks were already well aware of the potential benefits of pursuing expanded business activities in East Asia. Because it normally takes a Japanese company a minimum of three to five years to investigate possible overseas production bases, the fact that many moved production overseas so quickly after the Plaza Accord indicates that this option was already queued up in many business plans.

Top-Down Linkages

Ministries usually initiate policy debates through their relevant divisions and bureaus and involve external experts and organizational representatives. The government uses an established committee format to convey and exchange ideas on national and international policies affecting the business community. The names vary, but the *iinkai* consist of high-level business representatives from their respective constituencies, and various subcommittees (*shoiinkai*) consist of recognized practitioners and experts who digest a vast range of information and present timely issues relevant to the business concerns of committee members. The subsequent role of the committee members is to advise and disseminate information through their organizational and individual networks.

With the expansion of ODA and OOF ("other official flows") allocations in the mid-1980s to promote FDI, the ministries have had the resources to award increased contract research to various external organizations. On trade and investments issues, the METI tends to funnel ODA research funds through the Research Institute of Economy, Trade, and Industry, the Institute for Developing Economies, and the Japan External Trade Organization (JETRO). The Japan Bank for International Cooperation (JBIC, established after a merger between the Export-Import Bank and the Overseas Economic Development Fund) tends to disburse its OOF through the JBIC Institute and related organizations (see table 6.2). On infrastructure issues, the METI, JBIC, Japan International Cooperation Agency (JICA), and economic ministries commission consulting associations (e.g., Engineering Consulting Firms Association), industrial associations, and specialized think tanks to conduct feasibility studies. These institutions may in turn subcontract research to various research institutes and experts. Such activities allow a wider circle of "elites" to participate in the policy debate within Japan.

Economic ministries not only gather a wide range of information in this way but they can also mediate different interests, thus ensuring that the core policy positions of the ministry are represented in any final report. In the case of trade and investment issues, this information is summarized in government white papers issued by METI and JETRO. Issues emanating from the policy community often have funding for technical assistance attached, which the JICA, in particular, administers (Arase 1995). Staff seconded from the economic ministries to the Japanese embassies in East Asia can monitor the local situation and convey their agencies' core policy positions to host governments and at international forums. In addition, METI career bureaucrats often staff the senior positions in the JETRO overseas offices, which work closely with the local JCCI chapter.

The business community adheres to policy fashions to the extent that these speak to their needs, but firms also pursue their own interests through multilateral and bilateral forums with their counterparts in East Asia. The JCCI engages in multilateral economic cooperation with East Asia through the

ASEAN–Japan Economic Council, the Confederation of Asia-Pacific Chambers of Commerce and Industry, and seven bilateral business councils. Moreover, it has local chapters in each of the major cities in East Asia, where the keiretsu companies usually rotate leadership of the local chapter. The Keizai Doyukai has been active at the multilateral level, especially at the ASEAN–Japan Business Meeting, and in 1981, it established the Japan ASEAN (now Asia) Investment Company. In addition, Kankeiren has taken an active role in promoting ties between the Kansai region of Japan and East Asia, particularly Southeast Asia, through its annual Global Business Opportunity Conference meeting in Osaka (this meeting is now online) as well as bilateral business council meetings. The Nippon Keidanren participates in the Confederation of Asia-Pacific Employers (CAPE) and supports bilateral business councils between East Asian countries not covered by the JCCI. In turn, some East Asian governments have established trade representative offices in Tokyo, such as the Economic Development Board (Singapore), the Malaysia Industrial Development Authority, and the Hong Kong Trade Organization. Companies pursue their individual business interests outside these arenas when their interests do not match the collective framework. Such government and business arenas are important channels through which the bottom-up regionalization story begins to converge on the top-down regionalism story.

Geography of Regionalization

As a result of intergovernmental bargaining and regional business interactions, East Asian governments create economic spaces—that is, arenas for business activities—that take the form of subregional groupings and regional infrastructures. Japanese companies converge on these economic spaces in locating their GPNs.

Subregional Groupings

By the mid-1980s, government policies for the accumulation and allocation of physical and human capital in the region began to tip the FDI playing field in favor of East Asian countries vis-à-vis other developing regions of the world (UNCTAD 1992; Chowdhury and Islam 1993; World Bank 1993). One way East Asian countries have distinguished themselves from other developing regions is in their movement toward regional economic cooperation—that is, policies and schemes promoting the flow of goods, people, money, and information across national borders. Into this regional arena, the PBEC, Pacific Asia Free Trade and Development Conference (PAFTAD), and the Pacific Economic Cooperation Council (PECC) have at different times and in combination formed the crucible for formulating the rationale and policies for economic cooperation in the Asia-Pacific region. Eventually such cooperation was formalized in the APEC forum (Woods 1993; Patrick 1997).

East Asian governments have taken action by establishing economic zones (e.g., export-processing zones). This allows East Asian governments to experiment with trade and investment policies in a limited geographical area so as to control the impact of liberalization on their economy. Beginning in 1966, Taiwan opened the first export-processing zone in the southern port city of Kaohsiung, and over the next forty-five years other countries followed by establishing more than 150 economic zones in the region (Asian Productivity Organization 1997).

Government efforts to enlarge the economic space in East Asia through the use of growth triangles extended government experiences with economic zones. A growth triangle involves neighboring countries agreeing informally or formally to combine their comparative advantages in resources, labor, and infrastructure. In Northeast Asia, these understandings have been more informal and driven by companies, especially Japanese and ethnic Chinese business networks (Naughton 1997). In contrast, the Singapore–Riau Islands–Johore growth triangle is more formal and is based on intergovernmental agreements, particularly the leg extending from Indonesia through the Riau Islands (Thant, Tang, and Kakaku 1998).

A free trade agreement is an even bigger step toward expanding regional economic space. Southeast Asian countries adopted an ASEAN free trade agreement in 1992. Northeast Asia has lagged behind. In 2002, however, China signed a framework agreement with the member countries of ASEAN to establish an ASEAN–China free trade agreement. The Japanese government is deviating from its purely multilateral approach to trade and investment and negotiating a series of regional trade agreements (Munakata 2001). Although the think tanks with ties to the METI and the Ministry of Foreign Affairs are the intellectual center for promoting regional trade agreements, the business community, especially the Nippon Keidanren, is also playing an active supporting role through the top-down and bottom-up institutional mechanisms now in place to engage East Asian countries.

Such subregional groupings are not randomly distributed across East Asia but appear as the developing countries liberalize and engage the global economy. In a measured stepwise intergovernmental bargaining process, the East Asian countries have selectively opened subregional economic space and moved farther down the liberalization road than their counterparts in other developing regions of the world.

Regional Infrastructure

Another way companies map East Asia is the extent to which the infrastructure of a country is "online and en route." The segmentation of products and business functions opens opportunities to those East Asian countries that can link and facilitate the associated cross-border flows. Some rough measures are the volume of goods handled by container ports, the number of passenger arrivals at international airports, the volume of international telephone calls carried by submarine cables and communication satellites, and the volume of transactions in capital markets.

On these measures, Yokohama, Kobe, Hong Kong, Singapore, Pusan, Kaohsiung, and Keelung rank among the top ten container ports in the world (JANCPEC 1992). The facilities at Changi Airport (Singapore) consistently receive high marks in world rankings, and Narita (Tokyo), Hong Kong, and Don Muang (Bangkok) international airports are among the busiest in the world (Pacific Asia Travel Association 1999). Tokyo and Hong Kong have become major securities and bond markets, and Singapore is an important foreign exchange market in the international flow of capital and financial products (Tachiki 2000). Submarine cables with a capacity of more than a thousand voice channels link North America via Japan, Hong Kong, and Singapore. In addition, Hong Kong (AsiaSat), Indonesia (Palapa), and other satellites create large communication footprints covering much of the Asia-Pacific region (International Telecommunications Union 2000).

On all these measures, Tokyo, Hong Kong, and Singapore have emerged as the primary hubs for the subregional and interregional flow of trade and investment from the western side of the Pacific Ocean (JANCPEC 1992; Rimmer 1997). By packaging their geographical centrality among the subregional groupings with world-class physical and organizational infrastructures (e.g., specialized legal and financial services, repairs and maintenance, social networks), these three Asian hub cities provide vital linkages to the global economy (Tachiki 1998).

Trade and Investment Corridors

Variations in subregional groupings and regional infrastructures highlight the continuities and discontinuities in the FDI investment map of East Asia. Where a dense network of institutions has emerged, East Asian countries have made significant strides in easing cross-border flows of goods, people, money, and information. In contrast, bottlenecks due to national limitations on landing rights, visa restrictions, incompatible communications hardware and software, and regulations on capital flows inhibit cross-border flows (JANCPEC 2003). This patchy business environment across East Asia affects the location choices of Japanese and, presumably, other companies.

Most Japanese GPNs are concentrated in several trade and investment corridors. Figure 6.1 shows one such corridor in Northeast Asia that coalesced in the late 1970s and early 1980s. Anchored at one end by Tokyo, the corridor runs down the coastal areas of South Korea, Taiwan, and China, and is anchored at the other end by Hong Kong. A similar trade and investment corridor emerged in the 1908s in Southeast Asia. It extends from Chiang Mai (Thailand and some extension now to Vietnam) through the western side of the Malay Peninsula, curves around Singapore with a narrow extension to Manila (the Philippines), continues to Jakarta, and ends in Surabaya (Indonesia). Significantly, fewer GPNs are found outside these trade and investment corridors, essentially the "new frontier countries" falling within two broad bands. Both bands originate from the Kamchatka peninsula on the Russian Pacific and run through inland China, but one leg extends to Indochina and the other leg extends to South Asia. In between these bands are the new frontier countries/regions of the Pacific Russia, inner China, Mongolia, Vietnam, Cambodia, Laos, Myanmar, and the South Asian countries.

According to the Toyo Keizai databank (1991, 1996, 2001), nearly three-fourths of the Japanese companies operating in East Asia are concentrated in these trade and investment corridors. Where the new frontier countries are adopting the principles of economic cooperation, joining subregional groupings, and building world-class infrastructures, companies have already shown a willingness to move their labor-intensive products to these countries (UNCTAD 2001). For example, southern China has become a major producer of personal computer–related components, and Vietnam is attracting textiles and household electric/electronics companies. This geographical distribution of FDI and GPNs defines the business boundaries of East Asia.

Between FDI and Regionalism

In contrast to the plain FDI statistics, a mapping of East Asia through the business plans of Japanese companies shows a strengthening of Japan's economic ties with its regional neighbors. Although Japanese FDI waxed and waned in the postwar era, the benefits of FDI were becoming clearer to Japanese managers in the 1980s; the bursting of the bubble economy in the 1990s, however, weighed them down with bad assets and overcapacity. In an effort to clean up their corporate debt, Japanese managers shifted the emphasis in their business plans from maximizing profits to rationalization. The 1990s was a period of corporate reorganization, especially after the 1997 Asian financial crisis, in which companies repositioned their FDI to consolidate geographically, especially out of Europe and the United States and into China. Moreover, Japanese companies were diversifying into proven medium and medium-high technology products and slowing the development of new products (Parker and Lee 2002). This lack of attention to emerging technologies and products is one reason Japanese companies have been late to the Internet revolution (Tachiki 2004).

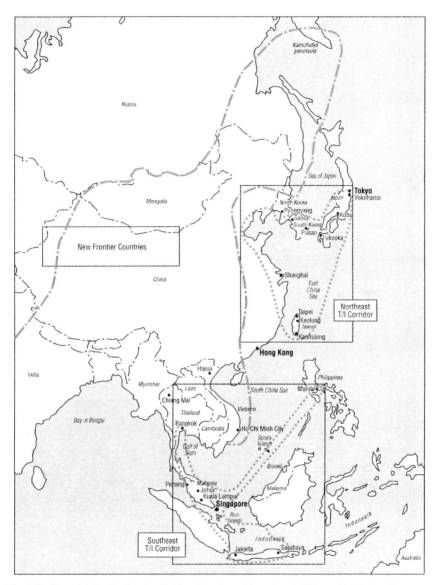

Fig. 6.1. Map of Asia showing the Northeast trade and investment (T/I) corridor (extending from Tokyo to Hong Kong), and the Southeast T/I corridor (from Chiang Mai, Thailand, to Surabaya, Indonesia, and Manila), and the New Frontier Countries of Pacific Russia, inner China, Mongolia, Vietnam, Cambodia, Laos, Myanmar, and South Asia.

As Japanese companies have entered the twenty-first century, they have been gradually focusing on the incorporation of information technology in their business practices. In the design segment, off-line concurrent engineering practices are giving way to online 3-D CAD/CAE techniques. In the manufacturing segment, Internet-based software for supply chain management and enterprise resource planning is merging with existing electronic data interchange–based just-in-time and *kamban* delivery systems. And in the sales and marketing segment, customer relations management software is expediting existing quality function deployment methods. Environmental management systems, especially life cycle assessment (from concept to market to disposal), are also affecting how companies organize their operations.

A rationalization strategy through FDI is just one dimension of a company's business plan. When we look at the diversification side of a business plan, we find that new products using nanotechnology, biotechnology, and information technology are becoming more evident in companies across industries. Since past experience suggests Japanese FDI follows rather than precedes diversification and domestic rationalization activities in a business plan, these emerging business strategies would lead us to expect in the future changes in the direction, scope, and depth of Japanese corporate economic regionalization activities in East Asia.

First, the organization of FDI into GPNs affects the direction of regionalism. As Japanese companies rotate the products in their GPNs in search of low-cost production bases, they will draw the new frontier countries—that is, Pacific Russia, inner China, Indo-China, and South Asia—closer into the regional economy. The easing of tensions on the Korean peninsula and the Taiwan Straits, the resolving of territorial disputes over the Northern Territories and the Spratly Islands, and economic cooperation in developing the Mekong Delta should eventually link the new frontier countries to existing trade and investment corridors and align them with the regional economy. In addition, the Japanese government has signed a free trade agreement with Singapore, and it is privately studying the possibility for bilateral free trade agreements with South Korea and Mexico. Such moves should create more opportunities for companies to expand their GPNs within the existing trade and investment corridors.

Second, the segmentation of GPNs affects the scope of regionalism. Japanese GPNs channel regional trade through a network of closely affiliated local suppliers and markets. As competitive pressures drive Japanese companies toward more open and decentralized GPNs, however, they are likely to seek access to local technology and business capacities (Kaburagi, Ikehara, and Izuishi 2000; JETRO 2002). Investment promotion agencies are restructuring to address this need by expanding their post-investment services. This is already requiring a repositioning of subregional groupings. A recent trend among economic zones involves a greater emphasis on capital and knowledge-intensive industries—for example, the Hsinchu Science-Based Industrial Park (Taiwan) and the Singapore Technology Park—signaling experimentation with science and technology policies. At the regional organization level, other issues affecting business that are attracting attention include a regional information technology infrastructure (e-Asia), regional security, and environmental protection.

Third, the institutional environments of GPNs affect the depth of regionalism. The FDI of Japanese companies is mainly concentrated in the manufacturing and commerce sectors, which biases regional policy discussions emanating from the private sector toward schemes for easing the intraregional flow of goods and services. Consequently there is a *broad* forum for regional integration on trade issues (ASEAN, APEC, PAFTAD, and PBEC), but the 1997 Asian financial crisis revealed the necessity to *deepen* it along monetary and political dimensions. The American and European MNCs are taking an active lead in the merger and acquisition of local financial services companies, which should deepen policy discussions to include the necessity for building a regional financial architecture and competition policy. In addition, some existing forums (e.g., APEC, ASEAN + 3, Asia–Europe Meeting) are taking up regional security issues and, especially since the events of September 11, 2001, those related to terrorism.

The 1985 Plaza Accord and the 1997 Asian financial crisis have had a significant impact on Japanese companies, but most surveys indicate that the majority will remain active in the region, with China the center of attention in the medium term (JETRO 2002; Marugami et al. 2003). This chapter has only sketched the broad features of Japanese GPNs and leaves for future studies the task of using the GPN as the unit of analysis to further articulate the ebb and flow in the direction, scope, and depth of the economic regionalization process.

7

The Regionalization of Southeast Asian Business:

Transnational Networks in National Contexts

NATASHA HAMILTON-HART

Business in Southeast Asia has had a regional dimension for a long time.[1] For businesses from Southeast Asia, regionalization involves a concentration of investment and trade interests in a loosely defined Asian region. For the global transnational corporations operating in Southeast Asia, regionalization means that their production processes and intra-firm structures are frequently organized on a regional basis. Europe and the United States are important economic partners, but transnational exchanges in Asia also have a regional orientation, particularly in terms of outward direct investment from Southeast Asia and firm-level trading and production systems. This chapter looks at the processes behind this internationalization and concurrent regionalization of business in Southeast Asia.

Investment and trade flows linking Southeast and Northeast Asia have been promoted by network-like relationships among firms and individuals. These relationships have fostered regionalization by reducing the costs and risks of transnational investment. Business strategies that involve a significant networking component are often analyzed in terms of the ethnic or national origins of the players involved: Japanese or, in the case of much of the investment carried out by individuals from Southeast Asia, Taiwan, and Hong Kong, ethnic Chinese. The familiar categorization of business systems as Chinese, Japanese, or Western, however, does not always correspond with differences in the way firms

I thank T. J. Pempel and other members of the Remapping Asia project who provided valuable comments at seminars sponsored by the Social Science Research Council and the Center for Global Partnership in February and June 2002.

1. Although this chapter looks at business activity from a Southeast Asian perspective, the relevant region here is not Southeast Asia but the western Pacific part of Asia.

operate in Asia because firms often change their strategies when they move to new institutional environments. Strategies such as forging personalized, non-market relationships are not equally rewarding in all national contexts, and business actors face incentives to adjust their behavior when they operate in different national jurisdictions. The interplay between firm and governmental attributes means that the processes behind regionalization in Asia are not static or uniform. Given this flexibility, the transnational economic linkages that have developed in Asia do not imply an exclusive or inward-looking region.

Business Networks, National Institutions, and Regional Integration

Networks describe a range of relationships that create linkages among firms or between firms and governments. They provide for exchanges that are neither strictly hierarchical (although they may be asymmetrical) nor conducted on purely arms-length, price-based terms.[2] These systems of exchange can provide benefits such as coordination, capital, risk minimization, and information. The different types of networking capacity that firms develop are commonly seen as a response to particular cultural forces or institutional conditions: embedded social norms, for example, or national governance systems that arise from economic endowments, political structures, and legal institutions (Orru, Biggart, and Hamilton 1997; Carney and Gedajlovic 2001). For example, where the legal system does not provide for secure property rights and reliable contract enforcement, private players have incentives to develop network-based alternatives that provide these functions. Businesses thus tend to acquire characteristics and strategies—including strategies of networking—that reflect the cultural and institutional contexts in which they are established.

What happens, however, when businesses with capacities derived from one context move abroad? One view is that they tend to bring their "national" business systems with them, with more or less economic success, depending on host-country conditions (Yeung 2002). For example, several observers have argued that as Japanese businesses expanded in Southeast Asia, interfirm relationships, *keiretsu* governance structures, and systems of collaboration with government actors—all developed in Japan—migrated with them. Enduring differences among transnational firms can be traced to national country of origin (Doremus et al. 1998). On the other hand, firms also adopt different strategies in different regional or national contexts (Encarnation 1992). Some firms in Southeast Asia pursue highly personalized network relationships in political and business spheres in both their home country and overseas; others acquire or jettison aspects of these strategies in different places.

---

2. Deyo and Doner (2001b, 6–21) provide a good theorized account of network forms of governance.

A firm's tendency to establish business and political networks is a product of firm-level attributes and strategic repertoires shaped by the context in which it was established, as well as more dynamic factors such as firm size and technological capacity. Whether these characteristics and strategies flourish overseas depends on at least two things. First is the *accessibility* of local networks in the host country. This in turn depends on how structurally open to outsiders they are and on the congruity between host-country business practices and those of the outside firm. Both private-sector (business–business) and political (government–business) networks vary in this regard. Interfirm governance systems in Japan, for example, do not seem to integrate non-Japanese actors easily. Governments also vary in terms of how easy it is for private actors to develop personal contacts with officials: some are relatively porous, making it easier for business actors to forge relationships with political actors; others are relatively closed to at least some forms of alliance with business.

Second, the *incentives* to penetrate host-country networks influence whether firms invest in doing so. The costs of failing to establish political connections, for example, may be relatively minor, or they may mean total exclusion from a market or uncertain legal protection. A firm moving into a country with a relatively liberal foreign investment regime and a consistent, rules-based regulatory system does not require special privileges or personalized political access. The more that national institutions provide secure property rights, contract enforcement, and transparency, the less do network forms of governance yield commercial advantages. Local alliances are more useful the more that regulatory systems create risks or obstacles for foreign investors.[3]

Taking these factors into account can help explain variations in business strategies. U.S. firms, for example, sometimes press for arms-length, rules-based institutions abroad, despite comparatively high levels of interfirm networking at home.[4] In contexts in which firms are outsiders, they may find that penetrating local networks involves adaptation costs that are higher than the costs of mobilizing "home" networks that grant them access to a wide range of economic and diplomatic resources. In addition, the extra-territorial reach of home country laws (such as the Foreign Corrupt Practices Act of 1977) may raise the costs associated with adaptation to local environments.[5] In contrast, where local networks are relatively open to U.S. firms (for example, microelectronics production networks involving Chinese and Taiwanese actors) or

3. Corruption, for example, makes foreign investors more likely to adopt joint venture partners than to establish wholly owned subsidiaries (Smarzynska and Wei 2000).

4. For example, in terms of both density and distance in patterns of interlocking board memberships, U.S. firms are similar to Hong Kong firms and considerably more deeply involved in interfirm networks than are British or Thai firms (Peng, Au, and Wang 2001, 168–70).

5. American firms do not seem to invest in relatively corrupt countries any less than do firms from other countries, but a recent analysis suggests they may be deterred from some forms of local networking (in this case, forming joint ventures with local partners) in these countries (Smarzynska and Wei 2000, 13).

where there are effective intermediaries (such as Hong Kong trading companies that occupy niche roles in facilitating market entry and distribution in China for Western firms), using local networks is a more rewarding strategy than bypassing them (Naughton 1997; Li 2001).

Similarly, although Japanese firms have made effective use of informal, personalized political access in countries such as Indonesia, such strategies are not characteristic of Japanese outward investment per se, even in Southeast Asia. No accounts of personal alliance building are found in descriptions of Japanese FDI in Singapore, and only rarely do they surface in relation to investments in Malaysia. In the United States, Japanese firms have invested a lot in attempts to gain political access, but they have done so in ways that show a general tendency to adapt to host-country practices by using lawyers, lobbyists, and public relations firms to protect their interests (Katzenstein and Tsujinaka 1995, 95–104).

The ability of firms to pursue a variety of networking strategies has allowed them to operate in a wide range of institutional conditions. Porous governing systems may fail to provide predictable, rule-based market and regulatory institutions, but they create scope for personalized cooperation with business actors, which can sometimes allow firms to circumvent national policies that restrict trade or investment flows. Weak and selective governing systems are also likely to motivate outward investment as a means of risk diversification and can facilitate other types of economic linkage. As Peter Dauvergne's (1997a) study of Japanese timber extraction in Southeast Asia has shown, the regulatory weakness of governments in Indonesia, the Philippines, and East Malaysia has been a critical factor sustaining this form of economic integration.

This does not mean that such regulatory environments are optimal, even for those who work profitably within them. Firms might prefer formal liberalization and impersonal regulation, but if these are not forthcoming, they may make use of (or acquire) networking capacities to secure informal concessions. This works only in sectors in which regulatory reliability is not important: resource extraction, for example, or low-technology manufacturing. Personalized interventions are unlikely to provide goods such as sophisticated public infrastructure, effective support for high-technology manufacturing, or guarantees that a joint venture partner will not use its superior ability to navigate the local legal system to the detriment of its foreign partner. Industries that depend on the provision of such benefits will probably not thrive in contexts in which they can secure only informal favors. Institutional context, therefore, is likely to influence the kind of transnational economic linkages that develop in particular locations, and it can help explain why regionalization in Asia has been consistent with significant asymmetries and widely varying national development trajectories.[6]

6. Whether extensive intercorporate and business–government networks are actually inimical to the creation of rules-based regulatory institutions is a separate issue from that of whether networks can themselves deliver the kind of functions associated with rules-based regulation.

Persistent Business Strategies and Regional Integration

The network governance systems of both Japanese and ethnic Chinese business have been important factors behind economic regionalization in Southeast Asia. Typically, ethnic Chinese business networks have some characteristics that differentiate them from Japanese networks (Hamilton 1996; Claessens, Djankov, and Lang 2000). For example, family control of the firm is typical of Chinese business, interfirm relationships tend to be personalized rather than institutionalized at the level of the firm, and collaboration with government actors is generally informal rather than publicly institutionalized. Most studies characterize Chinese businesses as more able to develop relationships with American and European firms than are Japanese firms, which are locked into more formalized interfirm collaborative structures, but there are many points of contact between Japanese and ethnic Chinese businesses in the region (Borrus, Ernst, and Haggard 2000; Deyo, Doner, and Hershberg 2001). Japanese and ethnic Chinese business actors have extended their presence in the region by using strategies that are broadly similar to those employed in their home environments. This kind of regionalization, in which an extant business model is transported overseas, is most evident where there is a level of congruence in the conditions provided by both home and host-country environments.

Japanese Firms in Southeast Asia

Japan's domestic business systems appear to have partially migrated to Southeast Asia in a process that began in the 1960s and accelerated with the surge of Japanese investment in the second half of the 1980s. The development of Japanese investment and trade in the region was supported by interfirm relationships, which provided coordination, capital, risk minimization, and information. These ventures also benefited from ties to Japanese governmental and quasi-governmental agencies (Pempel 1993; Arase 1995; Hatch and Yamamura 1996). The relationships among Japanese firms and between Japanese firms and the Japanese government can be seen as a set of informal institutions spanning public and private spheres. These institutions facilitated the regionalization of investment in Asia, where the Japanese government investment promotion efforts have also included many low-key initiatives involving host government officials (Doner 1997, 2001; Hatch 2002). The institutions structuring Japanese business activity have changed over time and for many firms are now less important. However, particularly in the case of early Japanese FDI in Southeast Asia, they provided coordination, infrastructural support, and access to capital, which facilitated the movement of relatively small firms, allowing them to reproduce overseas many of the conditions on which their economic success depended.

The extension of Japanese-style network forms of governance in the region was encouraged by a degree of fit between Japanese practices and local conditions. Strategies that included making use of personal links to political power holders, for example, were facilitated by a legacy of Japan's wartime presence in the region: a set of contacts in parts of Southeast Asia that were instrumental in paving the way for Japanese business involvement (Nishihara 1975; Shiraishi 1997). Local governing systems such as Indonesia's, with routines and structures that were already significantly personalized, were able to accommodate Japanese players relatively easily. Although there are plenty of cases in which Japanese firms have not been able to develop political relationships in Indonesia, there are also several cases of alleged direct payments by Japanese corporations to Indonesian political actors.[7] Even in countries where business–government ties are more formal and institutionalized, the widespread acceptance of government involvement in business in Southeast Asia means that the Japanese government's links to business are not, in general, perceived as problematic.[8] As widely noted, Japanese corporate governance systems that provide for management rather than shareholder control are well adapted to local requirements to take on joint venture partners.[9] Factors such as proximity, low costs, and pro-business governments provided the main incentive for investment, but more specific host-country conditions allowed Japanese actors to persist with broadly familiar business strategies in much of Southeast Asia.

Regional Investment by Ethnic Chinese Firms

By the 1990s, direct investment flows were dominated no longer by Japanese sources but by the newly industrialized countries of Northeast Asia and investors from lower-income but high-growth economies in Southeast Asia. Much of this investment was also structured by interfirm networks and network-like structures that provided information, distribution channels, finance, and political protection or favor. Most of this transnational business involving Southeast Asian, Taiwanese, and Hong Kong players was carried out by ethnic Chinese investors.

7. For example, several charges relating to payments by Japanese construction and other firms were investigated in both Japan and Indonesia in 1999. See Daily Yomiuri Online, April 8, 1999; Kompas, April 10, 14, 1991. Also, in early 1999, the head of the then governing Golkar Party, Akbar Tanjung, acknowledged that the party had received aid for agricultural projects from Japan's Liberal Democratic Party. This was denied by the Japanese embassy in Jakarta. See Kompas, March 25, 1999; Republika, March 26, 1999.

8. On convergence regarding some fundamental norms, including the acceptability of interfirm links and an active role for government in business, see Stubbs 1995.

9. In Malaysia, for example, Japanese transnational corporations have been comparatively willing to accept government requirements to take on locals in relatively passive ownership roles. See Jesudason 1989, 182–85. Restrictions on hiring Japanese management staff have been far more problematic.

Ethnic Chinese living in Southeast Asia make up a large part of the local private business sector. Their transnational, regionally focused operations are often built around relationships with other ethnic Chinese actors (Yeung 1998, 2002). As in the case of early Japanese FDI in Southeast Asia, interfirm relationships have allowed relatively small firms, which lack the resources to undertake transnational ventures individually, to move overseas. Most Taiwanese FDI in Southeast Asia, for example, has been carried out by small and medium enterprises that have relied on access to networks to provide business contacts and support, although they have not always been able to penetrate local informal networks successfully (Chen 1998).

Post-1978 reforms in China and increasing wealth in Southeast Asia allowed for the escalation of ethnic Chinese transnational trade and investment links. The growing density of these ties led to the emergence of a "greater China" economic area spanning southern China, Hong Kong, and Taiwan.[10] Some observers detected the contours of a larger "Chinese" economy stretching from southern China to Southeast Asia and parts of the wider Pacific area (e.g., Weidenbaum and Hughes 1996). An Asian orientation to the overseas business ties of ethnic Chinese can in part be attributed to earlier migration patterns from China, which disbursed family members, contacts, and know-how across the Pacific, but particularly in Southeast Asia (McKeown 1999). Complementarities between the business practices of ethnic Chinese in much of Southeast Asia and the requirements for operating in China can also explain a concentration of investment in the region. Many of Southeast Asia's ethnic Chinese businesspeople can draw on similarities (to some degree) in language and culture and, particularly in countries such as Indonesia, Thailand, and the Philippines, have developed skills useful for operating in opaque or discriminatory regulatory environments. Their resulting competitiveness in China, where the lack of a rules-based regulatory system means that the cultivation of personalized networks are an advantage, is part of the reason why ethnic Chinese account for a very high (albeit declining) share of total inward FDI to China (Wang 2001).

Individual firms have often been able to deploy business practices essentially similar to those developed at home. One example is provided by the Charoen Pokphand (CP) group, a Thai-based conglomerate with estimated group turnover in the mid-1990s of $6 billion to $7 billion per year.[11] Its main activity is agribusiness and related industries, but it also has interests in finance, manufacturing, and telecommunications. It began internationalizing its operations in the 1970s, first in Indonesia, then in Hong Kong, Singapore, and Taiwan. It made its first move into China in 1981, which by the

10. Although ethnic Chinese actors provided crucial linkages, American and other foreign investors were involved as partners in some of these transnational ventures. See Naughton 1997.

11. Unless otherwise specified, all information on CP comes from Pavida 2001.

mid-1990s was the primary source of group profits. Through the 1990s, it was reportedly the largest corporate investor in China (Peng, Au, and Wang 2001, 162). In China, CP followed a formula that had proved successful in Thailand and Indonesia: not only did it employ similar industry-specific strengths and sequencing strategies, but it also profited from playing the same role of intermediary between foreign suppliers of technology and local authorities. As Pavida argues, its networking strengths included being able to establish friendly ties that served as sources of finance, information, and political protection: "Similar to their domestic behavior, CP's ability to get involved in such diverse activities demonstrated the mastery of their networking skills. To Western or Thai companies that wanted to enter China but did not know the bureaucracy, CP's connections with Chinese authorities were extremely helpful" (Pavida 2001, 61).

Venturing into China is nothing new for many Southeast Asian businesses, whereas others have recently established enterprises there for the first time. Their willingness to do this reflects, in part, the sheer size and promise of the Chinese market. The ability to deploy skills and contacts acquired in home operations or prior activities in Hong Kong also makes investing in China promising. Malaysia-based Quek Leng Chan, for example, appears well positioned to move into China. In Singapore, his family owns the country's largest property developer and has a controlling interest in Hong Leong Asia, a publicly listed firm that, with the acquisition of three manufacturing and distribution firms in China at the end of 2001, realized more than 90 percent of its earnings in China (DBSVickers Securities, *Singapore Equity Research,* April 25, 2002). Quek Leng Chan controls the family's operations in Malaysia and owns extensive corporate assets in his own right. With the divestment of hotel assets in the United Kingdom and a particularly advantageous sale (for S$10 billion) of his bank in Hong Kong to Singapore's DBS Bank, Quek was said to be looking for new investment opportunities in China. In doing so, he is able to draw on years of experience managing and building up the operations of his bank and manufacturing interests in Malaysia. One of the skills that underpin his success there has been the ability to forge business and political alliances—and change them when necessary.[12]

The economic crises of 1997–98 caused a drop in outward investment from Southeast Asia, as many of the region's businesses struggled with high debt and drastic declines in profits. However, outward investment has partly revived and continues to maintain a regional orientation (Hamilton-Hart

---

12. In the 1970s, a local business ally introduced him to members of Malaysia's governing elite, who helped him acquire licenses for an insurance company and a finance company. In the early 1990s, Quek backed then finance minister Anwar Ibrahim and financially supported Anwar's business associates. With Anwar's fall in 1998, Quek switched his lobbying efforts to Mahathir. He was reportedly a major donor to the ruling coalition in its 1999 electoral campaign (Far Eastern Economic Review, August 9, 16, 2001).

2004). The strategies and capacities of many ethnic Chinese businesses in Southeast Asia still appear to work well in China. Among the players announcing plans to expand operations there are many of the region's wealthiest and most politically connected entrepreneurs, who have dense networks in both business and political fields.

The Widjaja Family: Sticking with a Familiar Formula

The benefits and risks of sticking with the same strategic repertoire across different institutional contexts can be highlighted by looking at Indonesia's Widjaja family. The Widjajas control what was one of Indonesia's largest conglomerates in the 1990s, a set of companies known as the Sinar Mas group, with major operations in banking, pulp and paper making, and agribusiness. The family's bank in Indonesia was, like most large private banks there, substantially nationalized in the wake of the financial crisis of 1998. Nonetheless, as late as 1999, the group looked set to weather the crisis much better than other Indonesian conglomerates. Instead, one of the Widjaja family's companies, Asia Pulp and Paper (APP), became Southeast Asia's single largest delinquent debtor when it stopped payment on liabilities of nearly $14 billion in March 2001.

Although many factors propelled the group's phenomenal expansion in the 1990s, a fairly constant business strategy can be discerned. The basic features of this strategy were majority ownership and management control by family members, connections with politically influential individuals, and maximum use of financial markets to raise funds from outsiders, both through gaining public listing and raising debt from banks and bondholders and through carrying out complex intra-group financial transfers.[13] Although no cases of fraud or illegal activity have been proved, the group has made a habit of testing regulatory limits. In contrast to some other ethnic Chinese businesses, most of the group's intercorporate connections are aimed at maintaining ties to politically influential people. For example, when their shared palm oil venture with Suharto's closest business ally, Liem Sioe Liong, ended in 1990, the elder Widjaja reportedly pressed hard to retain some connections with Liem's businesses, not for commercial reasons but because of Liem's personal influence with the president (Schwarz 1994, 114).

These practices have marked Widjaja family business activity both at home in Indonesia and abroad. Most of their actual operations in the paper and agribusiness industries are concentrated in Indonesia and China, where one

---

13. On the group's adroit use of rights issues that appeared to favor its majority shareholders, see Backman 1999, 114. In 1999 the family's previously insolvent bank in Indonesia was able to raise $677 million through a rights issue for recapitalization, possibly yielding as much as $100 million for the major shareholders (Far Eastern Economic Review, July 22, 1999).

family member (Peter Oei Hong Leong) also has an array of manufacturing and other investments, mostly joint ventures with state-owned enterprises. Oei Hong Leong is considered to have a wide set of personal political connections in China that date back to years spent there in the 1960s (Hamilton-Hart 2002, 133). High-level political contacts with Chinese officials continue to be visible. For example, Teguh Ganda Widjaja skipped a meeting with a group of creditors in Singapore in 2001 to meet Chinese prime minister Zhu Rongji, who was visiting Indonesia (*Far Eastern Economic Review*, February 14, 2002). APP continued to make investments in China, despite the company's creditors (to whom it was in default) having sought to halt all new borrowings. In May 2001, a subsidiary announced it had incurred liabilities of $225 million in the purchase of a 51 percent stake in a Chinese bank (*Straits Times*, May 4, 2001); and in early 2002, APP resumed construction of a pulp plant in China. Reportedly, the Chinese government helped arrange financing, which was secured through local Chinese banks (*Business Times*, May 28, 2002).

Widjaja family companies raised much of their finance on international markets. APP was listed on the New York Stock Exchange until 2001, when several class action suits were filed against it (and its auditors, Arthur Anderson, and investment bank Merrill Lynch) for failures to disclose liabilities (*Asiamoney*, November 2001). Singapore has been the family's main site for listing companies and arranging other forms of fund-raising. Their strategy there has involved some well-connected figures associated with the government. In January 1999, two former senior officials from the Monetary Authority of Singapore (the financial-sector regulator and de facto central bank) joined APP as advisers with a brief to focus on fund-raising, financial risk, and hedging (*Business Times*, January 23, 1999).[14] Also in 1999, a government MP and prominent businessman became a director of another Widjaja family company, publicly listed Asia Food and Properties (AFP).[15] He was also a director of a spin-off company, Golden Agri-Resources, which was able to raise about $350 million through its initial public listing that year. Golden Agri reportedly had joint venture agreements with one of the Singapore government's holding companies for oil palm industry investments in Asia (*Far Eastern Economic Review*, February 14, 2002).

14. One, Elizabeth Sam, had been a director of a large local bank, OCBC, for many years. The other, Koh Beng Seng, had left the MAS, of which he had been the deputy managing director, in mid-1997. Two former Indonesian central bank officials had been involved with the group's Indonesian bank (Bank Internasional Indonesia, Annual Report 1995).

15. Lew Syn Pau was an MP (1988–2001), businessman, and director of ten other companies in Singapore. He was also vice president of the Singapore Confederation of Industries (of which he became president in 2002). Between 1987 and 1994, he had held management positions in two companies owned by Singapore's primary union confederation (Asia Food and Properties, Annual Report 2001).

Problems at AFP and Golden Agri became apparent in 2001, when it became known that the two companies could not recover as much as $500 million placed with two privately held Widjaja family banks in offshore financial centers, which had lent this money to APP (*Asiamoney,* November 2001).[16] AFP's auditor issued a disclaimer on the company's 2001 financial statements, noting concerns about its S$2.8 billion in debts (assets at the time were valued at around $600 million) (*Business Times,* June 1, 2002). Widjaja family members and businesses have had some brushes with Singapore regulators. The country's commercial crime unit visited APP's headquarters in November 2001, but no action against the company was announced. Earlier that year, Oei Hong Leong's purchase of shares in a company at the time of its takeover by OCBC, a local bank of which he was a finance director, prompted OCBC to write to the Securities Commission. Oei launched a libel suit against OCBC but dropped the suit when OCBC withdrew its remarks and apologized (*Straits Times,* May 1, 2002).

The Widjaja family's persistence with the same business strategy at home and abroad is in one sense no different from the way other companies, like Thailand's CP group, have capitalized on their strengths. Like many firms from Southeast Asia, they have concentrated their businesses in locations where regulatory and market conditions are in some ways similar to those in the home context. Although incorporated in Singapore, the Widjajas' companies carry out their operations mainly in two locations: Indonesia and China. Singapore and New York, both used as fund-raising centers, appear to be rather different in terms of their regulatory institutions. Nonetheless, the Widjajas met with huge success and had few reasons to change their business practices; until the precarious nature of their companies' finances surfaced, they appeared credible to investors and creditors. Other business actors in Southeast Asia have either preemptively adjusted their business strategies according to environmental conditions or encountered more compelling incentives to do so.

Incentives to Adjust: Southeast Asian Businesses Abroad

Many businesses in Southeast Asia operate in a variety of institutional contexts. Because businesses are at least potentially flexible, however, regulatory and other differences have not posed insurmountable barriers to internationalization. Indonesian business actors, used to working in an uncertain and opaque regulatory environment at home, have responded to the challenges of working in different environments abroad. Singaporean firms operating

16. The exact amount is unclear. Other press accounts refer to "hundreds of millions of dollars" lent to these two banks. See Far Eastern Economic Review, February 14, 2002.

abroad also face incentives to adapt to the new institutional environments they encounter in places such as China.

Indonesian Businesses in Asia and the United States

Secure property rights regimes, politically friendly governments, and rules-based regulation have made Singapore and Hong Kong attractive destinations for investment from Indonesia. Although proximity, family relationships, and historical trading links have also encouraged investment, the contrast in political and regulatory conditions has been important. Singapore's role as a safe haven for regional investors—those anxious about unreliable government at home or simply wanting to avoid tax liabilities—is well known. It is something Singapore has encouraged by providing a stable environment and by limiting disclosure about the source of funds flowing into the country. Operating in Singapore's very different regulatory environment has prompted at least some inward investors to change strategies used in Indonesia and conform with local business practices.

The Singapore operations of Liem Sioe Liong illustrate this shift. The Liem family ran Indonesia's largest conglomerate, known as the Salim group, and gained notoriety for their close (and lucrative) personal connections to then president Suharto. Liem had business operations in Singapore since 1968 but retained a low profile there. In the late 1970s he took a stake in a major hotel and shopping center project, in conjunction with United Overseas Bank's Wee Cho Yaw as well as other ethnic Chinese businesspeople from Singapore and Hong Kong (*Straits Times,* December 5, 1979). Other shared interests with Wee include a stake in a large listed firm, United Industrial Corporation, acquired from fellow Indonesian Oei Hong Leong of the Widjaja family in 1990 (*Star,* January 3, 1991). In the mid-1990s, Liem's family used a Singapore-listed company to acquire a S$2.75 billion stake in their Indonesian assets (*Straits Times,* July 16, 1997). Liem thus has significant assets and operations in Singapore. His relationships there, however, have been limited to other corporate players; he does not appear to have recruited or cultivated government connections.[17] He has also maintained a clean reputation, avoiding allegations of insider trading or other improprieties.

The Liem family's ability to depersonalize their business is reflected in the management of First Pacific Company, their major investment vehicle in Hong Kong. In almost all accounts, First Pacific's management was substantially professional and the family had little involvement in its business decisions (Yeung

17. The fact that Lee Kuan Yew's brother held a stake in UIC has sometimes attracted comment. However, Lee sold his stake around the same time Liem bought into the company. Liem's intercorporate networking in Singapore has been less sustained than that of some other Indonesians who set up businesses there. See, for example, Liu 2001.

1998, 144). In the mid-1990s, ten out of twelve of its top executives came from foreign banks (*Business Week International,* September 2, 1996). Its chief executive, Manuel Pangilinan, was a professional manager originally from the Philippines. Through First Pacific, Liem was considered respectable enough to endow a chair at the Wharton School (where Pangilinan received his M.B.A. in 1968). Although First Pacific had a slow start, by the early 1990s it was thriving, having successfully turned around a Dutch trading company (acquired in 1983) and made several well-regarded investments in Asia. In 1998 the Dutch trading firm was sold for $1.7 billion (*Far Eastern Economic Review,* December 17, 1998), part of a declared refocusing of the group's assets toward Asia. One major post-1997 purchase was a controlling (24 percent) stake in PLDT, a large telecommunications firm in the Philippines, acquired for $750 million (*Business Times,* November 28, 1998). First Pacific also invested about $650 million for a 40 percent stake in one of the Liem family's Indonesian companies, Indofood, in 1999 (the stake was increased to 48 percent in 2001).

First Pacific's Pangilinan stood by these purchases even after its Southeast Asian strategy proved costly, with the company having to write off $1.7 billion in losses in 2001 (First Pacific, *Annual Report 2001*). The acquisition of Indofood confirmed the Liem family's ultimate influence over the company.[18] Earlier moves by First Pacific showed that its professional management kept an eye on changing political circumstances. With its post-1997 position in mind, the company sold a one-third interest in its Hong Kong bank to China's Ministry of Foreign Trade and Economic Cooperation in 1993. According to the bank's managing director, "It was almost a giveaway. We wanted to buy long-term stability" (*Business Week International,* September 2, 1996).

Pangilinan's ability to retain his image as a professional, Western-trained manager and simultaneously to capitalize on political connections where local conditions presented the opportunity was even more evident in his activity in the Philippines. Pangilinan had made some moves to cultivate former President Ramos in the early 1990s and had a personal connection with President Estrada, who was in power at the time First Pacific acquired its stake in PLDT. Pangilinan later admitted in an affidavit that he had issued a 20 million peso check for Estrada in November 1999.[19] He called it a "lawful election campaign contribution coming from my own personal funds," even though the donation was made seventeen months before elections were scheduled. PLDT was facing interconnection problems with a rival company

18. This potential for control was evident in the composition of its board of directors, which, in contrast to First Pacific's management, has always been dominated by long-term Liem family associates from Indonesia. The assertion of ownership control was dramatically illustrated in 2002, when First Pacific's decision to sell its major Philippine assets was openly opposed by Pangilinan (Philippine Daily Inquirer, May 30, 2002).

19. The following details are from the Philippine Center for Investigative Journalism 2002.

and a potential securities commission probe around this time. Both issues were settled after Pangilinan met with Estrada. According to another affidavit, earlier sales of PLDT shares by the government social security fund were made on Estrada's orders "for Manny [Pangilinan] to buy."[20] Pangilinan's continued flexibility and political engagement may be the reason why he largely escaped scrutiny in connection with official investigations into Estrada's alleged unlawful activities: he reportedly contributed a sizeable amount to help finance the protest rallies against Estrada that brought President Arroyo to power in January 2001.

Riady Family Ventures in Asia and the United States

The chameleon-like qualities of Liem Sioe Liong and Manuel Pangilinan are shared by another Indonesian business family, the Riadys. The Riadys' main businesses are carried out by various branches of the Lippo group, which was Indonesia's fourth-largest conglomerate in the 1990s. Lippo focused on financial services, investment, and property development. The group was established by an Indonesian banker, Mochtar Riady, and substantially run by his children. Although the Riadys are sometimes accused of employing an across-the-board strategy of cultivating personal political connections and exploiting minority shareholders (Backman 1999, 333–49), their business strategies in fact show some interesting variations according to location.

The Lippo group in Indonesia had good connections with government figures and other ethnic Chinese corporate actors. It was also able to thrive by taking advantage of buoyant market conditions and taking care to cultivate brokers and financial press analysts, which facilitated large-scale public fundraising exercises that left the family in control of the group's assets (Backman 1999, 334–45). However, the Riadys did not simply replicate these strategies in their U.S. or Singaporean operations. As revealed in the wake of a high-profile campaign finance scandal from 1997 onward, the Riadys actively sought political connections in the United States. The ways in which they did so, however, were largely in line with established practice there. If the Riadys had been U.S. nationals, their efforts to establish and maintain connections with President Bill Clinton and people associated with him would not have been abnormal.

The Riadys, who had established a bank with a local partner in Arkansas in the 1980s, were not the only people who followed Clinton to Washington after having financially supported his gubernatorial campaigns in the 1980s. Memos written by people associated with the Democratic Party suggest that

20. Despite healthy revenues, PLDT turned out to be costly for First Pacific. Its due diligence had failed to uncover extremely large debts of a subsidiary company (Far Eastern Economic Review, November 1, 2001).

it was normal to give consideration on the basis of financial support. For example, the organizer of a 1991 Democratic National Committee delegation to Hong Kong noted that James Riady's close associate in the United States, John Huang, "has agreed to host a high dollar event for us in Hong Kong with wealthy Asian bankers who are either U.S. permanent residents or with U.S. corporate ties. He will make sure that all of the hotel accommodations, meals, and transportation are paid for by his bank. He should be invited to be part of our delegation" (Committee on Government Reform and Oversight [CGRO] 1998, chap. 4, II.A.). The fact that fund-raising efforts would be rewarded by access to the president and positions within his administration again appeared entirely accepted. Hence John Huang's appointment to a position in the Department of Commerce came after a Lippo employee wrote to the deputy director of personnel that the Riadys had "invested heavily in the Clinton campaign. John is the Riady Family's top priority for placement because he is like one of their own" (CGRO 1998, chap. 4, III.A.). If the activities of many Americans associated with the Riadys are indicative, maintaining government contacts through employment, payment of generous retainers, and social visits forms part of established practice in Washington.[21] The Riadys do not seem to have imported anything foreign to the mix except themselves.

The fact that it all culminated in a major scandal—and that none of the Riadys' U.S. businesses were profitable—may suggest that their strategy was not effective. However, their commercial operations in the United States were very small in comparison with Lippo group interests in Asia. Further, they were successful in gaining what is probably the first consideration of any U.S. business that makes political donations: access. The fact that their access appears to have been used mainly for very general discussions is not surprising. The official enquiry into the affair could not uncover any material, personalized concessions granted to the family but argued that the administration's *policy* on issues such as most-favored-nation status for China might have been influenced by the Riadys. If so, the Riadys would have been only one of many corporate actors making their views on this matter known to the administration. This kind of benefit tends to confirm that political contacts are used in different ways in the United States and in Indonesia.[22]

---

21. These activities, many of which are apparently unrelated to advancing Riady family interests, are described in CGRO 1998, chap. 4. Offers to an incumbent president of a corporate directorship after he leaves office are not normally public news, which was the case for a reported offer by James Riady to Clinton (Far Eastern Economic Review, October 12, 2000), but movement between government and corporate positions is hardly unusual.

22. The U.S. Department of Justice's later case against James Riady and Lippo's California bank claimed that Riady sought more specific benefits at the local level (U.S. Department of Justice, press release, January 11, 2001). The California bank, however, did not avoid regulatory problems even during the Clinton administration.

The effectiveness of the Riady family's strategy in the United States can also be seen in terms of the gains it produced for them in Indonesia and China. Access to the administration probably "put the Riady family in a better position in Indonesia. For instance, surely the Riadys' stance with Indonesian President Soeharto grew when James Riady was able to organize a meeting between Clinton and Soeharto; something the Indonesian government appeared unable to do on its own" (CGRO 1998, chap. 4, IV.D). The concrete support from both political and business players that the Lippo group was able to achieve for some of its ventures in Indonesia confirms its considerable stature, which must have been strengthened by being able to display its connections to the U.S. president.

Even in the United States, the Riadys may have emerged relatively unscathed. After refusing to cooperate with the investigation into the campaign finance affair, James Riady eventually came to an agreement with the Department of Justice. In early 2001 he agreed to pay fines of $8.61 million levied against himself and Lippo Bank California to settle the case against him in connection with his campaign finance contributions (U.S. Department of Justice, press release, January 11, 2001). His personal liability for the fine, however, was reported elsewhere to be only $10,000, the rest being due from the former Lippo Bank California (*Business Times,* January 13, 2001). Riady had sold this bank for $16 million in 1998 (*Business Times,* November 11, 1998), and his ongoing liabilities to the bank are not publicly known.

The Riadys have not always been successful in their business ventures, but they do appear to be sensitive to the particular incentives and opportunities provided by different host countries. Operations in Singapore provide further evidence of their ability to adjust their approach. The family's main business in Singapore is a listed food-making and investment company, Auric Pacific, in which it acquired majority control in 1997. It was affected in 2001 by write-downs in the value of some investments, but apart from this modest loss, it has attracted very little attention. Auric has not cooperated with local business partners or cultivated people with Singapore government connections, even though most of its activity is in Singapore. Although a 22 percent stake in Auric was held by a government-linked company, Parkway Holdings, the Riadys have shown so little concern for this relationship that they ousted its representatives from the board in 2001.[23] Apart from the Parkway representatives, most of Auric's directors have been either Lippo family members or people whose high-level connections are not in Singapore. For example, Richard Woolcott, Australia's former ambassador to Indonesia, was brought onto the board in 2001 (but he lost his board seat, apparently due to Parkway's efforts, in 2002) (*Business Times,* May 23,

---

23. Parkway, primarily a health care provider, has since announced its intention to divest its interest in Auric.

2002). Two other directors are people with extensive personal connections, but they are almost entirely Hong Kong based.[24]

Singapore Businesses in Asia

Singaporeans have substantial direct investments in Asia, a pattern of outward investment that reflects both proximity and sustained home government support for developing the "external wing" of Singapore's economy (Rodan 1993; Department of Statistics 2001). Many of Singapore's largest companies, such as government-linked Singapore Telecommunications (SingTel) and the Development Bank of Singapore (DBS), have recently invested billions of dollars in the region to acquire assets, support existing partnerships, or establish new ventures in Australia, China, Hong Kong, the Philippines, and Thailand. SingTel now realizes about one-third of its operating revenue overseas, mostly in the broad Asian region, a proportion that has been rising steadily since the late 1990s (SingTel, *Full Financial Report 2000/2001,* press release, May 9, 2002). DBS has an explicit strategy of focusing on the region, declaring its mission to be "building the best bank in Asia," and has made several investments in banks in Southeast Asia and Hong Kong since the financial crisis (DBS, *Annual Report 2001*). Other government-linked companies (GLCs) have also invested in Thai banks since 1998, and one has been an important provider of capital to one of Thailand's most successful auto parts manufacturers (Deyo and Doner 2001a).

An increasing amount of Singaporean outward investment is going to China, where Singapore was, cumulatively, the fifth-largest investor by the end of the first quarter of 2002 (*Straits Times,* May 30, 2002).[25] How have Singaporean companies operated in a country that has a very different set of regulatory and legal institutions from those in Singapore? Singaporean investment in China has been substantially government led, part of an explicit policy of regionalization launched in the early 1990s (Rodan 1993). Although some investment in China had begun independently, a study of listed companies in Singapore showed that the pickup in their investments in the region lagged the government's policy (Tsang 2001). Government leadership and prodding for the regionalization drive included substantial direct investment by GLCs and statutory authorities (Yeung 2002).

In China, Singapore has also used senior politicians such as former prime minister Lee Kuan Yew to mobilize Chinese political support. Two major projects have been the establishment of industrial parks, one in Suzhou, the other

---

24. One was a director of one of Hong Kong's largest securities houses, the other a Lippo manager in Hong Kong who was also a member of the Hong Kong Broadcasting Authority and council member of the City University of Hong Kong.

25. The largest investors were the United States, Japan, Taiwan, and Hong Kong.

in Wuxi.[26] The industrial parks were to attract foreign investment—including investment from Singaporean manufacturing companies—by providing enclaves of reliable infrastructure and efficient, Singapore-style management. The companies that established the two Singapore-linked parks were both joint ventures between Singapore consortiums (led by GLCs) and local Chinese partners: a state-owned business in the case of the Suzhou Industrial Park, local government in the case of the Wuxi park. Although some firms were attracted by the Singapore brand name, both projects ran into significant problems arising in part from particular difficulties that Singapore GLCs faced in adjusting to the political and regulatory environment in China.

According to a manager of the company set up to develop the Suzhou Industrial Park, "normal" companies could use whatever means to make a profit: "You can be above table, under table, back door, front door or whatever you think of, but not for us. Number one we cannot embarrass the Singapore government" (quoted in Yeung 2000, 831–32). Indeed, an article in the Chinese press noted that because of "strict laws and regulations, and drawing on Singapore's experience of honest and clean government, not a single civil servant in the park's administrative committee has broken the law or committed a crime" (quoted in Yeung 2000, 831–32). Squeaky clean operations and high-level political support might underpin successful industrial parks in Singapore, but in China the lack of flexibility and attention to local government priorities caused problems for the Suzhou Industrial Park from the start. In particular, despite assurances of support from Beijing, the provincial government did not stop promoting its rival industrial park (*Business Times,* June 11, 2001).

After failing for years to resolve these problems, Singapore ceded its majority stake in the joint venture to the Chinese in January 2001. At that time, cumulative losses stood at $77 million in invested equity plus shareholders' loans of $160 million. Things started to change after the transfer of management control. This was attributed by the Singapore side to better support from the Chinese because their interests were now "better aligned." For example, when the park was controlled by the Singaporeans, in addition to contending with local government attempts to divert the same investors that the joint venture was pursing, they had had to take on full costs of providing basic infrastructure, which were expected to have been paid for by local authorities (*Business Times,* May 5, 2001; Yeung 2000). The park made its first profit ($7.6 million) in 2001 and looked set to realize further profits in 2002 (*Business Times,* May 29, 2002). Despite being judged a more successful venture because of greater autonomy and flexibility given to the Singaporean partners (Yeung 2000), the Wuxi park too ended up being transferred to majority

---

26. Unless otherwise stated, information on these industrial parks in China is drawn from Yeung 2000, 2002.

Chinese ownership. The park had shown losses ever since its first two years of operation (1993–95), and in early 2002, the Singaporean consortium cut its stake from 70 to 49 percent and gave up management control. According to the Singaporean GLC leading the venture until then, with the municipal government in charge, there would be a "better alignment of interests." The GLC intended to divest its interest completely once the price was right (*Straits Times*, May 14, 2002).

Clearly, Singaporean companies investing in China need to acquire skills and strategies that are different from those employed in Singapore. As shown by the example of Singapore's second largest bank, United Overseas Bank (UOB), venturing into China requires some adaptation even for private companies. A controlling interest in UOB is held by Wee Cho Yaw's family, which also owns substantial shares in a major diversified conglomerate and property companies. UOB acquired another large Singapore bank in 2001, Overseas Union Bank, and thereby became the largest foreign bank in Malaysia. After the financial crisis it also acquired major stakes in relatively small banks in the Philippines and Thailand. Wee Cho Yaw plays a significant role in running the family's assets, and his son plays a management role in UOB. In the past, Wee Cho Yaw enjoyed good relations and a number of personnel and joint venture connections with the Singapore government. He has also, at various times, been linked to several wealthy ethnic Chinese business actors from Hong Kong and Indonesia (Hamilton-Hart 2002, 94–96, 135). Despite this experience, Wee Cho Yaw expressed caution about entering China, where UOB was invited to take minority stakes in several local banks. He described his strategy there in these terms: "We build up contacts and then we work and grow together with the local banks. We will slowly build up there—to understand their culture and their system, then we can move into China and work with them" (*Business Times*, April 1, 2002).

The government is trying to help companies understand the culture and the system in places like China. In addition to financial incentives and support for overseas operations, government agencies are providing management training for Singaporean companies extending their operations in the region. For example, in 2000 the Economic Development Board, Singapore's lead industrial development agency, awarded aid to eighteen companies under its Overseas Enterprise Incentive initiative and trained 147 Singapore managers under a regionalization scheme (Economic Development Board, *Annual Report 2001*). A new program was launched in 2001 to train up to five hundred Singaporeans to be "Asian business experts." The minister of trade and industry said that the training program aimed to "build a core of future business leaders who have deep knowledge and strong links to the region." He said that Singaporeans needed to deepen their knowledge of important countries in Asia and widen their networks in the region (*Straits Times*, October 25, 2001). Despite being made up mostly of ethnic Chinese,

Singaporean companies apparently do not naturally have the skills to operate in the region.

Regional Implications

The processes of private sector–led economic integration described here suggest that regionalization in Asia continues to be facilitated by various forms of intercorporate and business–government collaboration. The network-like relationships that support transnational economic activity in the region tend to be informal and private, even when they include public-sector players. This does not mean that integrative trends are taking Asia toward a closed form of regionalism based on opaque, impenetrable networks. Rather, integrative processes at work point toward three implications at the regional level.

First, there is no uniform set of "Asian" business practices that prevails in the region. Outward investment from Southeast Asia is not replicating the earlier wave of Japanese FDI in the region, which was concentrated in long-term manufacturing projects. It is more sectorally diversified and, whether undertaken by medium-sized firms or units of large conglomerates, tends to be less institutionally coordinated. With the exception of some FDI by Singaporean firms, Southeast Asian outward investment also receives less support from home government initiatives than does Japanese manufacturing FDI in the region. In addition, there is variation that cuts across the familiar distinctions drawn between Japanese and ethnic Chinese business practices. Japanese and ethnic Chinese firms operating in Southeast Asia have expanded their overseas activity by using a variety of strategies involving different degrees of reliance on business and political networks. Their networking strategies are adaptive responses to environmental conditions. They are acquired, modified, and discarded according to time and place. As market conditions and the institutional environment in the region change, firms register strong incentives to change the way they do business. Although the examples given show that not all firms respond to these incentives, some modifications in firm strategy according to location are evident.

Second, the processes behind economic integration may be largely informal, but this does not preclude formal intergovernmental regional cooperation. Informal network governance systems face some inherent limits in what they can achieve and do not remove incentives for collective action on a range of issues, including managing the downstream effects of closer integration (Doner 1997). Private sector–led regionalization can thus stimulate demands for formal cooperation, which has become an increasingly important objective for Asian governments since 1997 (Stubbs 2002; Terada 2003). To the extent that formal cooperation creates a more open, transparent, and rules-based environment, it is likely to decrease the salience of network forms of governance that compensate for uncertain or restrictive regulatory environments. Other functions supplied by network governance systems, such as providing for reduced risk, information, or coordination, are likely to endure to the extent that market conditions make them rewarding.

Third, regionalization is not antagonistic to the development of broader trade and investment links. The current regional concentration of certain economic exchanges is partly based on a congruence between initial firm strengths and the business environment in parts of Asia. However, economic ties are also a function of proximity, growth potential, and economic complementarities. Given these incentives, firms will make efforts to adapt, if necessary, to different institutional environments. Although the cases of adaptation discussed in the preceding section involve firms from Southeast Asia, the ability to navigate political uncertainty by developing the right personal links and partnerships is not limited to firms with Asian origins. One example that illustrates this capacity on the part of non-Asian firms comes from the recent sale of a controlling stake in what had been Indonesia's largest private bank, Bank Central Asia (BCA).[27] After many delays, the winning bidder for BCA turned out to be a consortium headed by Farallon Capital, an American investment fund whose local partners were an Indonesian family that owns a cigarette-manufacturing company. Neither group had any experience running a bank (*Far Eastern Economic Review*, March 28, 2002). Standard Chartered Bank (British, but with a Southeast Asian businessman as its single largest shareholder) had been widely expected to win the bid: it was a well-run bank, familiar with the region, and able to provide BCA with technical expertise. According to the Indonesian minister overseeing the sale, its marginally higher offer was rejected because its conditions were too stiff. Another factor working in Farallon's favor turned out to have been securing the good offices of Hubert Neiss—at the time, chairman of Deutsche Bank Asia but better known as the IMF's representative who had dealt with Indonesia from 1997 onward.[28]

Such anecdotes are supported by the aggregate data on investment inflows to Asia: although there remains a regional concentration to some direct investment flows, American and European investors have made significant purchases and loans, especially since 1997 (Hamilton-Hart 2004). Some investors may be more able than others to develop appropriate business and political relationships in countries such as Indonesia and China, but investors

27. BCA, formerly owned by Liem and Suharto family members, was nationalized by the Indonesian government after massive runs on the bank in 1998.

28. According to Neiss, Deutsche Bank Asia had signed an agreement with Farallon to provide advisory and risk management services should it win the bid for BCA. Neiss was involved in the bidding process, personally explaining to the Indonesian authorities the role Deutsche Bank Asia would play if Farallon secured the bid and outlining its vision for how BCA would operate (Business Times, March 20, 2002).

from a variety of backgrounds have shown a capacity to develop these ties when necessary. It is the case that firms build on existing strengths and strategic repertoires, so some patterns distinguish prototypical firms from different ethnic or national backgrounds. Complementarity between network-based modes of business and governing systems in much of Southeast Asia and China has encouraged the diffusion of these business practices in the region. But political networking does not characterize all businesses operating in the region. If some investors have pursued similar, personalized, strategies regardless of where they are located, others have selectively modified their business strategies according to local conditions.

III

REGIONAL LINKAGES: INSTITUTIONS, INTERESTS, IDENTITIES

8

Between Regionalism and Regionalization: Policy Networks and the Nascent East Asian Institutional Identity

PAUL EVANS

The chapters in this volume share a common interest in the material forces of firm-driven trade, investment, and production that are deepening economic integration in proximate parts of continental and maritime Asia.

The less-developed twin of this integration from the bottom up is the process of state-led institution building from the top down. Over the past decade, the institutional fabric of East Asia has become richer and more densely textured. On a bilateral basis, the number of summits and exchanges has increased substantially. And on a multilateral basis, an incipient regionalism has developed in three layers: formal governmental organizations including ASEAN, APEC, the ASEAN Regional Forum (ARF), and, more recently, the Shanghai Cooperation Organization; various track II channels for dialogue on economic, political, security, environmental, and other transnational issues; and civil society–based activity involving actors such as NGOs, regional advocacy groups, and professional and business associations. "Although it is underdeveloped," observed a Korean academic, "regionalism in Asia is complicated enough" (Han 2002, 1).

The author is grateful to the Abe Fellowship program administered by the Social Science Research Council and the Canadian International Development Agency for research and travel support. Thanks also to some twenty-five officials and academics, twenty of them in Asia, for interviews on various aspects of East Asian regionalism. Special thanks to Amitav Acharya, Han Sung-Joo, John Ravenhill, Richard Stubbs, Simon Tay, T. J. Pempel, and the other authors in this volume for their comments on earlier drafts.

However complicated and innovative the new regionalism has been, the prevailing opinion inside and outside Asia is that regionalism is more talked about than acted upon and that the major intergovernmental institutions have lost momentum or stagnated. A recent review of ASEAN and APEC began with the question "Are the principal regional organizations in the East Asian and Asia-Pacific regions moribund or verging on it?" (Webber 2001, 340).

In contrast to the projects for building nation-states and national economies after the Second World War, the project for region building lacks a clear objective, a shared vision, and strong political support. Political leaders in East Asia express an awareness of regional developments and frequently float proposals for various kinds of joint projects and regional institutions. But they expend very little energy persuading domestic constituencies about the importance of these ideas and devote very few resources to their implementation.

The advocates of regionalism face a recurring conundrum. How do you create strong intergovernmental organizations in a context of exceptional diversity in which states are unwilling to transfer sovereignty to intergovernmental institutions, especially regional ones? The underlying premise of the "ASEAN Way" and its successor, the "Asia-Pacific Way," was that it is possible to have high levels of cooperation with low levels of institutionalization. Step-by-step incremental progress, a comfort level for all, consensus, and peer pressure were portrayed as superior to strong intergovernmental organizations with independent staffs and special expertise, rules, and enforcement mechanisms (Acharya 1997). The approach has proven unsuccessful in dealing with several recent problems, including the economic crisis, East Timor, and the haze problem, bringing into question the effectiveness of regional institutions. When swift action is needed on a regional issue in Southeast or Northeast Asia, the instruments and actors have almost always included extra-regional players, especially but not exclusively the United States.

If regionalization is the expression of increased commercial and human transactions in a defined geographical space, regionalism is the expression of a common sense of identity and destiny combined with the creation of institutions that express that identity and shape collective action. Caught between aspirations for building multilateral cooperation and political realities constraining it, regionalism in East Asia often takes hybrid forms that frequently blur the distinction between governmental and nongovernmental. In this context, the multiple forms of track II dialogues have special meaning. As agents of what Anthony Milner has called "a relentless conversation," they are playing essential roles in providing the rationale for regionalism, finding a consensus among policy elites for moving regionalism forward, and shaping the governmental institutions that aim to make regionalism effective.

This chapter considers both governmental (especially ASEAN + 3 [APT][1]) and nongovernmental initiatives to promote regionalism. Although some see East Asian regionalism as a competitor to an American-centered set of arrangements, I argue that the thrust of most of the track II processes is to find ways to make them compatible, at least in the short and medium term.

East Asian Regionalism and the APT

As T. J. Pempel outlines in his introductory chapter, the twentieth century spawned several attempts to create intra-Asian regionalism. Doing so on an East Asian basis has precedents in the Chinese imperial system and the Japanese-led Greater East Asian Co-Prosperity Sphere of the 1930s. It is a major conceptual and political leap to connect what in the postwar period has been seen as the separate regions of Southeast Asia and Northeast Asia. The current formulation of "East Asia" has its material foundations in the changing pattern of production, trade, and investment commencing in the mid-1980s after the Plaza Accord.[2] In 1990 Prime Minister Mahathir of Malaysia first advocated an East Asian economic grouping. Although the proposal met heavy resistance across the Pacific in North America and Australia and in several parts of Asia, it echoed in regional discussions throughout the 1990s, becoming, in the words of Lee Kuan Yew, "an idea that would not go away." The basic thrust of the proposal, minus the anti-Western rhetoric, was channeled into the East Asia Economic Caucus within APEC and then reappeared

1. I've chosen the phrase ASEAN + 3, and the acronym APT, mainly for the aesthetic symmetry with ASEAN and APEC. A characteristic feature of Asia Pacific institutions is that the names are often awkward (Asia-Pacific mixes continents and oceans), seldom complete (consider Gareth Evans's famous quip about APEC being four adjectives in search of a noun), and eternally contested (should Asia Pacific have a hyphen?). What I am calling APT is presented in most official forums as ASEAN + 3 and by other analysts in combinations that include ASEAN 10 + 3, 10 + 3, and, for the cheekier, 3 + 10. Sometimes this represents confusion, but there is also a hidden codethat using the numbers rather than letters signifies that the real unit of analysis is individual states rather than ASEAN as an organization. The term 3 + 10 highlights the role of the Northeast Asian three in providing the resources and primary initiative for the process.

2. For those educated in North America under the influence of John Fairbank and Edwin Reischauer or their students, the concept of East Asia in the APT context is very different from the idea of East Asia as the Sinic or Confucian culture area. American ideas about defining Southeast Asia have had a major impact inside Southeast Asia itself, but this has not been the case with the idea of East Asia. I speculate that much of the discussion of naming has been driven by English-speaking Southeast Asians (especially in Singapore) who were educated either in Europe or outside of Harvard. Key individuals from Japan, China, and South Korea were aware of the Sinic underpinnings of "East Asia" Harvard-style and redefined it to be more acceptable to their Southeast Asian colleagues worried about any return to Middle Kingdomism and Chinese hegemony. The Fairbank and Reischauer conception based on civilizational and cultural commonalities plus hierarchy has thus given way to a definition based on interactions and nominal equality forged within the region itself (Evans 2000).

in 1996 in the ASEAN-led Asian component of preparations for the Asia–Europe Summit (ASEM) process (Terada 2003). The definition of the region that includes the members of ASEAN plus China, Japan, and South Korea and excludes North America, Australia and New Zealand, and South Asia, has been contested but has proven durable and underwrites most of the contemporary initiatives promoting East Asian regionalism.

What explains the new interest in creating deeper cooperation on an *East Asian* basis? Most accounts begin with the deepening economic interactions that followed the Plaza Accord in 1985 and emphasize the material and psychological consequences of the economic crisis that began in 1997. Fred Bergsten argues that the advocates of East Asian regionalism are "motivated by a large number of factors in moving toward creating their own institutional identity," with part of the motivation "defensive and reactive while part is positive and even visionary" (Bergsten 2001, 7).

E. A 지역주의
가데고리.

The arguments in favor of East Asian regionalism normally fall into one of three categories, which Simon Tay has conveniently identified as function, identity, and geopolitical weight (Tay 2002, 104). The first argues for regionalism as a means of deepening functional cooperation to manage an increasingly interdependent regional economy and the political forces that accompany it.[3] A number of economists inside and outside East Asia have stressed the virtues of regional cooperation in areas such as trade facilitation and financial monitoring and surveillance (Dobson 2001; Pacific Economic Cooperation Council [PECC] 2002). In the eyes of many Asian economists, the mistakes that produced and, to some, amplified the economic crisis of 1997 should never again be allowed to reoccur. And a variety of business analysts not only see the increase in intra-regional trade but also endorse it to fuel future export growth. On a political level, functionalist arguments have taken several turns, one of them being that an East Asian process can go beyond ASEAN and APEC in establishing deeper societal involvement; in fostering developmental objectives related to poverty, illiteracy, equity, and social justice; and, most simply, in dealing with transnational problems that need concerted regional action. Other variants are that East Asian regionalism can revitalize a sagging ASEAN (Wanandi 1999), reposition ASEAN as the hinge of a balanced set of interregional institutions including ASEM, APEC, and Latin America (Soesastro 2001), and provide "new diplomatic glue" for Northeast Asia (Alatas 2001).

---

3. Although economists are persuaded that interactions within East Asia are increasing, they differ on whether the level of dependence and interdependence with countries outside East Asia, especially the United States, is decreasing. Every East Asian country except Japan does at least half of its trading with other countries in East Asia (and the percentage is rising), yet the United States remains the principal economic partner for most. A BRIE team states the case even more strongly: "the overwhelming direction of the principal axes of interaction . . . go[es] the wrong way: From one Asian nation after another, they run not to other Asian nations but to the United States" (Cohen 2002, 7).

2)   The second sees regionalism as a reflection and <u>amplifier of an underlying regional identity or consciousness</u>. This takes several forms. One is that there are common Asian aspirations and, for some, values that can unify the region and give it a distinctive character. The commonality of identity can take positive or negative forms. Simon Tay looks toward a new East Asia that can provide the space for a new generation of cosmopolitan Asians (Tay 2002, 103). Others see the commonality as the <u>"feeling of humiliation</u> shared by many East Asian countries" after the economic crisis (Kikuchi 2002, 17), the "politics of resentment" that came in its wake (Higgott 1998a; Bowles 2002), or, with a materialist twist, the preservation of a distinctive form of capitalism in the face of outside pressure (Stubbs 2002).[4]

3)   The third argument for regionalism is as <u>a collective call to action for increasing East Asian weight in the world</u> and, at least to some, <u>counterbalancing the influence of the United States</u>. Fred Bergsten points to the Asian desire to reduce excessive dependence on outside institutions, especially "the IFI's based in Washington, the authorities of the United States, and the private (predominantly Anglo-Saxon) markets that took their cues from both" (Bergsten 2000, 3). In part, this is an insurance policy in the event that the global trading system deteriorates or regional blocs in Europe and North America become more protectionist and assertive. Put in more positive form, there is the argument that East Asia needs to have a stronger voice in global institutions, including the WTO and the international financial institutions. The other side of the coin is the view that a stronger East Asia is necessary to defend Asian economic and security interests in an era of rising American power and to prepare the way for a more mature and self-regarding regional formation (Higgott 1998a).

Structures and Proposals

Although the APT aspires to play the central role in promoting East Asian regionalism, it is just one element of a much wider set of activities that have been developing since 1997 on an East Asian basis.[5] On the monetary and financial side, they include the Miyazawa Initiative of October 1998 for bilateral (as compared with regional) swap arrangements with Malaysia and South Korea; sustained support within several governments for the creation of some

---

4. Richard Stubbs has described this as "a form of capitalism that is quite distinct from either European or North American forms of capitalism. The East Asian form of capitalism, which is increasingly found in the APT countries, is rooted in business networks—both Japanese and ethnic Chinese networks—and is characterized by strong state-business links. It emphasizes production rather than consumption, and results rather than ideology, and tends to place a premium on market share as opposed to short-term profits. East Asian capitalism is also based much more on social obligation and social trust than the rule of law" (Stubbs 2002, 7).

5. These are in addition to the plethora of proposals for what in this context can be identified as separate "subregional" activities within Northeast Asia and Southeast Asia.

kind of Asian Monetary Fund; the Chiang Mai Initiative to create a regional arrangement for orchestrating currency swaps at moments of crisis; monetary cooperation through the Network of Bilateral Swap Arrangements; the Manila Framework Group focused on early warning mechanisms; regular meetings of groups such as the executives of East Asian and Pacific Central Banks (see Dobson 2001; Ravenhill 2002); and recent attempts to create an Asian bond market (Asian Development Bank 2003).

On the trade side, there have been numerous proposals for new arrangements on a bilateral and regional basis. Most significant are the proposal for a China–ASEAN free trade area and the organization of an ASEAN–China Trade Negotiating Committee to create a framework for implementation; the proposal by Prime Minister Koizumi for a Japan–ASEAN comprehensive economic partnership and the creation of an experts' group to examine implementation; proposals for a 10 + 3 free trade area as exemplified in the report of the East Asia Vision Group (EAVG); a proposal for a regional free trade area that would also include Taiwan; and the welter of proposals and negotiations for bilateral "free trade" or "economic partnerships," including examples such Singapore–Japan (Ravenhill 2003).

The ASEAN + 3 Process

APT is the most ambitious and comprehensive of the governmental efforts to create an institutional framework to support East Asian regionalism. Although only five years old, it is "generating a buzz" (Wain 2000, 4), according to journalists, and academics have claimed that it "now has the potential to become the dominant regional institution in East Asia" (Stubbs 2002, 441).[6] It appears to have high-level political support, as seen in the regular summits of heads of state, and combines procedural modesty with far-reaching ambitions. None of its proponents live or die on the basis of APT's success. Almost all have a realistic sense of proportion about its current prospects and capabilities and support it as nothing more than one pillar of the regional institutional architecture. Yet although APT is a call for economic cooperation, it is also in some minds a search for a new identity or, more precisely, elements of a new identity. As an institution, APT, like APEC before it, has the double burden of promoting pragmatic, interest-based cooperation at the

6. There is a small but well-informed and lively literature on the APT process and the broader theme of East Asian regionalism. For example, there is a debate between political economists and neo-classical economists about whether the principal motivation is East Asia defending a particular form of capitalism (Bowles 2002; Stubbs 2002) or, alternatively, adjusting to universal market realities in a new way (Dobson 2001). Beyond differences born of national perspective and personal temperament, there seem to be continental divisions on the significance of the process. Europeans tend to see it destined for failure until it takes the inevitable turn to supra-national institutionalization. North Americans sometimes share the skepticism but are not as consistent or demanding in spelling out prescriptions. Australians are skeptical but want in.

same time as building the rationale and instruments for deeper integration structured on some kind of "community" basis.

APT can be categorized as a consultative process involving thirteen governments. Its operational definition was inherited from the ASEAN-led effort to create a process for Asian consultation in advance of the ASEM. The ASEAN 10 (nine initially) were joined by the three most important economies in Northeast Asia, with Taiwan excluded for explicitly political reasons.

Most of the bureaucrats in individual ministries around the region handle APT issues in a broader portfolio that includes APEC, ASEM, and the associated track II activities. APT does not yet have a permanent secretariat or facility, although the ASEAN secretariat provides some element of coordination and the Malaysian government has been promoting Kuala Lumpur as the site of a new APT secretariat, offering US$10 million to establish the facility (Abdullah 2002). It currently functions as a rolling series of meetings at three levels. The first involves the heads of government and has included annual leaders' meetings (Kuala Lumpur, December 1997; Hanoi, November 1998; Manila, November 1999; Singapore, November 2000; Brunei, November 2001; Phnom Penh, November 2002). The second involves ministerial-level meetings of economic and finance ministers. The third involves senior officials from ministries and agencies, including patent offices, science and technology, and working groups. In addition, APT has commissioned various nongovernmental study groups, including the EAVG, and others looking at regionwide monetary integration and free trade. Although significant, activity at the governmental or track II level pales in comparison with that of the better-developed APEC process, with its working groups, meetings, and network of study centers.

The many obstacles to APT success and progress are frequently recited. The diversity of cultures, political and economic systems, and levels of development is only slightly less than in APEC. Unlike the EU, in APT there is no common aspiration to democracy, and there are enormous variations in administrative, technocratic, and intellectual capacity among the participating states, with little chance that these inequalities will be addressed or resolved in the near future. The inherent asymmetry between the economic clout of ASEAN and the Northeast Asian three is considerable, with the combined GDP of the latter some nine times higher than the former. On the political side, there is no single country capable of or, arguably, interested in leading the process. Indeed, it appears that APT can move forward only if no single state is seen as playing the dominant role. The reaction of Washington is also important, with most arguing that strong opposition to the APT, as in the case of the East Asian Economic Grouping and Asian Monetary Fund, would slow or stop its development. Others convinced that APT is essentially about economic cooperation believe that it will gradually disappear if the world trading system moves forward. Even its strongest boosters are modest about its significance and role. Han Sung-Joo, chair of the EAVG, predicted that "the process will go on, but a slow but steady pace" (Han 2002, 7).

Ranged against this APT skepticism is the widespread view that East Asia is an idea whose time has come. As phrased in the EAVG report, "While the pace of building an East Asian community is uncertain, the direction is clear and the trend currently underway is irreversible" (EAVG 2001, x). Several leaders are calling for the transformation of APT into an East Asian summit process, thus moving toward a new regional structure rather than just regional cooperation. "It is shameful," claims the Malaysian prime minister, "that the countries of East Asia have to hide behind other names like ASEAN plus Three in order for them to get together" (Mahathir 2002, para. 32).

Nongovernmental Policy Networks

The APT is a formal governmental process, and its main proponents have been national leaders, chief among them Prime Minister Mahathir bin Mohamad in Malaysia and, at an earlier point, then president Kim Dae-jung in South Korea.[7] There was no formal track II process organized on an East Asian basis preceding the APT, because the Pacific Economic Cooperation Council (PECC) preceded APEC and the Council for Security Cooperation in Asia Pacific (CSCAP) preceded the ARF. And the APT was initiated by government officials largely insulated and removed from expert groups. NGOs and the private sector (excepting Japanese, Korean, and Chinese trade associations interested in doing business in other parts of East Asia) have shown little interest in the process.

It is thus tempting to treat APT as a state-driven process playing catch-up with the on-the-ground economic realities of regionalization. It is similarly tempting to treat APT as the reflection of state interests in which national governments have defined the agenda, direction, and pace of East Asian regionalism, with the outside policy experts left to find a rationale and fill in the blanks. The reality is more complicated.

The APT claims the energies and imaginations of probably no more than five or six hundred people. Their interactions represent the connection between bottom-up (recognizing that "the bottom" comprises sophisticated societal elites) and top-down processes. Here there has been considerable activity and advocacy initiated by a shifting but coherent group of individuals and institutes in Asia and including some in Europe, Australasia, and North America. What role have nongovernmental and track II processes played in

---

7. Only Mahathir has provided consistent support for East Asian regionalism for more than a decade and made it a policy priority, as seen, for example, in the rejection of bilateral free trade agreements on the grounds that they will weaken ASEAN and a broader process like APT (Ravenhill 2003, 304).

the emergence of East Asian regionalism? And what have been the major debates inside them? Who are the actors? How are they connected?

Conceptualizing and categorizing these "nongovernmental" actors is a tricky enterprise. The idea of "epistemic communities" has the advantage of focusing on idea-based groups operating transnationally. The groups operating in Asia often do appear to share a set of normative and principled beliefs, a value-based rationale for their actions, a common policy enterprise, and similar discursive practices. But they rarely meet the exacting conditions of shared causal beliefs and shared notions of validity (Haas 1992, 3). Some of these groups do fit this more demanding definition, among them advocacy groups concerned with environmental, human rights, and nonproliferation issues as well as some of the economists, business groups (e.g., Pacific Asia Free Trade and Development Conference and Pacific Basin Economic Council), and professional associations. Yet the institutionalized track II processes, including PECC and CSCAP, function more as brokerage than advocacy groups. They reach consensus only at fairly high levels of abstraction and focus on building processes for exchange among policy elites on a range of issues without an agreed set of preferred policy outcomes.

More helpful, though less precise, is John Ruggie's idea of an episteme, adapted from Michel Foucault, which refers to a "dominant way of looking at social reality, a set of shared symbols and references, mutual expectations and a mutual predictability of intention" (Ruggie 1975, 569–70). If the episteme is treated as a process rather than a starting point, it accurately captures the evolutionary dialogue activities that are bringing together individuals from very different national settings who hold very different ideas and then move toward a kind of consensual knowledge that they hold in common.

Richard Higgott uses the ideas of policy networks and policy communities. A policy network is "constituted by its membership . . . and the linkages that structure interaction" (Higgott 1994, 373). A policy community is a more formalized relationship "characterized by the identification of an emerging set of institutionalized relations between non-governmental and governmental members of a policy network to facilitate policymaking and policy implementation" (373). Writing in 1994, he concluded that there were several policy networks in operation but that they had not yet reached the stage of policy communities.

Whether described as policy networks or epistemic communities (in the relaxed sense of the term), the groups promoting East Asian regionalism have several defining characteristics. With the single exception of the definition of the region (East Asia, not Asia Pacific), these are strikingly similar to the operation of policy networks in the broader Asia Pacific setting.

1. They primarily aspire to influence government decision making, usually at a national level and occasionally at the regional and global levels. In most minds

the objective is to influence governments rather than create a transnational civil society separate from them.

2. They are close to government in several ways. Governments often fund them, shape the agendas, select or influence the selection of participants, lend their prestige to the individuals from their countries, and are the principal targets of the policy advice emerging from discussions. The distinction between governmental and nongovernmental players is often blurred, with officials participating in various track II activities in their private capacities and, in several countries, with today's official becoming tomorrow's "outside expert," and the reverse. This produces some complex terminology: "unofficial but not nongovernmental," "quasi-governmental," "semi-governmental." The vocabulary of track I and track II is revealing not only because it accurately portrays the two processes as at least tending in the same direction but because it has now been refined and expanded to include "track 1.5," "track 1.25," and so forth, as well as the new "track III" (Capie and Evans 2002).

3. Although some of the participants can be considered "experts" on the basis of education and professional standing, especially among the economists who come close to having the theoretical consistency and standards that are the foundations for an epistemic community, most are generalists, some but not all with advanced education outside Asia in institutions in North America, Europe, and Australasia. If there are commonalities of opinion and outlook, they are as much a product of interaction in the incessant parade of meetings as they are of earlier upbringing or shared scientific training. This raises the possibility that there is indeed a core group of regionalists, veterans of years and in some cases decades of constant interaction in regional forums, creating a perspective different from their national ones. If and as this happens, networks can become communities. T. J. Pempel's observation that Asian elites have in the past been more likely to meet on American campuses than in Asia is no longer true: contemporary regionalists tend to congregate in Asian hotels around the hollow squares that host regional experts' groups or dialogues.[8]

4. The commonalities lie in the ability to operate in English (the working language of both East Asian and Asia Pacific regionalism) and in knowledge of regional issues as well as the policy context of their domestic settings. Digging deeper, there is usually a common commitment to internationalism, rationalism, and economic liberalism.[9]

Where and how have these policy networks or epistemic communities connected with East Asia? They fall into three categories. The first is processes that have been generated in an Asia Pacific context; the second in the context of

8. The Dialogue and Research Monitor (http://www.jcie.or.jp/drm/index.html) chronicles almost six hundred multilateral meetings on security matters alone in the period 1994–2002.

9. In outlook and worldview, there are a variety of similarities to the views analyzed in Tomoko Akami's thoughtful dissection of the main lines of thinking in the Institute of Pacific Relations in the 1920s and 1930s. The principal differences are the wider range of national perspectives and the almost unanimous support of market mechanisms and more liberalized trade in the contemporary discourse (Akami 2002; Woods 1993).

the Asia–Europe meetings; and the third in the context of state-sponsored and initiated processes within East Asia itself.

It is ironic that many of the formative discussions about East Asia have taken place in dialogue settings established with a different understanding of the geographical footprint of the "region for cooperation." The objectives and modalities of an East Asian regional grouping have been part of discussions in the context of APEC and around the margins of ASEAN meetings. At the track II or nongovernmental level, the idea of East Asia received extensive attention in dozens of meetings nominally organized on an Asia Pacific basis, including such annual events as the Asia-Pacific Roundtable in Kuala Lumpur.[10] The Asia Pacific Agenda Project organized by the Japan Center for International Exchange is instructive in that the vocabulary is Asia Pacific but the agenda and participants are heavily East Asian focused. At the annual meetings in Cebu in 2001 and Siem Reap in 2002, roughly only five of eighty participants came from outside East Asia.

Not all Asia Pacific dialogue channels are sympathetic to the arguments for East Asian regionalism, even when it is presented as compatible with and supportive of Asia Pacific institution building.[11] Some of the non-Asian participants are wary of any form of activity that will potentially compete with global multilateralism in the form of the WTO or the international financial institutions, and they are concerned about the political implications of "drawing a line in the Pacific." Some of the Asian participants do not see any need for an explicitly East Asian formulation, either because it has the potential to undercut ASEAN coherence or because it risks reducing American involvement in the region.

Yet most of the participants in Asia Pacific processes are either supportive or neutral concerning the creation of a separate East Asian process. And tellingly, many of the strongest Asian proponents of ASEAN, APEC, the ARF, and the attendant track II processes are also active proponents of East Asian regionalism and the APT.[12]

The ASEM process and its attendant track II process, the Council for Asia Europe Cooperation, were explicitly fashioned as "intercivilizational dialogues" and have provided multiple opportunities for the Asian participants

10. The use of a hyphen with the term Asia-Pacific was often code for defining the region on the basis of East Asia but including participants from other places (e.g., North America, Australia, Europe) in the discussions. For some, East Asia has always been the unspoken center of Asia-Pacific.

11. This becomes even more evident if we take into account the fact that policy makers in most Asian countries tend to see bilateral relations as more important to their immediate futures than any form of incipient multilateralism. See the study of Japan by Okawara and Katzenstein (2001).

12. Individuals who have supported Asia Pacific and East Asian institution building include Narongchai Akrasanee, Chia Siou Yue, Jesus Estanislao, Han Sung-Joo, Mohamed Jawhar Hassan, Carolina Hernandez, Hadi Soesastro, Noordin Sopiee, Tanaka Akihiko, Simon Tay, Jusuf Wanandi, Tadashi Yamamoto, and Zhang Yunling.

(defined operationally as East Asia) to meet regularly and with the intention of creating an "Asian" perspective or agenda. They have been acknowledged as the impetus for the current version of the idea of Asians meeting with Asians. This was a very rare occurrence in the four decades after the demise of the intra-Asian conferences in the mid-1950s, including the Bandung Conference in 1955.

On an explicitly East Asian basis, several channels for discussion have been created since 1997. There are a variety of experts' groups, involving research institutes from key countries, meeting bilaterally and regionally to look at issues including free trade arrangements. Several institutes in Asia, among them the Institute for Southeast Asian Studies in Singapore, the Korean Institute for Economic Policy, the ASEAN Institutes for Strategic and International Studies, the Nomura Research Institute, the institutes connected with METI in Japan, and the Chinese Academy of Social Sciences, have organized intra-Asian meetings on a bilateral and regional basis in the past five years, with East Asian regionalism and the APT process as main agenda items. The Boao Forum in Hainan and other explicitly "Asian" meetings (note that Australia is considered an integral part of East Asia for the purposes of the Boao meeting) are expanding in number, the most recent addition being the Asian Cooperation Dialogue led by the Thai prime minister and involving mainly foreign ministers from the APT countries (except for Myanmar) as well as Bahrain, Bangladesh, India, Pakistan, and Qatar.

The most intensive and comprehensive of these nongovernmental processes has been the East Asia Vision Group. Created in response to a proposal by then president Kim Dae-jung and chaired by Han Sung-Joo, a Korean academic who had served as foreign minister and later became ambassador to the United States, the EAVG consisted of two nongovernmental representatives selected by each of the thirteen countries in the APT. It held five meetings between the summer of 1999 and November 2001, when it delivered its report to the meeting of the thirteen heads of government in Brunei. It was tasked to deliberate on the ultimate goals of East Asian cooperation, how these goals could be achieved, and what institutional framework is required.

The final report staked out an ambitious objective: "We have reached a consensus that we should envision East Asia as evolving from a region of nations to a bona fide regional community, a community aimed at working toward peace, prosperity and progress. We are agreed on the necessity of such cooperation in all aspects of society." It then outlined more than seventy proposals for expanding cooperation in these areas, perhaps the most significant being the creation of an East Asian free trade area, expansion of the framework agreement on an ASEAN investment area, establishment of a self-help regional facility for financial cooperation, strengthening of the regional monitoring and surveillance process in East Asia, a focus on poverty alleviation, promotion of regional identity and consciousness, evolution of the annual

APT summits into an East Asian summit, and establishment of a nongovernmental East Asia forum to serve as the institutional mechanism for broad-based social exchanges.

The report did not define the ingredients of community except in abstract terms ("shared challenges, common aspirations and a parallel destiny") and did not mention the concepts of democracy, supra-national institutions, or civil society. Economics as the catalyst and the value of trust and understanding are familiar refrains in regional discussions. And although the report was state-centric, it also alluded to the need to go "beyond government efforts to involve the broader society and the people of the region." It went further than most of the APEC and ASEAN discourse in explicitly mentioning the value of NGOs, especially in the context of environmental issues, and in using ideas like "cooperative security," "human security," and "good governance." Although emphasizing the value of liberalization, market openness, and globalization, it supported a broader agenda that included poverty alleviation, developmental assistance, social justice, and equity.

The EAVG report was presented to the APT Summit in November 2001 and then referred to the East Asia Study Group (EASG), composed of senior officials, which was tasked to come up with concrete action. In its own analysis of the EAVG's fifty-seven recommendations, the EASG identified seventeen "implementable measures with high priority" and nine additional measures for medium- or long-term study, and it dropped thirty-one from further consideration. It deferred for later consideration the EAVG's principal recommendations of a free trade and investment area, a regional financing facility, coordination of exchange rates, NGO consultations, and the creation of an East Asian (as compared with an APT) summit. Reflecting the sometimes ephemeral nature of East Asian regionalism, the EAVG and EASG reports have been discussed in various dialogue meetings and among senior governmental officials but have attracted virtually no public attention.

Debating Regionalism

Within the EAVG and other nongovernmental discussion forums, a variety of fundamental issues have been debated. The debates, frequently more interesting than the reports and statements emanating from the meetings, center on five main issues.

The first is the definition of East Asia and the ensuing arguments about its geographic footprint and membership in a potential East Asian institution. There have been several proposals for including more countries in the APT process, with candidates including North Korea, Mongolia, India and Pakistan, and Australia and New Zealand. Whatever the political calculations involved, the underlying question is whether East Asia should be defined geographically (with accompanying criteria of historical experiences, common values, or civilizational perspectives) or functionally based on contemporary interactions and interests.

In one flexible formulation reminiscent of the earlier definition of Southeast Asia as "south of China and east of India," East Asia has been coyly defined as "larger than Southeast Asia but smaller than all of Asia" (Tay 2002, 99). Another suggestion from a Japanese scholar active in PECC and CSCAP is that "'East Asia' is more a functional concept than a geographical one. . . . Its geographical scope may be expanded or narrowed, depending upon the intensity of interactions in a specific issues area. So there is no need for the membership of the ASEAN + 3 forum to be fixed. . . . Such countries as the United States are essential parts of 'East Asia' given their political, security and economic roles" (Kikuchi 2002, 16).

The functional argument is inspired by a pragmatic and materialist commitment to solving practical problems and sidestepping the thorny issues of history, values, and identity. And it steps around accusations that the definition of the region as proposed by some follows racially defined boundaries. But it begs the question of why any new institutional arrangement is necessary, considering the existence of APEC and a range of other institutions facilitating functional economic cooperation.

The values/culture perspective comes in two variants. One can be summarized as the "Asian values" school, which focuses on distinctive characteristics emerging from East Asia's history. In the EAVG report, for example, East Asia is identified as "a distinctive and crucial region in the world" with "geographical proximity, many common historical experiences, and similar cultural norms and values." In the section of the report on cultural and educational programs, a paragraph "urges governments of the region to work together with their respective cultural and educational institutions to promote a strong sense of regional identity and an East Asian consciousness" (EAVG 2001, 98). It is telling that in the EAVG report, the geographical boundaries are assumed rather than stated, and no examples are given of common historical experiences, cultural norms, and values. Tommy Koh, Mahathir bin Mohamad, and others have provided detailed accounts of the "Asian values" that some feel to be the implicit core of an East Asian identity.

The second variant can be identified as the "cosmopolitan culture school." Yoichi Funabashi and others have made the case for an Asian consciousness and identity (Funabashi 1993). But rather than looking for it in history and values, they ascribe it to distinctive responses to universal processes such as globalization. Simon Tay, a Singaporean academic, makes the revisionist case that "Asia has no strong and enduring history of unity and accepted commonality, whether in polity, culture, language or religion." Rather than endorse a state-centered discourse of Asian values, he looks for commonalities in culture based on the interaction of peoples responding to modernity:

The new Asian culture will therefore not be found in a museum of Confucian analects or the speeches of octogenarian party cadres. It will instead be seen in the streets of Shanghai, Shibuya in Tokyo, and Singapore. My guess is that emerging with influences of J-pop, films by Ang Lee and others, and California roll sushi. It will grow as new Asians meet and communicate their similarities, differences and interdependencies. And, in all likelihood, they will do so in English, with their own particular accents. . . . It should not be the job of politicians in the region to stir Asian nationalism or to find some new excuse for their differences. The task will be to keep up with the trends, and prepare the institutions—economic, social, cultural and political—to give space to the cosmopolitan generation of Asians that is emerging. (Tay 2002, 104)

The idea of an "identity without exceptionalism" (Acharya 2001b) has proven very attractive to younger-generation liberals in many of the dialogue channels, although less compelling to their seniors.

The second debate centers on how comprehensive cooperation should be at this point. The case for various forms of financial and monetary cooperation is compelling. And there also seems to be consensus that the broader dimensions of cooperation, including developmental assistance, should be part of the agenda. The debate centers on how far political and security matters should be included. As seen in the EAVG report, the areas of "nontraditional" and human security have been increasingly important in intra-regional meetings. On the topic of "hard" security, including military doctrines, force deployments, arms control, and the like, most governments have tried to steer clear of detailed discussion in the absence of an American presence, citing the existence of security-specific forums such as the ARF, although rarely addressing them in depth in the ARF or any formal multilateral context. A few Chinese and Southeast Asian participants have argued that hard security matters should soon be featured more prominently, but at this point there is no mention of a longer-term move toward some kind of an *East Asian* security community, much less collective defense or collective security arrangements.

Third is the nature of the institutional structure that needs to be created. Not surprisingly, nongovernmental forums make the case for creating a parallel track II process (e.g., PECC and CSCAP) to what emerges at the formal governmental level. The contentious issue is how to give any East Asian institution teeth. Although APT is constructed as a consultative forum, it is already delving into areas that in due course will demand sophisticated policy coordination, adjudication, and enforcement mechanisms.

There is not yet a coherent answer about how to solve the institutionalization dilemma. The EAVG, for example, did nothing more than recommend establishing a parallel track II process, the East Asia Forum, and regularizing the APT summits as East Asian summits. It recommended "progressive institutionalization," acknowledging that "organizational capacity is crucial for effective formulation and implementation of programs" without providing any kind of sketch of what that institutionalization should look like. Other forums have produced a myriad of suggestions. Some have called for the restructuring of the APT along the lines of the Organisation for Economic Co-operation and Development, with a central administrative mechanism possessing some kind of permanent expertise (Dobson 2001, 1014). Jusuf Wanandi and several others have suggested that APT revisit European models of community building. And others have indicated that the idea of unanimity and consensus be replaced or supplemented by "coalitions of the willing" within the APT. One recommendation under active consideration is that APT employ a "sherpa system" of the kind used by the G7. A consensus has not been reached on how to proceed, but there is widespread acknowledgment that reliance on voluntarism, peer pressure, consensus, and avoidance of activist regional secretariats independent of national control is no longer a useful model but rather a hindrance.

The fourth is about leadership. Who, or more precisely, how, will the new process be led? From the perspective of interstate dynamics, it is clear that the balance of economic and political power lies in Northeast Asia. Southeast Asia has not shown the collective capacity for leadership that it did before the economic crisis. China and Japan are the natural leaders of East Asia, but for widely accepted reasons neither has the capacity to play such a role or the support from others in the region to do so (Stubbs 2002; Webber 2001). In this situation, South Korea along with individual Southeast Asian governments, especially those of Singapore and Malaysia, have played a middle power role in moving the process forward.

The leadership issue also relates to nonstate actors and individuals. It is difficult to find a Jean Monet or a Robert Schuman equivalent in contemporary East Asia. Mahathir bin Mohamad, Lee Kuan Yew, and Kim Dae-jung are the principal exponents of East Asian thinking, but unlike Charles de Gaulle and Konrad Adenauer, they do not lead major powers. Outside government, the intellectuals pushing the process are not single-minded in identifying East Asia as the unit of the future. Rather, their aim has been to advance East Asian regionalism by putting it in a larger context of multiple identities and a multilayered institutional architecture.

Nongovernmental processes are useful to state-led agendas and provide a wealth of technical expertise and contending points of view. They are the collective force for creating and shaping ideas and have the capacity to promote initiatives and establish a climate of opinion independent of any individual government. But they do not yet have the social foundation to create a transnational civil society that can drive regionalism separate from state elites willing to work with them.[13]

13. At least in Southeast Asia, some of the track II processes, especially the ASEAN Institutes of Strategic and International Studies, have recognized the problem and tried to make connections to the "track III" world of NGOs through mechanisms including the newly formed ASEAN People's Assembly. There is not yet evidence of this kind of connection taking place on an East Asian basis.

East Asian Regionalism and the Pacific Regional Order: Complementary or Competitive?

The future of East Asian regionalism is difficult to predict. In part this is because its trajectory is nonteleological and can take several different paths. It is also because the project remains precarious. Even its strongest supporters are aware that East Asian regionalism is at a modest and early stage of development, faces formidable obstacles, and is unlikely to be a key factor in the balance of economic and political power in the region, at least in the immediate future. It has made substantial progress in a little over a decade but is not operating in a vacuum, even in its own backyard. The United States is not just the vital external actor; it is the major force in the economic and security relations of the region. In 1990, during the late days of the administration of the first George Bush, U.S. officials reacted strongly and negatively to the initial Mahathir ideas for an East Asian Economic Grouping. And in 1997 and 1998, U.S. officials were decidedly negative about the prospects of some kind of Asian Monetary Fund. But in the final years of the Clinton administration and the early years of the George W. Bush administration, officials have been generally supportive of the APT process and the East Asian dialogue channels accompanying it.

It is therefore not surprising that the Asian promoters of East Asian regionalism have usually gone to great pains to defuse anti-American rhetoric, to emphasize the value of the American presence in the region, and to underline the continued importance of trans-Pacific institutions, including APEC and the ARF, in which the United States plays a major role. The imagery and aim are not Fortress Asia. Indeed, it is this pro-American approach that has permitted countries such as Japan, Singapore, and South Korea to play major roles in East Asian regionalism at the same time that they have maintained close relationships with Washington.

Looking beyond national tactics to more fundamental ideas, a key issue is how a nascent East Asian regionalism will connect with the existing Pacific order underpinned by the presence and power of the United States. Some advocates of East Asian regionalism, among them Prime Minister Mahathir, see it explicitly as a way of building a regional formation that can diminish or counter American influence. This is not a rejection of globalization, nor is it anti-Americanism; rather it is the view that for reasons of function, identity, and interest, a more self-regarding East Asian arrangement is needed. Several academics have concluded that the economic crisis of 1997 solidified concerns about too much American influence and led to the current phase of APT-led regionalism. In the words of one: "The contours of post-financial crisis regionalism are, by state design, aimed at restoring to Asia a greater degree of political power and autonomy vis-à-vis the rest of the world, and the U.S. and the international financial institutions it controls, in particular" (Bowles 2002, 231).

A second point of view is that whatever the feelings of resentment in Asia directed at the United States in the wake of the economic crisis, there is actually little likelihood that East Asia will soon emerge as an effective regional entity and certainly not one that is fundamentally at odds with the United States or Asia Pacific arrangements. This view emphasizes that the shared sense of identity in East Asia is fragile and thin, that East Asia is no more able to solve either the institutionalization dilemma or domestic intransigence to freer trade (especially in agriculture, fisheries, and forests) than was APEC, and that there are severe constraints on how far monetary and trade cooperation can proceed. Concludes one observer: "If, then, there exists a greater sense of East Asian identity post-crisis, for many of the governments of the region such a development need not come at the expense of linkages with extra-regional partners. The potential for the development of a closed East Asian economic bloc is no greater five years after the crisis than it was before then" (Ravenhill 2002, 193).

This is certainly the view of many governmental officials in the region, especially those from Singapore, South Korea, and Japan. It also is the view of the large majority of participants in the various track II policy networks supporting East Asian regionalism. They recognize the value of East Asian cooperation as useful in managing regional issues born of increased economic interdependence and as a means of developing bargaining power with outside institutions and governments, especially the United States and the European Union. But they are generally committed to a form of open regionalism, resistant to the idea of any kind of economic bloc (much less security arrangement), skeptical about claims of unique and common Asian values that would underpin a regional institution, and loath to see American withdrawal or disengagement from East Asia. Although aware of the limitations of Asia Pacific processes, including APEC and the ARF, and frequently concerned about surges of American triumphalism and arrogance, their aim has been to find ways to harmonize East Asian stirrings with Asia Pacific institutions. Put in broad terms, Asia Pacific and East Asian regionalism are conceived to be not competitors but opposite sides of the same coin.

Operationally, the purveyors of East Asian regionalism face a double challenge. One part of it is identifying the areas in which cooperation is necessary and feasible, overcoming the ghosts of a troubled history, and generating an awareness of regional commonalities if not identity. The second part is implementing a form of multilateralism that fits with regional conditions but that also produces the norms, rules, and procedures for effective, not just symbolic, cooperation. It is possible to have regionalism without multilateralism. Indeed, this was the East Asian experience in the eras of Chinese and Japanese imperial domination. But at the current moment, virtually all of the enthusiasts see regionalism and multilateralism as integrally linked.

The structure, rules, and principles of multilateralism are under review. The choice to broaden the range of institutions in eastern Asia, including the creation of the APT process, reflected economic realities and the desire to create something new. But broadening did not solve the problem of how to establish an *effective* regional institution, whatever the geographical boundaries of the organization. Rather than thinking that the solution to the institutionalization dilemma must come on an Asians-only basis, members of track II circles see the solution emerging in the overlap between Asia Pacific processes and East Asian ones. Advances in one presumably would spill over into the other. This is certainly the expectation of groups like the PECC Finance Forum, which has endorsed the Chiang Mai Initiative, and the Manila Framework Group; both groups organized on an East Asian basis as useful means for intensifying regional surveillance processes (PECC 2002).

China looms as an increasingly important power in East Asia. If there were to be a sustained challenge to American influence and the American order in the Pacific, it would come from China. China's embrace of multilateral institutions since 1996 has been substantial; indeed, it has moved in less than a decade from a defensive and wary neighbor to an engaged participant and now an active leader. The two principal reasons for this shift are that China is attempting to reassure anxious neighbors about its intentions and that it recognizes the value of multilateral cooperation in addressing a range of transnational issues. East Asia and the APT are just one of the geographical configurations for multilateral cooperation advanced by Chinese officials, with others operating on a trans-Pacific basis (e.g., China's involvement in APEC and the ARF), a pan-Asian basis (the Boao Forum), a central Asian basis (e.g., the Shanghai Cooperation Organization), or a "bilateral" basis (with individual countries and ASEAN as a collectivity).

The more subtle issue is whether Chinese officials and intellectuals are developing a distinctive approach to the form and rules of multilateral institutions in the region, something that might be called multilateralism with Chinese characteristics. The Shanghai Cooperation Organization, based in China and created mainly at Beijing's behest, gives some clues in that it is decidedly state-centric, committed to conventional principles of sovereignty and noninterference, and dedicated to defending state interests against perceived challenges from nonstate actors. It operates on principles similar to those of ASEAN. This particular formulation is neither innovative nor likely to be seen as palatable or productive by most countries or publics in a broader Asian setting.

This leads to the conclusion that China has neither the capacity nor vision at this point to create an independent multilateral framework that operates against the interests of the United States, at least in the short term. Nor is there the constituency in other countries in the region to support such a venture, even if it were China's intention. Instead, like those in all of the other countries in the region, Chinese officials and academics have not presented the issue as a zero-sum competition with the United States. Chinese efforts inside the ARF in 1997 and 1998 to use it as a means to undermine the system of America's bilateral alliances stopped fairly quickly. Those with their hands on the rudder of East Asian regionalism show few signs of traveling to an anti-American destination.

If there were to have been a strategic parallel to the economic anxieties about American power in the wake of the economic crisis, it is not visible even in the context of heavy American assertiveness, including the expanded presence of American forces in central and Southeast Asia after the events of September 11 and the invasion of Iraq. Although aspects of American policy have been criticized, almost all states support the efforts to suppress terrorism and accept a larger presence of American forces in the region. Indeed, the prospects for cooperation among the great powers are improving, albeit on a narrow basis of state-centered antiterrorism and antiseparatism. The rhetoric of regionalism is unchanged, but if there is counterbalancing, it is exquisitely subtle and well disguised.[14]

The American-led alliance system underpins the regional security order even as a more complex system is being constructed on the economic front. The compatibility of the two sets of arrangements has been an essential aspect of their success. All of the multiple forms of regionalism have germinated and developed in a post–Cold War setting involving unusually positive relations among the great powers. For the moment there is a virtuous cycle in which these positive relations encourage regional institutions and regional institutions provide a more positive foundation, albeit in limited ways, for cooperation among the great powers.

In the event of a major military conflict in the region, the viability of the regional institutions would be severely tested. If it involved a direct United States–China conflict or the creation of some kind of military alliance for the purpose of containing China, Asia Pacific and East Asian regionalism would shatter together. It is at least plausible that the geopolitical rationale for regional multilateralism is that it reduces the prospects of this kind of conflict or containment possibility.

Is there the prospect that the policy networks that interconnect East Asia and Asia Pacific will mature into policy communities that can promote a deeper regionalism and institutionalization? In part this depends on geopolitics and geo-economics. It will also depend on the imagination and capacity of the nongovernmental groups themselves. Calls for Community with a capital C and projects to create a vision, whether constructed on an East Asian or

---

14. The absence of counterbalancing is generating an interesting theoretical debate. David Kang argues that East Asians are more likely to join the bandwagon of a major power (China or the United States) than to counterbalance it because of a cultural and historical preference for hierarchy (Kang 2003a). Amitav Acharya argues that Asia's future will not include hierarchical arrangements, counterbalancing, or bandwagoning as key elements. Rather, he sees the development of regional interdependence, norms, and institutions within a neo-Westphalian framework as more likely and more durable sources of East Asian stability (Acharya 2003).

Asia Pacific basis, still tend to ring hollow. Nationalism remains much stronger than regionalism, and governments remain far more dominant than any constellation of transnational actors.

The regional institutional architecture can be expected to be complex and diverse in its next phase. It likely will be composed of multiple overlapping organizations at the governmental and nongovernmental levels. The slow march to building more effective institutions and identity is not proceeding on a single track. In the scribblings and imaginings of a handful of cosmopolitan Asian intellectuals and political leaders are the seeds of a deeper East Asian regionalism. The genius of the process is its pragmatism and realism. Its failing is that it has not yet captured the support of Asian publics or elites in looking beyond the differences of the past and toward a poststatist agenda that is at least a generation away.

9

The Political Economy of Environmental Regionalism in Asia

LAURA B. CAMPBELL

Although Asia has engaged in a process of environmental regionalization, until now it has primarily addressed cross-border pollution problems on an ad hoc basis. Asia's approach to environmental regionalism, which relies on voluntary cooperation, nonbinding agreements, and a weak institutional infrastructure, reflects the political economy of the region and individual Asian countries. Regional trade and investment patterns, a predominance of developing countries in the region, serious concerns about ceding sovereignty over environmental issues, lack of effective domestic political demand for strong environmental policy, and the absence of demands for upward harmonization of environmental standards by Japan or Singapore are key factors affecting the development of environmental regionalism in Asia.

The primary driver of Asian regionalism has been very severe transboundary air pollution, especially haze from forest burning and acid rain. The urgency and seriousness of this pollution have motivated governments to cooperate on the regional level to address these problems. However, because the air pollution does not affect all members of the region, cooperation has been limited to the countries directly involved. Although regionalism has not been successful in eliminating haze or acid rain, it has had important secondary effects on domestic policy. For example, Singapore has promoted the participation of NGOs in regional haze programs because of their value in focusing attention and creating pressure on Indonesia to address the problem. The ineffectiveness of the regional haze agreement has also highlighted the importance of domestic political capacity in tackling regional environmental problems and the need for binding treaties and effective enforcement mechanisms.

In contrast to Asia, the primary drivers of environmental regionalism in Europe and North America have been concerns about the effects of differences in environmental standards on national competitiveness and market access. Because of the lack of direct product competition in Asian markets, neither competitiveness nor market access concerns have driven environmental regionalism, despite a large volume of trade within the region and considerable variation in the stringency of national environmental rules.

Figures showing high levels of regional trade are not indicative of product competition within the Asian market because of regional trade and investment patterns. Historically, a large portion of regional trade can be attributed to cross-border transfers of goods for further processing (see the chapters in this volume by Tachiki, and MacIntyre and Naughton) and to export of raw materials, such as oil and timber, which do not compete with domestically produced goods. As these patterns change in ways that result in more direct competition within the region, the impetus for environmental regionalism is likely to increase.

Although the size and importance of regional trade are growing rapidly, global markets, particularly those of the United States and the European Union, historically have been much more significant for Asian countries. As a result, the environmental priorities advanced by the United States and the European Union have had a significant influence on the development of Asian environmental policy. To ensure market access, Asian countries have adapted to foreign environmental product standards such as emission limits on vehicles and energy efficiency requirements for appliances, and they have adopted multilateral treaties that heavily reflect the health and environmental priorities of powerful market economies.

The Montreal Protocol on Protection of the Ozone Layer is an example of an environmental treaty that affected market access for a variety of Asian exports, including electronics, computers, cars, and appliances. To encourage countries to join the treaty, the protocol banned trading with nonparties in ozone-depleting chemicals used for manufacturing as well as in products that contained these chemicals. Similarly, in order to become members of the WTO, Asian nations were required to adopt a package of treaties as a "single undertaking," including trade agreements affecting environmental and health standards.

Other external forces also influence the development of environmental policy in Asia, primarily by increasing domestic demand for stronger environmental protection rules and more openness and transparency in policy setting. These outside forces include internationalization of the NGO movement, NGO access to global treaty negotiations, creation of the Internet, foreign aid and foundation grants aimed at strengthening democratic institutions and influencing national environmental policy, and World Bank and Asian Development Bank environmental rules.

Several factors could significantly affect the future development of environmental regionalism in Asia. China's rise in the regional power structure, particularly if it opens its national market to regional imports, would provide the country with the capacity to demand regional harmonization of national environmental standards. China's interest in doing this, however, will largely hinge on the level of effective domestic political demand that China raise its own levels of environmental protection. Although in many respects Japan's influence has declined in Asia, the size of its domestic market still affords it the power to demand upward environmental harmonization, to the extent that it is open to regional imports. Even with open markets, trade-related environmental concerns will be an issue for China and Japan only if there is direct competition between domestic and imported products.

As transboundary environmental problems worsen in Asia, increasing dissatisfaction over the ineffectiveness of current forms of regionalism is likely to drive the development of deeper environmental integration. Awareness of its lack of success in addressing the haze problem has already generated discussion in the region about the need for stronger institutions and formal agreements, prompted the inclusion of NGOs in regional environmental activities, and highlighted the importance of domestic capacity building in solving transboundary environmental problems.

In analyzing Asian environmental regionalism, this chapter discusses the characteristics of the regional and domestic political economies that affect the process and outcomes of regionalism; regional responses to transboundary environmental problems in the cases of acid rain and haze from forest burning; the relationship between the Asian region and environmental globalization; and some external influences that affect the development of environmental regionalism.

The Political Economy of Environmental Regionalism in Asia

Environmental regionalism is often viewed as a more feasible, effective, and democratic approach for addressing environmental problems that transcend national boundaries than is globalization. Primarily because a smaller number of countries are involved, regionalism is seen as more likely to facilitate participation and represent the interests of all the parties, making it more democratic than a global approach. In addition, concerns about the potentially negative impacts on the multilateral trading system of linking trade and environment issues within the WTO have fostered the view that the regional level is a better place to address international environmental issues than is the global, and possibly in the context of regional trade agreements.

Underlying the view that regionalism is a more feasible way to manage international environmental problems are assumptions that regional commonalities such as geography, culture, values, and economic and political systems, combined with a smaller number of countries needed for consensus, will make agreement easier to reach on the regional than on the global level. Although a smaller number of parties can result in a more democratic process, this is not a given. Proponents of environmental regionalism also tend to assume the existence of regional institutions capable of addressing cross-border environmental issues. Other conditions, such as transparency in national and regional policy development and parity of negotiating power among the members of the region, also influence the process.

Although all Asian countries share the view that environmental issues should not be addressed within the WTO, this has not prompted the development of environmental regionalism as an alternative. This is because Asia does not currently have shared environmental priorities or concerns about competitiveness and market access that arise from differences in environmental standards—the strongest drivers of environmental regionalism.

Various aspects of the regional political economy influence the development of environmental regionalism. This chapter examines some general assumptions about why countries regionalize in light of the assumptions' relevance to Asia and analyzes how interdependent characteristics of the Asian region affect its process of environmental regionalism.

Geographic and Demographic Factors

Asia is defined primarily by political, not geographic, boundaries, and there is a great deal of physical variation within the region. To some extent, geographic similarities have resulted in shared environmental problems and led to regional cooperation. For example, the heavy concentration of population along coastal areas in most Asian countries makes them particularly vulnerable to a rise in sea level from climate change. This common environmental concern, combined with external aid aimed at engaging Asian countries in the prevention of climate change, has motivated countries in the region to undertake joint environmental research and monitoring activities.

Geographic proximity has affected the nature and seriousness of cross-border environmental problems in Asia. Proximity has resulted in pollution causing serious transboundary environmental damage, including degradation of shared waterways, acid rain, haze, and marine pollution. Geography also affects the distribution of transboundary pollution, which is generally not region wide. These geographic factors have, in turn, influenced the structure of regionalism in Asia, which primarily consists of nonbinding subregional agreements.

Shared Culture and Values

Although sharing common cultural assumptions and values in environment-related areas such as public health, property rights, civil liberties, and nature conservation does not guarantee that environmental regionalism will develop, such commonality is likely to promote convergence of national environmental policy. Whether shared culture and values are viewed as affecting Asia's approach to environmental regionalism depends heavily on what characteristics are defined as Asian. As Paul Evans points out in chapter 8, issues about whether Asians share common values and, if so, what those values consist of are both complex and unsettled. If, as Simon Tay has stated, preferences for nonbinding agreements, weak enforcement mechanisms, and informal institutions are characteristically Asian (Tay 1998), then these common values have had an important impact on the procedural and structural aspects of Asian environmental regionalism.

Although shared values about the environment and human health may influence the process of regionalism, a country's level of economic development is a more important factor in determining its national and regional environmental priorities. The Asian region is made up predominantly of developing countries with low levels of effective domestic environmental regulation. This scenario creates little incentive for regionalism, especially upward harmonization. Within Asia, greater priority has been attached to economic growth than to health and environmental protection, resulting in lower effective environmental standards in the less-developed economies.

The experiences of Japan and Singapore, both economically advanced countries with high environmental standards, illustrate that the willingness and capacity to address environmental problems tend to increase sharply with economic development. Lack of evidence indicating that these two countries share environmental values distinct from those of other Asian countries also highlights the importance of economic issues in setting national and regional priorities.

Transboundary Environmental Problems

The most important driver of environmental regionalism in Asia is transboundary air pollution, particularly acid rain from fossil fuel energy production and haze from forest burning. Climate change, also caused by fossil fuel combustion and forest fires, is another serious form of air pollution in the region, but it has not been as important in driving regionalism as have acid rain and haze, which produce more visible and immediate impacts. Even though the acid rain and haze problems are seen as extremely urgent, countries nevertheless have been reluctant to adopt binding regional standards governing air emissions and forest management. Concerns about ceding sovereignty over economic and land-use activities have had a major influence on the region's failure to take strong action to address these problems.

An important aspect of both the acid rain and haze problems is that each is caused primarily, although not solely, by one very large country in the region: China in the case of acid rain and Indonesia in the case of haze. Consequently, developing domestic political and technical capacity to reduce pollution in China and Indonesia is critical in addressing these issues on the regional level.

For transboundary problems such as acid rain and haze, which also have serious impacts on human health and the environment in the countries generating the pollution, domestic political demand for stronger protection can be an important driver behind regional cooperation. For example, although China is the primary source of acid rain in North Korea, South Korea, Vietnam, and the regional seas, 83 percent of its pollution remains within its own borders, causing tremendous damage to human health and the environment (Nautilus Institute and Center for Global Communications 2000; World Bank 1997).

Because of the connection between domestic political demand and regionalism, emphasizing the so-called dual benefits of addressing transboundary problems can be one of the most effective means of persuading polluting countries to cooperate regionally. Providing technical and financial assistance as part of an agreement to address the transboundary pollution, as was done in both the acid rain and haze agreements, can make regional cooperation more attractive by helping a government to meet domestic environmental demands.

Regional agreements on haze pollution and acid rain in Asia have included provisions for financial and technical assistance, information sharing, and joint environmental monitoring. Although countries are encouraged to take specific measures to reduce the pollution, the lack of legally binding regional environmental rules has left governments with broad discretion over national implementation of the agreements.

Haze from Forest Burning

Forest burning in Indonesia has caused severe transboundary air pollution, euphemistically referred to as haze, for a number of years. In 1991, 1994, 1997, and 1998, however, the haze was much worse than usual, causing severe consequences in Brunei Darussalam, Indonesia, Malaysia, and Singapore and lesser damage in Thailand and the Philippines. Although Indonesian officials suggested that the fires were caused by slash-and-burn activities of subsistence farmers and the effects of El Niño, satellite photos show that the vast majority of the haze came from land clearing by large logging companies. Economic losses caused by the 1997 haze have been estimated at well over US$1.4

billion. The haze also seriously affected human health, including contributing to millions of cases of respiratory illness and causing twenty-nine deaths in Indonesia alone (Cotton 1999; Tay 1998).

In 1998, ASEAN adopted the "Regional Haze Action Plan" to reduce the impact of the haze and prevent future occurrences. The primary objectives of the Haze Plan are (1) to prevent land and forest fires through better management policies and enforcement; (2) to establish operational mechanisms to monitor land and forest fires; and (3) to strengthen regional capabilities for fighting and mitigating land and forest fires.

Under the ASEAN Haze Plan, countries are required to strengthen national forest fire prevention and mitigation laws and policies and to develop plans to implement them. The plan also mandates that countries monitor compliance with and strictly enforce these laws. One of the most important elements of the Haze Plan is its authorization of the ASEAN Meteorological Center to compile and disseminate satellite imagery information for detecting and monitoring forest fires and haze. In global forums, Malaysia has led Asian countries in strongly opposing the use of satellite data for environmental purposes, particularly for monitoring changes in tropical forests. Although characterized by some countries as unauthorized spying, the data were used in regional negotiations to expose the effects of logging concessions and forest burning. The use of satellite imagery to refute the Indonesian government's statements about the cause and extent of the haze problem represents an enormous shift in thinking about the acceptable level of intrusion on a sovereign government in order to address environmental problems.

Institutional weaknesses in ASEAN contributed to the failure of the Haze Plan, but Indonesia's lack of domestic political capacity to address its forestry management practices was the most important factor. Although Indonesia has adequate laws to protect its forests, it has not been effective in enforcing compliance by the main logging concessionaires, who have close ties to politicians and government officials. In essence, Indonesia chose to appease domestic commercial interests instead of honoring its commitments to its regional neighbors under the Haze Plan (Cotton 1999).

Although the Indonesian central government retains control over the provinces in many areas, the National Environment and Planning Ministry has little capacity to enforce environmental laws. Ministry staff, although dedicated and hardworking, have been largely ineffective in changing the environmental behavior of state-owned facilities. Within the government, economic development has had priority over health and environmental concerns. The weak political capacity of the Environment Ministry in Indonesia, highlighted by its inability to enforce laws concerning forestry practices, has resulted in its failure to manage the haze problem. Consequently, neither domestic nor regional health and environmental problems caused by the haze have been addressed effectively (Cotton 1999).

Acid Rain

Acid rain, caused primarily by sulfur dioxide emissions from power plants, is one of the most serious environmental problems in Asia and results in damage to buildings, forests, lakes, rivers, and agriculture. Acid rain also causes severe effects on human health by transforming substances such as mercury into toxic compounds. Japan became aware of the transboundary acid rain problem in the early 1980s but did not definitively tie it to emissions from continental Asia until 1989 (Brettell 2001, 17–22). Soon after, Japan began to seek support for regional cooperation to address the problem from China and South Korea.

Within a few years, new research showed that Indonesia, Malaysia, Mongolia, the Philippines, Singapore, the Russian Federation, Thailand, and Vietnam were also affected by transboundary acid rain. The expansion of the scope of the problem beyond East Asia has made it particularly difficult to address acid rain because of the greater difficulties involved in achieving consensus and the weak domestic political capacity of many of the countries involved (Brettell 2001).

Beginning in 1993, Japan sponsored a series of intergovernmental meetings aimed at creating a regional scheme to monitor acid rain. These meetings resulted in the formal establishment of the East Asia Acid Deposition Monitoring Network (EANET) in 1998. Japan continued to coordinate EANET activities until 2001, when it arranged for the network's transfer to the United Nations Environment Programme's Regional Office for Asia and the Pacific (Interim Scientific Advisory Group of EANET 2000). Transferring the administration of EANET to the regional office of a United Nations organization was viewed as a means of enhancing its credibility by reducing the appearance that it was being controlled by Japan, its primary funder.

EANET relies on voluntary measures that consist primarily of joint monitoring, technical and financial assistance, and information sharing. Although establishment of the EANET represents real progress in creating an institutional framework to address the acid rain problem, it has not succeeded in actually reducing the air pollution that causes it. One reason for this is that Japan, the initiator of efforts to address the problem and a country with stringent air pollution control laws, does not have the political power within the region to demand upward harmonization of air emission standards. Recognizing the need for further action, Japan has proposed that a regional agreement similar to the European Convention on Long Range Transboundary Air Pollution (LRTAP) be adopted by Asia. Representatives from countries that are parties to LRTAP have attended EANET meetings and discussed their experience in developing the agreement.

LRTAP was negotiated within the United Nations Economic Commission for Europe in a period of détente after the breakup of the Soviet Union; it includes eastern European countries, Russia, and a number of former Soviet republics in its membership. Like a number of other environmental treaties, the LRTAP Convention creates a framework for cooperation. Binding air emission limitations are set out in eight separately negotiated treaties known as protocols. Parties to LRTAP may choose whether to adopt each of the protocols, and many parties have not ratified those dealing with acid rain. Unlike compliance with EU regulations on air pollution, which is very high, implementation of LRTAP has not been very successful in non-EU countries.[1] One lesson for Asia from the LRTAP experience is that binding standards are less likely to be effective when they are adopted outside a framework of political and/or economic integration.

The most serious impediment to addressing acid rain in Asia is China's position as the dominant polluter. China has huge coal reserves and is expected to rely heavily on coal-fired power plants to meet its energy needs for the foreseeable future. Although the majority of acid rain generated by China remains in the country, a great deal is also transported to other countries. Despite the seriousness of the problem in China, domestic political demand for pollution reduction has not been high enough to force the government to take serious action.

Regional Trade and Investment

In accord with the views of Steven Krasner (1983), that powerful nations set the agenda in international regimes, and Ernst Haas (1980), that new issues are often linked with previous areas of integration, trade and environment issues are usually linked on a regional basis when economic integration creates market access and competitiveness concerns within a unified market and/or countries with regional market power attach high priority to environmental protection (Steinberg 1997). For these reasons, economic integration has been accompanied by environmental regionalism in the EU and NAFTA. In these regions, countries with both market power and high environmental standards (for example, Germany and the United States) successfully promoted upward harmonization of environmental standards. Differences in the level of economic integration and relative power of the richer, greener countries within each region account for the variation in the form and depth of environmental regionalism (Steinberg 1997, 233).

In contrast to the EU and NAFTA, trade integration has not provided an impetus for environmental regionalism in Asia. Because of the historically

---

1. As members of the Economic Commission for Europe, Canada and the United States have also joined LRTAP. The United States has not ratified any of the three protocols dealing with acid rain, and Canada has not yet adopted the 1999 protocol on acidification. Canada's hope that the United States' membership in LRTAP would be more effective in reducing emissions from U.S. power plants in the Midwest than bilateral negotiations have been has not been fulfilled.

greater importance of global relative to regional trade, the process of environmental regionalism is less advanced in Asia than is globalization. Although the relevance of the trade and environment linkage for Asia has been addressed by regional policy makers in ASEAN, the primary focus has been on the effects of foreign and global environmental rules on market access.

Although statistics on the exact size of Asian regional trade vary based on the source of information, all figures show that it has increased significantly since the 1980s both in overall volume and relative to Asian trade with the rest of the world.[2] The available figures do not distinguish between cross-border shipments for further processing and trade in consumer products. In addition, data showing the volume of regional trade in competing products, important figures in evaluating the effect of regional trade patterns on the development of environmental regionalism, are not available.

A significant portion of intra-Asia trade is composed of transfers between related companies for further processing and export to countries outside the region (Tachiki, this volume). Because there is little direct product competition in the Asian market, the increased production costs caused by environmental regulation have not resulted in pressure for upward harmonization from the countries with high environmental standards, Japan and Singapore. For a country such as Japan, the manufacture of noncompeting products in other Asian countries and the restriction on importing goods that are domestically produced have actually enabled it to benefit from the lower environmental standards in Southeast Asia and China. By locating more polluting industries in low-standard countries in the region, Japan has reduced the costs of producing consumer goods for the Japanese and global markets and of obtaining intermediate inputs for goods made in Japan.

The absence of strong regional environmental process standards also influences the behavior of countries competing for incoming investment, especially developing countries with low effective levels of protection. Environmental process standards set rules governing environmental protection during manufacturing. Regulations concerning air and water pollution, waste disposal, and workplace safety are examples of process standards. Depending on the stringency of these standards, compliance can add significantly to the cost of production.

Competition for foreign direct investment within the region can inhibit countries from strengthening or enforcing environmental rules as they struggle to attract investment by minimizing production costs.

2. Although trade among ASEAN members grew significantly faster than did extra-regional trade in 2000, it still accounted for only one-quarter of total ASEAN trade. However, Asian regional trade is expected to continue to increase, and this could change the effect of environmental globalization on the region. The value of exports to the United States alone was more than 20 percent of GDP in Malaysia and 10 percent in Thailand in 2000 (WTO 2001).

In addition, Asian countries increasingly compete with each other in global markets, making it difficult to raise environmental process standards unilaterally without disadvantaging domestically produced goods. When there is product competition in a unified market among countries with differing levels of environmental protection, the most effective means of leveling the playing field is to adopt a single regional process standard. Referred to as harmonization, this approach ensures that prices reflect the same environmental costs regardless of where manufacturing takes place within the market.

Although harmonizing environmental rules can also be effective in addressing transboundary pollution, without a major economic benefit like market access to drive the process, this approach has not been adopted in Asia. Because Asia's trade and investment patterns have not generated the type of market access and competitiveness concerns that tend to drive harmonization of environmental rules, there has been little incentive to adopt regional standards.

Environmental product standards, such as the energy efficiency and recycling standards for appliances, can also affect market access by requiring a manufacturer to meet multiple standards in order to sell in different countries. In contrast to process standards, harmonization of product standards is a well-accepted means of facilitating trade and has taken place on the global level for many years. The International Standards Organization (ISO) was created to coordinate the development of common technical standards. In recent years, ISO has also adopted environmental standards, recognizing the potential for these standards to create barriers to trade. In keeping with their export-oriented economies, Asian countries have widely adopted ISO standards.

Economic Globalization and Asian Environmental Standards

In general, Asian countries have been more engaged in the globalization than the regionalization of environmental rules, which primarily reflects the greater relative importance of global trade for Asian countries as compared with regional trade. The *Second ASEAN State of the Environment Report* notes that although "globalization and free trade will bring greater benefits to ASEAN countries," they need "to be vigilant against the negative consequences as well," which include the potential effects on exports of foreign and global environmental rules (ASEAN Secretariat 2001a, 149).

Acknowledging that trade and environment are "fundamentally related" and that trade is an "increasingly important driver of environmental change," (p. 154) the ASEAN report also warns that "the proliferation of multilateral environmental agreements," WTO environmental rules, and the environmental preferences of consumers in major export markets pose major challenges to ASEAN trade and market access (ASEAN Secretariat 2001a, 149).

Because of Asia's heavy reliance on the U.S. and EU markets, environmental standards and consumer preferences in these countries have a significant influence on environmental policy development in the region.

Multilateral Environmental Agreements

Because activities that cause global environmental damage can take place within or across national boundaries, trade sanctions are sometimes included in multilateral environmental agreements in order to prevent relocation of polluters to nonparty states and to encourage countries to join the treaty. As a result, a number of environmental treaties contain a combination of restrictions on trade with nonparties and financial incentives to promote participation. In 1996, the WTO identified twenty multilateral environmental agreements that include trade provisions (WTO 1996).

A number of environmental treaties have the potential to significantly impact Asian trade, and this has been a strong, although certainly not the sole, motivation for Asian countries to participate in these treaties. The importance Asian countries attach to participation in global environmental rule making is shown by their membership is almost all of the major environmental treaties.

The Montreal Protocol on Protection of the Ozone Layer serves as a good example of the effects of an environmental treaty on the newly industrializing export-oriented economies of Asia. The protocol was adopted in 1985 after discovery that the atmospheric ozone was being destroyed by emissions of certain chemicals, primarily chlorofluorocarbons carbon tetrachloride, and halons. The ozone layer protects earth from excessive radiation from the sun, and its depletion causes serious health and environmental problems including skin cancer and agricultural damage. The so-called ozone-depleting chemicals (ODCs) were widely used in aerosols, refrigerators, air conditioning, fire fighting, and industrial solvents.

Because ODCs disperse in the atmosphere, emissions anywhere in the world contribute equally to the destruction of the ozone layer, and global cooperation is needed to address the problem. To encourage countries to cooperate, restrictions on trade with nonparties in ODCs and products containing or manufactured with these chemicals were included in the Montreal Protocol. Restricting trade in products manufactured using ODCs also prevented industry from relocating to a country that had not joined the treaty and then re-exporting goods back to countries that became parties.

In general, the level of consumption of ODCs increases along with economic development, because use of these chemicals is linked to manufacturing and the use of refrigerators, cars, air conditioning, and telecommunication and computer products. As a result, Organization for Economic Cooperation and Development (OECD) countries were the largest consumers and sole producers of ODCs before adoption of the protocol. In the industrializing countries of Asia, however, ODC production and use were rising, and this trend was expected to continue along with economic growth.

Asian countries, with the exception of Japan, were not particularly worried about the ozone layer and probably would not have joined the protocol except for the threat of trade sanctions and consumer boycotts by Western countries. Although the use of ODCs in Asian countries was not affected by the protocol, it would have banned export of products containing or made with ODCs to the United States, EU, and virtually all other developed country markets.

Scientific data about the differential impacts of ozone depletion on Asia and OECD countries provide further evidence that concerns about market access, not health and environmental issues, drove Asian participation in the protocol. Most Asians are less affected by ultraviolet radiation than Caucasians because of their generally higher levels of skin pigmentation, so the health effects of ozone depletion were not as serious in Asian countries as in those with a high population of northern Europeans. In addition, the thinning of the ozone layer was found to be uneven, with more depletion over areas above Australia and North America, both areas with large populations of Caucasians vulnerable to skin cancer.

Japan, China, Korea, Malaysia, Singapore, and other Southeast Asian countries were actively involved in negotiating the protocol. Japan, although initially reluctant to participate, became actively involved in the process, its interest bolstered by the early development of ODC substitutes by Japanese companies. All Asian countries are now parties to the protocol.

WTO Agreements and the Environment

The United States was the primary sponsor of the environmental provisions included in Article XX of the 1948 General Agreement on Tariffs and Trade (GATT) (Steinberg 1997, 240), and it continues to rely on these provisions to justify its unilateral trade sanctions imposed for environmental purposes. During the Uruguay Round, the United States, supported by the EU, returned to the issue of balancing trade and environmental concerns and successfully promoted adoption of the Technical Barriers to Trade Agreement (TBT) and the Sanitary and Phytosanitary Agreement (SPS). These agreements both guard against the use of health and safety rules for protectionist purposes while ensuring the right of countries to set standards at levels each considers appropriate (Steinberg 1997, 240–41).

Developing countries were strongly opposed to both TBT and SPS and were induced to sign them only by the "single undertaking" requirement created by the EU and United States during the negotiations. Under the terms of the single undertaking, a country had to adopt all of the Uruguay Round multilateral agreements as a package. The incentive to adopt the entire package was reinforced by a withdrawal from the 1948 GATT by all parties to the 1994 WTO agreements, thus eliminating existing trade preferences for countries that did not sign (Steinberg 1997, 241). The health and environmental rules in WTO agreements have a disproportionate impact on trade in agricultural and food products, which is particularly significant for many Asian countries.

Because the United States and EU have the political and market power to influence global policy, their domestic environmental priorities are heavily reflected in WTO agreements. Tommy Koh voiced concerns about this issue in *Asian Dragons and Green Trade,* stating that Asian countries must actively participate in the trade and environment debate within the WTO to avoid being bound by "rules that have been made without their consent by Americans and Europeans"(Koh 1996, viii–x). WTO has noted that product regulations and standards, including those related to health, safety, and environmental issues, are creating growing concerns about market access (WTO 2001, 36, 90–94), a view strongly shared by Asian countries. Nevertheless, there is increasing pressure from industrialized countries to strengthen environmental provisions during the Millennium Round of trade negotiations.

Sovereignty Concerns

In Asia, governments exercise strong national control over environmental issues and generally oppose any relinquishment of sovereignty in this area to a regional organization. Environmental issues are closely tied to energy security, natural resource use, economic development, and public health—areas closely guarded as being within the sovereign domain of all nations. Having lost control over natural resources under colonial rule, several Asian countries are particularly sensitive to ceding sovereignty that limits their authority in this area. Not coincidentally, the international legal principle of sovereignty over natural resources was conceived to justify repudiation of pre-independence natural resource contracts deemed unconscionable by postcolonial governments. The potential for environmental regionalism to increase national political demand for more democratic and transparent environmental policy setting also raises governmental apprehension about the indirect effects of relinquishing sovereignty to a regional institution.[3]

Of course, a decision to cede sovereignty over an environmental issue involves a balancing of the urgency of the need to be addressed through

---

3. Concerns about retaining sovereignty over national environmental policy are certainly not unique to developing countries. However, in industrialized countries, concerns tend to focus on the antidemocratic effects of regionalizing issues that are viewed as essentially national or local and the tendency to set lower regional standards to accommodate countries with low levels of environmental protection (Stein 2001).

regional cooperation against the benefits of retaining national control. As discussed earlier in the chapter, the economic benefits of market access have been large enough to cede sovereignty over a number of environmental and health issues on the global level. However, within Asia neither market access nor competitiveness concerns have been great enough to warrant any serious relinquishment of national sovereignty over environmental issues. Although serious transboundary pollution problems have motivated regional cooperation, the forms of environmental regionalism adopted in Asia to address these issues have been nonbinding and have involved very minimal ceding of sovereignty.

The Role of NGOs and Civil Society

Civil society and NGOs do not have a strong position in the domestic political economy of Asian countries. Lack of transparency and opportunity for participation in environmental policy making reflect Asian governments' view that NGOs and other members of civil society are not legitimate actors in political affairs. Public participation in policy development has been a major driver behind strengthening environmental protection in countries with high standards, and exclusion of NGOs has limited the development of stronger national and regional environmental rules in Asia.

The ineffectiveness of regional institutions in addressing the transboundary haze pollution of 1997–98 has begun to shift governmental attitudes about the role of NGOs in regional environmental policy development. Recognizing that Indonesia's lack of national political will to stop the forest burning was a major reason for the failure of the regional haze agreement, Singapore has promoted the participation of Asian and international NGOs in regional activities in order to increase political pressure on the Indonesian government. Singapore's action is particularly remarkable given the highly restrictive view it has taken in the past of the role of NGOs in domestic policy setting.

Extra-Regional Influences on Asian Environmental Policy

External forces also influence the development of environmental policy in Asia, primarily by increasing domestic demand for stronger environmental protection rules and more openness and transparency in policy setting. Some of the extra-regional influences on national and regional environmental policy include creation of the Internet, internationalization of the NGO movement, NGO access to global treaty negotiations, foreign aid and foundation grants aimed at strengthening Asian environmental policy and democratic institutions, and World Bank and Asian Development Bank environmental rules.

Probably the single most important external influence is the Internet, which has radically altered the context in which civil society and NGOs operate by providing broad access to information and a cheap means of communicating with parties within and outside the region. Often, Asian NGOs are able to obtain information from websites and international NGOs that is not available from their own governments. Extensive collaboration with international NGOs in Japan, Europe, and the United States, made economically feasible by the Internet, has introduced new ideas and raised the expectations of civil society and NGOs in Asia.

Beginning in the mid-1980s, NGOs were granted access to intergovernmental negotiations of environmental agreements. Over the past decade, Asian NGOs have become active participants in these negotiations, gaining access to foreign governments and valuable opportunities for networking with international and regional NGOs. Because of the global visibility obtained by participating in international negotiations, Asian NGOs had an indirect impact, sometimes referred to as a boomerang effect, on domestic environmental policy.

Coming together at international meetings has also affected regional activities among Asian NGOs. In addition to caucusing and developing regional positions on global environmental issues, Asian NGOs increasingly work together on regional problems. Until recently, regionalization of environmental issues by NGOs was generally unrelated to official environmental regionalism. This may be changing as a result of the haze crisis because some governments have come to view NGOs as important actors in reinforcing state regionalism.

In efforts to strengthen the role of civil society, foster democratization, and influence national environmental policy, foundations and foreign governments have funded the activities of environmental NGOs in Asia. One example of the use of foreign aid to support NGOs is a project funded by the U.S. Agency for International Development in Indonesia, which created a trust fund to provide long-term support for Indonesian NGOs working on biodiversity issues. Biodiversity conservation in Indonesia involves a number of politically sensitive issues, including land reform, governmental transparency, the role of civil society in environmental decision making, and forest management. Foreign aid is used to finance environmental NGOs in order to promote political change while also supporting environmental conservation.

Many international foundations include protection of human rights, promotion of civil society, and good governance within their funding priorities. As a result, these foundations often fund projects and NGOs working in these areas. Some examples of NGOs financed by the Rockefeller Brothers' Fund in 2000 illustrate its support for work on politically sensitive environmental issues: the Mekong Watch Japan, the Agrarian Reform Consortium in Indonesia, the Northern Development Foundation in Chiang Mai, the Tambuyog Development Center in the Philippines, and Wetlands International Asia-Pacific in Malaysia. This list of grantees also shows the role played by foundations in promoting regionalism by their funding of projects that involve multiple countries within Asia, as in the case of Mekong Watch.

Under pressure from Western governments and international NGOs, the World Bank and Asian Development Bank have adopted environmental guidelines covering their lending, grant, and technical assistance programs. Bank environmental policies provide for NGO participation in project development, monitoring and implementation, and public access to information about the project. NGOs often have more access to information and more opportunity to influence national project development through these multilateral development banks than through direct interaction with their own governments.

The Role of the Private Sector

The close relationship between government and industry in Asian countries retards environmental regionalism because industry is generally opposed to increased regulation and transparency. Ensuring that regional standards are nondiscriminatory would require transparency and openness in the rule-making process and could entail the involvement of NGOs. Increased transparency in environmental rule making could expose private-sector influence over a government's environmental decision making and strengthen domestic political demand for environmental protection, changes unlikely to be supported by industry.

Asian companies' influence on environmental regionalism is illustrated by the use of official development assistance to support Japanese business in Southeast Asia during the 1960s and 1970s (Dauvergne 1997a, 2–3). Officially, Japan stopped its tied aid practices in the late 1980s, but a high proportion of aid continued to support infrastructure projects that benefited Japanese companies, especially those related to energy and transportation (Dauvergne 1997a, 3), and was still "closely coordinated with the commercial agenda of private sector actors" in the mid-1990s (Arase 1995, 171–73). By financing infrastructure development to support environmentally intensive Japanese industry, the government enabled companies to take advantage of the lower environmental standards in Southeast Asia and China and minimized any motivation for upward harmonization to Japanese levels of environmental protection.

The effect of the private sector in Indonesia on national and regional environmental policy can be observed from the failure of the government to enforce the Regional Haze Action Plan and its own laws on forest management. In China, of course, government and industry are still one and the same in many cases, so it is difficult to assess the private sector's role in environmental policy separate from that of the government.

Although multinational corporations based in industrialized countries do not generally favor strong environmental regulation, for several reasons they tend to prefer global standards to national ones. To deflect strong criticism by Western NGOs, satisfy consumer demand for environmentally friendly products, and promote administrative efficiency, some large multinationals have adopted company-wide environmental standards on a global basis. Adopting a single standard, usually based on laws in the home country, minimizes charges that a company has located offshore to avoid environmental rules and facilitates transfer of technology and personnel among subsidiaries. Adhering to a high international standard can also help a multinational company minimize the difficulties associated with adopting numerous local standards developed in an opaque process and implemented in a potentially discriminatory manner. However, many multinationals have outsourced pollution-intensive activities to local companies to minimize their environmental liability.

As major sources of capital and investment in Asia, American and European companies can influence environmental policy in Asian countries by favoring global rules in environmental agreements and the WTO and by requiring their Asian suppliers and subcontractors to meet minimum environmental standards to assuage consumer concerns.

National and Regional Environmental Institutions

Weak institutional infrastructure on the national and regional level contributes to the current approach to environmental regionalism in Asia. On the national level, all Asian countries have created environmental agencies and adopted fairly stringent laws and regulations. With the major exceptions of Japan and Singapore, however, implementation and enforcement of environmental laws have not been effective. In all Asian countries, other ministries, including those dealing with finance, trade, construction, and energy, overshadow the environmental agency. Even in Japan, a country with stringent standards and high compliance rates, the Environment Ministry does not have the authority to enforce environmental laws.

In a chicken-and-egg situation, weak national institutions reflect the low level of effective political demand for environmental protection and retard its further development. Without national political support, it is also much more difficult for environmental officials to advance environmental issues on the regional level.

ASEAN, the primary institution in the region dealing with environmental issues, is a consensus-based organization that relies on voluntary cooperation to carry out its work. It does not have legislative powers, enforcement authority, or a binding dispute resolution mechanism. In the haze case, these institutional weaknesses badly hampered its ability to effectively address the problem. ASEAN does bring together environment officials from various levels of government to discuss issues and share information, and it has coordinated technical assistance in certain areas. ASEAN's environmental program is primarily aimed at building national capacity to manage environmental problems and fostering regional cooperation.

Regional Cooperation on Environmental Issues in International Negotiations

In general, Asian countries do not advance regional positions in global negotiations on environmental issues. The different levels of economic development of Asian countries is one important reason for this lack of regional solidarity. In most cases, a country's economic situation is a key indicator of its position on national, regional, and global environmental issues, although political relations and domestic environmental impacts are also important.

Japan, as an advanced industrial economy, usually participates in international negotiations along with other members of the OECD. Other Asian countries negotiate as members of the Group of 77 Developing Countries and China. For political and financial reasons, countries such as South Korea and Singapore have remained members of G-77, despite their economic advances. When Asian countries have taken a regional position in either environmental or trade negotiations, the "region" usually consists of ASEAN members. For example, ASEAN has taken a strong position within the WTO against linking trade and environmental issues and allowing NGOs to participate in its activities.

Future Prospects for Asian Regionalism

Given the ongoing economic and political changes occurring in the Asian region, it seems inevitable that environmental integration will deepen over time. Some important factors that will influence how environmental regionalism proceeds in Asia include changes in the level and composition of intraregional trade, increased access to Japanese and Chinese domestic markets, and tightening of national environmental laws in China.

China's increasing political and economic power in the region could lead to deeper environmental integration. If China's domestic market were opened to expanding regional trade, it would have the market power to demand regional harmonization of environmental standards. However, unless an increase in market power is accompanied by the adoption of stringent national environmental standards, competitiveness concerns will not be an impetus for China to demand harmonization. Given the severity of environmental problems in China today, it is not unreasonable to project that domestic political demand could increase enough to force the government to significantly strengthen environmental rules.

Japan's domestic market is increasingly open to Asian exports. If this trend continues, competition between Japanese and imported products could rise. With both stringent environmental standards and a large domestic market, Japan could demand upward harmonization on the regional level.

10

The War on Terrorism in Asia and the Possibility of Secret Regionalism

DAVID LEHENY

In the initial weeks after the terrorist attacks of September 11, 2001, in Washington and New York, which together claimed over 3,100 lives, media attention focused on the long reach of al Qaeda, the group that was immediately accused of the attacks. That the movement would have branches scattered throughout the Middle East, northern Africa, and central Asia surprised few, but commentators seemed alarmed that the network's reach extended as well to Southeast Asia. Of course, this bewilderment owed something to the popular misconception that the group's focus is on the conflict between Israelis and Palestinians, but it also reflected the marginalization of Southeast Asia in discussions of Islam, especially those concerning Islam's political influences (Hefner 1997). The January 2002 arrest of apparent members of the Southeast Asian terrorist group Jemaah Islamaiah (JI; translated as Islamic Group), which was linked to al Qaeda, set off international repercussions, provoking a new wave of crackdowns across states in Southeast Asia and helping to justify an American military presence in the region. In April 2002, the Malaysian government arrested fourteen suspected JI members, and the government of the Philippines arrested an Indonesian bomb expert alleged to be a JI militant (Baguiro 2002).

Shortly after the attacks, international relations scholar Stephen Walt referred to the U.S.-led "war on terrorism" as "the most rapid and dramatic change in the history of U.S. foreign policy" (Walt 2001–2, 56). At the very least, it presents important opportunities and constraints to governments around the world, because the United States remains the only truly global superpower. Rather than predict the "outcome" of the war on terrorism in Asia, which may be partly contingent on decisions made in Tel Aviv, Ramallah, or Baghdad, I explore in this chapter what these opportunities and constraints might be. In so doing, I investigate the relationship between terrorism and politics as well as the potential for regional security institutions that focus primarily on the internal security concerns of member states. I also hope to shed light on the role in Asia of political Islam, or the various movements that have sought to replace the secular state in predominantly Muslim areas with a theocracy guided by religious leaders ruling through strict interpretations of the Koran (see Kepel 2002).

Two caveats are in order. First, although this chapter deals specifically with Islamist movements, I do not mean in any way to equate Islam with terrorism, a tactical style of violence used at one time or another in virtually every geographical, political, religious, and ethnic context. But the "war on terrorism" is about American struggles with Islamist movements, and it is impossible to talk meaningfully about one without the other, especially after the September 11 attacks. Second, this chapter should not be taken as a full discussion of the problems of terrorist violence, regional security, or political Islam in Southeast Asia. I hope only that it will untangle some of the more important strands of a remarkably complex phenomenon, one that will bedevil policy makers around the world for years to come.

Asia-Pacific Security Institutions, Terrorism, and Theories of Security

In a widely cited article, Aaron Friedberg argues that security in Asia presents a troublesome prospect because of the complex balance of forces, legacies of historical mistrust, and the absence of meaningful international institutions capable of mitigating the vexing consequences of international anarchy (Friedberg 1993). Friedberg thus represents one side of the debate over Asian security; against him are those who would argue that since the end of the Cold War, there has been more international conflict in "peaceful" Europe than in the Asia-Pacific. The fact that Asia has not experienced a frenetic arms race or a massive interstate war does not mean that Friedberg is wrong, but the absence of an Asian version of NATO does not mean he is right. The difficulty of assessing whether Asia's regional security is in good or bad shape mirrors our problems in defining what the region's security institutions are.

One perspective sees Asia-Pacific security as marked by an important balancing game primarily between the United States and China, with Japan, North and South Korea, and Taiwan occupying critical supporting roles (e.g., Cha 2000; Collins 2000; Mendl 1995). In this view, groups such as ASEAN and the ASEAN Regional Forum (ARF) are largely impotent talking shops that have either abdicated security goals in favor of less troublesome topics or are so weakly institutionalized as to have no real import. In contrast, defenders of these institutions argue that the comparison to NATO is overly facile and that these groups can be significant in ways that are often invisible when seen in terms of materialist conceptions of power and politics. Iain Johnston (1999), for example, suggests that ARF's role appears to be the socialization of China into a peaceful and stable region, by encouraging Chinese leaders to identify concerns through consultation rather than to act unilaterally. These contrasting positions mirror debates in the field of international security—between those who focus primarily on the rational pursuit of materially defined interests (e.g., Waltz 1979) and those who emphasize the socially constructed nature of international politics (Katzenstein 1996b).

Although they will hardly settle the debate, recent volumes edited by Muthiah Alagappa (1998, 2001) draw on a broad array of theoretical positions to guide detailed empirical research on the changing security environment of Asia. The risk of interstate conflict looms especially large in Northeast Asia, whereas Southeast Asian governments have been forced to confront primarily internal security conflicts, including separatist movements, the occasional leftist insurgency, and religious violence. In his study of Japanese security, Katzenstein (1996a) argues that a more robust conception of security politics would include state orientations to internal and external threats alike. Given ASEAN's history as an organization devoted to meeting the threat of communist insurgency faced by Southeast Asian governments in the 1960s and 1970s, it is perhaps surprising that the literature on Asian security institutions has tended not to make the link. By the same token, throughout the 1980s and 1990s, neither did the policy makers themselves, at least in their public pronouncements.

As a topic, terrorism demands a rethinking of this gap. Groups that use terrorism often have had primarily local goals (e.g., British withdrawal from Northern Ireland, creation of an Islamic state in Egypt) but may find it tempting to operate internationally. Since the 1972 Munich Olympics—when the Black September group kidnapped and ultimately murdered eleven Israeli athletes—terrorist organizations have found that international acts have sometimes drawn useful attention to their demands, resulting in important organizational benefits such as financial support and expanded recruitment pools. Moreover, a terrorist group might include among its enemies foreign governments and organizations believed to provide support to the local regime or population it opposes. A global scale for its conflict provides a terrorist group with a rich array of targets. For these reasons, the literature on terrorism has long chronicled the potential interest of terrorist groups in international action (see, e.g., Hoffman 1998).

It has not, however, linked terrorism to broader theoretical discussions of security. Some researchers on terrorism began to specialize in local conflicts or in specific groups (e.g., Bell 2000), while others approached the issue conceptually. Among the latter category are Martha Crenshaw, whose work best defines research on the politics of terrorism (Crenshaw 1983, 1985, 1995), and Jerrod Post, whose examination of individual terrorist group leaders is aimed at creating useful psychological profiles of terrorists (Post 1998). Especially after 1995, when the Aum Shinrikyo cult released sarin gas in the Tokyo subway system, the terrorism literature began to show a preoccupation with the use of weapons of mass destruction (Laqueur 1999; Stern 1999). Because terrorism specialists have found that their audiences have been those policy makers forced to confront terrorism as a security threat, especially in the United States, their work has been more practical and empirical than theoretical (Leheny 2002).

The absence of terrorism in discussions of regional security thus results both from the neglect by international security scholars of the relationship between internal and external security, and from terrorism specialists' focus on audiences outside the academy. As Katzenstein (2002) points out, the September 11 attacks suggest a need to broaden conceptions of security to include such issues as societal security or comprehensive security, for which sociological or anthropological insights might be of value. Even if one chooses to adopt a narrow definition, leaders' and scholars' views of international security must now engage not simply interstate but also nonstate conflict capable of inflicting grievous harm on superpowers, not to mention on smaller, more vulnerable states. The U.S. war on terrorism has already changed the conditions under which other states and international institutions operate, and it will likely do so for several years. If regionalism refers to top-down efforts to allow a set of states to cooperate within a specified geographic framework (see Pempel's introductory chapter to this volume), international terrorism may provide the impetus for a new security regionalism in Asia.

Al Qaeda as a Loose Ideational Network

The other side of the regional coin is regionalization, or bottom-up processes of integration, usually viewed as economic in nature. Revelations about the Qaeda network, however, suggest that it is worth thinking about the possibility of ideational regionalization, specifically through the construction of religious identities that cross national boundaries. The existence of an organization like the JI does not necessarily mean that there has been significant ideational regionalization around an Islamist identity in Asia; JI might simply be an isolated, marginalized group of militants. But the nature of al Qaeda makes it extraordinarily difficult to determine which groups are affiliated with it and how deep the links run; they may be little more than shared experience at training camps and the potential to operate in tandem. Equally important, even the clear existence of al Qaeda cells might say little about the strength and popularity of political Islam in a region, although such cells might pose a significant security threat anyway.

Since the September 11 attacks, al Qaeda has been characterized in varied ways, including as a terrorist organization, a network, a group, an army, and a faction. This terminological problem emerges in part from the entity's clandestine nature, making it difficult to know precisely what it looks like "underneath," as well as from its novelty. Put simply, there has never been a phenomenon quite like al Qaeda (the Base), a militant Islamic movement that combines aspects of states, formal organizations, and networks in its stated goal of reestablishing fully Islamic governments in predominantly Muslim areas.[1] Al Qaeda is certainly more than a simple organization; it links perhaps dozens of fundamentalist organizations, all of which have different proximate political goals but ostensibly are united in the broader effort to establish political communities dominated by Islamic law and free of other religious forces, especially Christianity and Judaism. They can perhaps be best understood as a culturally defined network, one that links members in part through shared references and goals, but not always in formal or even mutually understood structures.

Since September 11, 2001, popular awareness of al Qaeda has increased exponentially. The rudimentary foundation of al Qaeda was created in 1987, after the split of two factions of the mujahedeen (holy warriors) fighting against the Soviet presence in Afghanistan (Engelberg 2001). During the 1980s, the Reagan administration (which simultaneously warned of Islamic fundamentalism in Iran) generously funded the anti-Soviet insurgence, using fundamentalism to entice potential recruits from around the region (Gerges 1999, 69–73). With financial support from the United States and also Saudi Arabia, members of the Pakistani security services began to establish training centers on the Pakistani–Afghani border, calling the fight against the Soviets a jihad.[2] Offering payment and the opportunity to take part in a meaningful struggle, the leaders of the mujahedeen movement attracted Muslim recruits from around the Middle East, northern Africa, central Asia, and as far away as Southeast Asia. In the brutal civil war that followed the withdrawal of the Soviet Union, many of the non-Afghani fighters joined a militia known as the Taliban (Students) because of its members' strongly fundamentalist bent, built through years of study and training at the madrassas (religious training centers) in the border region (Rashid 2000).

Among the militants drawn to Afghanistan during the insurgency against the Soviet Union was wealthy Saudi dissident Osama bin Laden. Bin Laden's

1. In a fascinating interview with Middle East Report (Mubarak 1997), one leader of the radical Tal'at Fu'ad Qasim (Islamic Group) explains the movement's goals, the fight in Afghanistan, and the roles of Ayman al Zawahiri (of Egyptian Islamic Jihad) and Osama bin Laden.

2. The term jihad (holy war, struggle, effort) is widely debated in the wake of September 11. My use of it here is designed to correspond to its use within the jihadi movement, which views struggle in primarily violent terms. I do not mean to imply that this is the correct interpretation of the term, or that Islam espouses violence more so than do other monotheistic faiths. See Stern 2000 for a discussion of the jihadi movement in Pakistan.

considerable financial resources and his clever use of rhetoric made him an important force in Islamist politics (a term used to describe militant Islamic political views) from the late 1980s onward. Many of the Islamic fighters drawn to Afghanistan during and after the anti-Soviet campaign had larger concerns at home. The most important group among these, Egyptian Islamic Jihad (EIJ), had risen to prominence because of its assassination of President Anwar Sadat in 1981. EIJ's criticism of the United States for supporting the regime of Hosni Mubarak—a secular ruler it claims is highly corrupt—as well as for supporting Israel dovetailed with bin Laden's anger at the United States for basing troops in Saudi Arabia during and after the Persian Gulf War (Mac-Farquhar 2001). Significantly, bin Laden's and EIJ's main goals—to remove the United States from the Saudi holy land and to replace the Mubarak regime with a religious one that followed Islamic law—differed, and might even have been contradictory had an Egyptian revolution encouraged even more American involvement in Riyadh. Bin Laden's skill was to focus on the common external enemy to Islam, in essence arguing that by first removing the infidels from Muslim territory, the EIJ could further its long-term interests in Egypt itself (Gerecht 2002). This connection, arguably the most important for members of "the Base," is emblematic of al Qaeda's strategy throughout the 1990s.

Indeed, the camps in Afghanistan and the madrassas in Pakistan trained thousands of students and fighters from around the world, including Arabs, Asians, Turks, Africans, Europeans of North African descent, and in one celebrated case, a young Californian. Al Qaeda was hardly the only actor involved, and not all of the products of these programs ended up working with bin Laden's organization. But its militant, quasi-millennial interpretations of the Koran (Juergensmeyer 1993), in combination with its tactical training in weapons, explosives, surveillance, and planning, attracted members of Islamist movements with different local concerns and provided a global perspective for their work. No longer were they simply religious Egyptians struggling to replace a corrupt, secular government; no longer were they just Moros trying to win independence from a repressive Philippine state and a Catholic majority. Instead, their local concerns were part of a broader struggle against "Jews and crusaders," a struggle generally portrayed as one with the United States and Israel. Among the aspects of al Qaeda that have astonished terrorism experts in recent years has been the distinctly international flavor of its cells; indeed, the cells that supported the attacks on New York and Washington may have included citizens of Saudi Arabia, Egypt, France, Indonesia, and other nations. Al Qaeda's special role was in uniting members of local groups, bringing them together under the common banner of a global Islamist movement that would benefit them all.

Of course, it would have been extraordinarily difficult to verify whether al Qaeda might have been capable of achieving this kind of global revolution, even before it incurred the full wrath of U.S. military forces working in conjunction with British special forces and anti-Taliban militias in Afghanistan. Its methods and means for developing loyalty to a remarkably amorphous idea, however, are instructive. One terrorism specialist, Jessica Stern (2000), has paid special attention to the role of the madrassas in promoting extreme interpretations of the Koran and deeply anti-American rhetoric. Perhaps equally important were the training camps in Afghanistan, many of which were funded by bin Laden and the financial networks he helped to establish for al Qaeda. Indeed, U.S. retaliatory cruise missile strikes in the aftermath of the 1998 East African bombings of U.S. embassies attacked (inaccurately, we have since learned) bin Laden's camps. Scholars of state formation have emphasized not only the importance of armies for the creation of state bureaucracies (Tilly 1992) but also the relevance of military drills and training for forging a common identity capable of overcoming regional divisions that threaten to polarize national armies (McNeill 1984). In other words, al Qaeda's role has largely been to take militants with primarily local political concerns and to convince them that they are part of a global struggle for Islam. By training and working together in military camps and in the Afghani campaigns, Islamists developed loyalty to the idea of a global jihad, one that would inform the ways in which they pursued local actions as well.

That terrorism can be motivated by identity concerns seems obvious. After all, nationalist movements using terrorist tactics (from the I.R.A. to the Tamil Tigers) remind us that "identity politics" can be a topic of considerably more global immediacy than campus discussions of multiculturalism might sometimes imply. The success of al Qaeda has been in building an Islamist identity that transcends state boundaries and even the murky perimeters of regions. Those organizations affiliated with al Qaeda may be predisposed toward attacking the governments of Egypt, or the United States, or Uzbekistan, or the Philippines, but they do not necessarily define themselves as central Asian, Middle Eastern, or Southeast Asian groups. They are instead engaged in local campaigns that can be simplified and reconstructed as elements of a global struggle to protect the faithful from the infidels.

As Gilles Kepel points out, however, al Qaeda's actions reflect not the strength of political Islam but rather its weakness (Kepel 2002). After all, al Qaeda was long based in the only swath of territory available—Taliban-controlled Afghanistan. Political Islam has, in most cases, found itself in conflict with secular republics, monarchies, or socialist governments, and its forces have usually been on the losing side. Even when al Qaeda's attacks on the United States—seen as a corrupt superpower intent on bringing harm to Muslims—find wide popular support in Muslim nations, the goal of establishing strict Islamist regimes has been notably less successful. For reasons of recruiting members and maintaining outside support, terrorist groups may carry out brutal attacks even when conditions seem inauspicious for their causes

(Crenshaw 1985). Whether or not bin Laden viewed the strikes on Washington and New York as an effort in a losing campaign is impossible to say, but they do not necessarily imply that political Islam has strength beyond a critical network of clandestine movements and their supporters.

The clandestine nature of terrorist organizations makes research on them difficult under any circumstances, but any empirical work on al Qaeda must remain sensitive to three significant features. First, al Qaeda's history as a loose network based on a common, diffuse ideology, as well as on military and religious training in Pakistan and Afghanistan, suggests that it is difficult to define precisely what it means for a group to be "linked" to al Qaeda. Sometimes the links will be as obvious as they are with the EIJ, but in other cases they may rely on long-dormant personal connections forged in Afghanistan and on the opportunistic pooling of resources and missions when opportunities arise. Second, the terrorist movements linked to al Qaeda will usually focus on local rather than global conflicts, meaning that their activities will likely differ across national contexts. Finally, there is no clear correlation between the strength of political Islam and the ability of al Qaeda's cells to operate, meaning that the presence or absence of one ought not be taken as evidence of the other.

Political Islam and Terrorism in Southeast Asia

The local campaigns in Southeast Asia differ from one another and also from those taking place in the Middle East and central Asia. Islamist political violence in Asia has in general not worked to reconstruct national governments as the servants of religious leaders pursuing shari'a law. It has instead served to highlight distinctions between ethnic and religious communities in the region, aiming at secession or at the suppression of groups that threaten the long-term goal of Islamization of the polity. This means that the political dynamics of Islamic terrorism in Southeast Asia differ from those of efforts elsewhere, even as the global jihad against the West has mobilized supporters from Malaysia, Singapore, Indonesia, and the Philippines. These groups have mostly concerned themselves with local disputes, and their cooperation appears to be oriented toward the global mujahedeen struggle rather than toward creating a distinctively Southeast Asian religious movement. Singapore's arrest of apparent JI militants, most of whom are from Malaysia and Singapore, combined with the discovery of alleged Indonesian members, indicates that group members from different nations can align themselves to organize attacks against Western targets in the region. In these cases, however, the "collective action frame" (Babb 1996) that allows them to cooperate is drawn from the global jihadi movement and has shaped the way that militants conceptualize their grievances. The idea of a struggle against global enemies of Islam therefore informs the groups' rhetoric and their selection of targets, though it has not in itself established a region-wide identity of the movements as "Southeast Asian Islamists." Indeed, the JI's alleged choice of major bombing targets—a nightclub crowded with Australians and other foreigners in Bali in 2002, and a branch of an American hotel chain in Jakarta in 2003—suggests the importance of these Western symbols in the group's ideology.

None of the terrorist groups in question can be understood without attention to the specific religious and political contexts in which they are embedded. Especially visible among them, particularly with the deployment of U.S. forces to the Philippines to combat them, is the Abu Sayyaf Group (ASG). Secessionist violence in Mindanao was traditionally led by the Moro National Liberation Front (MNLF), a movement that used terrorist violence throughout the 1980s and early 1990s to promote the secession of predominantly Muslim Mindanao from the otherwise Catholic Philippines (Schloss 2001). Like other secessionist movements using terrorist tactics (such as the IRA in Northern Ireland, the Basque region's ETA, or the Tamil Tigers of Sri Lanka), the MNLF enjoyed wide popular support from its surrounding ethnic community, especially when the repressive Marcos regime cracked down on the region and failed to honor treaties and agreements between the government and Mindanao's Muslims (McKenna 1998). For years, the government of the Philippines was concerned primarily with the larger MNLF and its more aggressive offshoot, the Moro Islamic Liberation Front (MILF). The MNLF, under its leader Nur Misuari, brokered a peace treaty with the government, providing Muslim-controlled Mindanao with a certain amount of autonomy in exchange for security guarantees.[3]

The ASG, which has operated at the fringes of the Moro movement on Jolo and Basilan islands, has never been as large scale a threat as either the MILF or the MNLF. Even so, its eagerness to continue the armed struggle has made it a persistent thorn for the government of the Philippines. Founded in 1991, the ASG has also earned the attention of U.S. counterterrorism authorities because of its apparent connections with the Qaeda network and its fund-raising tactics. In 2000, ASG members traveled by speedboat to a Malaysian beach resort and kidnapped European vacationers. After months, the hostages were freed in part through the efforts of the Libyan government, which paid a ransom of $17 million to the organization (Parry 2000). After that, the ASG went on a remarkable kidnapping spree, taking hostage other travelers, including an American visitor freed after nearly a year, and two American missionaries—with one killed in the rescue mission that freed the other. ASG leaders have apparently used their ransom windfalls at times to pay off members of the military to avoid capture.[4]

---

3. The content of the agreements can be found in Ferrer 1997.

4. This is still a rumor, but the miraculous escape of many ASG militants after they were surrounded by Filipino forces in a hospital seems inexplicable without reference to bribery. See Parry 2001.

This emphasis on kidnapping for ransom has led to the ASG's reputation as a group of bandits perhaps more than terrorists. A number of factors, however, have convinced U.S. counterterrorism authorities in particular that the ASG maintains close, possibly operational, ties to al Qaeda. Ramzi Yousef, a Pakistani affiliate of al Qaeda convicted in the United States of the 1995 bombing of the World Trade Center, apparently ran a bomb factory discovered in Manila in 1995; he was also convicted of the 1994 bombing of an airliner in the Philippines in which one Japanese traveler was killed. Filipino authorities claim that the ASG cooperated in the plan to destroy more airliners (Schloss 2001). Moreover, the group's late commander, Abdurajak Abubakar Janjalani, trained and fought in the Afghani campaign, during which time he evidently received financial support from Osama bin Laden to build his own movement upon his return to the Philippines. The group's political motives remain murky, and it is hard to avoid the suspicion that the core of the ASG leadership is more concerned with financial benefits and survival than with the prosecution of a vigorous campaign of secessionist terror.

During much of the struggle over autonomy for Mindanao, the Malaysian government has walked a perilous tightrope. Its own security would have been threatened through the escalation of hostilities in nearby Mindanao, especially given the flood of Moro refugees already arriving in the state of Sabah in the 1960s (Nair 1997, 182–93). Although careful not to alienate the government of the Philippines, the Malaysian government also faced pressure from domestic Muslim groups that believed the Moros had been treated appallingly, especially during the Marcos years. Former prime minister Mahathir bin Mohamad ultimately worked to limit international Islamic condemnation of the Philippines while quietly pressuring the Filipinos to grant more autonomy to Mindanao. Even so, when Nur Misuari, at that point the governor of the Autonomous Region in Muslim Mindanao (ARMM), fled to Malaysia in late 2001 after leading an MNLF revolt to prevent an election that would have chosen his successor, the Malaysian government turned him over to Filipino authorities.

The role of Islam in Malaysia is unusual. The religion of neither a secessionist minority nor a dominant majority, as is the case, respectively, in the Philippines and Indonesia, Islam represents the faith of most of the country's ethnic Malays, roughly half of the Malaysian population. The government's efforts to craft a uniquely Malaysian national identity—one that can absorb the ethnic distinctions between Malays, Chinese, Indians, and smaller indigenous groups—have relied to some degree on the political use of Islam to support its Bumiputera policies, or those initiatives that favor the indigenous Malays. Islam is thus given a special place in the Malaysian constitution and has received institutional support from the Malaysian government (Nair 1997, 18–41).

Even so, Western-oriented development policies, political repression, and the growing economic divide between wealthier Chinese and the still poor Malays combined to produce a series of limited resistance movements in the late 1960s and early 1970s. The most successful of these were student groups that crystallized around the idea of *dakwah* (to call), becoming quasi-missionary movements pressing for the revitalization of strict Islamic codes in Malaysian society (Shamsul 1997, 213–22; Nagata 1980). Consisting predominantly of educated and increasingly middle-class members, the dakwah movement grew in political importance, partly to the detriment of rural "ordinary Muslims," who found themselves in some regions pressured into adopting visible markers of Islam in their public lives (Peletz 1997). The primary goal of the Mahathir government's stance on Islam became the co-optation of the language and ideas of the dakwah movement while preventing its more ambitious leaders from challenging the authority of the ruling coalition (Abu Bakar 1981; Mauzy and Milne 1983–84; Camroux 1996).

This approach has been a tense one, made even more so by Mahathir's 1998 arrest of his deputy, Anwar Ibrahim. Anwar, who had himself been brought into the government because of his standing among young Muslims and intellectuals (Keppel 2002, 88–98), had challenged Mahathir's handling of the 1997 economic crisis and was seen as an overly eager heir apparent. Indeed, the Malaysian government has meted out rough treatment to Islamist forces only when they seem to threaten Mahathir's hold on power. In 1994, his administration banned a dakwah group, al Arqam, because its leader announced that in one of his apparently periodic conversations with the prophet Muhammad, the prophet had predicted Mahathir's downfall (Tan 2000, 93–105).

In the aftermath of the September 11 attacks, Mahathir targeted the Parti Islam SeMalaysia (PAS), the fundamentalist Muslim party that serves as the main electoral rival to Mahathir's own United Malays National Organization (UMNO); the PAS had itself gained adherents after Anwar's arrest. Shortly after the attacks in New York and Washington, the Malaysian government announced that it would detain Nik Adli Nik Abdul Aziz, the son of the PAS's spiritual leader, alleging that he was a member of Kumpulan Militan Mujahideen (Chapter of Militant Holy Warriors, or KMM). The KMM has been blamed for attacks in Jakarta, including the 2000 bombing of the Philippines embassy (*Asiaweek*, October 5, 2001). Another wave of arrests of its members followed the unraveling of the Singapore plot, with the Malaysian government alleging that KMM was largely behind the efforts. That KMM was involved with JI in Singapore seems likely, although Mahathir certainly stood to benefit from an easily justified roundup of regime opponents.

The KMM's alleged activities in Jakarta bear only a shaky connection to the Indonesian Islamist movements most commonly discussed with reference to the war on terrorism. Like Abu Sayyaf and, apparently, the KMM, Indonesia's violent groups include members who trained in Afghanistan and may be connected to al Qaeda. Their struggle is not secessionist, nor is it aimed immediately at the reconstruction of the national government as an Islamic authority respecting shari'a law. Instead, in Indonesia—the world's most populous predominantly Muslim nation—militant movements have engaged in sectarian battles against other religious communities, and their relationship to the government thus lacks the hostility found in both Malaysia and the Philippines.

Islam's role in Indonesia has been complicated by the continuing relevance of indigenous mystical traditions, many of which have merged with a particularly Indonesian form of Sufism (Howell 2001). This syncretic blend of Islam and inherited religious traditions has endowed the nation with unique cultural resources, although it has also left it vulnerable to charges that it is somehow not "Islamic" enough. Indeed, Indonesian Islamic leaders trained in and sometimes funded by Saudi Arabia have pushed for an Islamic resurgence in Indonesia along the lines pursued by PAS members in Malaysia. In both nations, Islam has become a useful frame for articulating critiques of a government's orientation toward modernity, development, and the West. And, as in Malaysia, the government has had to be wary of the possible threat that a popular reformist Islam would present to a leader's authority. For this reason, during much of his nearly three-decade tenure, President Suharto worked cagily between his professed devotion to indigenous mystical traditions and his declared scholarship in Arabic texts and the lessons of the Koran. When faced with threats from student militants pushing for an enhanced role for Islam, for example, Suharto did his best to co-opt the movement, even placing his trusted lieutenant (and eventual successor) B. J. Habibie in the core of a new association of Muslim intellectuals (Hefner 2000; Liddle 1996). Even so, the New Order's Social Organization Act of 1985 helped to drive the creation of antiregime tendencies among the nation's Islamic movements, because of its requirement that all organizations—including religious groups—recognize the nationalist Pancasila ideology as their "sole organizing principle" (Woodward 1993, 579).

The election of Abdurrahman Wahid, head of the Nahdlatul Ulama (NU, the country's association of "traditionalist" Islamic scholars), to the presidency in 1999 suggested to some hopeful observers that the country was moving to embrace Wahid's own tolerant and pluralistic version of Islam (Hefner 2000; Hedman 2002). Even so, fundamentalist movements—motivated in part by the secessionist struggles in East Timor, Aceh, and elsewhere—had moved toward the use of violence against non-Muslim communities, partly in order to establish areas of clear control by shari'a law and partly to deny the possibility of further efforts to break away from Indonesia. The most visible of these, Laskar Jihad (Militia of the Holy War) even operated a welcome desk at Ambon airport to greet foreign mujahedeen who had flown in to join the jihad against the Christians of the Maluku Islands (Sim 2001). The now jailed head of the organization, Ja'far Umar Thalib, is an Indonesian of Yemeni descent who trained and fought in the anti-Soviet campaign in Afghanistan. He denies any straightforward connection with al Qaeda, even going so far as to criticize Osama bin Laden, although he has expressed support for the attacks on the United States (Paddock 2001).[5]

The tentative stance of Megawati Sukarnoputri's administration, which had voiced some support of Washington's position but was slow to challenge Laskar Jihad and other jihadi groups, reflects tensions underlying the coalition government. Although the military authorized a small crackdown on Laskar Jihad shortly before Megawati's ascension to the presidency in 2001 (Hedman 2002, 42), the government did not clamp down more firmly on the movement until spring 2002, and perhaps only in order to extract more military aid from the United States. The nation's second largest party, the United Development Party (PPP), represents a constituency consisting largely of urban "modernist Muslims," or those who observe a purer form than the Sufist blend preferred in the countryside. Indonesia's vice president under Megawati, Hamzah Haz, heads the PPP and has his own designs on the presidency, which he cannot attain without his party's support. Playing to this conservative Muslim vote, he visited Thalib in jail shortly after the Laskar Jihad leader's arrest. It was, he reported, his duty to his "Muslim brother."

Even the PPP is hardly an Islamist party of the type preferred by bin Laden and his ilk, and fundamentalists have lost ground in Indonesia to secular and other Muslim parties alike (Hedman 2002, 41). The 2004 election, which witnessed very limited support for fundamentalist organizations, suggests that Islamist parties are far from a popular majority. But the government's institutional fragility, the still imposing role of the armed forces, as well as the fractured nature of the party system will together make it important that leaders consider Islamists' potentially pivotal role. Indonesia's religious fundamentalists will likely not be in a position to achieve any far-reaching religious turn for the country, though they are too important to ignore and perhaps even to marginalize.

This does not mean that the United States serves its best interest by pursuing its war on terrorism in Southeast Asia, just that the threat posed by Islamist movements is something other than a fiction to justify American intervention. Throughout the region, Islamist forces are at best beleaguered, able to achieve some political success only in secessionist conflicts heavily imbued with ethnic tensions. It is at present unclear whether the October 2002 Bali bombing and the attack on the Marriott hotel in Jakarta in 2003 will do anything for JI other than to encourage a government crackdown that enjoys substantial popular support. And the connections between separatist rebels in

---

5. In his testimony before Congress, Boston University's Robert Hefner, a specialist on Islam in Indonesia, said that the denial was unpersuasive (Bonner and Perlez 2002).

the Philippines, radical regime opponents in Malaysia, and Islamists with murky ties to the military in Indonesia may be purely emotional rather than strategic, financial, or operative. Even so, in a struggle that has now featured a Briton of Jamaican descent trying to destroy an airliner with explosives hidden in his sneakers, it is safe to say that stranger things have happened. American policy makers are likely to pursue all available avenues for suppressing al Qaeda; the demonstrated presence of Islamist militants and lack of effective state control in certain areas together make Southeast Asia a region of intense concern in the war on terrorism.

Re-regionalism in Asia

It was the amorphous worry about connections between rebels and Islamists that framed the U.S. decision to deploy more than six hundred members of its special forces to provide military training in the Philippines. According to the U.S. government, the move targets the ASG, which has been linked publicly (most recently in 1995) to al Qaeda. To be sure, the ASG remains an important security threat to U.S. citizens in the region, mainly because of its kidnapping tactics. It does not, however, appear to be an especially "political" branch of the Qaeda movement, nor did the 2002 plot in Singapore implicate the ASG as an important component of the plan. Indeed, it is hard to see how the U.S. mission will significantly reduce the Qaeda network's ability to target American assets in the long term.

What it will do, however, is give the U.S. government a reasonably sympathetic environment in which to pursue the international war on terrorism. Although memories of American imperialism and post-imperial support for repressive regimes left many Filipinos ambivalent about the reentry of U.S. troops, the ASG is a deeply unpopular movement in most parts of the Philippines, and anti-American protests quickly declined except among students in madaris (religious schools similar to the Pakistani madrassas) in Mindanao (Brooke 2002; BBC Monitoring 2002). The presence of U.S. forces would thus aim primarily at a popularly supported goal, something the Bush administration might not have been able to count on elsewhere in the region. The initial deployment in Southeast Asia thus might be an effort to establish a good precedent—that the United States stands ready to assist other governments in their efforts to eradicate troublesome violent movements.

On its face, this ought to be an appealing pledge. After all, states can usually agree on very little, but presumably they all prefer states to nonstates, or at least to the nonstate movements that might threaten them. Even with ASEAN, however, the idea of tight transnational collaboration against domestic threats has been a tough sell. By early 2002, Malaysia and Singapore were already beginning to push ASEAN on the always nettlesome topic of tighter security cooperation. ASEAN was itself established in 1967 to serve as a bulwark against the encroachment of communism (Shee 1977), but its unusual focus on a "common internal threat" rather than an external one made it difficult to establish the genuine defense coordination found in a more traditional alliance (Acharya 1991). Focusing more on political, diplomatic, and even economic coordination, ASEAN has proved reluctant to enforce security obligations that seemingly infringe on the sovereignty of member states. An informal meeting of ASEAN foreign ministers in Thailand in February 2002 yielded a pledge of joint action against terrorism and was followed by a Special Ministerial Meeting on Terrorism in Kuala Lumpur in May 2002 (Abdullah 2002; "ASEAN Foreign Ministers" 2002).

It was a tense series of meetings. The government of Singapore initially criticized Indonesia for its reluctance to arrest Indonesian cleric Abu Bakar Bashir, seen as an important leader of the JI (Roberts 2002). The area of shared interests is at best limited, since the participants include more aggressive opponents of political Islam such as Singapore and the Philippines, an Indonesian government criticized by neighbors for not doing enough to clamp down on militants, and a Malaysian government needing to support Islam while at the same time vilifying Islamists. As a result, ASEAN cooperation has focused on more limited issues, such as calls to adhere to UN counterterrorism conventions (Abdullah 2002), rather than on more ambitious efforts like shared or coordinated antiterrorist units.

The absence of tight ASEAN cooperation is emblematic of the problems that a seemingly uncontroversial goal—such as a world without terrorism—has when it confronts other domestic and regional priorities for Asia-Pacific governments. Outside the relatively placid waters of the ASEAN member states, the problem is trickier still. The often maligned ARF, which includes the ASEAN states as well as most other Asia-Pacific nations, has itself adopted strong language against terrorism and pledged future cooperation, which may at the least raise the costs of allowing terrorist groups to operate. But the most powerful members of ARF will likely have radically different views of how the war on terrorism should proceed.

Even before the September 11 attacks, the U.S. approach to terrorism was ostensibly highly activist in nature, although it was often poorly coordinated and remained a low priority among American security commitments (see, e.g., Carter 2001–2; Tucker 1997). It was unsurprising, therefore, that the U.S. response would include not simply an assault on al Qaeda's facilities in Afghanistan but a larger offensive aimed at its network and its putative state sponsors. American activities in the Asia-Pacific might thus reflect only the goal of eradicating terrorism, but it is not improper to speculate that the United States might have larger regional security goals in mind. Security cooperation in the Philippines might help to reestablish an American presence at the Subic Bay naval base, bolstering the United

States's ability to act in the event of an East or Southeast Asian military crisis. Moreover, cooperation in the central Asian republics of Uzbekistan, Kyrgyzstan, and even Tajikistan might simply be aimed at eradicating al Qaeda's presence in that region. By the same token, it might give Washington an important military foothold in an area of great strategic value vis-à-vis rivals such as China and Russia.

Because of the importance it places on its diplomatic standing and on international agreements, the Japanese government has publicly adhered to UN and G-8 conventions on international terrorism. Even so, it faces enormous constitutional and political constraints on the development and use of police or military force against terrorist groups, both at home (Katzenstein and Tsujinaka 1991) and abroad (Itabashi, Ogawara, and Leheny 2002). In part because of these limits on fighting terrorism, and in part because of a widespread public belief that the government should place the safety of Japanese citizens first, the Japanese government has occasionally paid ransoms to rescue Japanese hostages.[6] When the U.S. government requested international support for the campaign against Afghanistan, Japanese prime minister Junichiro Koizumi quickly pledged military assistance beyond anything yet provided by Japan to an international mission. Although subsequent Diet negotiations delayed the promised deployment of an Aegis-equipped cruiser, Japan still escaped the punishing ridicule it received during the Persian Gulf War, when its pledge of financial assistance came too late to save it from merciless attacks, especially in the U.S. media. Even so, Southeast Asia is not Afghanistan—and Japan would be hard-pressed to provide active support of U.S. efforts in Southeast Asia if these would make the thousands of Japanese residing in the region targets of KMM, JI, or ASG attacks (Leheny 2001–2). Moreover, because of Japan's bitter history with armed conflict in the region and the normative proscriptions on the use of force, any further steps it takes toward counterterrorism cooperation in Asia will carry symbolic implications both at home and abroad.

China, to give the most obvious example, would eye Tokyo's moves with great suspicion; the world's largest nation currently finds itself in a deeply ambivalent position in the war on terrorism. After the September 11 attacks, China's mild support for U.S. actions in Afghanistan has been premised on its own desire to crack down on Muslim militants in Xinjiang Province. This traditionally Uighur stronghold has displayed secessionist tendencies, and

---

6. In 1977, the Japanese government openly paid the Japanese Red Army $6 million to end a hijacking drama in Dacca, Bangladesh; it had not yet signed international conventions banning such concessions to terrorist groups. In 1999, it denied paying the Islamic Movement of Uzbekistan a ransom to free three Japanese aid workers kidnapped in rural Kyrgyzstan. Japanese newspapers, however, reported that a ransom of $2–5 million was paid. See Itabashi, Ogawara, and Leheny 2002.

the Chinese government had long sought a free hand to crack down on Uighurs pushing for independence or autonomy (Agence France Presse 2001). One of China's regional initiatives—the Shanghai Cooperative Organization (SCO), which includes China, Russia, Uzbekistan, Kyrgyzstan, Tajikistan, and Kazakhstan—has focused largely on Islamist threats in central Asia. Even so, the deployment of U.S. forces in Uzbekistan, Kyrgyzstan, and Tajikistan, combined with their reappearance in the Philippines, has alarmed Beijing that the United States is using the war on terrorism to encircle China. Japan's historic decision to support the United States in Afghanistan has left many in China convinced that it must react to the threat of a newly assertive United States–Japan alliance operating in tandem with China's other neighbors (Friedberg 2002). Partly in response, China has met with the SCO to try to ensure that the American stay on its western flank will be brief and limited, by pointedly saying that those fighting terrorism should not have double standards and that Afghanistan should be a "neutral" country.[7]

American efforts probably received a boost from the atrocity at the Bali nightclub in October 2002. Because nearly 90 of the 202 killed were Australians, the Australian government—which has publicly and repeatedly allied itself with the U.S.-led war on terrorism—had special reason to push the Indonesian government after the attack. The international pressure combined with local outrage together appear to have encouraged the Australian government to confront Islamists more directly; police even arrested Abu Bakar Bashir, charging him in connection with a different series of bombings. The subsequent trial of a purported JI militant named Amrozi concluded with a guilty verdict and a death sentence. The almost simultaneous bombing of the Marriott hotel in Jakarta suggests that the Indonesian government will continue to face intense foreign pressure to arrest militants, share intelligence, and publicly support antiterrorist initiatives. Whether these will lead to broader transnational agreements is still unclear.

The war on terrorism has created a bewildering array of possibilities for states and new security institutions in Asia, although this is primarily because it adds a new layer to existing tensions, not because it replaces them. If Washington pursues primarily bilateral arrangements, as it has with the Philippines and will likely do in other troop deployments, it risks encouraging further reactions, particularly by China, that would engender new regional institutions that exclude or challenge American hegemony. If, on the other hand, Washington pursues regional agreements, it may find that the interests of other governments are simply too diverse to promote much coordination beyond the limited form currently under debate at ASEAN.

---

7. A BBC Monitoring Report of a Xinhua article included this point. See "China: Foreign Ministry Spokesman on Shanghai Six Consensus," financial news information, BBC Monitoring Reports of a Xinhua report, January 2, 2002; accessed through Lexis-Nexis.

Reactive Regionalization

The prospects for bottom-up regionalization are, in some ways, more uncertain and worrisome than those Washington faces in its efforts to promote regional agreements among states. As noted earlier, in spite of the arrest of JI in Singapore or the occasional appearance of Indonesian Islamists in Malaysia or the Philippines, there is little evidence that fundamentalist movements have succeeded in socially regionalizing Muslim Southeast Asia. The concerns of groups in the region still appear to be predominantly local. But through intentional action or simple mishap, the U.S. government and other states might succeed where al Qaeda itself has not—in encouraging the creation of an Islamist region. In the U.S. initiative against the Taliban, policy makers seemed genuinely attuned to the concern that military action might further weaken America's already shoddy standing among the bizarrely labeled "Arab street." The Taliban, however, turned out to occupy a far more rickety structure than many had expected, and U.S. military successes came so quickly that the "image" concern turned to the humiliating speed with which U.S. forces could crush their enemies, rather than focusing on massive numbers of civilian deaths. In the initial months after deployment, U.S. forces in the Philippines deliberately maintained a low profile, serving as "trainers" rather than as an active contingent. President Gloria Arroyo too went out of her way to deny that U.S. forces would have a combat role.

Even so, Americans are training and working in an area in which at least two major separatist movements, in addition to the targeted ASG, operate. In the event of an unlucky firefight in which U.S. forces engage members of the MILF or the MNLF, especially if there are fatalities on either side, it would be difficult to keep the number of U.S. forces in the hundreds. It would be more difficult still to prevent Islamist leaders in the region from capitalizing on the attack. Political Islam has been a limited force in Southeast Asia, but much of its strength has derived from clumsy efforts at crackdowns, such as those by Ferdinand Marcos in Mindanao or, more recently, Mahathir bin Mohamad in Malaysia. Should movement leaders credibly identify an "anti-Muslim" alliance between the United States and distrusted governments in the region, they might well be able to establish the makings of a genuinely regional Islamist identity that would encourage cooperation between local organizations in attacks on regionwide targets.

This need not arise from a firefight gone wrong. The JI members arrested in Singapore appear to have been a singularly unlucky lot, and they were unwise to plan their moves in the most heavily and competently policed state in Southeast Asia. With the Indonesian government having taken extraordinary steps to arrest even respected Islamist leaders for their roles in political violence, militants may find Southeast Asia to be particularly inhospitable to their more violent activities. Indeed, an annual meeting of Islamists, including many loyal to Bashir, was poorly attended in 2003, with virtually none of the major government figures, such as Hamah Haz, who had put the congress on their schedules in previous years (Perlez 2003). But the Marriott bombing in Jakarta suggests that there are still militants with access to weapons who are ready to carry out violent acts against Western interests. And a heavy government crackdown might even provoke an Islamist backlash.

New Regionalism, Secret Regionalization

None of these grim scenarios is inevitable, and it would be foolhardy to predict outcomes in East and Southeast Asia. In fact, conditions in the region may be affected dramatically by distant but very public events, such as the American occupation of Iraq and tensions between Israelis and Palestinians. If either proceeds exceptionally peacefully, or if either becomes a bloodbath with primarily Muslim victims, Islamic movements and states alike would confront radically different opportunities or constraints for furthering their political goals. But the war on terrorism adds a new layer to the internal and external security calculations of governments throughout the region, and it is unlikely to end anytime soon. No U.S. president wants to be labeled as the one who allowed "a second September 11" to take place, meaning that it is unlikely that even the next few administrations will declare a clear end to counterterrorism action in the Asia-Pacific. The security recalculations taking place from Washington to Pyonyang, and from Tashkent to Kuala Lumpur, will likely continue for years to come.

This discussion has set aside what should probably be the most important question of all to the most powerful actor in this crisis: will the war on terrorism in Southeast Asia make the United States safer in the long run? Ultimately, the answer is unknowable, and for a reason that goes beyond the usual metaphysical one of whether we can really predict future security. Terrorist groups are, by nature, clandestine, and even their existence can be a jealously guarded secret. Even cooperation with the intense military might of the U.S. government will be insufficient in the medium term to guarantee that the region's governments have clear, uncontested control over their territory. In the absence of this kind of control and the transparency it might bring, U.S. policy makers will cling to the worry that a failure to act aggressively might be the failure that leads to disaster.

So the campaign that is driving the reevaluation of security relations in the Asia-Pacific might be considered Sisyphean, given the inability to achieve final, verifiable success. American security specialists, who essentially created the bilateral "hub-and-spoke" structure of Asian security relations, may be unconcerned with the possible effects of U.S. actions on the Asia-Pacific. But political actors in the region will continue to make choices about how Islamic militancy or state responses might benefit from transnational cooperation that promotes tighter regional linkages. This will hardly be the goal of American action, which will be marked by efforts to tighten security and then, possibly in response to an attack, tighten it some more—to push the boulder up the hill, just to watch it roll back down again. For the United States, to paraphrase Albert Camus, it is the effort that matters. The trick for governments and political movements in the region will be to determine how it matters for them.

11

Conclusion: Tentativeness and Tensions in the Construction of an Asian Region

T. J. PEMPEL

In this conclusion I do not summarize the preceding chapters but rather draw from them to do three main things. First, I highlight the continual tensions within East Asia between the competing pulls of nationalism and regionalism. Absent a deeply rooted Asian identity and lacking an agreed-upon regional project, East Asian regional linkages have remained less deeply institutionalized and more fluid than those in the European Union. Yet links across Asia are being forged by multiple actors and on multiple levels, so that the most overt and explicitly political institutions of East Asian regionalism are but a small part of the cumulative linkages that have developed across the region.

Second, I underscore the extent to which the boundaries defined by any combination of East Asian links are in flux, differing considerably by problem and over time. There is less a clear-cut and well-defined East Asian bloc than a series of East Asian nodes and networks that frequently, but not always, overlap, reinforce, and spin out from one another. On balance, far more of these are biased toward "open" as opposed to "closed" regional ties, leaving the outer boundaries of East Asia, however defined, far fuzzier than its inner core.

Finally, I address the impact of these regional changes over time, focusing primarily on the links among regional economic development, connectedness, and power.

Uncontestable linear trends are less evident across East Asia than are ebbs and flows that reflect political, social, and economic changes. East Asian regional ties remain highly contested and deeply politicized. But at the same time, despite the specific institutional forms that these ties take or the specific boundaries that are shaped, East Asia overall has become a far richer, more peaceful, and more influential piece of global real estate since the end of World War II.

National Interests versus Regional Ties : nationalism vs. regionalism

National interest and national identity continue to be powerful forces throughout East Asia. The region's emerging connections have hardly displaced them. A century or more of social, cultural, and political fragmentation long impeded any sense of common identity or commonly agreed-upon goals across the region. Even the "imagined communities" that are East Asia's nation-states were late in crystallizing (Anderson 1983). More problematic still has been any imagined community that is regional in nature. That has been changing, but slowly and with uneven pervasiveness.

For most of the postwar period, East Asia was composed primarily of countries devoid of unambiguously accepted national identities and strong national governments. The majority of today's East Asian countries still lacked even basic national independence as World War II drew to a close. Residual social, ethnic, and religious differences—often aggressively aggravated by colonial powers—stood as formidable barriers against any collective national identity or national governmental purpose. Strong states were the norm in Japan, the two Koreas, Taiwan, and Singapore, but more pervasive throughout the region were far weaker states with constricted policy capacity. The Cold War further handicapped many of the region's governments from enhancing their capacity for independent action. Guerilla wars and domestic territorial disputes engulfed wide swaths of both Northeast and Southeast Asia, and neighboring governments often meddled in these domestic disputes. The divisive residues of the Cold War continue to be reflected in the divisions on the Korean peninsula and within "greater China," while other territorial borders remain contested within the area of the South China Sea and in several Southeast Asian countries haunted by internal fragmentation.

Not surprisingly, such conditions meant that throughout the early postwar years, many East Asian political elites devoted their attention and resources to nation and state building: the creation of stable and reliable armies and police forces, the consolidation of domestic bureaucratic control and extractive capabilities, the inculcation of a spirit of national loyalty, the securing of national borders, and the promotion of economic development. Shoring up the banks of potentially eroding sovereignties took precedence over constructing new bridges to foreign shores.

Furthermore, the two largest powers in the region—China and Japan—despite their increasing economic linkages to the region and to one another, had then, and continue to have today, few incentives to permit their foreign policy goals to be hemmed in by regional agreements dominated by their smaller neighbors. Economics and culture remained similarly national or sub-national in the early postwar years. State-owned and private corporations struggled to enhance their domestic production facilities and to gain shares of national markets rather than to become global producers seeking world-wide markets. Pan-Asian culture was far more convincing as a sweeping abstraction than as the reflection of any comprehensively shared conscious-ness that shaped the day-to-day activities of most citizens.

In short, politically, economically, and culturally, East Asia in the early years after World War II lacked compelling motivations to pursue cross-regional linkages. Far more dominant were concerns about the inculcation of national consciousness, enhancement of national governmental capacity, and the pur-suit of national interests.

Virtually all chapters in this book make clear that such starting points were not insurmountable bulwarks against the tentative expansion of ties across the region. But absent any integrative pan-regional project, most governments pursued regional linkages gingerly while jealously guarding national sover-eignty. This was certainly apparent in the creation and early actions of ASEAN, the most extensively institutionalized regional body in East Asia. The 1976 Treaty of Amity and Cooperation in Southeast Asia forbade the threat or use of force against member states, pressuring all of them to resolve their disputes through peaceful means while enshrining the principles of mutual respect for political independence, territorial integrity, national identity, and noninter-ference in each other's internal affairs (Alagappa 1998, 657; Acharya 2001a). Regional ties in Southeast Asia were unquestionably bolstered by the creation of ASEAN, but as a body, ASEAN was deeply deferential to national sover-eignty. ASEAN's actions typically relied on creating "coalitions of the willing" rather than on collectively enforcing compliance.

Despite such narrowly national concerns, as MacIntyre and Naughton make clear, resource-producing countries of Southeast Asia, including Indonesia, began by the early 1980s to shift away from this preponderantly introspective focus. With domestic state powers more substantially in place and with import-led growth more problematic as a long-term strategy, these countries began to revise their domestic regulations to encourage incoming investment and trade. Financial interactions began to crisscross the region. As such countries gained larger stakes in the regional economy, and as their national economic well-being improved, many governments began to devote increased effort to fostering closer regional interactions. This was particularly striking among Southeast Asian countries in the creation of a variety of arrangements from ASEAN to AFTA to the recent enthusiasm for an ASEAN Economic Community and for negotiating an ASEAN–China free trade pact. A number of ASEAN countries also became more willing with time to criticize other members whose national conduct they perceived to be hindering broader regional progress.

Private firms were even more active regionalizers than were governments, and they were particularly active in expanding their investments across national borders following the enhanced value of the Japanese, Korean, and Taiwanese currencies in the mid-1980s. No longer was it just firms from the few largest economies that moved abroad. Any number of corporations based in Indonesia, Singapore, and Malaysia increased their overseas investing. The result was an ever thicker network of bottom-up webs of production, trade, and cross-border services. In many cases, these investments began at the behest of, or quickly drew into the process, their governmental supporters and opponents both at home and in their targeted investment locales. Many activities that began as simple corporate economic arrangements took on an explicit political complexion as a result. The Japanese, Singaporean, and Taiwanese governments, for example, generated numerous official policies to support their companies' moves abroad. Additionally, as Hamilton-Hart makes clear, different Southeast Asian firms continually confronted the dilemma of whether to seek political intermediation as they sought to penetrate locally based business networks. But for the most part, with the notable exception of Taiwan, any challenges such corporate activities may have posed to national sovereignty remained at the margins of political debate in ways that formal membership in regional organizations did not.

The broader political climate certainly became more conducive to regional cooperation. Today's political leaders in Asia recite, with increasing frequency, the slogans of regional unity and harmony. Thus, at the 1999 Manila meeting of APEC, the Philippines' president spoke of "the dream" of "an East Asian Common Market, an East Asian currency and one East Asian community." The South Korean president talked of the need to find ways to "nurture East Asia into a single community of cooperation" and to promote an "East Asian Economic Cooperation System." The Chinese premier declared his preference for "closer East Asian cooperation" to "strengthen and deepen" what he called this "effective dialogue mechanism." Indeed the chief executive of the Hong Kong Monetary Authority called for an Asian currency unit that would replicate the ECU (Chu 1999).

Even more vigorously, in seeking to differentiate the region from the United States and Europe, several East Asian leaders have put forward strong public arguments that Asians are joined together in support of certain values, typically those associated with Confucian ideals. Lee Kuan Yew of Singapore, Mahathir bin Mohamad of Malaysia, and Ishihara Shintaro of Japan, for example, have been persistent spokesmen for such allegedly distinctive "Asian values." These, they contend, provide common social glue within individual countries and across the region's borders. Among the most important things stressed are widespread acceptance of communal needs over individuality, deference to authority over citizens' rights, devotion to hard work over leisure, and worker–manager cooperation over conflict. Such values, it is argued, differ sharply from those prevalent in the West. In the words of Kishore Mahbubani (1995), they represent "the Pacific Way." Such contentions resonate with the arguments of Huntington (1996) about the values and norms that underlie competing "civilizations." Yet although they promote a constructivist counterweight to potentially challenging "Western" values such as pluralism, individualism, human rights, and laissez-faire economics (Thompson 2001), such arguments are often redolent with self-justification for authoritarianism at home.

A number of empirical studies of national and regional values have shown that citizens in East Asian countries differ far more widely on many key norms than the proponents of allegedly harmonizing Asian values suggest. A University of Michigan survey, for example, assessed national values in more than seventy countries along two major axes: traditional values and quality of life (*Economist,* January 4, 2003, 18–20). The former centers on the importance of religion, family, and country; the latter on the importance of economic and physical security as opposed to self-expression and individualism. Although hardly exact surrogates for the "Asian values" put forward by Lee, Mahathir, Ishihara, and others, they are sufficiently close to warrant attention. When the countries of East Asia are mapped on these two axes, they form nothing like a single, discrete cluster. South Korea, Taiwan, and China group together around certain allegedly Confucian commonalities, most notably anti-individualism, much as Asian values' advocates would predict. But Japan is much closer to many Western European countries in its combination of individualism and secularism than it is to those countries identified as Confucian. Meanwhile, Thailand, Indonesia, Vietnam, and Malaysia, although close to one another in norms and values, are vastly more traditional than any of the Northeast Asian countries. Empirically, therefore, values, at least those examined by the University of Michigan study, hardly transcend all East Asian borders. National or subregional differences across East Asia are far more striking.

Nationalist sentiments remain conspicuously stronger in Northeast Asia, where they have been particularly detrimental to the development of closer institutional connections (Moon 2003). Japan, China, and South Korea share expanding trade and investment ties, membership in several formal bodies, and informal links that include joint military visits and exchanges of top-level foreign ministry officials, among other measures of cooperation. Still, historical memories militate against the creation of deeper and more formalized links. Chinese and Korean officials remain dubious about the persistence of right-wing nationalism in Japan. Japanese politicians fear the domestic consequences of low-cost Chinese imports in both agricultural and manufactured goods as well as the rising military threat implicit in an economically powerful China. China and Japan compete for trade privileges in Southeast Asia, while South Korea has recently concentrated more national attention on reintegration of the peninsula than on enhancing ties with its two Northeast Asian neighbors. Korea's regional economic agenda also presumes itself the center of any Northeast Asian banking, financial, logistical, and regional institutions. Compared with Southeast Asia, therefore, Northeast Asia has remained more resistant to the pulls of regionalism.

Despite the many impediments, East Asia has become a region with far more intra-regional institutions than were in place one or two decades ago. At the same time, existing institutions continue to reflect national differences as well as nationally defined self-interests. As a result, they have often been feckless in coping with regionwide problems. For example, APEC was widely lauded by the United States and others as a key instrument of trans-Pacific trade liberalization in the early 1990s, but it was institutionally irrelevant in coping with the crisis of 1997–98, and its economic momentum came to a standstill in subsequent years. By the time of the 2001 APEC meetings in Beijing, President Bush barely made the trip; the Taiwanese representative was blocked by Chinese opposition; and the agenda was politically and economically vacuous. ASEAN too was ineffective during the 1997–98 crisis, leading many to declare it politically moribund. In the aftermath of the crisis, the ASEAN + 3 (APT) meeting has become formalized and is gaining credibility as a transregional monetary coordinating body, but its powers too remain more limited than is implied by the boldface headlines of regionalist publications. The ASEAN Regional Forum (ARF) has played at best a minimal role in resolving security problems. Moreover, in the eyes of Asian leaders, the European Union, with high levels of institutionalization and broad agreement on collective goals, remains far from their image of an ideal Asia. To the extent that such leaders exert power over events, they make it unlikely that East Asia will follow in Europe's footsteps.

National self-interest also persists in the economic sphere, where Asian regionalization is the most highly developed. Unable to overcome the nationalist protectionisms that have impeded more comprehensive regionwide trade liberalization, and frustrated with the fecklessness of such bodies as APEC and AFTA, some East Asian governments have begun to push ahead with a wave of bilateral free trade agreements (FTAs). But many economically logical FTAs have foundered on domestic protectionism, leaving it unclear if the future will see an ever-expanding number of bilateral FTAs that might bolster regional integration or a more limited number centered on a few key players, thereby reinforcing nationally based differences in approaches to intra-regional trade.

East Asian regional linkages consequently present a mixed picture. Regional ties advance, but on highly specific and typically noninstitutionalized bases; meanwhile, national self-interests and differences continue to retain a high priority for many national leaders. And in the case of FTAs, national interest and regional connectedness may well be advancing synchronistically.

As Evans makes clear, even East Asia's deeply entrenched nationalisms are now contending with a number of governmental and quasi-governmental processes that bring together leading East Asians who share a commitment to enhancing regional ties. Such individuals meet regularly and share ideas on commonly perceived problems. The result, he suggests, is an elite cluster of pan-regional cosmopolitans. Preferences change as a result of ongoing inter-actions, and many shift endogenously by the very process of meeting regularly (Wendt 1994). Furthermore, all major powers in the region (except for Tai-wan) participate actively in ARF, and as Tsunekawa catalogs, even military cooperation has expanded throughout the region and now includes port visits by various navies, mutual exchanges by foreign and defense ministry officials, the sharing of military information, and a host of other confidence-building measures.

Intra-regional contacts at the mass level are expanding in areas such as tele-phone and mail communication, shipping and aviation, tourism, television and satellite broadcasts, and legal and illegal migration (Cohen 2002). Such cross-border interactions constitute precisely the kinds of social communica-tions that Karl Deutsch (1957, 1966) and his followers found were most likely, with increasing density of interaction, to generate shared identities and ulti-mately new perceptions of community. Symbolically, however, as late as 2002, only two East Asian capitals (Seoul and Tokyo) were directly connected by Internet hookups; all other messages within the region had to be routed through other countries, most notably the United States. East Asia is far more linked than in the past, but often in ways that involve connections that pass through other parts of the world.

More iconic contributors to an East Asian identity have arisen from the pas-tiche of pan-Asian cultural commonalities that now span the region, engross-ing its citizens at the popular, rather than the elite, level—Japanese cartoons and karaoke, Korean pop music, Star television, soap operas and cartoons, multinational Asian singing groups, pirated software, and the like. Such link-ages certainly contrast with the situation only a few decades ago, when vari-ous governments, such as those in Korea, China, Taiwan, and Malaysia banned movies and songs from neighboring countries. Thus, at the level of mass or popular culture, Asians today enjoy a much wider variety of common cultural experiences than did their parents or grandparents. Moreover, many more East Asian elites and citizens treat other parts of Asia as important ref-erence points. It is not only to the United States or Western Europe that many of them now turn for policy ideas, vacation spots, and Internet chat rooms.

In addition, as McNicoll's data make clear, much of East Asia, particularly its cities, has become increasingly middle class, with a consequent impact on values among general citizens. As he puts it, "What [East Asians consume] looks much the same from Seoul to Jakarta: high-rise housing and new durables such as cars and computers. The middle class also have become consumers of entertainment, and of news—of their country, the region, and the world—with values and perceptions echoed, and in some measure shaped, by the media." The implications are twofold. On the one hand, there is an obvious decrease in the sense of fragmentation and singularity that once divided East Asia. But on the other hand, many East Asian consumers have begun to resemble one another and to share a consequent mind-set; what unites them with one another ties them as strongly to their middle-class counterparts elsewhere in the world, thus providing little that is distinctively "East Asian."

In this sense, much of the rise in a collective Asian identity remains embryonic and bottom up and must be balanced against two contradictory trends. First, the cultural unifiers within East Asia are often more global than particularly regional in nature. As a result, they integrate East Asia narrowly, but they also weave East Asia into broader consumerist and economic trends worldwide rather than fostering any sense of East Asian distinctiveness. And second, despite such integrative elements, East Asia collectively still remains a collage of very different political and economic regimes, many with strong legacies of hostility toward one another. Equally, many of Asia's various citizenries remain highly diverse on other vital normative identities, including religious, ethnic, linguistic, and cultural self-definitions. Indeed, many East Asian countries remain highly divided internally, a point driven home, as David Leheny makes clear in his chapter, by the rising influence of radical Islamist movements, most notably of late in Indonesia and the Philippines, which also, along with Singapore and Malaysia, harbor cells of fundamentalist Islamic terrorists linked to al Qaeda. Such tendencies militate against the quick emergence of any common East Asian identity, inhibiting the collective pursuit of all but the most uncontroversial goals.

Most importantly for regionalism, although many corporations, financial institutions, NGOs, and track II bodies are spinning transregional webs, few governments in East Asia systematically define their national self-interests in ways that demand rapid enmeshment in the region as a whole (Job 2002). Indeed, in one comparative examination of regional developments, Haggard (1997) finds "little evidence for the theory that higher levels of interdependence generate the demand for deeper integration" or that trade generates dilemmas that only regional institutions can resolve. East Asian regionalism through formal, legal institutions, with its accompanying rules and constrictions on the autonomy of national governments, thus continues to have less of the appeal that it enjoys in most capitals of Western Europe (Grieco 1997; Mattli 1999). The European Union, as Schmidt (2003, 4) notes, has developed a single currency, a single market, a single voice in international trade negotiations, a single antitrust authority, common policies on environmental protection, worker safety, and health, and even the beginnings of a common foreign policy and security policy. Yet the EU is the only geographical region to have achieved such comprehensive integration. Far more pervasive within

East Asia, as in most other regions, and in accord with Solingen's analysis in chapter 2, have been governmental acceptances of expanding but relatively less constricting de facto networks with their origins and driving forces outside government (see also Katzenstein 1996c). Indeed when East Asian governments have become members of formal regional organizations, most have continued to press for sharp delimitations on the legal and secretarial powers of those bodies.

Finally, the balance between regional and national pulls has often shifted suddenly. Most recently, the relative inability of loosely constructed regional institutions to ward off the worst effects of the 1997–98 economic crisis, or to take remedial actions once the crisis hit, stimulated second thoughts among many Asian governments about the previously assumed benefits of informality and the dangers of institutionalization. More worried about the economic challenges from the United States and global financial actions than about the potential military threats from their immediate neighbors, many East Asian governments discovered a measure of enhanced agreement in collectively facing down what they often viewed as an overweening Western arrogance. Both Evans and Solingen underscore the ways in which the APT process has gained extensive support from governments across East Asia as one manifestation of this more regionalist rethinking (see also Stubbs 2002). In addition, China, Japan, South Korea, and Russia have demonstrated previously unimagined cooperation in bringing both the United States and the DPRK to the bargaining table over the threat of a North Korean nuclear program. But whether such cooperation will transcend the specifics of the current crisis remains uncertain.

ASEAN members have also become less deferential to national sovereignty, as noted by their increasing criticisms of the human rights record of the military government in ASEAN member Myanmar. Deviating from the longstanding policy of noninterference in the domestic affairs of one another, the ASEAN governments were particularly embarrassed by the detention of democracy advocate Aung San Suu Kyi. Even then Malaysian prime minister Mahathir, normally one of the strongest advocates of intra-ASEAN harmony, warned that Myanmar might be expelled from the regional body if Suu Kyi continued to be held in detention (*Far Eastern Economic Review*, August 14, 2003). Such moves suggested a heightened willingness to enter into more formalized and less consensually sensitive regional bodies as well as some erosion of the sanctity of sovereignty.

Yet even post-crisis Asia has hardly shown linear movement toward closer integration at the expense of national pulls. Most governments involved in the APT process, not surprisingly, remain highly responsive to national rather than regional issues and interests. Japan, despite being active in APT, spent most of the late 1990s and early 2000s self-absorbed by its overwhelming domestic economic problems. Indonesia, once among the staunchest advocates of closer regional ties, was quick to adopt an inward focus in response to economic and sociocultural problems at home. Malaysia, often an outspoken advocate of closer regional ties, was quick to end earlier currency convertibility so as to defend its national economy against capital outflows. In 2001, Thailand reversed its earlier openness to foreign direct investment in areas such as telecommunications and retail. Additionally, individual corporations and banks follow their perceived self-interest, and their moves across borders have gone in both directions as a result. From the present vantage point, Asian regional ties seem likely to strengthen, but largely from the bottom up, and faced with the strong and competing top-down counter pull by governments that are responsive primarily to domestic political concerns less amenable to resolution through regional deepening. But even as governments and their representatives meet and learn to cooperate, the very process of interaction continues to reshape their agendas and their levels of mutual trust.

Bounding East Asia: Open versus Closed Regional Ties

The outer boundaries of any "East Asian" region have been fuzzy. Indeed, varied terms describe nuanced, although often overlapping, entities. Paul Evans (2000, 7) provides an extensive list of the more frequently used terms that encompass this particular geographical area, and no one label coincides with most internal or external actors' own perceptions of reality.

Because they are on the periphery, the republics of central Asia, Mongolia, the DPRK, Myanmar, Australia, and New Zealand are periodically "in" but just as often "out" of East Asian institutions and networks. Regional institutions are most extensive among what might be thought of as a core of East Asian countries; there is a heavy overlap of membership in ASEAN, APT, and ARF, for example. The outer limitations of East Asia expand but are blurred at the periphery when the focus becomes trade, investment, and ad hoc cooperation over environment or health. Moreover, bodies like the Shanghai Cooperative Organization link together China, Russia, and four central Asian states, creating an important "noncore" institutional arrangement. Even among the core components of any East Asian regional arrangement, institutional ties remain thin, and in the economic sphere, where intra-Asian ties are strongest, Asia has no institution focused on intra-regional trade preferences. As John Ravenhill (2000, 329) has observed, "East Asia is the only major region that lacks its own economic organization committed to trade liberalization on a discriminatory basis." With the rise in bilateral free trade pacts as well as the return to prominence of Asian–U.S. security links, there are even more reasons for understanding East Asia as marked by fluid and flexible outer boundaries.

On the other side of the ledger, the legacy of the economic crisis and the subsequent enhancement of the APT process show that on certain issues, but most notably on matters of economic security, many in East Asia remain dubious about an unbounded and completely open definition of regional interests. Certainly, one of the central questions that has driven discussion of East Asian regionalism and regionalization has been whether emerging links will be open or closed. Would East Asia create a "reactive regionalism" aimed primarily at protecting a core of presumptively Asian interests against a not necessarily accommodating global environment? Or would regional ties serve as an intermediate building block destined in the long run to integrate East Asia with the broader world? In short, will the outer boundaries of any Asian region be exclusively "Asian," or will they be "Pan-Pacific?" (Berger 1999; Bergsten 2000; Funabashi 1993; Katzenstein 2003; Ravenhill 2001).

Whether East Asia would be open or closed was most dramatically played out in the vigorous debate about the East Asian Economic Caucus (EAEC) versus Asia-Pacific Economic Cooperation (APEC) (Higgott and Stubbs 1995). Fears of growing integration in Europe starting in the late 1980s led many Asian business and government leaders to consider closer and more formalized cooperation with one another. Adoption of the Single Europe Act in 1987 and speedy progress toward "Europe 1992" deepened fears that a "Fortress Europe," might wall off Asian imports. Concerns grew with the enlargement of the EU and the ratification of the Maastricht Treaty on European Monetary and Political Union and became more worrisome still when NAFTA linked the United States, Canada, and Mexico in a second huge regional trade arrangement (Mattli 1999, 166). Malaysian prime minister Mahathir proposed to create a largely closed East Asian regional economic organization capable of countering these two bodies. Ultimately, however, it was APEC and open regionalism that prevailed over Mahathir's vision of a closed EAEC.

The creation of APEC, with membership that included the United States, Canada, Australia, and New Zealand, bolstered open regional approaches. APEC therefore had a transregional agenda as well as a regional one. The motivations for this open APEC were as much global as regional and were heavily influenced by the economic agenda of the United States. Certainly the U.S. goals were not shared evenly across the organization.

The United States sought constantly to transform APEC from a discussion forum focused on trade facilitation and economic cooperation favored by many Asian leaders into a results-oriented body pressing trade targets and number-specific economic openings. To the United States, only one of APEC's three nominal goals deserved serious pursuit. Trade liberalization took priority over trade facilitation and economic cooperation. Asian critics meanwhile asked whether an APEC in pursuit of such a specific agenda was little more than "a Tool for U.S. Regional Domination" (Nesadurai 1996). As the United States, along with Canada and Australia, sought to institutionalize APEC as a formal body applying strict rules, it ran into conflict with Southeast Asian members who pressed APEC to follow ASEAN principles, namely, institutional informality and mutual respect for national sovereignty.

As a regional organization that traversed the Pacific and included the United States and Canada from the start, and that subsequently admitted Chile and Mexico, APEC was explicitly compatible with the GATT and its successor, the WTO. It gave a strong institutional boost to both the principles and membership of an "open East Asian region." APEC was a logical institutional manifestation of the trans-Pacific regionalization developed by corporations over the previous decades—open but not deeply institutionalized. Yet its narrow focus on trade liberalization left many Asian governments dubious about allowing themselves to be seriously constrained by an organization whose agenda was so overweeningly dominated by the United States.

APEC proved incapable of projecting even its own trade liberalization agenda. This was particularly true in the case of the Early Voluntary Sector Liberalization at the Kuala Lumpur meeting of 1998. The United States failed in its effort to bundle and push forward the liberalization of trade in several politically sensitive sectors, making it clear that the U.S. agenda of open trade and rapid liberalization was not shared throughout the APEC membership (Krauss 2004). APEC and open regionalism both failed this important test.

The issue of East Asia's open or closed character has been regularly complicated by the question of institutionalization. Whether East Asia should advance portions of any collective regional agenda through formal institutions has been a singularly contentious issue. And all issues of institution creation have been forced to address the issue of open or closed membership. ASEAN eschewed formal rules and relied heavily on informality and "coalitions of the willing"; although the organization eventually included members beyond its original core, it currently shows no likelihood of expanding its boundaries beyond Southeast Asia. APEC, along with ARF, was thinly institutionalized but with much more expansive Asian-Pacific (open) memberships. The bias against formal, legally binding organizations with extensive secretariats remains strong across East Asia. Still, this is hardly unusual in comparative terms. As Kahler (2000b) has argued, heavily legalized regional institutions such as the EU are anomalous islands in a generally less legalized world.

Boundary and institutionalization questions have hardly been resolved. The evidence presented by the chapters in this book shows that different governments, and more importantly, different corporations, NGOs, and groups of citizens, have diverse perceptions and preferences on regional linkages. Thus, for example, it is much more difficult to attract well-established Asian corporate investment to develop energy resources than to put up manufacturing plants. As a result, countries with large labor pools and limited energy potential are far more able to restrict their search for investment partners to an inner

Asian core than are the energy-rich countries that are magnets for global multinational energy companies. Similarly, the middle-class values that unite Asians are perforce openly shared with other middle-class citizens worldwide. Intra-Asian trade has risen sharply, as has cooperation on certain specific problems such as health care or the environment. But even in these areas, much Asian trade remains Pan-Pacific, and many of the most notable health and environmental problems are global rather than region specific. As Evans has demonstrated, even track II members who are preponderantly oriented toward exclusively "Asian" solutions have differed as to whether these should be primarily Southeast Asian, East Asian, or Asia-Pacific solutions. The outer boundaries of any Asian regionalism shift with issues, institutions, and advocates.

The question of open versus closed regionalism hit another critical crossroads in the wake of the painfully negative effects of the economic crisis of 1997–98. No event in recent political economy has been more devastating to Asia's collective regional well-being. The inability of APEC to intervene successfully to avert or end the crisis, combined with the general reluctance of many relatively well-off Asian countries to use their foreign reserves to bail out their less well-to-do neighbors, underscored the extent to which existing "open" regional ties did little to trump perceptions of national self-interest on the one hand or to deflect outside forces on the other. The debate was even reflected in competing labels for the crisis. Within policy circles in North America and Europe, what occurred was an "Asian contagion," "Asian cronyism," or an "Asian economic crisis." For the West, the source of the problems lay primarily within the affected East Asian countries and their failure to adopt American-style market economies.

In contrast, within many circles in Asia, the same events were understood as the outgrowth of insensitive and draconian policies pursued by the United States, the IMF, and the World Bank, with their collective commitment to a "Washington consensus." This Washington consensus, it was argued, threatened the goals of most East Asian countries. To the latter, there was hardly an Asian crisis but rather an IMF crisis (Higgott and Breslin 2000). Indeed, as the *Economist* (2000, 109–10) put it, "the International Monetary Fund is so unpopular in East Asia that it now has an entire economic crisis named after it." Such perceptions generated widespread support within that narrower Asia to create institutional mechanisms that would foster closer and closed ties, particularly in finance, that might serve as an effective counterweight to the power of "extra-Asian" actors.

In light of the experiences of 1997–98, many Asian leaders also began to reexamine the global financial architecture with renewed skepticism. Not a little of this concern involved the perspective that existing "global" institutions were only minimally reflective of recent increases in Asia's relative economic weight. To many Asian leaders, international economic institutions had failed to provide East Asia with a role consistent with its decades-long economic progress. The United States and the EU dominated GATT and continue to dominate the WTO, while in the IMF and the International Bank for Reconstruction and Development, both larger and smaller Asian countries are grossly underrepresented. For example, Japan has an economy one-half that of the United States or Europe, but its special drawing rights quota is one-third that of the United States and one-fifth that of the EU. China now has the world's second largest economy in purchasing power and the seventh largest at market exchange rates, but it ranks eleventh in the quota lineup. Korea's quota is so small that its rescue package in 1998–99 has to be a record—1,900 times its quota.

One tangible result of this reexamination of the global financial architecture was at least a temporary reassertion of the benefits of a more closed regionalism. In the Chiang Mai Initiative of May 2000, the APT forum was chosen to mobilize intra-Asian capital and foreign reserves, creating an Asia-specific buffer against a repeat of 1997–98. This, it was hoped, would keep East Asia free of the constraints of loan conditionalities that might be imposed by the IMF. For many Asian elites and rulers, their national and regional economic security had become at least as problematic as the security of their national borders. Their collective response was to circle the East Asian wagons against the presumably hostile forces outside (Henning 2002). Still, it is easy to overemphasize the significance of APT as an "anti-Western" or "closed Asian" institution. The amounts of money outside national control remain relatively small, while most actions that can be taken by APT must still be IMF-congruent (Amyx 2004).

More immediately relevant is the fact that if a narrowly defined East Asia seeks collectively to influence the global financial architecture, it is far more likely to search for remedies through a recalibration of weights within global financial institutions than by creating closed and tightly legalized institutions with membership drawn only from the APT group (Eichengreen 1999; Kahler 2000c). In this sense, any probable Asian regional problem is likely to require resolution not through exclusive and closed regional bodies but simultaneously through "open" multinational organizations.

An additional counterweight to the seemingly closed character of APT can be found in the rise of bilateral free trade agreements by various Asian countries. The number of FTAs entered into by Asian countries has expanded considerably since the late 1990s. Many of these ties involve exclusively Asian nation-states (e.g., the Singapore–ASEAN pact or the proposed China–Japan pact). Yet far more reflect some version of open regionalism. Certainly a number of Asian countries have developed or are exploring trans-Pacific bilateral trade pacts such as those proposed by Japan and Singapore with Mexico and Chile.

If Asian regional ties have become somewhat narrower and more tightly bounded in the economic and financial spheres, within the security arena they remain vastly more open and unquestionably dependent on the United States. The United States remains the major Pacific superpower, with an extensive naval presence and basing rights in numerous East Asian countries. U.S. hegemony remains the preponderant shaper of regional military activities across Asia. This fact was reinforced in the wake of the September 11 attacks on the United States. Although different Asian governments have collaborated with one another against regional terrorist networks, the primary lines of cooperation have been between individual Asian countries and the United States, largely in efforts to eradicate potential fundamentalist terrorist networks within various Asian borders, as detailed by David Leheny.

Indeed, countries such as Australia, Japan, Singapore, and the Philippines, all of which had shown periodic predispositions toward a narrower definition of the region, moved quickly in the wake of September 11 to shore up their military and defense ties with the United States as the latter moved to advance its new doctrine of preemptive war. Many of these countries, which had made previous rhetorical genuflections to Asia, narrowly defined, found themselves moving quickly toward wholehearted endorsement of the new American definition of security and support for American military actions in the Middle East. They moved away from identification with their immediate Asian neighbors and toward what is globally the most powerful country.

The Australian government sent troops to Afghanistan and Iraq, while the Japanese government abandoned fifty years of defense policy and sensitivity to the security concerns of neighboring Asian countries so as to send support ships to Afghanistan and troops to Iraq. Despite strong domestic opposition, President Arroyo of the Philippines worked closely with U.S. Department of Defense officials to allow American military "advisors" to join antiguerilla activities in Mindanao. And Singapore won the speedy signing of a bilateral free trade pact with the United States as a result of its explicit support for U.S. security policy. In contrast, countries such as Malaysia, Indonesia, China, and to a lesser extent Thailand remained more critical of U.S. military strategies but were unable to generate any collective regional response to the new U.S. military policy. The result has been enhanced fragmentation on security within the core East Asian region.

Finally, on the question of nuclear proliferation by North Korea, and the U.S. reaction, there was a somewhat surprising measure of agreement among China, Russia, South Korea, and Japan. Indeed, Russia's participation marked a clearly larger role in East Asian regional diplomacy than it had previously enjoyed. All four worked to bring both the United States and the DPRK to a regional bargaining table, despite the particularly strong objections of the DPRK to multilateralism and the truculence of the United States toward any negotiations with a "rogue regime" and a member of the supposed axis of evil.

In a similar way, intra-regional production patterns, trade, and investment flows that crisscross East Asia remain consistently counterbalanced by the reliance of most of the expanding markets of Northeast and Southeast Asia on exports to the United States. For the most part, U.S. markets remain largely open to Asian products, and the United States remains the ultimate destination for a substantial portion of the goods exported from East Asia. With fluctuations over time, the United States has consistently absorbed between 25 and 33 percent of Asia's exports. More importantly, on a bilateral basis, the United States remains the largest or second largest market for the exports of nearly a dozen Asian countries. In most instances, the United States absorbs from two to six times as much of the exports of these Asian counties as do their second largest markets (Pempel 1997). Additionally, nearly 30 percent of U.S. exports go to the ASEAN 5, South Korea, Taiwan, China, and Japan. The United States has also remained a paramount contributor of investment capital to much of Asia's economic development. For East Asia to consider a closed regionalism in the face of such links would be economic suicide.

At the same time, the rapid economic growth of China has made that country an increasingly important market for exports from much of the rest of East Asia. And more and more Chinese exports are now destined for Asia as well as the United States.

Debates about the merits of various outer boundaries for East Asian regional ties continue within East Asia. These shift from issue to issue. Many relatively uninstitutionalized areas of interaction such as trade as well as even more institutionalized areas such as antiterror initiatives remain heavily open in character. In other key areas such as finance and investment, however, many East Asian elites feel a strong centripetal pull toward intra-Asian cooperation. National and intra-national differences across Asia remain great. As a consequence, recent developments continue to be driven less by common agreement among Asians on any underlying values or norms than by efforts to preserve national choices while creating barricades against perceived Western encroachments.

Asian Regionalism: Internal Linkages and Collective Power

Postwar East Asia shows unmistakable evidence of three striking trends. First, the region has become vastly richer and more globally influential. East Asia now accounts for a substantially larger share of world GNP and world trade, and its citizens have much higher standards of living than was the case three decades ago. Second, the region has become more interconnected. Finally, although not without important exceptions, the region has become generally more peaceful as state-to-state conflicts have been ameliorated. This final section examines the synergistic connections among these three trends and suggests how they are shaping East Asia's future.

One of the most fundamental achievements of the East Asian region has been its economic success. To appreciate the magnitude of this achievement, it is vital to understand how unusual this economic improvement is compared with the rest of the developing world. In contrast to virtually every other geographical region of the nonindustrialized world in the postwar period, Asia as a whole has done remarkably well in closing the economic gap between itself and the advanced countries of the West.

For most of the postwar years, the poorest parts of the world fell deeper into poverty while the richer parts gained larger shares of world GNP. In 1960, for example, the richest fifth of the world's population held thirty times more of the world's income than did the poorest fifth. This ratio widened to 32 to 1 in 1970, 45 to 1 in 1980, and 59 to 1 in 1989 (Frieden and Lake 2002, 417). The stunningly rapid advance of the many economies in East Asia marked the only substantial and sustained deviation from this otherwise worldwide trend. In 1960, Asia accounted for only 4–5 percent of world GNP, compared with 37 percent for the United States, Canada, and Mexico. By the early 1990s, the combined economies of Japan, South Korea, Taiwan, the ASEAN countries, and greater China contributed roughly 30 percent of world GNP, approximately the same share as that contributed by North America on the one hand and Western Europe on the other. Northeast and Southeast Asia saw similar jumps in their shares of world trade, their attraction of foreign direct investment, and their gains in per capita GNP. Broadly speaking, Asia closed a substantial part of the yawning economic gap between itself and the richer parts of the world by increasing its domestic productivity and enhancing its share of world GNP and trade; in the process it improved the economic well-being of its citizens while simultaneously bolstering its share of world power both militarily and economically.

This rise in Asia's economic power has not always been reflected in alterations of long-standing allocations of influence within international bodies such as the United Nations, the IMF, or the World Bank. But it is unmistakable in trade, investment flows, and holdings of foreign reserves and in the attention paid to Asia by foreign offices and defense departments worldwide. To a large extent, redressing such imbalances provides a substantial part of any future agenda for Asia as a whole. The literature of the late 1990s trumpeting the arrival of the "Pacific century" was unquestionably overwrought. Nevertheless, economic success has catapulted East Asia into a new level of collective importance globally.

East Asia's increased interconnectedness in the last two decades has been vital in enhancing its collective global influence. The chapters in this book have demonstrated many of the ways in which this occurred. The increase in these connections, however, has been neither linear nor devoid of internal tensions. The previous sections of this conclusion highlighted the ebb and flow of ties over time and over different issues. East Asia's diverse cultural roots and the region's absence of any common regionwide agreement on underlying values make it logical that regionalization and regionalism have been, and will be, somewhat problematic. Existing connections remain highly sensitive to the centrifugal forces of national autonomy and continue to be biased toward informal rather than deeply institutionalized mechanisms for cooperation.

Despite the plethora of economic ties as well as the increasing number of formal institutions that have been established across the Asian region in the military and security sphere, state-to-state relations in Asia continue to retain numerous vestiges of Cold War animosities and competing territorial claims. Likewise, outstanding debates continue over the contemporary problems of nonstate terror and the proliferation of weapons of mass destruction. At the same time, as linkages deepen across East Asia, ever stronger pulls exist for defining certain problems, such as financial cooperation, trade, investment, or the Korean nuclear threat, in ways that are distinctly "East Asian."

Finally, Asia has been enjoying a somewhat "long peace," of nearly thirty years. Direct wars between nation-states in East Asia have diminished, the last notable conflicts being those in and around Vietnam in the 1970s, although the resolution of the Vietnamese occupation of Cambodia did not end until 1991. Without a doubt, state-to-state relations are rife with the potential for conflict in several parts of the region. Still, compared with relations during the years immediately following World War II, East Asia has generally become a far less war-riven region.

Both Taiwan and the People's Republic of China have moved, in recent years, to enhance the capital flows, trade, and people-to-people exchanges across the Taiwan Straits that previously were impossible. They have hardly become "one China," but Taiwanese newspapers are now filled with ads for real estate in Shanghai and with stories of second families being maintained by Taiwanese businessmen in south China. Chinese missiles were fired over Taiwan as recently as 1996; the Chen government on Taiwan has slowly advanced a separate Taiwanese identity movement; diplomatic spats and threats of recriminations from both sides continue as of this writing in early 2004. The seemingly smallest issues—from visas to membership in the WHO to air travel—remain contentious. Nevertheless, for the moment at least, both sides appear to share a commitment to nonmilitary solutions in resolving their relationship.

Relations on the Korean peninsula have been more militarily problematic, despite the 1994 KEDO Accord aimed at deflecting DPRK nuclear weapons development, South Korean president Kim Dae-jung's Nobel Peace Prize–winning efforts to reduce frictions though his so-called Sunshine Policy, and the follow-on efforts to improve North–South relations by his successor, Roh Moo-hyun. Yet on August 31, 1998, North Korea fired a Taepo Dong missile over Japan. In early January 2002, the Japanese Coast Guard sank an alleged North Korean spy ship after the ship had breached Japan's territorial waters. The North Koreans, during a visit by Prime Minister Koizumi in September 2002, acknowledged a long-standing though defunct program of kidnapping Japanese civilians. And most troubling, following the famous "axis of evil" denunciation by George W. Bush in his January 2002 State of the Union Speech and the DPRK's (often ambiguous) statements that it had developed nuclear weapons, North Korea and the United States began a testy standoff that quickly escalated into regional tensions with the potential for nuclear proliferation across Northeast Asia. Multinational talks have begun, and there are clear outlines for a possible solution under which the DPRK would surrender its nuclear ambitions in exchange for guarantees of military security for the current regime by the United States as well as the DPRK's regional neighbors. Financial and technological aid from South Korea, Japan, and perhaps China would be integral parts of any settlement. Still, it is far from clear that the United States would provide acceptable regime guarantees or that North Korea would abandon all aspects of its nuclear program when it appears that nuclear weapons may provide the only ironclad guarantee in the modern world against outside attack (Harrison 2002).

Indonesian territorial integrity remains far from guaranteed, as was shown by the revolt and eventual independence of East Timor and tensions in Aceh. And increased ties across Southeast Asia have been weakened by disparate governmental responses to the rise of nonstate terror from various Islamist sects. Meanwhile, Northeast Asia remains unclear about how best to cope with the threat of weapons of mass destruction. These issues have played out in domestic politics from Indonesia, the Philippines, Thailand, and Malaysia to South Korea, Japan, and China, as each has opted for a rather different—and usually noncollective—response.

At the same time, this chapter suggests that the complex evolution of Asian regionalism and regionalization is resulting in a newly emerging order in the Pacific, albeit one that still has many gaps in its level of internal cohesion and one that remains subject to the heavy influence of extra-regional actors such as the United States over financial and military matters.

Asia collectively has expanded its military spending considerably over the past two decades, and many of its militaries are technologically sophisticated and capable of utilizing advanced weaponry and tactics. Nevertheless, Asian military power collectively remains vastly inferior to that of the United States, and it has been largely marginal in the resolution of most recent security tensions in the area (e.g., Hughes 2000; Schambaugh 2002).

Thus, it was the presence of the U.S. Seventh Fleet and U.S. destroyers that proved critical in easing tensions across the Taiwan Straits after China, upset over what it saw as excessive moves toward Taiwanese independence, began "missile tests" over the island. It was the United States that took the lead in challenging North Korea's nuclear program. The United States under George W. Bush undercut existing longstanding military security doctrines and nuclear nonproliferation treaties with its press to introduce Theater Missile Defense into Asia. And it is the United States that has been in the forefront of the so-called war against terrorism, injecting troops into the Philippines and possibly into Indonesia, despite government reluctance and massive public protests. Indeed, the Quadrennial Defense Review of 2001 and the National Security Strategy of September 2002 made it clear that the United States is seeking global military primacy and is prepared to pursue additional policies of preemptive attack such as those carried out in Afghanistan and Iraq. On balance, U.S. strategy has returned to a heavier reliance on unilateralism over multilateralism. Given the overwhelming military power of the United States, that shift will certainly limit the short-range ability of Asia to act collectively—particularly if and when such actions conflict with U.S. military goals.

Nonetheless, the Asian region collectively has gained global influence as a consequence of its combined economic, technological, political, and military strength. Intra-regional territorial disputes have not ended, but shooting wars between states have become less likely. To the extent that these elements of East Asian power move in a generally common and peaceful direction rather than at cross purposes, the collective power of the region as a whole is sure to be enhanced. Despite the demonstrated weakness of East Asian regional institutions in the economic crisis of 1997–98 and despite the most sweeping claims of certain globalist literature, U.S.-dominated markets have by no means gained uniform acceptance by leaders across Asia. Rather, most Asian governments have enhanced, not surrendered, their ability to regulate a host of economic and social activities within their borders. Most retain continued authority and power even as they have entered into formal regional arrangements or found themselves enmeshed in complex economic webs that some might have anticipated would confine their autonomy (Vogel 1998).

This was clear during the crisis; it seems to be even more evident in its wake. Asian governments were struck by the uncertain waves of economic globalization in 1997–98, but they appear to be gaining increased ability to keep from being swamped the next time such external waves pose a threat. Such abilities remain thinly institutionalized and heavily responsive to nationally defined objectives. Still, many of those national objectives have come to be more commonly shared across the region.

East Asian connectedness alone will not lead to the region's enhanced global influence. But connectedness combined with peace and prosperity is likely to make East Asia a more integrated and powerful player on the global arena. Ongoing interactions across East Asia help to identify common perceptions of collective problems. Whether or not East Asian cohesion will continue to develop remains uncertain, of course. But compared with the fragmented condition the region's main players previously faced, the situation today is vastly improved.

References

Aarts, Paul. 1999. "The Middle East: Eternally Out of Step with History." In *Racing to Regionalize: Democracy, Capitalism, and Regional Political Economy*, edited by Kenneth P. Thomas and Mary Ann Tétreault, 201–10. Boulder, CO: Lynne Rienner.

Abdullah, Ashraf. 2002. "KL to Give RM38m for Secretariat." *New Straits Times*, June 6.

Abe, Makoto, Yukihito Sato, and Mamoru Nagano. 1999. *Keizai kiki to Kankoku/Taiwan* (Economic Crisis and South Korea/Taiwan). Chiba: Institute of Developing Economies.

Abshire, David. 1990. "The Nature of American Global Economic Leadership in the 1990s." In *The Global Economy: America's Role in the Decade*, edited by W. Brock and R. Hormats. New York: W. W. Norton.

Abu Bakar, Mohamed. 1981. "Islamic Revivalism and the Political Process in Malaysia." *Asian Survey* 21, 10: 1040–59.

Acharya, Amitav. 1991. "The Association of Southeast Asian Nations: 'Security Community' or 'Defence Community?'" *Pacific Affairs* 64, 2 (Summer): 159–78.

——. 1992. "Regionalism and Regime Security in the Third World: Comparing the Origins of the ASEAN and the GCC." In *The Insecurity Dilemma—National Security of Third World States*, edited by Brian L. Job, 143–66. Boulder, CO: Lynne Rienner.

——. 1997. "Ideas, Identity and Institution-Building: From the 'ASEAN Way' to the 'Asia-Pacific Way.'" *Pacific Review* 10, 3: 319–46.

——. 1999. "Culture, Security, Multilateralism: The 'ASEAN Way' and Regional Order." In *Culture and Security: Multilateralism, Arms Control, and Security Building*, edited by Keith R. Krause, 55–84. London: Frank Cass.

——. 2001a. *Constructing a Security Community in Southeast Asia: ASEAN and the Problem of Regional Order*. London: Routledge.

——. 2001b. "Identity without Exceptionalism: Challenges for Asian Political and International Studies." Address to the inaugural workshop of the Asian Political and International Studies Association, Kuala Lumpur. November 1–2.

——. 2003. "Will Asia's Past Be Its Future?" *International Security* 28, 3: 149–64.

Acharya, Amitav, and Sola Ogunbanwo. 1998. "The Nuclear Weapon—Free Zones in South-East Asia and Africa." In *Yearbook 1998: Armaments, Disarmament, and International Security*, by Stockholm International Peace Research Institute, 443–56. Oxford: Oxford University Press.

Agence France Presse. 2001. "China Orders Xinjiang 'Terrorists and Religious Extremists' to Surrender." December 21. Accessed through Lexis-Nexis.

Aggarwal, Vinod K. 1995. "Comparing Regional Cooperation Efforts in the Asia-Pacific and North America." In *Pacific Cooperation: Building Economic and Security Regimes in the*

Asia-Pacific Region, edited by Andrew Mack and John Ravenhill, 40–65. Boulder, CO: Westview Press.

Aggarwal, Vinod K., and K. C. Lin. 2001. "APEC as an Institution." In *Assessing APEC's Progress: Trade, Ecotech and Institutions*, edited by R. E. Feinberg and Y. Zhao, 177–90. Singapore: Institute of Southeast Asian Studies.

Aggarwal, Vinod K., and Charles E. Morrison. 1998. *Asia-Pacific Crossroads: Regime Creation and the Future of APEC*. New York: St. Martin's.

Akami, Tomoko. 2002. *Internationalizing the Pacific: The United States, Japan and the Institute of Pacific Relations in War and Peace, 1919–45*. London: Routledge.

Akao, Yoji, ed. 1991. *Hoshin Kanri: Policy Deployment for Successful TQM*. Cambridge: Productivity Press. [Originally published by Japanese Standards Association as *Hoshin kanri katsuyo no jissai*.]

Alagappa, Muthiah. 1993. "Regionalism and the Quest for Security: ASEAN and the Cambodian Conflict." *Journal of International Affairs* 46, 2 (Winter): 439–67.

——. 1995. *Political Legitimacy in Southeast Asia: The Quest for Moral Authority*. Stanford: Stanford University Press.

——, ed. 1998. *Asian Security Practice: Material and Ideational Influences*. Stanford: Stanford University Press.

——, ed. 2001. *Coercion and Governance: The Declining Political Role of the Military in Asia*. Stanford: Stanford University Press.

Alatas, Ali. 2001. " 'ASEAN plus Three' Equals Peace plus Prosperity." Statement at the Regional Outlook Forum, Singapore. January 5.

Almonte, Jose T. 1997–98. "Ensuring the 'ASEAN Way.' " *Survival* 39, 4 (Winter): 80.

Alter, Karen J. 2000. "The European Union's Legal System and Domestic Policy: Spillover or Backlash?" *International Organization* 54, 3 (Summer): 489–518.

Alvarez, Jose. 2002. "The WTO as Linkage Machine." *American Journal of International Law* 96, 1 (January): 146–58.

Amsden, Alice H. 2001. *The Rise of "the Rest": Challenges to the West from Late-Industrializing Economies*. Oxford: Oxford University Press.

Amyx, Jennifer. 2004. "Japan and the Evolution of Regional Financial Arrangements in East Asia." In *Beyond Bilateralism: U.S.—Japan Relations in the New Asia-Pacific*, edited by Ellis S. Krauss and T. J. Pempel. Stanford: Stanford University Press.

Anderson, Benedict. 1983. *Imagined Communities: Reflections on the Origin and Spread of Nationalism*. London: Verso.

——. 1998. "From Miracle to Crash." *London Review of Books* 20 (April 16): 3, 5–7.

Arase, David. 1995. *Buying Power: The Political Economy of Japan's Foreign Aid*. Boulder, CO: Lynne Rienner.

"ASEAN Foreign Ministers Announce an Anti-Terrorism Stance." 2002. *Financial Times*, information from Thai press reports, March 14. Accessed through Lexis-Nexis.

ASEAN Secretariat. 1998. "Regional Haze Action Plan." http://www.asean.or.id.

——. 2001a. *Second ASEAN State of the Environment Report, 2000*. Jakarta.

——. 2001b. *ASEAN Investment Report, 2001: Foreign Direct Investment and Regional Integration*. Jakarta.

"Asian Currencies: Swapping Notes." 2000. *Economist*, May 13.

Asian Development Bank. 2001. "The Crunch: In the Aftermath of September 11, Malaysia Gets Tough with Its Homegrown Radicals." *Asiaweek*, October 5. Accessed through Proquest.

——. 2003. "The Asian Bond Market Initiative." http://aric.adb.org/docs/asiabondmarket/acd/asp.

"Asian Nations Agree on Currency Protection Swap." 2000. *Korea Times* (Seoul), May 8, 1 (*FBIS-EAS*-2000–0508).

Asian Productivity Organization (APO). 1987. *Export Processing Zones and Science Parks in Asia*. Tokyo: Asian Productivity Organization.

Ayoob, Mohammed. 1999. "From Regional System to Regional Society: Exploring Key Variables in the Construction of Regional Order." *Australian Journal of International Affairs* 53, 3: 247–60.

Babb, Sarah. 1996. "'A True American System of Finance': Frame Resonance in the U.S. Labor Movement, 1866 to 1886." *American Sociological Review* 61, 6 (December): 1033–52.

Backman, Michael. 1999. *Asian Eclipse: Exposing the Dark Side of Business in Asia*. Singapore: John Wiley.

Baguiro, Brendan Pereira Luz. 2002. "Terror Sweep in Region Stepped Up." *Straits Times*, April 19. Accessed through Lexis-Nexis.

Bagwell, Kyle, Petros C. Mavroidis, and Robert W. Staiger. 2002. "It's a Question of Market Access." *American Journal of International Law* 96, 1 (January): 56–76.

Ball, Desmond. 1993–94. "Arms and Affluence: Military Acquisitions in the Asia-Pacific Region." *International Security* 18, 3: 78–112.

Bank of Japan (BOJ). 1985, 2003. *Bank of Japan Quarterly Bulletin*. Tokyo.

Banister, Judith. 2001. Impacts of Migration to China's Border Regions." In *Demography and National Security*, edited by Myron Weiner and Sharon Stanton Russell, 256–304. New York: Berghahn Books.

Barnett, Michael, and F. Gregory Gause III. 1998. "Caravans in Opposite Directions: Society, State, and the Development of a Community in the Gulf Cooperation Council." In *Security Communities*, edited by Emanuel Adler and Michael Barnett, 161–97. Cambridge: Cambridge University Press.

Bayley, David. 1978. *Forces of Order: Police Behavior in Japan and the United States*. Berkeley: University of California Press.

BBC Monitoring of International Reports. 2002. "Philippines: 35,000 Muslim Students Volunteer to Fight U.S. Military Presence." January 24. Accessed through Lexis-Nexis.

Beeson, Mark. 1999. "Reshaping Regional Institutions: APEC and the IMF in East Asia." *Pacific Review* 12, 1: 1–24.

Bell, J. Bowyer. 2000. *The IRA, 1968–2000: Analysis of a Secret Army*. London: Frank Cass.

Bello, Walden, and Shea Cunningham. 1994. "Trade Warfare and Regional Integration in the Pacicfic: The USA, Japan and the Asian NICs." *Third World Quarterly* 15, 3: 445–58.

Berger, M. T. 1999. "APEC and Its Enemies: The Failure of the New Regionalism in the Asia-Pacific." *Third World Quarterly* 20, 5 (October): 1013–30.

Bergsten, C. Fred. 2000. "East Asian Regionalism: Towards a Tripartite World." *Economist*, July 15.

——. 2001. "The New Asian Challenge." Institute for International Economics Working Paper. March.

Bernard, Mitchell. 1994. "Post-Fordism, Transnational Production, and the Changing Global Political Economy." In *Political Economy and the Changing Global Order*, edited by Richard Stubbs and Geoffrey R. D. Underhill, 216–29. London: MacMillan.

——. 1996. "States, Social Forces, and Regions in Historical Time: Toward a Critical Political Economy of Eastern Asia." *Third World Quarterly* 17, 4: 649–65.

Bernard, Mitchell, and John Ravenhill. 1995. "Beyond Product Cycles and Flying Geese: Regionalization, Hierarchy, and the Industrialization of East Asia." *World Politics* 47, 2: 171–209.

"A Billion Consumers—A Survey of Asia." 1993. *Economist,* October 30, 1–18.

Blechinger, Verena, and Jochen Legewie, eds. 2000. *Facing Asia: Japan's Role in the Political and Economic Dynamism of Regional Cooperation.* Munich: Verlag Judicium GmbH.

Bloom, David, and Jeffrey G. Williamson. 1998. "Demographic Transitions and Economic Miracles in Emerging Asia." *World Bank Economic Review* 12, 10: 419–56.

Bobrow, Davis B. 1998. "The U.S. and ASEM: Why the Hegemon Didn't Bark." CSGR Working Paper 17. December.

Bonner, Raymond, and Jane Perlez. 2002. "Qaeda Moving into Indonesia, Officials Fear." *New York Times,* January 23, A1, A8.

Borrus, Michael, Dieter Ernst, and Stephan Haggard, eds. 2000. *International Production Networks in Asia: Rivalry or Riches?* London: Routledge.

Bowie, Alasdair, and Danny Unger. 1997. *The Politics of Open Economies: Indonesia, Malaysia, the Philippines, and Thailand.* Cambridge: Cambridge University Press.

Bowles, Paul. 2002. "Asia's Post-Crisis Regionalism: Bringing the State Back in, Keeping the (United) States Out." *Review of International Political Economy* 9, 2 (May): 230–56.

Bracken, Paul. 1999. *Fire in the East: The Rise of Asian Military Power and the Second Nuclear Age.* New York: HarperCollins.

Breslin, Shaun. 2000. "Decentralization, Globalization and China's Partial Re-Engagement with the Global Economy." *New Political Economy* 5, 2: 205–26.

Breslin, Shaun, Richard Higgott, and Ben Rosamond. 2002. "Regions in Comparative Perspective." In *New Regionalisms in the Global Political Economy: Theories and Cases,* edited by Shaun Breslin, Christopher W. Hughes, Nicola Philipps, and Ben Rosamond, 1–19. London: Routledge.

Breslin, Shaun, Christopher W. Hughes, Nicola Philipps, and Ben Rosamond, eds. 2002. *New Regionalisms in the Global Political Economy: Theories and Cases.* London: Routledge.

Brettell, Anna. 2001. "Energy and the Environment: The Atmospheric Link." Paper prepared for the Project on Environmental Security in East Asia, Tokyo, United Nations University.

Brooke, James. 2002. "Opposition to U.S. Forces Is Fading in the Philippines." *New York Times,* January 24. Accessed through Lexis-Nexis.

Buckley, P. J., and Mark Casson. 1985. *The Economic Theory of Multinational Enterprise.* London: Macmillan.

Buzan, Barry, and Gerald Segal. 1994. "Rethinking East Asian Security." *Survival* 36, 2 (Summer): 3–22.

Campos, Jose Edgardo, and Hilton L. Root, eds. 1996. *The Key to the Asian Miracle: Making Shared Growth Credible.* Washington, DC: Brookings Institution.

Camroux, David. 1996. "State Responses to Islamic Resurgence in Malaysia: Accommodation, Co-optation, and Confrontation." *Pacific Affairs* 36, 9 (September): 852–68.

Capie, David, and Paul Evans. 2002. *The Asia-Pacific Security Lexicon.* Singapore: Institute of Southeast Asian Studies.

Carney, Michael, and Eric Gedajlovic. 2001. "Corporate Governance and Firm Capabilities: A Comparison of Managerial, Alliance and Personal Capitalisms." *Asia Pacific Journal of Management* 18, 3: 335–54.

Carter, Ashton B. 2001–2. "The Architecture of Government in the Face of Terrorism." *International Security* 26, 3 (Winter): 5–23.

Cha, Victor D. 2000. *Alignment Despite Antagonism.* Stanford: Stanford University Press.

Chalk, Peter. 1997. "Grey-Area Phenomena in Southeast Asia: Piracy, Drug Trafficking, and Political Terrorism." Canberra Papers on Strategy and Defence. Australian National University, Canberra.

Cheeseman, Graeme. 1999. "Asian-Pacific Security Discourse in the Wake of the Asian Economic Crisis." *Pacific Review* 12, 3: 333–56.

Chen, Tain-Jy, ed. 1998. *Taiwanese Firms in Southeast Asia: Networking Across Borders.* Cheltenham, UK: Edward Elgar.

Chia, Siow Yue. 1996. "The Deepening and Widening of ASEAN." *Journal of the Asia Pacific Economy* 1: 59–78.

Chin, Kin Wah. 1997. "ASEAN: The Long Road to 'One Southeast Asia.'" *Asian Journal of Political Science* 5, 1: 1–19.

"China, ASEAN Pact on Free Trade Gets Arroyo's Support." 2002. *Wall Street Journal,* May 22, A20.

"China Investment and Trade: Buying Fast into Southeast Asia." 2002. *Far Eastern Economic Review,* March 28.

Chowdhury, Anis, and Iyanatul Islam. 1993. *The Newly Industrialising Economies of East Asia.* London: Routledge.

Christensen, Thomas J. 1999. "China, the U.S.-Japan Alliance, and the Security Dilemma in East Asia." *International Security* 23, 4 (Spring): 49–80.

———. 2001. "China." In *Strategic Asia, 2001–2: Power and Purpose,* edited by Richard J. Ellings and Aaron L. Friedberg. Seattle: National Bureau of Asian Research.

Chu, Yun-han. 1999. "Surviving the East Asian Financial Storm: The Political Foundation of Taiwan's Economic Resilience." In *The Politics of the Asian Economic Crisis,* edited by T. J. Pempel. Ithaca: Cornell University Press.

Claessens, Stijn, Simeon Djankov, and Larry H. P. Lang. 2000. "The Separation of Ownership and Control in East Asian Corporations." *Journal of Financial Economics* 58: 1–2, 81–12.

Cohen, Stephen S. 2002. "Mapping Asian Integration: Transnational Transactions in the Pacific Rim." *American Asian Review* 20, 3 (Fall): 1–30.

Collins, Alan. 2000. *The Security Dilemmas of Southeast Asia.* Basingstoke, UK: Palgrave.

Committee on Government Reform and Oversight (CGRO). 1998. *Investigation of Political Fundraising Improprieties and Possible Violations of Law: Interim Report.* Sixth report by the CGRO, U.S. Congress. November 5.

Cotton, James. 1999. *ASEAN and the Southeast Asian 'Haze': Challenging the Prevailing Modes of Regional Engagement.* Australian National University, Department of International Relations.

Crawford, John, and Saburo Okita. 1976. *Australia, Japan, and Western Pacific Economic Relations: A Report to the Governments of Australia and Japan.* Canberra: Australian Government Publishing Service.

Crenshaw, Martha. 1983. *Terrorism, Legitimacy, and Power.* Middletown, CT: Wesleyan University Press.

———.1985. "An Organizational Approach to the Analysis of Political Terrorism." *Orbis* 29, 3 (Autumn): 473–87.

———, ed. 1995. *Terrorism in Context.* University Park: Pennsylvania State University Press.

Crone, Donald. 1993. "The Politics of Emerging Pacific Cooperation." *Pacific Affairs* 65, 1: 68–83.

Cumings, Bruce. 1984. "The Origins and Development of the Northeast Asian Political Economy." *International Organization* 38, 1: 1–40.

———. 1993. "Japan's Position in the World System." In *Postwar Japan as History,* edited by Andrew Gordon, 34–63. Berkeley: University of California Press.

Dauvergne, Peter. 1997a. *Shadows in the Forest: Japan and the Politics of Timber in Southeast Asia.* Cambridge, MA: MIT Press.

——. 1997b. "Weak States and the Environment in Indonesia and the Solomon Islands." Australian National University, Department of International Relations.

——. 1998a. *Environmental Insecurity, Forest Management, and State Responses in Southeast Asia.* Australian National University, Department of International Relations.

——. 1998b. "The Political Economy of Indonesia's 1997 Forest Fires." *Australian Journal of International Affairs* (April).

——. 2001a. *Loggers and Degradation in the Asia-Pacific: Corporations and Environmental Management.* Cambridge: Cambridge University Press.

——. 2001b. "The Rise of an Environmental Superpower? Evaluating Japanese Environmental Aid to Southeast Asia." In *Japan and East Asian Regionalism,* edited by S. J. Maswood, 51–67. London: Routledge.

Davies, Ian. 2000. *Regional Cooperation in Northeast Asia: The Tumen River Area Development Program, 1990–2000. In Search of a Model for Regional Economic Co-operation in Northeast Asia.* North Pacific Policy Papers 4. Program on Canada—Asia Policy Studies, University of British Columbia.

De Brouwer, Gordon. 2002. "Research Focus: Strengthening the Policy Dialogue in East Asia." *APEC Economies* (newsletter) 6 (January): 1.

de Jonquieres, Guy. 1994. "Different Aims, Common Cause." *Financial Times,* November 18.

Dent, Christopher M. 2003. "Networking the Region? The Emergence and Impact of Asia-Pacific Bilateral Trade Agreement Projects." *Pacific Review* 16, 1: 1–28.

Department of Statistics (Singapore). 2001. *Singapore's Investment Abroad, 1998–1999.* Singapore: Department of Statistics, Ministry of Trade and Industry.

Deutsch, Karl W. 1957. *Political Community and the North Atlantic Area: International Organization in the Light of Historical Experience.* Princeton: Princeton University Press.

——. 1966. *Nationalism and Social Communication: An Inquiry into the Foundation of Nationality.* 2nd ed. Cambridge, MA: MIT Press.

Deyo, Frederic, and Richard Doner. 2001a. "Dynamic Flexibility and Sectoral Governance in the Thai Auto Industry: The Enclave Problem." In *Economic Governance and the Challenge of Flexibility in East Asia,* edited by Frederic Deyo, Richard Doner, and Eric Hershberg, 107–35. Lanham, MD: Rowman and Littlefield.

——. 2001b. "Introduction: Economic Governance and Flexible Production in East Asia." In *Economic Governance and the Challenge of Flexibility in East Asia,* edited by Frederic Deyo, Richard Doner, and Eric Hershberg, 1–32. Lanham, MD: Rowman and Littlefield.

Deyo, Frederic, Richard Doner, and Eric Hershberg, eds. 2001. *Economic Governance and the Challenge of Flexibility in East Asia.* Lanham, MD: Rowman and Littlefield.

Dhume, Sadanand. 2002. "Chinese State Concerns Broaden Indonesian Oil and Gas Holdings." *Wall Street Journal,* May 1 (online edition).

DiMaggio, Paul J., and Walter W. Powell. 1991. "The Iron Cage Revisited: Institutional Isomorphism and Collective Rationality in Organization Fields." In *The New Institutionalism in Organizational Analysis,* edited by Paul J. DiMaggio and Walter W. Powell, 63–82. Chicago: University of Chicago Press.

Dobson, Wendy. 2001. "Deeper Integration in East Asia: Regional Institutions and the International Economic System." *World Economy* 24, 8 (August).

Dobson, Wendy, and Chia Siow Yue, eds. 1997. *Multinationals and East Asian Integration.* Toronto: International Development Research Centre; Singapore: Institute of Southeast Asian Studies.

Doner, Richard. 1991. *Driving a Bargain: Automotive Industrialization and Japanese Firms in Southeast Asia.* Berkeley: University of California Press.

——. 1997. "Japan in East Asia: Institutions and Regional Leadership." In *Network Power: Japan and Asia,* edited by Peter J. Katzenstein and Takashi Shiraishi, 197–233. Ithaca: Cornell University Press.

——. 2001. "Regionalization and Regionalism in Southeast Asia: Implications of the Disk Drive and Auto Industries." Paper presented at the Annual Meeting of the Association for Asian Studies, Chicago. March 22–25.

Doremus, Paul, William Keller, Louis Pauly, and Simon Reich. 1998. *The Myth of the Global Corporation.* Princeton: Princeton University Press.

Drysdale, Peter. 1988. *International Economic Pluralism: Economic Policy in East Asia and the Pacific.* Sydney: Allen and Unwin.

——. 1991. "Open Regionalism: A Key to East Asia's Economic Future." Pacific Economic Paper 197. Australia-Japan Research Center, Australian National University.

Drysdale, Peter, and Andrew Elek. 1997. "APEC: Community-Building in East Asia and the Pacific." In *From APEC to Xanadu: Creating a Viable Community in the Post—Cold War Pacific,* edited by Donald C. Hellman and Kenneth B. Pyle, 37–69. New York: M. E. Sharpe.

Drysdale, Peter, and Hugh Patrick. 1979. "Evaluation of a Proposed Asian-Pacific Regional Economic Organization." In *An Asia Pacific Regional Economic Organization: An Exploratory Concept Paper,* Congressional Research Service, paper prepared for the Committee on Foreign Relations, United States Senate. Washington: U.S. Government Printing Office.

Dunning, John H. 1992. *Multinational Enterprises and the Global Economy.* Reading, MA: Addison-Wesley.

Dupont, Alan. 2001. *East Asia Imperilled: Transnational Challenges to Security.* Cambridge: Cambridge University Press.

East Asian Study Group. 2002. *Final Report of the East Asian Study Group.* http://www.aseansec.org.

East Asian Vision Group (EAVG). 2001. *Towards an East Asian Community: Region of Peace, Prosperity and Progress.* October. http://www.aseansec.org.

Eichengreen, Barry. 1999. *Toward a New International Financial Architecture: A Practical Post-Asia Agenda.* Washington, DC: Institute for International Economics.

Emmerson, Donald K. 1996. "Indonesia, Malaysia, Singapore: A Regional Security Core?" In *Southeast Asian Security in the New Millennium,* edited by Richard J. Ellings and Sheldon W. Simon. Armonk, NY: M. E. Sharpe.

——. 2001. "Goldilock's Problem: Rethinking Security and Sovereignty in Asia." In *The Many Faces of Asian Security,* edited by Sheldon Simon, 89–111. Latham, MD: Rowman and Littlefield.

Encarnation, Dennis. 1992. *Rivals beyond Trade: America versus Japan in Global Competition.* Ithaca: Cornell University Press.

——. 1999. "Asia and the Global Operations of Multinational Corporations." In *Japanese Multinationals in Asia: Regional Operations in Comparative Perspective,* edited by Dennis Encarnation, 46–86. Oxford: Oxford University Press.

Engelberg, Stephen. 2001. "One Man and a Global Web of Violence." *New York Times,* January 14. Accessed through Lexis-Nexis.

Ernst, Dieter. 1994. "Carriers of Regionalization: The East Asian Production Networks of Japanese Electronics Firms." BRIE Working Paper 73. Berkeley Roundtable on the International Economy, University of California, Berkeley.

Esty, Daniel C. 1996. "Environmental Regulation and Competitiveness: Theory and Practice." In *Asian Dragons and Green Trade,* edited by Simon S. C. Tay and Daniel C. Esty, 33–48. Singapore: Times Academic Press.

Evans. Paul. 2000. "The Concept of Eastern Asia." In *Eastern Asia: An Introductory History*, 3rd ed., edited by Colin Mackerras. Melbourne: Longman Australia.

——. 2003. "Nascent Asian Regionalism and Its Implications for Canada." Paper prepared for the Asia Pacific Foundation of Canada's Roundtable on the Foreign Policy Dialogue and Canada—Asia Relations. March 27.

Fairbank, John K., ed. 1968. *The Chinese World Order: Traditional China's Foreign Relations*. Cambridge: Harvard University Press.

Fawcett, Louise, and Andrew Hurrell, eds. 1995. *Regionalism in World Politics: Regional Organization and International Order*. Oxford: Oxford University Press.

Feinberg, Richard E. 2003. *APEC as an Institution: Multilateral Governance in the Asia-Pacific*. Singaopore: Institute of Southeast Asian Studies.

Feinberg, Richard E., and Ye Zhao. 2001. *Assessing APEC's Progress: Trade, Ecotech and Institutions*. Singapore: Institute of Southeast Asian Studies.

Felker, Greg, and K. S. Jomo. 1999. "New Approaches to Investment Policy in the ASEAN4." Paper prepared for the Asian Development Bank Institute's conference High-Level Dialogue on Development Paradigms. Tokyo.

Ferguson, Yale. 1984. "Cooperation in Latin America: The Politics of Regional Integration." In *The Dynamics of Latin American Foreign Policies: Challenges for the 1980s*, edited by Elizabeth G. Ferris and Jennie K. Lincoln, 37–56. Boulder, CO: Westview.

Ferrer, Miriam Coronel. 1997. *Southern Philippines Council for Peace and Development: A Response to the Controversy*. Manila: University of the Philippines Center for Integrative and Development Studies.

Findlay, Christopher, Haflah Pei, and Mari Pangestu. 2003. "Trading with Favourites: Risks, Motives, and Implications of FTAs in the Asia Pacific." Paper presented at the East Asia Trade Policy Seminar, Asia-Pacific School of Economics and Government, Australian National University, March 20–21.

Flynn, Stephen E. 1998. "Asian Drugs, Crime, and Control: Rethinking the War." In *Fires across the Water: Transnational Problems in Asia*, edited by J. Shinn, 18–43. New York: Council on Foreign Relations.

Foot, Rosemary. 1998. "China and the ASEAN Regional Forum." *Asian Survey* 38, 5: 425–40.

Frankel, Jeffrey A., and Miles Kahler, eds. 1993. *Regionalism and Rivalry: Japan and the United States in Pacific Asia*. Chicago: University of Chicago Press.

Frenkel, Stephen, ed. 1993. *Organized Labor in the Asia-Pacific Region: A Comparative Study of Trade Unionism in Nine Countries*. Ithaca: Cornell University Press.

Friedberg, Aaron. 1993. "Ripe for Rivalry: Prospects for Peace in a Multipolar Asia." *International Security* 18, 3 (Winter): 5–33.

——. 2002. "11 September and the Future of Sino-American Relations." *Survival* 44, 1 (Spring): 33–50.

Frieden, Jeffry A., and David Lake, eds. 2002. *International Political Economy: Perspectives on Global Power and Wealth*. New York: St. Martin's Press.

Friedman, John. 1986. "The World City Hypothesis." *Development and Change* 4, 10: 12–50.

Friman, Richard. 1993. "Awaiting the Tsunami? Japan and the International Drug Trade." *Pacific Review* 6, 1: 41–50.

——. 1999. "Obstructing Markets: Organized Crime Networks and Drug Control in Japan." In *Illicit Global Economy and State Power*, edited by Richard Friman and P. Andreas, 173–97. Lanham, MD: Rowman and Littlefield.

Fruin, W. Mark, ed. 1998. *Networks, Markets, and the Pacific Rim: Studies in Strategy*. Oxford: Oxford University Press.

Funabashi, Yoichi. 1993. "The Asianization of Asia." *Foreign Affairs* 72, 5 (November/December): 75–85.

——. 1995. *Ajia Taiheiyo fyujon* (Asia Pacific Fusion). Tokyo: Chuo Koron-sha.

Gamble, Andrew, and Anthony Payne, eds. 1996. *Regionalism and World Order.* London: MacMillan.

Garnaut, Ross. 1996. *Open Regionalism and Trade Liberalization.* Singapore: Institute of Southeast Asian Studies.

Gartzke, E., Q. Li, and C. Boehmer. 2001. "Investing in the Peace: Economic Interdependence and International Conflict." *International Organization* 55, 2 (Spring): 391–38.

Geddes, Andrew. 2000. *Immigration and European Integration: Toward Fortress Europe?* Manchester, UK: Manchester University Press.

Gerecht, Reuel Marc. 2002. "The Gospel According to Osama bin Laden." *Atlantic Monthly,* January, 46–48.

Gereffi, Gary, and Miguel Korzeniewicz, eds. 1995. *Commodity Chains and Global Competition.* Westport, CT: Praeger.

Gerges, Fawaz A. 1999. *America and Political Islam.* New York: Cambridge University Press.

Gershman, John. 2000. "In Focus: Asia Pacific Economic Cooperation." *Foreign Policy in Focus* 5, 9 (November). Available at https://wwwc.cc.columbia.edu/sec/dlc/ciao/pbei/fpif/gej01.html.

Gilpin, Robert. 2000. *The Challenge of Global Capitalism: The World Economy in the Twenty-first Century.* Princeton: Princeton University Press.

Goldstone, Jack. 2001. "Demography, Environment, and Security: An Overview." In *Demography and National Security,* edited by Myron Weiner and Sharon Stanton Russell, 38–61. Oxford: Berghahn Books.

Gordon, Bernard K. 2001. *America's Trade Follies: Turning Economic Leadership into Strategic Weakness.* London: Routledge.

Gould, Erica R., and Stephen D. Krasner. 2002. "Germany and Japan: Binding versus Autonomy." In *Embedded Capitalism: Japan and Germany in the Postwar Period,* edited by Kozo Yamamura and Wolfgang Streeck. Ithaca: Cornell University Press.

Graham, Edward M. 2000. "Globalization, Foreign Direct Investment, and the Environment." In *Fighting the Wrong Enemy: Antiglobal Activists and Multinational Enterprises,* edited by Edward M. Graham. Washington, DC: Institute for International Economics.

Grieco, Joseph M. 1997. "Systemic Sources of Variation in Regional Institutionalization in Western Europe, East Asia, and the Americas." In *The Political Economy of Regionalism,* edited by Edward D. Mansfield and Helen Milner, 164–87. New York: Columbia University Press.

——. 1998. "Political—Military Dynamics and the Nesting of Regimes: An Analysis of APEC, the WTO, and Prospects for Cooperation in the Asia-Pacific." In *Asia-Pacific Crossroads: Regime Creation and the Future of APEC,* edited by Vinod K. Aggarwal and Charles E. Morrison, 235–56. New York: St. Martin's Press.

Gruber, Lloyd. 2000. *Ruling the World: Power Politics and the Rise of Supranational Institutions.* Princeton: Princeton University Press.

Guerrieri, Paolo. 1998. "Trade Patterns and Regimes in Asia and the Pacific." In *Asia-Pacific Crossroads: Regime Creation and the Future of APEC,* edited by Vinod K. Aggarwal and Charles E. Morrison, 65–86. New York: St. Martin's Press.

Haas, Ernst. 1964. *Beyond the Nation State: Functionalism and International Organization.* Stanford: Stanford University Press.

——. 1980. "Why Collaborate: Issue Linkage and International Regimes." *World Politics* 32.

Haas, Peter. 1992. "Introduction: Epistemic Communities and International Policy Coordination." *International Organization* 46, 1 (Winter).

Haggard, Stephan. 1997. "Regionalism in Asia and the Americas." In *The Political Economy of Regionalism,* edited by Edward D. Mansfield and Helen V. Milner, 20–49. New York: Columbia University Press.

——. 2000. *The Political Economy of the Asian Financial Crisis.* Washington, DC: Institute of International Economics.

Haggard, Stephan, and Robert R. Kaufman. 1995. *The Political Economy of Democratic Transitions.* Princeton: Princeton University Press.

Hall, Peter A. 1986. *Governing the Economy: The Politics of State Intervention in Britain and France.* New York: Oxford University Press.

Hall, Peter [G.] 1997. "Megacities, World Cities and Global Cities." The First Megacities Lecture, The Hague. Available at http://www.megacities.nl/lecture_1/lecture.html.

Hamashita, Takeshi. 1997. "The Intra-Regional System in East Asia in Modern Times." In *Network Power: Japan and Asia,* edited by Peter J. Katzenstein and Takashi Shiraishi, 113–35. Ithaca: Cornell University Press.

Hamilton, Gary, ed. 1996. *Asian Business Networks.* Berlin: Walter de Gruyter.

——. 1999. "What Alan Greenspan Doesn't Know about Asia." In *The Politics of the Asian Economic Crisis,* edited by T. J. Pempel. Ithaca: Cornell University Press.

Hamilton-Hart, Natasha. 2002. *Asian States, Asian Bankers: Central Banking in Southeast Asia.* Ithaca: Cornell University Press.

——. 2004. "Capital Flows and Financial Markets in Asia: National, Regional or Global?" In *Beyond Bilateralism: The U.S.–Japan Relationship in the New Asia-Pacific,* edited by Ellis Krause and T. J. Pempel. Stanford: Stanford University Press.

Han, Sung-Joo. 2002. "East Asian Regional Cooperation." Notes for a presentation to the Carnegie Council. January 30.

Harris, Stuart. 1993. "The Economic Aspects of Pacific Security." Adelphi Papers 275. Institute for Strategic Studies, London.

——. 1994. "Policy Networks and Economic Cooperation: Policy Coordination in the Asia-Pacific." *Pacific Review* 7, 4: 381–95.

——. 2000. Asian Multilateral Institutions and Their Response to the Asian Economic Crisis: The Regional and Global Implications. *Pacific Review* 13, 3 (August): 495–516.

Harris, Stuart, and R. N. Cooper. 2000. "The U.S.–Japan Alliance." In *America's Asian Alliances,* edited by Robert D. Blackwill and P. Dibb, 31–60. Cambridge, MA: MIT Press.

Harrison, Selig. 2002. *Korean Endgame: A Strategy for Reunification and U.S. Disengagement.* Princeton: Princeton University Press.

Hatano, Sumio. 1998. "Sengo nihon no Ajia gaiko" (Japan's Foreign Policy toward Asia in the Postwar Era). In *Higashi Ajia kokusai kankei no dainamizumu* (Dynamism of International Relations in East Asia), edited by M. Saito, 89–111. Tokyo: Toyo Keizai Shinposha.

Hatch, Walter. 2000. "Rearguard Regionalism: Protecting Core Networks in Japan's Political Economy." Ph.D. dissertation, University of Washington.

——. 2002. "Regionalizing the State: Japanese Administrative and Financial Guidance for Asia." *Social Science Japan Journal* 5, 2: 179–97.

Hatch, Walter, and Kozo Yamamura. 1996. *Asia in Japan's Embrace: Building a Regional Production Alliance.* Cambridge: Cambridge University Press.

Hatsuse, Ryuhei. 1999. "Regionalisms in East Asia and the Asia-Pacific." In *Globalism, Regionalism, and Nationalism,* edited by Yoshinobu Yamamoto, 105–25. Malden, Mass.: Blackwell.

Haufler, Virginia. 1993. "Crossing the Boundary between Public and Private: International Regimes and Non-State Actors." In *Regime Theory and International Relations,* edited by Volker Rittberger, 94–111. Oxford: Clarendon Press.

Hedman, Eva-Lotta. 2002. "The Threat of 'Islamic Terrorism'? A View from Southeast Asia." *Harvard Asia Quarterly* 6, 2 (Spring): 38–43.

Hefner, Robert W. 1997. "Islam in an Era of Nation-States: Politics and Religious Renewal in Muslim Southeast Asia." In *Islam in an Era of Nation-States,* edited by Robert W. Hefner, 3–40. Honolulu: University of Hawai'i Press.

———. 2000. *Civil Islam: Muslims and Democratization in Indonesia.* Princeton: Princeton University Press.

Hemmer, Christopher, and Peter J. Katzenstein. 2002. "Why Is There No NATO in Asia? Collective Identity, Regionalism, and the Origins of Multilateralism." *International Organization* 56, 3 (Summer): 575–607.

Henderson, Jeffrey, Peter Dicken, Martin Hess, Neil Coe, and Henry Wai-chung Yeung. 2002. "Global Production Networks and the Analysis of Economic Development." GPN Working Paper 1. Manchester Business School, Manchester University, UK.

Henning, C. Randall. 2002. *East Asian Financial Cooperation.* Washington, DC: Institute for International Economics.

Higashi, Shigeki. 2000. "Tai no keizai kaihatsu to kinyu seido" (Economic Development and Financial System in Thailand). In *Hatten tojokoku no kokka to keizai* (The State and Economy in the Developing Countries), edited by Shigeki Higashi, 99–142. Chiba, Japan: Institute of Developing Economies.

Higgott, Richard A. 1993. "Competing Theoretical Approaches to International Cooperation: Implications for the Asia-Pacific." In *Pacific Economic Relations in the 1990s: Cooperation or Conflict?* edited by Richard Higgott, Richard Leaver, and John Ravenhill, 290–311. Boulder, CO: Lynne Rienner.

———. 1994. "Ideas, Identity and Policy Coordination in the Asia-Pacific." *Pacific Review* 7, 4.

———. 1997a. "*De Facto* or *de Jure* Regionalism: The Double Discourse of Regionalization in the Asia Pacific." *Global Security: Journal of Interdisciplinary International Relations* 11, 2: 65–83.

———. 1997b. "Regional Integration, Economic Cooperation or Economic Policy Coordination in the Asia Pacific? Unpacking APEC, EAEC and AFTA." In *The Regionalization of the World Economy and Consequences for Southern Africa,* edited by Heribert Dieter, 237–76. Marburg, Germany: Metropolis-Verlag.

———. 1998a. "The Asian Economic Crisis: A Study in the Politics of Resentment." *New Political Economy* 4, 1.

———. 1998b. "The International Political Economy of Regionalism: Europe and Asia Compared." In *Regionalism and Global Economic Integration: Europe, Asia and the Americas,* edited by W. D. Coleman and G. R. D. Underhill. London: Routledge.

———. 1999. "The Political Economy of Globalisation in East Asia: The Salience of "Region Building." In *Globalisation and the Asia-Pacific: Contested Territories,* edited by Kris Olds, Peter Dicken, Philip F. Kelly, Lily Kong, and Henry Wai-chung Yeung, 91–106. New York: Routledge.

Higgott, Richard A., and Shaun Breslin. 2000. "Studying Region: Learning from the Old, Constructing the New." *New Political Economy* 5, 3: 333–52.

Higgott, Richard, and Richard Stubbs. 1995. "Competing Conceptions of Economic Regionalism: APEC vs. EAEC." *Review of International Political Economy* 2, 3:549–69.

Hill, Hal. 1993. "Southeast Asian Economic Development: An Analytical Survey." Economics Division Working Papers, 93/4, Research School of Pacific and Asian Studies. Canberra: Australian National University.

Hirschman, Albert O. 1970. *Exit, Voice and Loyalty: Responses to Decline in Firms, Organizations, and States.* Berkeley: University of California Press.

Hoffman, Bruce. 1998. *Inside Terrorism.* New York: Columbia University Press.

Howell, Julia Day. 2001. "Sufism and the Indonesian Islamic Revival." *Journal of Asian Studies* 60, 3 (August): 701–29.

Hughes, Christopher W. 2000. "Japanese Policy and the East Asian Currency Crisis: Abject Defeat or Quiet Victory?" *Review of International Political Economy* 7, 2 (Summer): 219–53.

Huntington, Samuel P. 1996. *The Clash of Civilizations and the Remaking of World Order.* New York: Simon and Schuster.

Hurrell, Andrew. 1992. "Latin America in the New World Order: A Regional Bloc of the Americas?" *International Affairs* 68, 1 (January): 121–39.

——. 1995a. "Explaining the Resurgence of Regionalism in World Politics." *Review of International Studies* 21, 4.

——. 1995b. "Regionalism in Theoretical Perspective." In *Regionalism in World Politics,* edited by Louise Fawcett and Andrew Hurrell. New York: Oxford University Press.

Huxley, Tim, and Susan Willett. 1999. *Arming East Asia.* Adelphi Paper 329. London: International Institute for Strategic Studies.

Hymer, Stephen. 1976. *The International Operations of National Firms: A Study of Direct Foreign Investment.* Cambridge, MA: MIT Press.

Ikenberry, John. 2001. *After Victory: Institutions, Strategic Restraint, and the Building of Order after Major Wars.* Princeton: Princeton University Press.

Ikenberry, John, and Michael Mastanduno, eds. 2003. *International Relations Theory and the Asia Pacific.* New York: Columbia University Press.

Inoguchi, Takashi, ed. 2002. *Japan's Asia Policy: Revival and Response.* New York: Palgrave.

Interim Scientific Advisory Group of EANET. 2000. "Report on the Acid Deposition Monitoring of EANET during the Preparatory Phase." Acid Deposition and Oxidant Research Center, Niigata, Japan.

International Institute for Strategic Studies (IISS). 2000. *The Military Balance.* London.

International Law Enforcement Academy (ILEA). 2001. *International Law Enforcement Academy Bangkok, 2001.* Bangkok.

International Monetary Fund. 2002. *Direction of Trade Statistics.* Washington, DC: IMF.

International Telecommunications Union (ITU). 2000. *International Telecommunications Union Yearbook.* Geneva.

Itabashi Isao, Ogawara Masamichi, with David Leheny. 2002. "Japan." In *Combating Terrorism: Strategies of Ten Countries,* edited by Yonah Alexander. Ann Arbor: University of Michigan Press.

Ivanova, Tamara. 2000. "Ivanov Says Shanghai 5 Good Example of Subregional Cooperation." *Itar-Tass News Wire,* April 20. Accessed through Lexis-Nexis.

"Japan Braces for a 'Designed in China' World. 2002. *New York Times,* April 21.

Japan Defense Agency. 1999. *Bouei hakusho, 1999* (Defense of Japan, 1999). Tokyo.

——. 2001. *Bouei hakusho, 2001* (Defense of Japan, 2001). Tokyo.

Japan Environmental Council (JEC). 2000. *Ajia kankyo hakusho, 2000–2001* (White Paper on Environment in Asia, 2000–2001). Tokyo: Toyo Keizai Shinposha.

Japan External Trade Organization (JETRO). 1990, 2002. *White Paper on Foreign Direct Investments.* Tokyo.

Japan Institute of International Agency (JIIA). 2000. *Yakubutsujihan taisaku no tame no chousa kenkyu hokokusho: Chugoku* (Research Report for Drug Control Policy: China). Tokyo.

Japan International Cooperation Agency (JICA). Division of Environment and Gender. 2001. "JICA no kankyo kanren kyouryoku" (Environment-Related Cooperation by JICA). Mimeo. Tokyo.

Japan National Committee for Pacific Economic Cooperation (JANCPEC). 1992. *Economic Development of the Pacific Region and Triple-T Networking.* Tokyo.

———. 2003. *An Assessment of Impediments to Foreign Direct Investment in APEC Member Economies.* Tokyo.

Japan Small Business Research Institute (JSBRI). 2000. "White Paper on Small and Medium Enterprises in Japan: A Wake-up Call to Small Business—Building a Self-Sustaining Enterprise." Tokyo: Small and Medium Enterprise Agency, METI.

Jayasuriya, Kanishka. 2001. "Southeast Asia's Embedded Mercantilism in Crisis: International Strategies and Domestic Coalitions." In *Non-Traditional Security Issues in Southeast Asia,* edited by A. T. H. Tan and J. D. K. Boutin, 26–53. Singapore: Institute of Defence and Strategic Studies.

Jervis, Robert, Richard Ned Lebow, and Janice Gross Stein, eds. 1985. *Psychology and Deterrence.* Baltimore: Johns Hopkins University Press.

Jesudason, James. 1989. *Ethnicity and the Economy: The State, Chinese Business and Multinationals in Malaysia.* Singapore: Oxford University Press.

Jin, Chang Soo. 2003. "En no kokusaika seisaku: Kiseikanwa kara taigai keizai seisaku he" (Policy for Internationalization of the Yen: From Deregulation to Foreign Economic Policy). In *Nihon to Ajia no seijikeizai* (Political Economy of Japan and Asia), edited by Michio Muramatsu and Keiichi Tsunekawa, 71–89. Kyoto: International Center for Japanese Studies.

Job, Brian. 2002. "The Track II Process in Asia." In *Asian Security Order: Instrumental and Normative,* edited by Muthiah Alagappa. Stanford: Stanford University Press.

Johnson, Chalmers. 1982. *MITI and the Japanese Miracle.* Stanford: Stanford University Press.

———. 1987. "Political Institutions and Economic Performance: The Government–Business Relationship in Japan, South Korea, and Taiwan." In *The Political Economy of the New Asian Industrialism,* edited by Frederick C. Deyo, 136–64. Ithaca: Cornell University Press.

Johnson, D. Gale. 2000. "Agricultural Adjustment in China: Problems and Prospects." *Population and Development Review* 26, 10: 319–34.

Johnston, Alastair Iain. 1999. "The Myth of the ASEAN Way? Explaining the Evolution of the ASEAN Regional Forum." In *Imperfect Unions: Security Institutions over Time and Space,* edited by Helga Haftendorn, Robert O. Keohane, and Celeste A. Wallander, 286–324. Oxford: Oxford University Press.

———. 2003. "Socialization in International Institutions: The ASEAN Way and International Relations Theory." In *International Relations Theory and the Asia Pacific,* edited by G. John Ikenberry and Michael Mastanduno, 107–62. New York: Columbia University Press.

Joint Ministerial Statement of the ASEAN + 3 Finance Ministers Meeting. 2003. Issued by the APT finance ministers, Makati, August 7. http://www.mof.go.jp/.

Joint Statement on East Asia Cooperation. 1999. Issued by the heads of government, Manila, November 28. http://www.aseansec.org.

Jones, David M., and Michael L. R. Smith. 2001. "Is There a Sovietology of South-East Asian Studies?" *International Affairs* 77, 4 (October): 843–63.

Juergensmeyer, Mark. 1993. *The New Cold War? Religious Nationalism Confronts the Secular State.* Berkeley: University of California Press.

———. 2000. *Terror in the Mind of God.* Berkeley: University of California Press.

Kaburagi, Shinji, Satoshi Ikehara, and Shiro Izuishi. 2000. "Japanese Manufacturing Companies Show Their Intention to Expand Overseas Business Operations as They Continue Domestic and International Management Reformation at Brisk Pace." *JBIC Review* 5 (June): 1–76.

Kaburagi, Shinji, Shiro Izuishi, Takeshi Toyoda, and Mayumi Suzuki. 2002. "JBIC FY2001 Survey: The Outlook for Japanese Foreign Direct Investment (13th Annual Survey)." *JBIC Review* 6 (June): 1–57.

Kahler, Miles. 1995. "Institution-Building in the Pacific." In *Pacific Cooperation: Building Economic and Security Regimes in the Asia-Pacific Region,* edited by Andrew Mack and John Ravenhill. Boulder, CO: Westview.

———. 2000a. "Conclusion: The Causes and Consequences of Legalization." *International Organization* 54, 3 (Summer): 661–84.

———. 2000b. "Introduction: Legalization and World Politics." *International Organization* 54, 3 (Summer): 385–99. With Judith Goldstein, Robert O. Keohane, and Anne-Marie Slaughter; contribution to the special issue "Legalization and World Politics."

———. 2000c. "The New International Financial Architecture and Its Limits." In *The Asian Financial Crisis and the Structure of Global Finance,* edited by Gregory W. Noble and John Ravenhill, 235–60. Cambridge: Cambridge University Press.

———. 2000d. "Legalization as Strategy: The Asia-Pacific Case." *International Organization* 54, 3 (Summer): 549–72.

Kamiya, Matake. 1998. "Reisengo no Nihon no anzenhosho seisaku (National Security Policy of Japan after the End of the Cold War)." In *Higashi Ajia kokusai kankei no dainamizumu* (Dynamism of International Relations in East Asia), edited by M. Saito. Tokyo: Toyo Keizai Shinposha.

Kang, David. 2003a. "Getting Asia Wrong: The Need for New Analytic Frameworks." *International Security* 27, 4: 57–85.

———. 2003b. "Hierarchy and Stability in Asian International Relations." In *International Relations Theory and the Asia-Pacific,* edited by G. John Ikenberry and Michael Mastanduno. New York: Columbia University Press.

Kassim, Azizah. 2001. "Integration of Foreign Workers and Illegal Employment in Malaysia." In *International Migration in Asia: Trends and Policies,* 113–35. Paris: Organisation for Economic Co-operation and Development.

Katada, Saori. 2004. "Japan's Counterweight Strategy: U.S.–Japan Cooperation and Competition in International Finance." In *Beyond Bilateralism: U.S.–Japan Relations in the New Asia-Pacific,* edited by Ellis S. Krauss and T. J. Pempel. Stanford: Stanford University Press.

Katzenstein, Peter J. 1977. *Between Power and Plenty.* Madison: University of Wisconsin Press.

———. 1996a. *Cultural Norms and National Security: Police and Military in Postwar Japan.* Ithaca: Cornell University Press.

———, ed. 1996b. *The Culture of National Security.* New York: Columbia University Press.

———. 1996c. "Regionalism in Comparative Perspective." *Cooperation and Conflict* 31, 2: 123–59.

———. 1997. "Introduction: Asian Regionalism in Comparative Perspective." In *Network Power: Japan and Asia,* edited by Peter Katzenstein and Takashi Shiraishi, 1–44. Ithaca: Cornell University Press.

———. 2002. "September 11 in Comparative Perspective: The Antiterrorism Campaigns of Germany and Japan." *Dialog-IO*, Spring, 45–56.

———. 2003. "A World of Regions: Asia and Europe." Ithaca, NY. Manuscript.

Katzenstein, Peter, and Nobuo Okawara. 2000. "Japan and Asian-Pacific Security: Regionalization of Entrenched Bilateralism and Incipient Multilateralism." *Pacific Review* 13, 3: 165–94.

Katzenstein, Peter J., and Takashi Shiraishi, eds. 1997. *Network Power: Japan and Asia.* Ithaca: Cornell University Press.

Katzenstein, Peter, and Yutaka Tsujinaka. 1991. *Defending the Japanese State: Structures, Norms and the Political Responses to Terrorism and Violent Social Protest in the 1970s and 1980s.* Ithaca: Cornell University East Asia Program.

———. 1995. " 'Bullying,' 'Buying,' and 'Binding': U.S.–Japan Transnational Relations and Domestic Structures." In *Bringing Transnational Relations Back In: Non-State Actors, Domestic Structures and International Institutions,* edited by Thomas Risse-Kapen, 79–111. Cambridge: Cambridge University Press.

Keohane, Robert O. 1984. *After Hegemony: Cooperation and Discord in the World Political Economy.* Princeton: Princeton University Press.

Kepel, Gilles. 2002. *Jihad: The Trail of Political Islam.* Translated by Anthony F. Roberts. Cambridge: Harvard University Press.

Khong, Yuen Foong. 1997a. "ASEAN and the Southeast Asian Security Complex," in *Regional Orders: Building Security in a New World,* edited by D. Lake and P. Morgan, 318–42. University Park: Pennsylvania State University Press.

———. 1997b. "Making Bricks without Straw in the Asia Pacific?" *Pacific Review* 10, 2: 289–300.

Kikuchi, Tsutomu. 2002. "East Asian Regionalism: A Look at the 'ASEAN plus Three' Framework." *Japan Review of International Affairs*, Spring, 1–23.

Kim, Sun Hyuk. 1999. "Civic Mobilization for Democratic Reform." In *Institutional Reform and Democratic Consolidation in Korea,* edited by Larry Diamond and Doh Chull Shin, 279–303. Stanford: Hoover Institution Press.

Kimura, Michio. 2000. "ASEAN Expectations toward Japan's Role in the Consensual Process of Regional Integration: The Case of the East Asian Economic Caucus." In *Facing Asia: Japan's Role in the Political and Economic Dynamism of Regional Cooperation,* edited by Verena Blechinger and Jochen Legewie. Munich: Verlag Judicium Gmb.

Kishimoto, Shuhei. 2001. "Ajia kinyu senryaku no tenkai" (Unfolding of the Financial Strategy toward Asia). In *Ajia seijikeizairon: Ajia no naka no Nihon wo mezashite* (Political Economy of Asia: Searching for Japan in Asia), edited by Akira Suehiro and Susumu Yamakage, 289–319. Tokyo: NTT Shuppan.

Kodama, Fumio, and Lewis H. Branscomb. 1995. *Emerging Patterns of Innovation: Sources of Japan's Technological Edge.* Cambridge: Harvard Business School Press.

Koh, Tommy T. B. 1996. Foreword to *Asian Dragons and Green Trade,* edited by Simon S. C. Tay and Daniel C. Esty, vii–x. Singapore: Times Academic Press.

Kojima, Kiyoshi. 1971. *Japan and a Pacific Free Trade Area.* London: MacMillan.

Komiya, Ryutaro, Masahiro Okuno, and Kotaro Suzumura, eds. 1988. *Industrial Policy of Japan.* Tokyo: Harcourt, Brace, Jovanovich.

Korhonen, Pekka. 1998. *Japan and Asia Pacific Integration: Pacific Romances, 1968–1996.* London: Routledge.

Krasner, Steven. 1983. "Structural Causes and Regime Consequences: Regimes as Intervening Variables." In *International Regimes,* edited by Steven Krasner, 1–21. Ithaca: Cornell University Press.

———. 1999. *Sovereignty: Organized Hypocrisy.* Princeton: Princeton University Press.

Krause, Lawrence, and Sueo Sekiguchi, eds. 1980. *Economic Integration in the Pacific Basin.* Washington, DC: Brookings Institution.

Krauss, Ellis S. 2000. "Japan, the U.S., and the Emergence of Multilateralism in Asia." *Pacific Review* 13, 3 (September): 473–94.

———. 2004. "The United States and Japan in APEC's EVSL Negotiations: Regional Multilateralism and Trade." In *Beyond Bilateralism: U.S.–Japan Relations in the New Asia-Pacific,* edited by Ellis S. Krauss and T. J. Pempel. Stanford: Stanford University Press.

Krauss, Ellis S., and T. J. Pempel, eds. 2004. *Beyond Bilateralism: U.S.–Japan Relations in the New Asia-Pacific.* Stanford: Stanford University Press.

Kurogane, Kenji, ed. 1993. *Cross-Functional Management: Principles and Practical Applications.* Tokyo: Asian Productivity Organization. [Originally published by the Japan Standards Association in 1988 under the title *Kinobetsu kanri katsuyo no jissai.*]

Kwan, C. H. 2001. "The Rise of China as an Economic Power: Implications for Asia and Japan." In *Japan and China: Cooperation, Competition and Conflict,* edited by Hanns Gunter Hilpert and Rene Haak, 12–31. New York: Palgrave.

Lake, David A., and Patrick M. Morgan. 1997. *Regional Orders: Building Security in a New World.* University Park: University of Pennsylvania Press.

Laqueur, Walter. 1999. *The New Terrorism.* New York: Oxford University Press.

Lavely, William. 2001. "First Impressions from the 2000 Census of China." *Population and Development Review* 26, 10: 755–69.

Lawrence, Robert. 1991. "Emerging Regional Arrangements: Building Blocks or Stumbling Blocks?" In *Finance and the International Economy,* edited by Richard O'Brien, 24–36. Oxford: Oxford University Press.

———. 1996. *Regionalism, Multilateralism, and Deeper Integration.* Washington, DC: Brookings Institution.

Lawrence, Susan. 2002. "China-ASEAN Trade: Enough for Everyone." *Far Eastern Economic Review,* June 13.

Lawson, Fred H. 1999. "Theories of Integration in a New Context: The Gulf Cooperation Council." In *Racing to Regionalize: Democracy, Capitalism, and Regional Political Economy,* edited by Kenneth P. Thomas and Mary Ann Tétreault, 7–32. Boulder, CO: Lynne Rienner.

Lee, Hiro, and David W. Roland-Holst, eds. 1998. *Economic Development and Cooperation in the Pacific Basin.* Cambridge: Cambridge University Press.

Lee, Seunghwan. 2001. "Public Awareness, NGOs, and Environmental Security in Northeast Asia." Prepared for the Project on Environmental Security in East Asia, United Nations University, Tokyo.

Lee, Shin-wha. 2002. "Building Environmental Regimes in Northeast Asia: Progress, Limitations, and Policy Options." In *International Environmental Cooperation: Politics and Diplomacy in Pacific Asia,* edited by Paul G. Harris, 203–20. Boulder: University Press of Colorado.

Leheny, David. 2001–2. "Tokyo Confronts Terror." *Policy Review* 110 (December/January): 37–47.

———. 2002. "Symbols, Strategies, and Choices for International Relations Scholarship after September 11." *Dialog-IO,* Spring, 57–50.

———. 2003. *The Rules of Play: National Identity and the Shaping of Japanese Leisure.* Ithaca: Cornell University Press.

Leifer, Michael. 1989. *ASEAN and the Security of South-East Asia.* London: Routledge.

——. 1996. *The ASEAN Regional Forum: Extending ASEAN's Model of Regional Security.* Oxford: Oxford University Press for the International Institute for Strategic Studies.

Li, Lee. 2001. "Networks, Transactions, and Resources: Hong Kong Trading Companies' Strategic Position in the China Market." *Asia Pacific Journal of Management* 18, 3: 279–93.

Liddle, R. William. 1996. "The Islamic Turn in Indonesia: A Political Explanation." *Journal of Asian Studies* 55, 3 (August): 613–34.

Lincoln, James. 1984. *Japanese Industrial Policies: What Are They, Do They Matter, and Are They Different from Those in the United States?* Washington, DC: Japan Economic Institute of America.

Linden, Greg. 2000. "Japan and the United States in the Malaysia Electronics Sector." In *International Production Networks in Asia: Rivalry or Riches?* edited by Michael Borrus, Dieter Ernst, and Stephan Haggard, 198–225. London: Routledge.

Lipson, Charles. 1991. "Why Are Some International Agreements Informal." *International Organization* 45, 4 (Autumn): 495–538.

Liu, Hong. 2001. "Social Capital and Business Networking: A Case Study of Modern Chinese Transnationalism." *Southeast Asian Studies* 39, 3: 358–83.

Lo, Fu-chen, and Peter J. Marcotullio. 2001. "Globalization and Urban Transformations in the Asia Pacific." In *Globalization and the Sustainability of Cities in the Asia Pacific Region,* edited by Lo and Marcotullio. Tokyo: United Nations University Press.

Lutz, Ellen L., and Kathryn Sikkink. 2000. "International Human Rights Law and Practice in Latin America." *International Organization* 54, 3 (Summer): 633–60.

MacFarquhar, Neil. 2001. "Islamic Jihad, Forged in Egypt, Is Seen as bin Laden's Backbone." *New York Times,* October 4. Accessed through Lexis-Nexis.

MacIntyre, Andrew. 1994. "Power, Prosperity, and Patrimonialism: Business and Government in Indonesia." In *Business and Government in Industrialising Asia,* edited by Andrew MacIntyre. Ithaca: Cornell University Press.

——. 1997. "Southeast Asia and the Political Economy of APEC." In *The Political Economy of Southeast Asia,* edited by Gary Rodan, Richard Robison, and Kevin Hewison. Melbourne: Oxford University Press.

——. 2003. *The Power of Institutions: Political Architecture and Governance.* Ithaca: Cornell University Press.

MacIntyre, Andrew, and Budy P. Resosudarmo. 2003. "Survey of Recent Developments." *Bulletin of Indonesian Economic Studies* 39, 2: 133–56.

Mack, Andrew, and Pauline Kerr. 1995. "The Evolving Security Discourse in the Asia-Pacific." *Washington Quarterly* 18, 1: 123–40.

Maddison, Angus. 2003. *The World Economy: Historical Statistics.* Paris: Development Centre, Organisation for Economic Co-operation and Development.

Mahathir bin Mohamad, D. S. 2002. "Malaysia and Asia: Seeking a Balance between Peace and Prosperity." Speech delivered to the 30th Williamsburg Conference, Kuala Lumpur. April 11. Available at http://www.smpke.jpm.my.

Mahbubani, Kishore. 1995. "The Pacific Way." *Foreign Affairs* 74, 1 (January/February): 100–111.

——. 1998. "The Pacific Impulse." In Mahbubani, *Can Asians Think?* Singapore: Times Editions.

Malley, Michael. 2002. "Indonesia in 2001: Restoring Stability in Jakarta." *Asian Survey* 42, 1.

Manning, Robert A. 1996. "Security in East Asia." In *Asian Security Handbook: An Assessment of Political-Security Issues in the Asia-Pacific Region,* edited by William M. Carpenter and D. G. Wiencek, 21–31. Armonk, NY: M. E. Sharpe.

Mansfield, Edward D., and Helen V. Milner, eds. 1997. *The Political Economy of Regionalism*. New York: Columbia University Press.

Marugami, Takashi, Takeshi Toyoda, Takeshi Kasuga, and Mayumi Suzuki. 2003. "Survey Report on Overseas Business Operations by Japanese Manufacturing Companies." *JBIC Review* 7 (August): 1–78.

Mason, Mark. 1999. "The Origins and Evolution of Japanese Direct Investment in East Asia." In *Japanese Multinationals in Asia: Regional Operations in Comparative Perspective*, edited by Dennis J. Encarnation, 17–45. Oxford: Oxford University Press.

Mathews, John A., and Dong-Sung Cho. 2000. *Tiger Technology: The Creation of a Semiconductor Industry in East Asia*. Cambridge: Cambridge University Press.

Mattli, Walter. 1999. *The Logic of Regional Integration: Europe and Beyond*. Cambridge: Cambridge University Press.

Mauzy, Diane K., and R. S. Milne. 1983–84. "The Mahathir Administration in Malaysia: Discipline through Islam." *Pacific Affairs* 56, 4 (Winter): 617–48.

McCoy, Alfred W. 1991. *The Politics of Heroin: CIA Complicity in the Global Drug Trade*. New York: Harper and Row.

McKendrick, David, Richard Doner, and Stephan Haggard. 2000. *From Silicon Valley to Singapore: Location and Competitive Advantage in the Hard Disk Drive Industry*. Stanford: Stanford University Press.

McKenna, Thomas M. 1998. *Muslim Rulers and Rebels*. Berkeley: University of California Press.

McKeown, Adam. 1999. "Conceptualizing Chinese Diasporas, 1842 to 1949." *Journal of Asian Studies* 58, 2: 306–37.

McKinnon, Ronald, and Gunther Schnabl. 2003. "Synchronized Business Cycles in East Asia and Fluctuations in the Yen/Dollar Exchange Rate." Available at http://www.stanford.edu/~mckinnon/papers/BusinessCycles_EastAsia.pdf.

McNeill, William H. 1984. *The Pursuit of Power*. Reprint. Chicago: University of Chicago Press.

McNicoll, Geoffrey. 1999. "Population Weights in the International Order." *Population and Development Review* 25, 10: 411–42.

Mearsheimer, John J. 2001a. "The Future of the American Pacifier." *Foreign Affairs* (September/October): 46–61.

———. 2001b. *The Tragedy of Great Power Politics*. New York: Norton.

Mendl, Wolf. 1995. *Japan's Asia Policy: Regional Security and Global Interest*. London: Routledge.

Milner, Anthony. 2000. "Our Dignity in Asia." *Australian*, August 1.

Ministry of Economy, Trade, and Industry (Japan) (METI). 1999, 2000, 2001, 2002, 2003. *Waga kuni kigyo no kaigai jigyo katsudo* (Survey of Overseas Business Activities). Vols. 27–30. Tokyo.

Ministry of the Environment (Japan). 2001. *Kankyo hakusho 2001* (White Paper on the Environment, 2001). Tokyo.

Ministry of Finance (Japan). 1977, 1989, 1991. *Kokusai kinyu nenpo* (Annual Report of International Finance). Tokyo: Institute for Monetary and Fiscal Policy.

———. 2004. *Foreign Direct Investment Statistics*. http://www.mof.go.jp/english/e1c008.htm.

Ministry of Foreign Affairs (Japan). 1957. *Waga gaiko no kinkyo Showa 32nen ban* (Blue Book on Foreign Policy). Tokyo.

———. 2003a. "AFTA ni tsuite" (On ASEAN Free Trade Area). Mimeo. Bureau of Asia and the Pacific, Division of Regional Policy.

——. 2003b. "Chugoku–ASEAN jiyu boueki chiiki ni tsuite" (On ASEAN–China Free Trade Area). Mimeo. Bureau of Asia and the Pacific, Division of Regional Policy.

Ministry of International Trade and Industy (MITI). 1999. *Tsusho hakusho heisei 11 nenban* (White Paper on Trade, 1999). Tokyo.

——. 2000. *Tsusho hakusho heisei 12 nenban* (White Paper on Trade, 2000). Tokyo.

Mittelman, James H. 1999. "Resisting Globalization: Environmental Politics in Eastern Asia." In *Globalization and the Asia-Pacific: Contested Territories,* edited by Kris Olds, Peter Dicken, Philip F. Kelly, Lily Kong, and Henry Wai-chung Yeung, 72–87. London: Routledge.

Mochizuki, Mike. 1995. "Japan as an Asia-Pacific Power." In *East Asia in Transition: Toward a New Regional Order,* edited by Robert Ross. Armonk, NY: M. E. Sharpe.

Montgomery, John D. 2000. "The Pacific Basin as an Environmental Region." Seikyo series. Pacific Research Center. Available at http://www.ap.harvard.edu/pbrc/new/seikyo/env.html.

Moon, Chung-in. 2003. "Regionalism and Nationalism in Northeast Asia." Paper delivered at the annual convention of the American Political Science Association, Philadelphia. August 27–31.

Mori, Minako. 2002. "The New Strategies of Vehicle Assemblers in Thailand and the Response of Parts Manufacturers." *Pacific Business and Industries RIM* 2, 4: 27–40.

Mubarak, Hisham. 1997. "What Does the Gama'a Islamiyya Want?" In *Political Islam: Essays from the Middle East Report,* edited by Joel Beinin and Joel Stork, 314–34. Berkeley: University of California Press.

Mukoyama, Hidehiko. 1994. "Active Investment by Japanese Parts and Materials-Process Industries in Asia: Exploring the Backgrounds of Their Moves in Thailand and China." *Pacific Business and Industries RIM* 2, 44: 31–49.

Munakata, Naoko. 2001. "Evolution of Japan's Policy toward Economic Integration." Washington, DC: Center for Northeast Asian Policy Studies, Brookings Institution.

Nagata, Judith. 1980. "Religious Ideology and Social Change: The Islamic Resurgence in Malaysia." *Pacific Affairs* 53, 3: 405–39.

Nair, Shanti. 1997. *Islam in Malaysian Foreign Policy.* London: Routledge.

Nakamura, Takafusa. 1981. *The Postwar Japanese Economy: Its Development and Structure.* Tokyo: University of Tokyo Press. [Originally published by the University of Tokyo Press in 1980 under the title *Nihon keizai: Sono seicho to kozo.*]

Nam, Sangmin. 2002. "Ecological Interdependence and Environmental Governance in Northeast Asia: Politics versus Cooperation." In *International Environmental Cooperation: Politics and Diplomacy in Pacific Asia,* edited by Paul G. Harris, 167–202. Boulder: University Press of Colorado.

National Bureau of Statistics, People's Republic of China. 2003. *Zhongguo Tongji Nianjian* (China Statistical Yearbook). Beijing: Tongji Chubanshe.

National Institute for Research Advancement (NIRA). 2000. *Directory of Think Tanks in Japan.* Tokyo.

——. 2003. Shinkutanku nenpo 2004 (Annual Review of Japanese Think Tanks). Tokyo: NIRA, 2003.

National Police Agency (NPA). 1999. *Keisatsu hakusho heisei 11 nenban* (White Paper of Police, 1999). Tokyo.

——. 2000. *Keisatsu hakusho heisei 12 nenban* (White Paper of Police, 2000). Tokyo.

——. 2001. *Keisatsu hakusho heisei 13 nenban* (White Paper of Police, 2001). Tokyo.

Nau, Henry R. 2002. *At Home Abroad: Identity and Power in American Foreign Policy.* Ithaca: Cornell University Press.

Naughton, Barry. 1995. *Growing Out of the Plan: Chinese Economic Reform, 1978–1993*. New York: Cambridge University Press.

——. 1996. "China's Emergence and Future as a Trading Nation." *Brookings Papers on Economic Activity* 2: 273–344.

——. 1997. *The China Circle: Economics and Technology in the PRC, Taiwan, and Hong Kong*. Washington, DC: Brookings Institution.

——. 1999. "China: Domestic Restructuring and a New Role in Asia." In *Economies*, edited by T. J. Pempel, 203–23. New York: Free Press.

——. 2001. "Changing Horses in Midstream? The Challenge of Explaining Changing Political Economy Regimes in China." In *China Rising: Implications of Economic and Military Growth in the PRC*, edited by Jaushieh Joseph Wu, 37–65. Taipei: Institute of International Relations, National Chengchi University.

Nautilus Institute and Center for Global Communications. 2000. *Energy, Environment and Security in Northeast Asia: Defining a U.S.–Japan Partnership for Regional Comprehensive Security*. Berkeley.

Nesadurai, Helen E. S. 1996. "APEC: A Tool for U.S. Regional Domination?" *Pacific Review* 9, 1: 31–57.

Ng, Francis, and Alexander Yeats. 2003. "Major Trade Trends in East Asia: What Are Their Implications for Regional Cooperation and Growth?" Washington, DC: World Bank Policy Research Working Paper #3084, June.

Ng-Quinn, Michael. 1986. "The Internationalization of the Region: The Case of Northeast Asian International Relations." *Review of International Studies* 12: 107–25.

Nishihara, Masashi. 1975. *The Japanese and Sukarno's Indonesia: Tokyo–Jakarta Relations, 1951–1966*. Honolulu: University Press of Hawai'i.

Noble, Gregory, and John Ravenhill, eds. 2000. The Asian Financial Crisis and the Architecture of Global Finance. Cambridge: Cambridge University Press.

Nye, Joseph S. 1995. "The Case for Deep Engagement." *Foreign Affairs* 74, 4: 90–102.

——. 2001. "The 'Nye Report': Six Years Later." *International Relations of the Asia-Pacific* 1, 1: 95–103.

Ogasawara, Takayuki. 1998. "Ajia Taiheiyo no riijonarizumu" (Regionalism in the Asia-Pacific). In *Higashi Ajia kokusaikankei no dainamizumu* (Dynamism of International Relations in East Asia), edited by M. Saito, 161–83. Tokyo: Toyo Keizai Shinposha.

Ohba, Mie. 2001. "Chiikishugi to Nihon no sentaku (Regionalism and Japan's Options)." In *Ajia seijikeizairon: Ajia no naka no Nihon wo mezashite* (Political Economy of Asia: Searching for Japan in Asia), edited by Akira Suehiro and Susumu Yamakage, 259–88. Tokyo: NTT Shuppan.

——. 2002. " 'Ajia-Taiheiyo' chiiki heno dotei: Nichigou no seisaku tantosha to chishikijin no 'jiko housetsuteki chiiki' no mosaku" (Formation of the "Asia-Pacific" Region: Japanese and Australian Policymakers and Intellectuals' Search for "Self-Enclosing Region"). Ph.D. dissertation, Graduate School of International and Social Studies, University of Tokyo.

Ohmae, Kenichi. 1995. *The End of the Nation State: The Rise of Regional Economies*. New York: Free Press.

Okawara, Nobuo, and Peter Katzenstein. 2001. "Japan and Asian-Pacific Security: Regionalization, Entrenched Bilateralism, and Incipient Multilateralism." *Pacific Review* 14, 2.

Oneal, John R., and Mark A. Elrod. 1989. "NATO Burden Sharing and the Forces of Change." *International Studies Quarterly* 33, 4 (December): 435–56.

Organisation for Economic Co-operation and Development (OECD). 2001. *Trends in International Migration*. Paris.

Orr, Robert, and Bruce Koppel. 1993. "A Donor of Consequence: Japan as a Foreign Aid Power." In *Japan's Foreign Aid: Power and Policy in a New Era,* edited by B. Koppel and R. Orr, 1–18. Boulder, CO: Westview.

Orru, Marco, Nicole Woolsey Biggart, and Garry Hamilton, eds. 1997. *The Economic Organization of East Asian Capitalism.* Thousand Oaks, CA: Sage.

Osada, Hiroshi. 2001. "Indonesia: Aratana keizai unei no mosaku" (Indonesia: A Search for New Economic Management). In *Ajia keizairon* (Asian Economies), edited by Yonosuke Hara, 324–53. Tokyo: NTT Publishers.

Overholt, William H. 1999. "China in the Balance." Hong Kong: Nomura Securities Hong Kong Strategy Paper, May 12.

Pacific Asia Travel Association (PATA). 1999. *Annual Statistical Report, 1998.* Honolulu: Pacific Asia Travel Association.

Pacific Economic Cooperation Council (PECC). 2002. "Finance Forum Recommendations to the APEC Finance Ministers on Their Agenda for 2002–3." Memorandum. August 26.

Paddock, Richard C. 2001. "Indonesian Extremist Backs Terror." *Los Angeles Times,* September 23. Accessed through Lexis-Nexis.

Paddock, Richard C., and Bob Drogin. 2002. "A Terror Network Unraveled in Singapore." *Los Angeles Times,* January 20. Accessed through Lexis-Nexis.

Page, Sheila. 1995. "The Relationship between Regionalism and the Multilateral Trading System." UNCTAD/ITD/14. United Nations Conference on Trade and Development, Geneva. September 28.

Pangestu, Mari, and Kurnya Roesad. 1996. "Experiences from Indonesia and Other ASEAN Countries." In *Asian Dragons and Green Trade,* edited by Simon S. C. Tay and Daniel C. Esty, 99–106. Singapore: Times Academic Press.

Parker, Steve, and Sung Ho Lee. 2002. "Did East Asian Developing Economies Lose Export Competitiveness in the Pre-Crisis 1990s? Assessing East-Asian Export Performance from 1980 to 1996." ADBI Research Paper 34. Asian Development Bank Institute, Tokyo.

Parry, Richard Lloyd. 2000. "Abu Sayyaf at Heart of Islamic War after $17M Hostage Deal Puts Rebel Centre Stage." *Independent* (UK), August 29. Accessed through Lexis-Nexis.

——. 2001. "Philippines Army Took 'Terror Bribe.' " *Independent* (UK), August 25. Accessed through Lexis-Nexis.

Patrick, Hugh. 1997. "From PAFTAD to APEC: Economists' Networks and Public Policymaking." APEC Study Center Discussion Paper No. 2. Columbia University, New York.

Pavida, Pananond. 2001. "The Making of Thai Multinationals: A Comparative Study of the Growth and Internationalization Process of Thailand's Charoen Pokphand and Siam Cement Groups." *Journal of Asian Business* 17, 3: 41–70.

Peletz, Michael G. 1997. "'Ordinary Muslims' and Muslim Resurgents in Contemporary Malaysia: Notes on an Ambivalent Relationship." In *Islam in an Era of Nation-States,* edited by Robert W. Hefner and Patricia Horvatich, 231–73. Honolulu: University of Hawai'i Press.

Pempel, T. J. 1993. "From Exporter to Investor: Japanese Foreign Economic Policy." In *Japan's Foreign Policy after the Cold War: Coping with Change,* edited by Gerald Curtis, 105–36. Armonk, NY: M. E. Sharpe.

——. 1997. "Trans-Pacific Torii: Japan and the Emerging Asian Regionalism." In *Network Power: Japan and Asia,* edited by Peter Katzenstein and Takashi Shiraishi, 47–82. Ithaca: Cornell University Press.

——. 1998. *Regime Shift: Comparative Dynamics of the Japanese Political Economy.* Ithaca: Cornell University Press.

———. 1999a. "The Developmental Regime in a Changing World Economy." In *The Developmental State,* edited by Meredith Woo-Cumings. Ithaca: Cornell University Press.

———, ed. 1999b. *The Politics of the Asian Economic Crisis.* Ithaca: Cornell University Press.

Peng, Mike, Kevin Au, and Denis Wang. 2001. "Interlocking Directorates as Corporate Governance in Third World Multinationals: Theory and Evidence from Thailand." *Asia Pacific Journal of Management* 18, 2: 161–81.

Perlez, Jane. 2003. "Militant Islamic Congress Is Sparsely Attended in Indonesia." *New York Times,* August 10, A3.

Perrez, Franz Xaver. 1986. "The Relationship between 'Permanent Sovereignty' and the Obligation Not to Cause Transboundary Environmental Damage." *Environmental Law* 26, 4: 1187–1212.

Petri, Peter A. 1993. "The East Asian Trading Bloc: An Analytical History." In *Regionalism and Rivalry: Japan and the United States in Pacific Asia,* edited by Jeffrey A. Frankel and Miles Kahler, 21–48. Chicago: University of Chicago Press.

Philippine Center for Investigative Journalism. 2002. "The Estrada Plunder Case, Year 1," January 16–18, 2002. Available at http://www.pcij.org.

Post, Jerrold M. 1998. "Terrorist Psycho-Logic: Terrorist Behavior as a Product of Psychological Forces." In *Origins of Terrorism,* edited by Walter Reich, 25–40. Baltimore: Johns Hopkins University Press.

Pyle, Kenneth. 1998. "Restructuring Foreign and Defense Policy: Japan." In *Asia-Pacific in the New World Order,* edited by A. McGrew and C. Brook, 121–36. London: Routledge.

Quah, Euston. 2002. "Transboundary Pollution in Southeast Asia: The Indonesian Fires." *World Development* 30, 3: 429–41.

Rashid, Ahmed. 2000. *Taliban: Militant Islam, Oil, and Fundamentalism in Central Asia.* New Haven: Yale University Press.

Ravenhill, John. 1998. "The Growth of Intergovernmental Collaboration in the Asia-Pacific Region." In *Asia-Pacific in the New World Order,* edited by Anthony McGrew and Christopher Brook, 248–70. London: Routledge.

———. 2000. "APEC Adrift: Implications for Economic Regionalism in Asia and the Pacific." *Pacific Review* 13, 2: 319–33.

———. 2001. *APEC and the Construction of Pacific Rim Regionalism.* Cambridge: Cambridge University Press.

———. 2002. "A Three Bloc World? The New East Asian Regionalism." *International Relations of the Asia-Pacific* 2, 2: 167–95.

———. 2003. "The New Bilateralism in the Asia-Pacific." *Third World Quarterly* 24, 2: 299–317.

Richardson, Michael. 2000. "Asians Cautious on Forming New Regional Partnerships for ASEAN." *International Herald Tribune,* Systems: Spatial Structure and Corporate Control since the Mid-1980s." Paper presented at the Third Euro-Asia Conference Port City Governance, Regional Networks November 27, 11.

Rimmer, Peter J. 1997. "The Asia-Pacific Rim's Transport and Telecommunications and Deregulation Policies in East Asia." Tokyo.

Roberts, John. 2002. "U.S. Pressure on Jakarta May Backfire." *Bangkok Post,* March 10. Accessed through Lexis-Nexis.

Rodan, Garry. 1993. "Reconstructing Divisions of Labour: Singapore's New Regional Emphasis." In *Pacific Economic Relations in the 1990s: Cooperation or Conflict?* edited by Richard Higgott, Richard Leaver, and John Ravenhill, 223–49. Boulder, CO: Lynne Reinner.

Rosecrance, Richard. 1986. *The Rise of the Trading State.* New York: Basic Books.

——. 1999. *The Rise of the Virtual State*. New York: Basic Books.

——. 2001. "Has Realism Become Cost-Benefit Analysis? A Review Essay." *International Security* 26, 2 (Fall): 132–54.

Royal Commission on the Economic Union and Development Prospects for Canada. 1985. Report. Ottawa: Canadian Government Publishing Centre.

Rozman, Gilbert. 1998. "Flawed Regionalism: Reconceptualizing Northeast Asia in the 1990s." *Pacific Review* 11, 1: 1–27.

——. 2004. *Northeast Asia's Stunted Regionalism: Bilateral Distrust in the Shadow of Globalization*. Cambridge: Cambridge University Press.

Ruggie, John. 1975. "International Responses to Technology." *International Organization* 29 (Summer).

——. 1998. "What Makes the World Hang Together? Neo-Utilitarianism and the Social Constructivist Challenge." In *Exploration and Contestation in the Study of World Politics*, edited by Peter J. Katzenstein, Robert O. Keohane, and Stephen D. Krasner, 215–46. Cambridge, MA: MIT Press.

Saxenian, Anna L. 1999. "The Silicon Valley–Hsinchu Connection: Technical Communities and Industrial Upgrading." Manuscript. Stanford Institute for Economic Policy Research, Stanford University.

Sayigh, Yezid. 1991. "The Gulf Crisis: Why the Arab Regional Order Failed." *International Affairs* 67, 3 (July): 487–507.

Schambaugh, David. 2002. *Modernizing China's Military: Progress, Problems, and Prospects*. Berkeley: University of California Press.

Schloss, Glenn. 2001. "Seeds of Terror in Asia." *South China Morning Post*, September 13. Accessed through Lexis-Nexis.

Schmidt, Vivian. 2003. "The European Union: Democracy Legitimacy in a Regional State." Manuscript. Boston University.

Schoppa, Leonard. 2001. "Japan, the Reluctant Reformer." *Foreign Affairs* September–October.

Schreurs, Miranda A. 2000. "Environmental Security and Co-operation in Asia." In *Comprehensive Security in Asia: Views from Asia and the West in a Changing Security Environment*, edited by K. W. Radtke and R. Feddema, 134–58. Leiden: Brill.

Schwarz, Adam. 1994. *A Nation in Waiting: Indonesia in the 1990s*. Sydney: Allen and Unwin.

Sciolino, Elaine. 2002. "Taking a Rare Peek Inside the Royal House of Saud." *New York Times,* January 28, A4.

Seki, Mitsuhiro. 1994. *Beyond the Full-Set Industrial Structure: Japanese Industry in the New Age of East Asia*. Tokyo: LTCB International Library Foundation.

Shaller, Michael. 1985. *The American Occupation of Japan: The Origins of the Cold War*. New York: Oxford University Press.

Shamsul, A. B. 1997. "Identity Construction, Nation Formation, and Islamic Revivalism in Malaysia." In *Islam in an Era of Nation-States*, edited by Robert W. Hefner and Patricia Horvatich, 207–27. Honolulu: University of Hawai'i Press.

Shee Poon-Kim. 1977. "A Decade of ASEAN, 1967–1977." *Asian Survey* 17, 8 (August): 753–70.

Shiba K. K., ed. 1991. *Zenkoku kakushu dantai menkan* (Handbook of Industrial Association in Japan). Tokyo: Yokoyama Printers K.K. .

Shigemasa, Koichi. 1998. "Takokukan anzenhosho mekanizumu no naka no daini torakku gaiko" (Second Track Diplomacy in a Multilateral Security Mechanism). *International Relations* (Japan Association of International Relations) 119: 70–94.

Shinn, James, ed. 1996. *Fires across the Water: Transnational Problems in Asia.* New York: Council on Foreign Relations.

——. 2000. "Nitwits in Pinstripes vs. Barbarians at the Gate: Capital Market Integration and Corporate Governance in Japan, Germany, and South Korea." Manuscript. Princeton, N.J.

Shiraishi, Takashi. 1997. "Japan and Southeast Asia." In *Network Power: Japan and Asia,* edited by Peter Katzenstein and Takashi Shiraishi, 169–94. Ithaca: Cornell University Press.

——. 1999. "Asia: Back to What Basics?" *Nation,* July 30.

Sim, Susan. 2001. "Jakarta Now under Pressure to Act." *Straits Times,* September 17. Accessed through Lexis-Nexis.

Simmons, Beth A. 2001. "The International Politics of Harmonization: The Case of Capital Market Regulation." *International Organization* 55, 3 (Summer): 589–620.

Simon, Sheldon W. 1998. "Security Prospects in Southeast Asia: Collaborative Efforts and the ASEAN Regional Forum." *Pacific Review* 11, 2: 195–212.

——. 2001a. "Asian Armed Forces: Internal and External Tasks and Capabilities." In *The Many Faces of Asian Security,* edited by Sheldon W. Simon, 49–87. Latham, MD: Roman and Littlefield.

——. 2001b. "Southeast Asia." In *Strategic Asia, 2001–2: Power and Purpose,* edited by Richard J. Ellings and Aaron Friedberg, 269–98. Seattle: National Bureau of Asian Research.

Sioris, George. 2000. "ASEAN plus 3 Gives Asia Hope for the Future." *Japan Times,* October 9.

Smarzynska, Beata, and Shang-Jin Wei. 2000. "Corruption and Composition of Foreign Direct Investment: Firm-Level Evidence." World Bank Working Paper 2360.June.

Soesastro, Hadi, ed. 1995. "ASEAN in a Changed Regional and International Political Economy." Centre for Strategic and International Studies, Jakarta.

——. 2001. "Asia at the Nexus: APEC and ASEM." *Panorama* 4.

Soeya, Yoshihide. 1997. "Beikoku no Ajia Taiheiyo seisaku ni okeru ASEAN" (ASEAN in American Asia-Pacific Policy). *International Relations* 116: 114–29.

——. 1998. "Japan: Normative Constraints versus Structural Imperatives." In *Asian Security Practice: Material and Ideational Influences,* edited by Muthiah Alagappa, 198–233. Stanford: Stanford University Press.

Solingen, Etel. 1998. *Regional Orders at Century's Dawn: Global and Domestic Influences on Grand Strategy.* Princeton: Princeton University Press.

——. 1999. "ASEAN, *Quo Vadis?* Domestic Coalitions and Regional Cooperation." *Contemporary Southeast Asia* 21, 1 (April): 30–53.

——. 2000. "The Multilateral Arab–Israeli Negotiations: Genesis, Institutionalization, Pause, Future." *Journal of Peace Research* 37, 2 (March).

——. 2001a. "Mapping Internationalization: Domestic and Regional Impacts." *International Studies Quarterly* 45, 4.

——. 2001b. "Middle East Denuclearization? Lessons from Latin America's Southern Cone." *Review of International Studies* 27, 3: 375–94.

——. 2002. "Regional Conflict and Cooperation: The Case of Southeast Asia." Teaching with Columbia International Affairs Online (CIAO) module at http://www.ciaonet. org/teach. New York: Columbia University Press.

——. 2003. "The Triple Logic of the European-Mediterranean Partnership: Hindsight and Foresight." *International Politics* 40, 2 (June): 179–94.

——. 2004a. "Regional Institutions: Origins, Purpose, Effects." Department of Political Science, University of California, Irvine.

——. 2004b. "Southeast Asia in a New Era: Domestic Coalitions from Crisis to Recovery." *Asian Survey* 44, 2: 189–212.

Springer, Allen L. 2002. "Indonesian Forest Fires: Internationalizing a National Environmental Problem." In *International Environmental Cooperation: Politics and Diplomacy in Pacific Asia,* edited by Paul G. Harris, 291–315. Boulder: University Press of Colorado.

Stares, Paul B. 1996. *Global Habit: The Drug Problem in a Borderless World.* Washington, DC: Brookings Institution.

Stein, Eric. 2001. "International Integration and Democracy: No Love at First Sight." *American Journal of International Law* 95: 489–534.

Steinberg, Richard H. 1997. "Trade-Environment Negotiations in the EU, NAFTA, and WTO: Regional Trajectories of Rule Development." *American Journal of International Law* 91: 231.

Sterling, Claire. 1981. *The Terror Network.* New York: Holt, Rinehart.

Stern, Jessica. 1999. *The Ultimate Terrorists.* Cambridge: Harvard University Press.

——. 2000. "Pakistan's Jihad Culture." *Foreign Affairs,* November/December. Available at http://ksghome.harvard.edu/~.jstern.CSIA.KSG/pakistan.htm.

Stiglitz, Joseph E. 1996. "Some Lessons from the East Asian Miracle." *The World Bank Research Observer* 11, 2 (August): 151–77.

Stubbs, Richard. 1995. "Asia-Pacific Regionalization and the Global Economy: A Third Form of Capitalism?" *Asian Survey* 35, 9: 785–97.

——. 1999a. "States, Sovereignty and the Response of Southeast Asia's 'Miracle' Economies to Globalization." In *States and Sovereignty in the Global Economy,* edited by D. A. Smith, D. J. Solinger, and S. C. Topik. London: Routledge.

——. 1999b. "War and Economic Development: Export-Oriented Industrialization in East and Southeast Asia." *Comparative Politics* 31, 3: 337–55.

——. 2002. "ASEAN plus Three: Emerging East Asian Regionalism?" *Asian Survey* 42, 3: 440–55.

Sturgeon, Timothy. 1999. "Turnkey Production Networks: Industrial Organization, Economic Development, and the Globalization of Electronics Contract Manufacturing." Ph.D. dissertation, Department of Geography, University of California at Berkeley.

Suehiro, Akira. 2000. "Zaisei kinyu seisaku: Chuo ginko no dokuritsusei to soshiki no nouryoku" (Fiscal and Financial Policy: Autonomy and Organizational Capacity of the Central Bank). In *Tai no keizai seisaku* (Economic Policy of Thailand), edited by Akira Suehiro and Shigeki Higashi, 59–114. Chiba: Institute of Developing Economies.

Suehiro, Akira, and Susumu Yamakage, eds. 2001. *Ajia seiji keizairon: Ajia no naka no Nihon wo mezashite* (Political Economy of Asia: Searching for Japan in Asia). Tokyo: NTT Shuppan.

Sumiya, Mikio, ed. 2000. *A History of Japanese Trade and Industry Policy.* Oxford: Oxford University Press.

Tachiki, Dennis S. 1985. *Total Quality Control: The Japanese Approach to Continuous Improvement.* Tokyo: Sakura Institute of Research.

——. 1993. "Striking up Strategic Alliances: The Foreign Direct Investments of the NIEs and ASEAN Transnational Corporations." *Pacific Business and Industries RIM* 21 (September): 22–36.

——. 1994. "Relationship between Direct Foreign Investment and High Level Manpower Policies." In *Human Resource Development Outlook, 1994–1995: Investment and Labour Flows in Selected Pacific Economies,* edited and compiled by Linda Low, 52–73. Singapore: Times Academic Press.

——. 1998. "Modes of Corporate Internationalization: Japanese FDI Strategies in the Asia-Pacific Region." In *Japanese Management in the Low Growth Era: Between External Shocks and Internal Evolution,* edited by Daniel Dirks, Jean-Francois Huchet, and Thierry Ribault, 73–89. Berlin: Springer Verlag.

——. 1999. "The Business Strategies of Japanese Production Networks in Asia." In *Japanese Multinationals in Asia: Regional Operations in Comparative Perspective,* edited by Dennis J. Encarnation, 183–212. Oxford: Oxford University Press.

——. 2000. "Options for Strategic Change: The Importance of Internal, Debt, and Equity Financing for Multinational Corporations." In *Corporate Strategies for Southeast Asia after the Crisis,* edited by Jochen Legewie and Hendrik Meyer-Ohle, 187–98. London: Palgrave.

——. 2004. "The Diffusion and Impacts of the Internet and E-Commerce in Japan." Global E-Commerce Survey Paper. Irvine: Center for Research on Information Technology and Organization, University of California at Irvine.

Tachiki, Dennis S., and Akira Aoki. 1992. "The Competitive Status of Japanese Subsidiaries: Building a Presence in Regional Markets." *Pacific Business and Industries RIM* 18 (December): 28–39.

Takahashi, Wakana. 2002. "Problems of Environmental Cooperation in Northeast Asia: The Case of Acid Rain." In *International Environmental Cooperation: Politics and Diplomacy in Pacific Asia,* edited by Paul G. Harris, 221–48. Boulder: University Press of Colorado.

Takenaka, Heizo. 1991. *Contemporary Japanese Economy and Economic Policy.* Ann Arbor: University of Michigan Press.

Tan, Andrew. 2000. *Armed Rebellion in the ASEAN States: Persistence and Implications.* Canberra Papers on Strategy and Defence. Canberra: Australian National University.

Tay, Simon S. C. 1998. "ASEAN: The Haze, Economics and the Environment." *Bridges: Between Trade and Sustainable Development* 2, 2 (March): 1, 14. [Published by the International Centre for Trade and Sustainable Development.]

——. 2001. "ASEAN plus 3: Challenges and Cautions about a New Regionalism." Paper prepared for the Asia Pacific Roundtable, Kuala Lumpur, organized by the ASEAN-ISIS.

——. 2002. "ASEAN plus 3: Challenges and Cautions about a New Regionalism." In *Asia Pacific Security: Challenges and Opportunities in the Twenty-first Century,* edited by Mohamed Jawhar Hassan, Stephen Leong, and Vincent Lim, 99–117. Kuala Lumpur: ISIS Malaysia.

Tay, Simon S. C., Zulkifli Baharudin, and Cherian George. 2000. "Role of Civil Service in Civil Society." *Straits Times,* February 17.

Terada, Takashi. 2003. "Constructing an 'East Asian' Concept and Growing Regional Identity: From EAEC to ASEAN + 3." *Pacific Review* 16, 2: 251–77.

Terry, Edith. 2000. "The World Bank and Japan: How Godzilla of the Ginza and King Kong of H Street Got Hitched." JPRI Working Paper 70. August.

——. 2002. *How Asia Got Rich: Japan, China and the Asian Miracle.* Armonk, NY: M. E. Sharpe.

Thambipillai, Pushpa. 1994. "Continuity and Change in ASEAN: The Politics of Regional Cooperation in South East Asia." In *The Political Economy of Regional Cooperation,* edited by Andrew Axline, 105–35. London: Pinter Publishers.

——. 1998. "The ASEAN Growth Areas: Sustaining the Dynamism." *Pacific Affairs* 11, 2: 249–66.

Thant, Myo, Min Tang, and Hiroshi Kakaku. 1998. *Growth Triangles in Asia: A New Approach to Regional Economic Cooperation.* 2nd ed. Hong Kong: Oxford University Press.

Thayer, Carl. 2000. "ASEAN Ten plus Three: An Evolving East Asian Community?" *Pacific Forum CSIS Comparative Connections*, 4th quarter. [An e-journal on East Asian bilateral relations.]

Thompson, Mark. 2001. "Whatever Happened to Asian Values?" Journal of Democracy 12, 4: 154–65.

Tilly, Charles. 1992. *Coercion, Capital, and European States, A.D. 990–1992*. Oxford: Blackwell.

Toyo Keizai. 1980, 1985, 1990, 1991, 1995, 1996, 2000, 2001, 2003. *Kaigai shinshitsu kigyo soran* (Statistics on Overseas Japanese Companies). Tokyo.

Trachtman, Joel P. 2002. "Institutional Linkage: Transcending 'Trade and . . .' " *American Journal of International Law* 96, 1 (January): 77–93.

Trezise, Philip H., and Yukio Suzuki. 1976. "Politics, Government and Economic Growth in Japan." In *Asia's New Giant: How the Japanese Economy Works*, edited by Hugh Patrick and Henry Rosovsky, 753–812. Washington, DC: Brookings Institution.

Tsang, Eric W. K. 2001. "Annual Report Disclosure and Corporate Legitimacy: A Study of Singapore Companies' Responses to the Government's Call for Venturing Abroad." *Asia Pacific Journal of Management* 18, 1: 27–43.

Tucker, David. 1997. *Skirmishes at the Edge of Empire*. Westport, CT: Praeger.

United Nations. 1972. "Report of the United Nations Conference on the Human Environment." A/Conf. 48/14/Rev.1. Stockholm.

———. 2000. *Replacement Migration: Is It a Solution to Declining and Ageing Populations?* New York: UN Population Division.

———. 2001a. *World Population Prospects: The 2000 Revision*. New York: UN Population Division.

———. 2001b. *World Urbanization Prospects: The 1999 Revision*. New York: UN Population Division.

———. 2002. *International Migration, 2002*. New York: UN Population Division.

United Nations Conference on Trade and Development (UNCTAD). 1991, 1992, 2001. *World Investment Report*. New York.

United Nations Drug Control Programme (UNDCP). 2000a. "China Country Profile." Pamphlet. Bangkok.

———. 2000b. "International Congress in Pursuit of a Drug Free ASEAN 2015, Sharing the Vision, Leading the Change: Summary Report." Pamphlet. Bangkok.

———. 2000c. "Thirty Years Fighting Drugs through Leadership and Participatory Cooperation." Pamphlet. Bangkok.

———. 2002a. *Global Illicit Drug Trends, 2002*. New York: United Nations.

———. 2002b. "Indonesia Country Profile." Pamphlet. Bangkok.

———. 2002c. "Regional Drug Control Profile for Southeast Asia and the Pacific." Pamphlet. Bangkok.

United Nations Economic Commission for Europe. 1999. *Strategies and Policies for Air Pollution Abatement*. Geneva.

United Nations Economic and Social Commission for Asia and the Pacific. 1997. *Regional Cooperation and Response Actions to Climate Change in Asia and the Pacific*. Bangkok.

Urata, Shujiro. 1999. "Intra-Firm Technology Transfer by Japanese Multinationals in Asia." In *Japanese Multinationals in Asia: Regional Operations in Comparative Perspective*, edited by Dennis J. Encarnation, 143–62. Oxford: Oxford University Press.

———. 2001. "Global Strategies of Electronics Firms." Paper presented at the FRI-MIT-SOFI conference Can Japan Be a Global Player? Fujitsu Research Institute, Tokyo.

Urata, Shujiro, and Toru Nakakita. 1991. "Industrial Development in Japan and Its Implications for Developing Countries." In *Industrial Adjustment in Developed Countries and*

Its Implications for Developing Countries, edited by Ippei Yamazawa and Akira Hirata, 13–142. Tokyo: Institute for Developing Economies.

U.S. Department of State. 2000. *International Narcotics Control Strategy Report, 2000.* Washington, DC: Government Printing Office.

Vernon, Raymond. 1971. *Sovereignty at Bay: The Multinational Spread of U.S. Enterprises.* New York: Basic Books.

Viner, Jacob. 1950. *The Customs Union Issue.* New York: Carnegie Endowment for International Peace.

Vogel, Steven K. 1998. Freer Markets, More Rules: Regulatory Reform in Advanced Industrial Countries. Ithaca: Cornell University Press.

Wain, Barry. 2000. "Building an East Asian Identity." *Asian Wall Street Journal,* May 19–21.

Wallace, William. 1995. "Regionalism in Europe: Model or Exception?" In *Regionalism in World Politics: Regional Organization and International Order,* edited by Louise Fawcett and Andrew Hurrell. Oxford: Oxford University Press.

Walt, Stephen M. 2001–2. "Beyond Bin Laden: Reshaping U.S. Foreign Policy." *International Security* 26, 3 (Winter): 56–78.

Waltz, Kenneth. 1979. *Theory of International Politics.* New York: McGraw Hill.

Wan, Ming. 2001. *Japan between Asia and the West: Economic Power and Strategic Balance.* Armonk, NY: M. E. Sharpe.

Wanandi, Jusuf. 1999. "ASEAN's Challenges for Its Future." *PacNet* 3, January 22.

Wang, Hongying. 2000. "Multilateralism in Chinese Foreign Policy: The Limits of Socialization?" In *China's International Relations in the Twenty-first Century: Dynamics of Paradigm Shifts,* edited by W. Hu, G. Chan, and D. Zha, 71–91. Lanham, MD: University Press of America.

———. 2001. *Weak State, Strong Networks: The Institutional Dynamics of Foreign Direct Investment in China.* Oxford: Oxford University Press.

Watanabe, Akio. 1992. *Ajia Taiheiyo no kokusai kankei to Nihon* (Japan and International Relations in Asia and the Pacific). Tokyo: University of Tokyo Press.

———. 2001. "Japan's Position on Human Rights in Asia." In *Japan and East Asian Regionalism,* edited by S. J. Maswood, 68–89. London: Routledge.

Webber, Douglas. 2001. "Two Funerals and a Wedding? The Ups and Downs of Regionalism in East Asia and Asia-Pacific after the Asian Crisis." *Pacific Review* 14, 3.

Weber, Max. 1949. " 'Objectivity' in Social Science and Social Policy." In *Max Weber on the Methodology of the Social Sciences,* translated and edited by Edward A. Shils and Henry A. Finch. Glencoe, IL: Free Press.

Weidenbaum, Murray, and Samuel Hughes. 1996. *The Bamboo Network: How Expatriate Chinese Entrepreneurs Are Creating a New Economic Superpower in Asia.* New York: Free Press.

Wendt, Alexander. 1994. "Collective Identity Formation and the International State." *American Political Science Review* 88, 2 (June): 384–96.

Wickramasekara, Piyasiri. 2001. "Labour Migration in Asia: Issues and Challenges." In *International Migration in Asia: Trends and Policies,* 35–59. Paris: Organisation for Economic Co-operation and Development.

Wines, Michael. 2001. "Chinese Creating a New Vigor in Russian Far East." *New York Times,* September 23.

Winters, L. Alan. 1998. "Regionalism and the Next Round of Multilateral Trade Negotiations." Paper presented at the Conference on the World Trade System at Fifty, April 15. World Bank, Washington, DC.

Womack, James P., Daniel T. Jones, and Daniel Roos. 1990. *The Machine That Changed the World.* New York: Macmillan.

Woo-Cumings, Meredith. 1999. *The Developmental State*. Ithaca: Cornell University Press.

Woods, Lawrence T. 1993. *Asia-Pacific Diplomacy: Nongovernmental Organizations and International Relations*. Vancouver: University of British Columbia Press.

Woodward, Mark R. 1993. "Textual Exegesis as Social Commentary: Religious, Social, and Political Meanings of Indonesian Translations of Arabic Hadith Texts." *Journal of Asian Studies* 52, 3 (August): 565–83.

World Bank. 1993. *The East Asian Miracle: Economic Growth and Public Policy*. Oxford: Oxford University Press.

———. 1997. *Clear Water, Blue Skies: China's Environment in the Twenty-first Century*. Washington, DC.

———. 2001. *World Development Indicators*. Washington, DC.

———. 2002. *World Development Report, 2002*. Washington, DC.

———. World Trade Organization (WTO). 1996. "Report of the Committee on Trade and Environment." WTO Doc. PRESS/TE no. 14. Geneva.

———. 2001. *Overview of Developments in the International Trading Environment* Geneva.

Yamakage, Susumu. 1991. *ASEAN: Sinboru kara shisutemu he* (ASEAN: From a Symbol to a System). Tokyo: University of Tokyo Press.

———. 1997. *ASEAN pawaa: Ajia Taiheiyo no chukaku he* (ASEAN Power: Toward the Core of Asia and the Pacific). Tokyo: University of Tokyo Press.

———. 2001. "Nihon no ASEAN seisaku no henyo" (Transformation of Japan's Policy toward ASEAN). *International Affairs* (Japan Institute for International Affairs) 490: 57–81.

Yamamoto, Nana. 2001. "Ajia Taiheiyo no takokukan anzenhosho to Ohsutoraria: 'Ajia Taiheiyo rashisa' no mosaku" (Australia and Multilateral Security Cooperation in Asia and the Pacific: A Search for "Asia-Pacific-ness." *Studies on International Relations* (Society of International Relations Studies) 17: 35–56.

Yamamoto, Yoshinobu, and Tsutomu Kikuchi. 1998. "Japan's Approach to APEC and Regime Creation in the Asia-Pacific." In *Asia-Pacific Crossroads: Regime Creation and the Future of APEC,* edited by Vinod K. Aggarwal and Charles E. Morrison, 191–212. New York: St. Martin's Press.

Yamazawa, Ippei. 1992. "On Pacific Economic Integration." *Economic Journal* November:102.

Yeung, Henry Wai-chung. 1998. *Transnational Corporations and Business Networks: Hong Kong Firms in the ASEAN Region*. London: Routledge.

———. 2000. "Local Politics and Foreign Ventures in China's Transitional Economy: The Political Economy of Singaporean Investments in China." *Political Geography* 19: 809–40.

———. 2002. *Entrepreneurship and the Internationalisation of Asian Firms: An Institutional Perspective*. Cheltenham, UK: Edward Elgar.

Yeung, Yue-man, and Fu-chen Lo. 1996. "Global Restructuring and Emerging Urban Corridors in Pacific Asia." In *Emerging World Cities in Pacific Asia,* edited by F. Lo and Y. Yeung, 17–47. Tokyo: United Nations University Press.

Yoshihara, K. 1988. *The Rise of Ersatz Capitalism in Southeast Asia*. Singapore: Oxford University Press.

Zhang, Yujin. 2000. "Economic Globalization and State Sovereignty." *Foreign Affairs Journal* (Beijing) 58 (December): 16–21.

Zhu, Yan. 2000. "IT Sangyo ni okeru Chukoku to Taiwan no bungyo kankei to" (The Division of Labor between China and Taiwan in the IT Industry). FRI Kenkyu Report no. 96. Fujitsu Research Institute, Tokyo.

Index

The letters *f* and *t* following page numbers indicate figures and tables.

ad hoc problem-oriented coalitions: and bottom-up/top-down processes, 22; and boundaries of East Asia, 265; characteristics of, 102; and environmental issues, 18, 23, 106, 216; and regional institutions, 46; and regional integration, 6, 11, 13–15, 17–18, 145, 148, 267. *See also* track II groups

Afghanistan, 23, 106, 240–243, 245, 247–248, 250–252, 270, 275

APEC (Asia-Pacific Economic Cooperation): and APT, 201; and Asian economic crisis of 1997–98, 4, 94, 102, 261, 268; and consensus, 36, 45, 49, 77, 84–85, 96, 97, 97n12, 102; and cultural issues, 39; and environmental issues, 137; and informality, 33–34, 45, 267; and Japan, 34, 47, 81, 96, 124, 126, 127, 130, 143; membership in, 14f, 15f, 27, 126, 211, 266; as multinational organization, 13; and open regionalism, 37, 49, 52; and private input, 124–125, 125n5; and regional economic links, 126, 164, 259; as regional institution, 32; and regional integration, 20, 143; and regionalism, 6, 195, 198, 205, 266; and security and defense, 43–44; and trade and investment liberalization, 33–34, 127, 266–267; weakening of, 94–97

APT (ASEAN + 3): and boundaries of East Asia, 208; characteristics of, 13–14; and consensus, 97; and demographic factors, 56; European Union compared to, 101; and financial and monetary cooperation, 133–134, 147–148; and framework for dialogue, 94, 96; and Japan, 132; membership of, 15, 15f, 25, 265; and open regionalism, 38, 49, 269; as regional institution, 32, 53, 144, 261, 264; and regionalism, 196–197, 196n1, 199–203, 200n6, 205–206, 209–211, 213

ASEAN (Association of Southeast Asian Nations): and ASEAN way, 33, 39, 196; and Asian economic crisis, 4, 33, 102, 261; brand-to-brand complementation program, 101, 156; and consensus, 35, 36, 39, 45, 49, 50, 59, 81, 85; creation of, 10, 32–33, 108–109; and demographic factors, 56; and drug trafficking, 121–122; and East Asia definition, 197; and environmental issues, 23, 134–135, 140–141, 142, 144–146, 216, 222, 224, 226, 233, 234; and informality, 34, 45, 267; Institutes of Strategic and International Studies, 110–111, 206, 210n13; and legalization, 48–49; membership of, 13, 14f, 15f, 25, 265, 267; and national

CORNELL STUDIES IN POLITICAL ECONOMY

A series edited by

Peter J. Katzenstein